TWENTY LESSONS IN ENVIRONMENTAL SOCIOLOGY

SECOND EDITION

Kenneth A. Gould

Brooklyn College of the City University of New York

Tammy L. Lewis

Brooklyn College of the City University of New York

New York   Oxford

OXFORD UNIVERSITY PRESS

Oxford University Press is a department of the University of Oxford.
It furthers the University's objective of excellence in research,
scholarship, and education by publishing worldwide.

Oxford   New York
Auckland   Cape Town   Dar es Salaam   Hong Kong   Karachi
Kuala Lumpur   Madrid   Melbourne   Mexico City   Nairobi
New Delhi   Shanghai   Taipei   Toronto

With offices in
Argentina   Austria   Brazil   Chile   Czech Republic   France   Greece
Guatemala   Hungary   Italy   Japan   Poland   Portugal   Singapore
South Korea   Switzerland   Thailand   Turkey   Ukraine   Vietnam

For titles covered by Section 112 of the US Higher Education
Opportunity Act, please visit www.oup.com/us/he for the
latest information about pricing and alternate formats.

Published in the United States of America by

Oxford University Press
198 Madison Avenue, New York, NY 10016
http://www.oup.com

Oxford is a registered trade mark of Oxford University Press.

Library of Congress Cataloging-in-Publication Data
Gould, Kenneth Alan.
   Twenty lessons in environmental sociology / Kenneth A. Gould,
Brooklyn College of the City University of New York, Tammy L. Lewis,
Brooklyn College of the City University of New York. -- Second edition.
      pages cm
   ISBN 978-0-19-932592-4
   1. Environmental sociology. 2. Human ecology. 3. Nature--Effect of
human beings on. I. Lewis, Tammy L. II. Title.
   GE195.G68 2015
   304.2--dc23
                                                        2014005112

Printing number: 9 8 7 6 5 4 3 2 1

Printed in the United States of America
on acid-free paper

The First edition was dedicated to Anna and Isabel.
The Second edition is dedicated to Allan Schnaiberg.

Contents

Part 1   Theory

Part 2   Systemic Causes of Environmental Disruption

This book was artisanally crafted in Brooklyn, NY

Annotated Table of Contents

making a fast connection on the Internet; and a person physically dismantling a computer that has been "thrown away" in the United States and exported to an "e-waste processing center" in another country. Although these snapshots are only three out of many possibilities, they offer an excellent opportunity to connect structures across time and space and to learn about the insights and creative uses of theory in environmental sociology.

Part 2   Systemic Causes of Environmental Disruption

less pluralist than one might hope. Offering a sampling of theories of environment–society relationships, social inequality, and state formation, it proposes that to better understand how contemporary U.S. policies result in environmental racism and inequality, one must consider the historical, legal, economic, and cultural roots and evolution of the U.S. nation-state itself. Such an exploration suggests that the United States remains an imperial presence in the Americas and globally, and this has dire consequences for any effort to produce social and environmental justice here or elsewhere. In this way, we might locate the deeper origins of the environmental state and, in turn, think through a different set of questions that might achieve reform or transformation of those practices. It concludes by offering thoughts for how individuals and groups might address these challenges, drawing on recent and ongoing cases in North America.

Increasing labor productivity has come to be viewed by political, economic, and academic elites as a panacea for economic progress. Yet this perspective represents only one view of increasing production by workers. The mechanisms by which labor productivity is achieved typically include substantial labor reduction, involving downsizing and shifts of the benefits of productivity away from workers and consumers and toward investors and senior management. Moreover, because replacing human labor with mechanical, chemical, and electronic technologies often requires heightened use of energy and water and increased disposal of wastes into natural systems, ecological disruption is typically associated with growing labor productivity through changes in production technology.

Transnational corporations (TNCs) are the most dominant and powerful social actors in the global political economy. Their main goal is to access markets, cheap labor, and resources to maximize their profit margin and returns to shareholders. They have been successful in eroding or delaying local, national, regional, and global environmental and public health protection mechanisms through powerful special interest groups that lobby governments and global institutions. The largest TNCs have more political and economic power than many developing countries. In the absence of strong state regulations, TNCs' power in the 21st century has served to undermine social welfare benefits, job security, public health, and environmental standards.

This has not been widely reported in the global news media since the media are increasingly controlled by these same TNCs. It is not in the interests of TNCs to critique the social and environmental consequences of their growing influence in the global economy. Corporate control over news and information strongly shapes what the public knows and does not know about key social and environmental issues. The control of news, media, and information is a critical form of power in environmental conflicts.

Demography is the discipline dedicated to studying how human population changes over time. The relationship between human population and the environment is complex and is not related simply to the number of people alive at any given time. Malthus described the relationship between human population growth and the environment as negative; he believed that increasing numbers of people would create pressures on the food supply. In turn, this would lead to famine, war, and disease that would bring human populations back into balance with the food supply. Malthus's narrow focus on food supply failed to take into account that human technologies could increase the amount of food available. The Green Revolution in agriculture did this, by using biotechnology and chemical inputs to raise productivity, albeit with negative environmental consequences. Malthus also failed to account for changing norms about family size; in many places, higher standards of living have led to slower rates of population growth, a process described as a demographic transition. Neo-Malthusians have attempted to account for these processes, most notably through Paul Ehrlich's I = PAT equation, which predicts environmental impact (I) as a product of population (P), affluence (A), and technology (T). Neo-Malthusian models have been widely criticized for latent racism and classism, particularly given the lack of attention to equitable distribution of environmental goods and bads (including food). The relationship between population and environment is examined in detail with reference to deforestation patterns in Ecuador. Simple analysis of forest loss over time would suggest that population growth has a linear and negative relationship with forest cover. However, more detailed analysis indicates that forests in this country are divided among coastal, Andean, and Amazonian forests, each with different human population pressures. This case demonstrates the importance of understanding how people interact with their environment rather than assuming that population growth invariably causes degradation.

This lesson examines the interactions between energy, society, and the environment, with particular attention given to the hidden costs of energy production. The lesson begins with an overview of global energy consumption patterns and then discusses the social, environmental, and public health costs of each of the major sources of energy. There are tremendous problems associated with oil, coal, natural gas, and nuclear energy production throughout the entire lifecycle of each of these energy sources. Extraction of fossil fuels poses great risks to water resources and causes widespread ecosystem destruction, as does the mining of uranium for nuclear energy production. Oil, coal, and natural gas all release carbon dioxide, one of the primary contributors to global warming, when they are burned. In addition, nuclear energy and all three of the fossil fuels create enormous quantities of toxic waste that pose tremendous health risks to nearby communities. While renewable energy sources, such as solar, wind, and hydroelectricity, provide improvements over fossil fuels and nuclear energy in a number of ways, they are not without their own costs to society and the natural world. Our energy-related social, environmental, and public health problems will not be solved by simply moving to renewable energy sources. The root of the problem is that we live in an over-powered world, and we continue to expand both the amount of energy we produce and the amount of energy we consume. We must shift national and international policy discussions away from trying to find ways to reduce carbon emissions without reducing our levels of energy consumption to finding ways to reduce our overall energy demand. The lesson concludes with some ideas for how to begin this change and invites the reader to think about ways that life could actually be *improved* if we were to reduce the amount of energy we consume on a daily basis.

Part 3   Some Social Consequences of Environmental Disruption

health paradigms. It reviews several landmark cases that have shaped our understanding of environmental illness and reviews how tragedies and chronic mishaps reveal the way that toxins in our environment cause illness. To illustrate some of the obstacles to understanding and dealing with environmental illness, this lesson describes illnesses caused by heat waves— a critical issue that exemplifies how environmental conditions affect human health. Ultimately, the cases discussed demonstrate how those who suffer environmental illness often first make connections between health and the environment. For them to gain compensation for their losses and to stop these exposures, public officials must also accept their claims. These instances reflect power differences based on race, class, and gender, as well as macro-level structures in society.

Most of the food people eat today arrives on their plates through a food and agriculture system that is globalized, corporatized, and industrialized. The first part of this lesson outlines how such a food and agriculture system came to be and what it means to say that food is globalized, corporatized, and industrialized. The second part of the lesson examines the social and environmental implications of food and agriculture today. This includes the significant environmental degradation resulting from intensive resource use and high chemical use, the dangers of farm work, and the persistence of hunger and the rise of obesity. The effects of food and agriculture on development are also analyzed, including the depopulation of rural areas, the privatization and commodification of formerly public goods, and the rise of slums in the Global South. The last part of the lesson examines efforts to make food and agriculture more sustainable, just, and healthy—that is, what is commonly referred to as alternative food and agriculture movements. In particular, the focus is on the increasing use of market-based approaches, and whether people can shop their way to a just and sustainable food and agriculture system.

Farms do not leap to mind as significant polluters. Yet, pollution from agriculture and especially livestock operations may now be the largest contaminant of America's waterways. This lesson uses the transformation of eastern North Carolina's pork industry as a case study to explain how industrialized agriculture has become a leading polluter. The lesson describes the recent growth and restructuring of that industry and its widespread adoption of confined animal feeding operation technologies. The concept of "externalities of scale" is introduced, which encompasses the various economic, social, and environmental harms associated with large-scale production and absent in smaller operations. The lesson then describes how this industry has negative impacts on the health, quality of life, and economic well-being of surrounding communities. Exploring the issue further, the authors describe how this industry has affected the ecology of eastern North Carolina, an environment particularly vulnerable to this form of production. They also detail the political struggle surrounding the industry, highlighting the roles of various stakeholders in both promoting and opposing these changes. The authors conclude that the transformation of hog production in eastern North Carolina and the associated negative consequences are illustrative of broader trends in how animals are being raised throughout industrialized nations.

Human communities may be vulnerable to floods and hurricanes for a variety of intersecting reasons. While coastal areas and low-lying floodplains have a natural physical vulnerability based on their geography, many of the components of flood and hurricane vulnerability are caused by human activities. These include overdevelopment and unsafe building practices in flood-prone areas, flood insurance and other recovery programs that encourage rebuilding in hazard zones, a stubborn refusal to acknowledge the extent of a community's risk, and perhaps most importantly, social inequalities based on sex, race, ethnicity, income, and age. The impacts of Hurricanes Katrina and Sandy, though they occurred in very different parts of the country, provide strikingly similar examples of these difficulties and disparities, and of the problems involved in choosing mitigation strategies that both diminish disaster risk and respect social justice concerns.

Global warming is the most significant environmental issue of our time, yet public response in Western nations has been meager. Why have so few taken any action? This lesson draws upon interviews and ethnographic data from a community in western Norway during an unusually warm winter to describe how knowledge of climate change is experienced in everyday life. That winter the first snowfall was two months later than usual;

ice fishing was impossible; and the ski industry had to invest in artificial snow-making. Stories in local and national newspapers linked the warm winter to global warming. Yet residents did not write letters to the editor, pressure politicians, or cut down on use of fossil fuels. This lesson describes the emotions of guilt, helplessness, and fear of the future that arose when people were confronted with the idea of climate change. The lesson presents a model of socially organized denial to describe how people normalized these disturbing emotions by deploying conversation norms and discourses that served as "tools of social order." Most studies of public response to climate change have focused on information deficit approaches. Many in the general public or environmental community have also presumed that the failure to engage is a function of lack of concern. Instead, this research describes how for the highly educated and politically savvy residents global warming was both common knowledge and unimaginable. "The social organization of climate denial" is described through multiple levels, from emotions to cultural norms to political economy. The research from Norway is supplemented by comparisons to the United States, telling a larger story behind the public paralysis in the face of today's alarming predictions from climate scientists. The lesson describes the lack of response as an active process the author calls "socially organized denial." As a result, information about climate science is known in the abstract but disconnected from political, social, and private life.

Part 4   Some Social Responses to Environmental Disruption

16. U.S. Environmental Movements   263

Robert J. Brulle

The U.S. environmental movement is perhaps the largest, longest-lived, and most complex social movement in the United States. To understand this movement from a sociological viewpoint requires an analysis of the different belief systems or "discursive frames" that define the different communities that make up this movement. This lesson starts with a description of these discursive frames. Using this perspective, it then describes the historical development of the different communities and their relative levels of economic resource mobilization.

17. Labor and the Environment   283

Brian K. Obach

Beliefs about the need for environmental protection are influenced by many factors, including one's economic position.

Workers may feel that environmental policies either advance or threaten their economic interests. Many people are employed in fields related to environmental protection or otherwise benefit from environmental policies. Some political leaders have supported environmental regulation and financial assistance for "clean industries," arguing that this type of development will ensure a healthy and sustainable economy. But not everyone agrees that environmental measures are beneficial economically. Some sectors of the economy are threatened by environmental policies that could curtail their operations. Conservative political leaders often oppose pro-environmental policies on the grounds that such measures impose burdensome costs on employers and weaken the economy, resulting in job loss. Workers in these occupations, often encouraged by employers who see environmental regulation as a threat to profits, may mobilize politically to oppose policies supported by environmentalists, setting off so-called "jobs versus the environment" conflicts. Labor unions can play an important role in shaping how workers perceive environmental issues, and they are positioned to help build a broad movement for a just and sustainable economy. However, labor unions have been in decline for decades due to technological developments, economic globalization, and a general assault on organized labor by employers. The structure of the labor relations system and the history of unionism in the United States have yielded a mixed record on environmental issues. At times unions have allied with environmental advocates and provided key support for environmental policies, but in other instances unions have sided with employers in opposition to environmental measures. Increasingly, unions have joined with environmentalists in support of policies that promise both environmental and economic benefits. Environmental measures are not likely to succeed unless workers believe that their economic fate is tied to a healthy environment.

18. Environmental Movements in the Global South   300

Tammy L. Lewis

Environmentalism in the Global North differs from that in the Global South in terms of their historical roots. In the Global North, early environmentalism began as an affluent movement to protect recreational spaces, whereas in the Global South, poor people's livelihood struggles are at the roots of environmentalism. Cases from India, Nigeria, and Bolivia illustrate key components of Southern movements. Additional cases from Brazil and Ecuador show the complicated relationship between globalization and environmentalism. Livelihood struggles in the Global South share characteristics of environmental justice struggles in North America. Organizations in environmental movements in the Global South are becoming increasingly professionalized. Alternatives to the established global environmentalism paradigm and global development model are emerging in the Global South and contesting dominant conceptions of "good living."

This lesson presents an anthropological approach, consisting of a comparative, holistic, intersubjective, and processual perspective, to the study of the environmental relations of indigenous peoples. The author questions the dichotomy and domination generally assumed by members of Western cultures to exist between people and nature and contends that more reciprocal material and ideational relations with the environment are also conducive to greater development and sustainability of benign environmental conditions. Whether or not people are "closer to nature" in their ideologies, the lesson proposes that environmental practices that contribute to resilience and possibilities for replenishment are also dependent upon types of environmental knowledge that emphasize balance, connectedness, interdependence, responsibility, and continuity. Not only do many forms of environmental relationships found among contemporary indigenous peoples deserve greater respect and legal status, but the author contends that the forms of "ecological wisdom" they practice should become a common element of Western environmental thought and practice for decision makers and public citizens.

This lesson begins with a discussion of the always multiple, sometimes vague, and often-conflicting definitions of "sustainable development." The authors connect this profusion of viewpoints to the inevitable tensions between the three basic goals of sustainable development: economic growth, environmental protection, and social equity. The lesson then uses two detailed examples of ecotourism development in Belize to illustrate these trade-offs and highlight how and by whom decisions regarding the goals of sustainable development are made. Three primary critical perspectives on sustainable development—free market environmentalism, policy/reformist, and critical structural—are also described and applied to the state of ecotourism in Belize. Finally, the conditions under which ecotourism can form the basis of a sustainable development trajectory are assessed.

Conclusion: Unanswered Questions and the Future of Environmental Sociology 353
Kenneth A. Gould and Tammy L. Lewis

In the conclusion, interlinking themes from throughout the book are briefly highlighted and analyzed. Those themes are brought to bear on the question of how we can/should act on the socioenvironmental knowledge that we have, with reference to the frameworks provided by the founding thinkers in environmental sociology. The authors then suggest areas of research that need to be pursued by environmental sociologists in the future and address concerns about what can practically be accomplished in the present. Students are encouraged to continue both their study of environmental sociology and their participation in the contemporary social, political, and environmental worlds. The lesson concludes by suggesting that the subfield of environmental sociology would benefit from the creation of structures to increase North–South intellectual exchange.

Acknowledgments

We thank the people of Akwesasne for grounding us in the reality of what it means to be engaged in the struggle for physical, social, cultural, and environmental health.

Thanks also to our colleagues Jeff Broadbent, Stella Čapek, and Mike Mascarenhas for convincing us of the need for a book such as this. We thank our colleagues who used the first edition of the book, and especially those who provided us with suggestions for the second edition. A big thanks, too, to the contributors of both editions for their commitment to clearly communicating environmental sociology to the next generation.

Over the years, our students at the University of California-Davis, Northwestern University, Denison University, Muhlenberg College, St. Lawrence University, and Brooklyn College of the City University of New York have inspired us to create effective means to communicate the importance of sociology in understanding environmental issues.

For ongoing encouragement, enthusiasm, and cheese, we thank our editor at Oxford University Press, Sherith Pankratz.

Finally, for their ongoing support, we thank our family.

About the Contributors

Luiz Barbosa is a Professor of sociology at San Francisco State. He is also affiliated with the Environmental Studies Program at the same institution. He is the author of several journal articles on the Brazilian Amazon rainforest, focusing on the effects of globalization, development, and environmental mobilization on preservation of the forest. He is also the author of the book *The Brazilian Amazon Rainforest: Global Ecopolitics, Development, and Democracy*. He is working on a second book manuscript on the situation in Brazilian Amazonia.

Diane C. Bates is an Associate Professor of Sociology at The College of New Jersey. Her research on land use change in the Ecuadorian Amazon has been published in journals such as *Latin American Research Review, Rural Sociology, Latin American Perspectives, Human Organization*, and *Ecuador Debate*. This research documents the complexity of the process through which small producers make decisions about their agricultural land based on economic opportunities within the household unit. In addition, she has researched a variety of environmental controversies in the United States, including deforestation in the San Jacinto (Texas) watershed, flooding along the Delaware River, New Jersey's controversial bear hunt, and the human ecology of smaller industrial cities.

Shannon Elizabeth Bell is an Assistant Professor of sociology at the University of Kentucky. Her research falls at the intersection of environmental sociology, gender, and social movements, with a particular focus on understanding the ways in which environmentally destructive industries acquire and maintain their power and discovering strategies for increasing the political participation of communities most affected by environmental injustices. She is author of *Our Roots Run Deep as Ironweed: Appalachian Women and the Fight for Environmental Justice* (University of Illinois Press, 2013) and is the 2013 recipient of the Practice and Outreach Award and the Robert Boguslaw Award for Technology and Humanism, both from the Environment & Technology Section of the American Sociological Association. In 2011 she received the Best Article Award from the Rural Sociological Society and Honorable Mention for the Allan Schnaiberg Outstanding Publication

Award from the Environment & Technology Section of the American Sociological Association.

Robert J. Brulle is a Professor of Sociology and Environmental Science in the Department of Culture and Communications, and an affiliate Professor of Public Heath in the School of Public Health at Drexel University in Philadelphia, Pennsylvania. He has a B.S. degree in Marine Engineering from the U.S. Coast Guard Academy, an M.A. in Sociology from the New School for Social Research, an M.S. in Natural Resources from the University of Michigan, and a Ph.D. in Sociology from George Washington University. His research focuses on the U.S. environmental movement, critical theory, and public participation in environmental policymaking. He is the author of over 70 articles in these areas and is the author of *Agency, Democracy and the Environment: The U.S. Environmental Movement from the Perspective of Critical Theory*, as well as co-editor, with David Pellow, of *Power, Justice and the Environment*. Prior to his employment in the academic field, Dr. Brulle served as a commissioned officer in the U.S. Coast Guard for 24 years, where his area of expertise was in the field of environmental response and pollution prevention.

Elizabeth H. Campbell received her Ph.D. from Binghamton University. Her dissertation focused on urban refugee protection, livelihoods, and possibilities for local integration in Kenya. She has published her findings in various journals and edited book collections. Her second area of focus is environmental sociology. As a graduate student, she designed and developed several courses on political economy, development and ecology, and human rights. As a Fulbright Scholar, she was based at the office of the United Nations High Commissioner for Refugees in Nairobi. She also worked on two separate occasions in Kakuma Refugee Camp in Kenya. Prior to that she worked for a monthly news magazine at the Alternative Information Center in Jerusalem. She has served as Director of Refugee Council USA, a coalition of 23 nongovernmental organizations focused on refugee policy, and Senior Advocate for Refugees International, where she focused on the Middle East and the Horn of Africa. She is now working as a Senior Humanitarian Advisor in the Bureau of International Organization Affairs at the Department of State.

Stella M.Čapek is Professor of Sociology in the Department of Sociology/Anthropology at Hendrix College. She has a B.A. from Boston University and an M.A. and Ph.D. in Sociology from the University of Texas at Austin. She teaches courses on Environmental Sociology, Social Change/Social Movements, Medical Sociology, Urban/Community Sociology, Images of the City, Gender and Family, Food, Culture, and Nature, and Sociological Theory. She is especially interested in interdisciplinary environmental studies, environmental justice, ecological identity, social constructions of nature, and sustainable community design. She has published articles on environmental justice, tenants' rights, urban/community issues, local interactions with wildlife, green design, and health and environment. She has taught about sustainability and ecotourism in Costa Rica and in the U.S. Southwest. She has co-authored two books, *Community Versus Commodity: Tenants and the American City* (1992) and *Come Lovely and Soothing Death: The Right To Die Movement in the United States* (1999). She has also published environmentally themed creative nonfiction.

Adam Driscoll is a doctoral candidate in sociology at North Carolina State University in Raleigh, NC. He received his M.A. in sociology from East Carolina University and his B.S. in biology from Drexel University. His research in environmental sociology explores the various ways in which the structure of human social relations and the natural world mutually shape one another, particularly in the realm of agriculture. He also conducts research within the scholarship of teaching and learning, examining online pedagogical practices and the efficacy of online education. His work has appeared in *Teaching Sociology* and the *Journal of World-Systems Research*.

Bob Edwards is a Professor of sociology at East Carolina University in Greenville, NC. He received his Ph.D. in sociology in 1995 from The Catholic University of America in Washington, DC. A longstanding interest in understanding the social organization of inequalities integrates his research on social movements, organizations, social capital, and civil society with his work on environmentalism, environmental justice, and the social impact of natural disasters. He has published over 60 refereed articles and chapters appearing in *American Sociological Review, Annual Review of Sociology, Social Problems, Social Forces, Mobilization, Teaching Sociology, Journal of Democracy, Journal of Public Policy*, and *Natural Hazards Review*. He is co-editor of *Beyond Tocqueville: Civil Society and the Social Capital Debate in Comparative Perspective* and of four thematic issues of *American Behavioral Scientist*.

Kenneth A. Gould is Professor of Sociology at Brooklyn College of the City University of New York, and Professor of Sociology, and Earth and Environmental Sciences at the CUNY Graduate Center. His work focuses on the political economy of environment, technology, and development and is best known for its contribution to the development of the "treadmill of production" model of socioenvironmental dynamics. Gould's research examines the responses of communities to environmental problems, technology and social change, the role of inequality in environmental conflicts, and the impacts of economic globalization on efforts to achieve ecologically and socially sustainable development trajectories. He is co-author of *Environment and Society: The Enduring Conflict* (1994), *Local Environmental Struggles: Citizen Activism in the Treadmill of Production* (1996), and *The Treadmill of Production: Injustice and Unsustainability in the Global Economy* (2008) and co-editor, with Tammy L. Lewis, of *Thirty Readings in Introductory Sociology* (2013), and *Ten Lessons in Introductory Sociology* (2014). His recent work examines ecotourism, nanotechnology, and green gentrification.

Maki Hatanaka is an Assistant Professor in the Department of Sociology at Sam Houston State University. Her recent research examines how changing forms of governance (e.g., standards, certification, and labeling) and new forms of supply chain management are affecting agrifood producers, communities, and the environment. Specifically, her focus is on the ways that farmers and farm workers as well as social and environmental movements resist, adjust, and accommodate such changes in the global agrifood system. Her work has been published in several edited volumes and numerous academic journals, including *Food Policy, World Development, Agriculture and Human Values, Journal of Rural Studies, Sociologia Ruralis,* and *The Local Environment.*

Jason Konefal is an Assistant Professor in the Department of Sociology at Sam Houston State University. His research examines the relationship between political economic structures and practices and opportunities for social change. Specifically, he is interested in how neoliberalization and globalization are affecting governance processes, and possibilities for equality, justice, sustainability, and democracy in food and agriculture. Dr. Konefal's recent publications have appeared in *Sociologia Ruralis, Journal of Rural Studies, Agriculture and Human Values,* and *Organization & Environment.*

Tammy L. Lewis is Professor of Sociology and Directory of Macaulay Honors College at Brooklyn College, and Professor of Sociology and Earth and Environmental Sciences at the CUNY Graduate Center. She teaches courses on urban sustainability, social movements, environmental sociology, and research methodology. Her research examines the effects of globalization on social movements and sustainability, with a focus on Latin America. Closer to home, she examines the processes of urban greening in Brooklyn. With Kenneth A. Gould she is co-editor of *Ten Lessons in Introductory Sociology* (2014) and *Thirty Readings in Introductory Sociology* (2013). She is co-author of *Environment, Energy, and Society* (2002) with Craig R. Humphrey and Frederick H. Buttel. Her work has appeared in *Conservation Biology, Mobilization, Social Science Quarterly,* and *Teaching Sociology,* among others. She has been a council member of the Environment and Technology section of the American Sociological Association and served on the board of the Society for Conservation Biology's Social Science Working Group.

Michael Mascarenhas is an Associate Professor in the Science and Technology Studies Department at Rensselaer Polytechnic Institute. He is a sociologist with scholarly interests in the fields of Post-colonial and Development Studies, Environmental Justice and Racism, and Science and Technology Studies. His research examines the political, social, and environmental tensions and controversies surrounding recent transnational changes in the governance of water regimes. He is the author of *Where the Waters Divide: Neoliberalism, White Privilege, and Environmental Racism in Canada.*

Sabrina McCormick is Associate Professor in the Department of Environmental and Occupational Health in The George Washington University School of Public Health and Health Services. She is a sociologist and documentary filmmaker. Dr. McCormick's first two books, *No Family History* and *Mobilizing Science*, investigated how social movements use science to improve environmental outcomes. Her current work takes an in-depth, sociological approach to addressing climate change adaptation and mitigation, such as in the areas of heat waves, climate-related illnesses, and the adoption of renewable technologies. She has produced and directed award-winning film projects in these areas, including for *The Years of Living Dangerously*, a Showtime series on climate change.

Kari Marie Norgaard is Associate Professor of Sociology and Environmental Studies at the University of Oregon. Her research on climate denial, tribal environmental justice, and gender and risk has been published in *Sociological Forum, Gender and Society, Sociological Inquiry, Organization and Environment, Rural Sociology, Race, Gender & Class*, and other journals, as well as by the World Bank. Her research has also been featured in *The Washington Post, National Geographic*, and *High Country News*, and on National Public Radio's "All Things Considered." Her first book, *Living in Denial: Climate Change, Emotions and Everyday Life*, was published by MIT Press in 2011. Norgaard is the recipient of the Pacific Sociological Association's Distinguished Practice Award for 2005.

Brian K. Obach is an Associate Professor of Sociology and chair of the department at the State University of New York at New Paltz. He specializes in the study of social movements, environmental sociology, and political economy. He is the author of *Labor and the Environmental Movement: The Quest for Common Ground*, in which he examines the promise and pitfalls of cross-movement alliance building. His other work focuses on political economy, especially as it relates to the environment. He is currently conducting research on the organic agriculture movement.

David Naguib Pellow is Professor of Sociology at the University of Minnesota. His teaching and research focus on ecological justice issues in the United States and globally. His books include *The Slums of Aspen: Immigrants vs. the Environment in America's Eden* (with Lisa Sun-Hee Park), *Resisting Global Toxics: Transnational Movements for Environmental Justice; The Silicon Valley of Dreams: Environmental Injustice, Immigrant Workers, and the High-Tech Global Economy* (with Lisa Sun-Hee Park); and *Garbage Wars: The Struggle for Environmental Justice in Chicago*. He has served on the Boards of Directors for the Center for Urban Transformation, Greenpeace USA, and International Rivers.

Allan Schnaiberg was Professor of sociology at Northwestern University, Evanston, Illinois, from 1969 to 2009. His work in what later became known as "environmental sociology" (and still later "environmental justice") started in 1971. Trained as a demographer and earlier as a chemist and metallurgical engineer, he was able to mediate between the sociopolitical expressions by natural scientists in the 1970s and the later analyses by social scientists of the societal–environmental dialectic. His development of the "treadmill of production" model of socioenvironmental dynamics greatly influenced the field of environmental sociology. The treadmill model was further developed in his collaborations in later years with Kenneth Gould, Adam Weinberg, and David Pellow. The common thread in his research was the ways in which both environmental problems and environmental protections have been infused with social inequalities. He traced these inequalities through his analyses of sociology of science, energy crises, appropriate technology, sustainable development, recycling, and environmental impact assessment. He died in 2009.

Bahram Tavakolian studied cultural ecology at UCLA with Dr. Walter Goldschmidt, and he has conducted field research on pastoral nomads in Afghanistan, urban migration in Turkey, women's labor force participation in Scotland, and Native American acculturation in the United States. He is at present Visiting Professor of anthropology at Willamette University in Salem, Oregon, and he is Professor Emeritus of sociology/anthropology and a former director of the Environmental Studies Program at Denison University in Granville, Ohio. His current writing projects include a manuscript on the relationships between gender and nomadism in the Middle East and central Asia and another on British India's impact on tribe–state relations in Afghanistan. A recent essay on "Nomads" will be published in *Vocabulary for the Study of Religion* (Brill).

Richard York is Professor of Sociology and Environmental Studies at the University of Oregon. He is Chair of the Environment and Technology Section (ETS) of the American Sociological Association (ASA). His research focuses on the social structural forces that affect the natural environment and the philosophy, history, and sociology of science. He has published dozens of articles, including ones in *American Sociological Review, Ecological Economics, Conservation Biology, Nature Climate Change, Social Problems, Sociological Theory*, and *Theory and Society*. He has published three books with Monthly Review Press: *The Critique of Intelligent Design* and *The Ecological Rift*, both with John Bellamy Foster and Brett Clark, and *The Science and Humanism of Stephen Jay Gould* with Brett Clark. In recognition of his research, he has twice (2004 and 2007) received the Outstanding Publication Award and once (2011) the Honorable Mention for the same award from the ETS of the ASA, and the Rural Sociology Best Paper Award (2011) from the Rural Sociological Society. He has also received the Teaching and Mentorship Award (2011) from the ETS of the ASA.

Nicole Youngman received her PhD in sociology from Tulane University and is a sociology instructor at Southeastern Louisiana University, specializing in environmental sociology and sociology of disaster. Her research focuses on the historical relationship among municipal growth machines, canal development, and flood risk in New Orleans.

An Introduction to Environmental Sociology

Kenneth A. Gould and Tammy L. Lewis

THE ORIGIN AND PURPOSE OF THIS BOOK

The idea for this reader emerged from a discussion among a small group of environmental sociology professors en route to visiting Akwesasne, the St. Regis Mohawk reservation, to learn more about their struggles with toxic contamination from nearby industrial plants. On the ride to Akwesasne we started to talk about our environmental sociology courses and how dissatisfied we were with the undergraduate, introductory-level readers (edited books with chapters from various authors) in our subfield. The point of a reader is to bring together exemplary works in a given subfield to expose students to the range of ideas, concepts, theoretical approaches, and empirical research, without requiring them to read a large number of individual books. For us, the problem with the traditional reader is that the chapters are usually drawn from professional journal articles, written by sociologists for sociologists. That is, the materials used to speak to undergraduate students, whom we don't expect to be familiar with the subfield, are the same materials that professional, trained sociologists use to speak to professional, trained sociologists, whom we rightly *do* expect to be quite familiar with the language, theories, data, and debates in the subfield. The result is that the audience for whom the initial materials were written is poorly matched to the audience for the collected reader. Granted, the versions of professional journal articles included in most readers have been edited to make them more accessible to the undergraduate. But still, the bulk of each chapter originates in professor-to-professor communication rather than professor-to-student communication. And neither the professors nor the students are particularly happy with the outcomes.

As we drove in a university van to the Mohawk reservation, we were struck by how odd it was that sociology professors, who largely earn their living by finding ways to explain their field to undergraduate students, are stuck assigning readings that are clearly not designed for that purpose. Each of us in the van taught environmental sociology to undergraduates. We decided that it would be much more useful to have an undergraduate reader that was based on our most successful professor-to-student communications

1

(our classes) rather than our most impressive professor-to-professor communications (our published professional journal articles).

It was at that point that two of us decided to launch the project that has resulted in this book. We made a list of what we thought were the most important topics to include in an undergraduate environmental sociology course. We then approached our environmental sociology colleagues whom we knew were enthusiastic teachers and had successfully taught undergraduate-level courses in environmental sociology. We asked them to choose among the topics and match them with their favorite class lectures, the ones both they and their students seemed to enjoy and get the most out of. Then, rather than asking them to give us their best professional research paper on that topic, we instead asked them to grab their lesson notes and write up the lesson as closely as they could to the way they actually teach it in class. We told them that what we wanted was the best approximation of a favorite class lecture in environmental sociology in written form.

To our knowledge, this is a completely new approach to creating an undergraduate reader, one that starts with the classroom experience rather than being forced to fit into that experience. As editors, a big part of our job was to remind our contributors that the audience for their writing is undergraduate students. After all, when professors write in their subfield, it is almost always for other professors. That is, we know how to talk to you about what we do and what we know, but we generally have less practice in writing to you about that.

Given our histories as U.S.-based professors, our network of colleagues tends to be U.S.-based, which resulted in a collection from a U.S. perspective. We discuss this more in the concluding lesson of the book.

Oxford University Press is a not-for-profit publisher, and we think that is an important model in a time of high-cost, high-debt, high-profit higher education. Oxford has been enthusiastic about the project and committed to keeping the cost of the book as low as possible for students.

Oxford published the first edition of this book in 2009, and much to our delight, it was well received by students and professors taking and teaching environmental sociology courses. Also to our delight, the subfield of environmental sociology continued to expand, with many more sociology departments adding or expanding course offerings in environmental sociology. Less delightful has been the continuing deterioration of the global environment in the years since the book's first publication. When we were asked to create the updated second edition that you are reading now, we took stock of what has gotten better, what has gotten worse, and what the important developments in environmental sociology have been since 2009. We gathered feedback from students and faculty who have used the book and applied their insights to guide us through the revision process. All of the lessons in the second edition have been updated or are new. In particular, the second edition expands our focus on issues of energy and food, two contested areas of environment–society interactions that are particularly vital to global sustainability. This edition of *Twenty Lessons in Environmental Sociology* also includes a glossary index to help you to more quickly and easily familiarize yourself with the key terms and concepts of the subfield. What all of us who have contributed to this new edition hope we have achieved is an even more user-friendly introduction to what we think is one of the most critical areas of human inquiry in the 21st century.

Our hope is that you will find the lessons in this book accessible, interesting, and challenging and that the fact that each lesson was originally written specifically for undergraduate students will make the experience of taking a course in environmental sociology more enjoyable, engaging, and beneficial.

WHAT IS ENVIRONMENTAL SOCIOLOGY?

Put most succinctly, environmental sociology is the study of how social systems interact with ecosystems. Of course, since environmental sociology explores all of the ways that these two very complex systems affect each other, it is a very wide field of scientific investigation. Just trying to understand social systems or ecosystems alone is a daunting task. Trying to understand how the two affect each other is a monumental effort indeed. Ecosystems, their qualities and changing dynamics, affect social systems in many ways, from the way we organize language to the way we organize economic systems. Similarly, social systems and their qualities and shifting dynamics also affect ecosystems in numerous ways, from the organization of backyard gardens to the disorganization of global climate systems.

That social systems and ecosystems are deeply interconnected may seem obvious, but the intellectual history of sociology over the past 150 years or so provides little evidence that the depth and breadth of this dynamic interaction has been fully appreciated by sociologists. Similarly, the intellectual history of the science of ecology over roughly the same period also provides little evidence that the full scope of the impact of social systems on ecosystems had been well incorporated. Part of the reason for this lack of focus had to do with the need to first develop some fairly workable understandings of both social systems and ecosystems separately, before attempting to understand how they interact. However, since they do interact a lot, it is still surprising that our explanations of each developed with little reference to the other.

Another part of the explanation of this lack of synthesis has to do with the notion of bifurcation. That is, in Western tradition, nature and society tend to be thought of as separate domains. This has been referred to as the **nature–society dichotomy**. Society happens in some places and nature in others, and the two are examined separately by different groups of researchers. For example, it is common for people to think of the city as a place where society happens, and the "wild" frontier as a place where nature happens. Natural scientists didn't pay much attention to urban environments, and social scientists didn't pay much attention to the wild. Yet another part of the reason for the failure to treat the two systems as dynamically intertwined has to do with the nature of academic organization. This is especially true for sociology, which emerged as a discipline much later than the natural sciences.

In seeking to carve out a distinct intellectual and organizational niche for itself within the academy, and thus establish itself as a legitimate field of scholarly pursuit, sociologists put much effort into defining sociology as something distinct from the natural sciences. That is, sociologists intentionally tried to separate their field of study from the already established fields that studied physical nature, such as biology and chemistry. As a result, any attempt at incorporating the natural world within sociology was seen as ceding intellectual ground to natural science, and thus undermining the effort to establish sociology as a distinct field of study with a separate area of investigation.

Despite the social barriers to fully integrating the study of social systems and ecosystems, over time the increasing confidence of sociology as a fully established and legitimate discipline created the social space for the emergence of environmental sociology. At the same time, both the increasing urgency of the negative impacts of social systems on ecosystems and the resulting negative impacts of ecosystem disorganization on human societies created the social need for the emergence of environmental sociology. Thus, as sociology matured, and as environmental problems became more and more prevalent and affected communities around the world, sociologists began to systematically examine nature–society connections.

All that said, it is important to note that environmental sociology is not equally rooted in sociology and ecology. Environmental sociology remains a subfield of sociology, one in which its practitioners are more open to including ecological variables within their analyses and have chosen to apply and develop sociological analysis precisely where social systems and ecosystems intersect. Environmental sociologists bring the sociological lens and apply their sociological imaginations to the ways in which social systems generate and respond to ecological change. They are not ecologists and are not prepared to address the deep complexity of ecosystems. Instead, their training is in the study of the deeply complex ways that social systems are organized and change. Their special focus is on how social systems are organized and change in response to the natural world, just as the changes they produce in the natural world force them to further respond and change.

A BRIEF HISTORY OF ENVIRONMENTAL SOCIOLOGY

One social response to environmental change has been the institutionalization of the study of social system–ecosystem interactions. The brief history we present here highlights the institutional trajectory of environmental sociology. We focus on the development of organizational structures intended to sustain the **subdiscipline**. In elaborating this history, we touch upon the key social forces that led to its emergence and how it fits into the broader context of sociology. The institutions are clearly tied to key individuals in the field. However, rather than focus on these individuals, we focus on the "real-world" events and intellectual concerns embedded in the era in which the subfield emerged.

Environmental sociology has been an officially recognized subfield within sociology only since around 1976, with its institutionalization as one of the American Sociological Association's topical sections. Prior to that time, "the environment" was not considered within the purview of sociology. Indeed, as noted earlier, in developing sociology as a discipline, the "founding fathers" sought to distance the study of "social facts" (Emile Durkheim) from studies of the biophysical world in order to legitimize the new "science of society," sociology (see Lesson 1). In the late 1800s, the environment was not part of sociology. When we consider that a key concern of classical sociology was to understand the broad-scale social changes brought about by industrialization and modern state bureaucracies, the omission of "the environment" and examination of "environmental inequalities" seems impossible from our contemporary perspective. Today, environmental sociologists study how social institutions interact with the environment and ask how industrial capitalism and modern state bureaucracies affect social and environmental inequalities and vice versa.

If we revisit the "classics" in sociology, searching to discover to what degree the founders may have looked at the environment, we do not see much in the analyses of Max Weber or Émile Durkheim. For example, we could stretch to see that Durkheim analyzed the effects of "cosmic factors"—season, temperature, etc.—on suicide rates (though he dismissed their causal relevance), but there really is not much there. Contemporary research by John Bellamy Foster and others suggests that Karl Marx was more attentive to the environment, though this was not a central focus and is certainly not Marx's legacy. In the 1970s, bringing the environment into sociological analysis occurred consciously and deliberately.

The institutional history of environmental sociology coincides with the emergence of the modern "ecology movement." Both were born in the late 1960s and early 1970s. Within a relatively short span of time, the professional organizations of sociologists incorporated formal niches for environmental sociology. The Rural Sociological Society's Natural Resources Research Group formed in the mid-1960s (it has had numerous name changes). The Society for the Study of Social Problems started a group on environmental problems in 1973, and the American Sociological Association's Environment and Technology section formed in 1976 (originally it was called the section on "environmental sociology").

The institutionalization of environmental sociology reflected the growing attention of society in general, and social scientists in particular, to issues of the environment. Intellectuals working in the fields of human ecology, rural sociology, and urban sociology and researching topics such as social movements found their intellectual interests intersecting with real-world events during this time period. This same era witnessed numerous environmental "crises," such as the energy crisis of the early 1970s, the Santa Barbara oil spill (1969), toxic wastes being discovered in the residential neighborhood of Love Canal (1978), and the accident at the nuclear power plant at Three Mile Island (1979).

Coupled with these crises was rising public concern regarding the environment and the resulting emergence of environmental organizations, including the Environmental Defense Fund (1967), Friends of the Earth (1969), and the Natural Resources Defense Council (NRDC, founded 1970). Political actions were also taking place. In 1969, Congress passed the National Environmental Policy Act, which President Nixon signed into law in 1970. The Environmental Protection Agency (EPA) was established in 1970, followed by the passage of key environmental laws: the Clean Air Act (1970), the Clean Water Act (1972), the Pesticide Control Act (1972), and the Resource Conservation and Recovery Act (1976). The year 1970 also marked the first Earth Day. Political attention was not just national but international, including the 1972 United Nations Conference on the Human Environment held in Stockholm. Environmental sociologists were not immune to their surroundings. They, too, responded to socioenvironmental changes and began researching the causes of environmental degradation, public opinion regarding the environment, and the social responses of the public and institutions to environmental changes.

Just as early sociology sought to distinguish itself from other sciences, early environmental sociology tried to distinguish itself from "mainstream sociology." Writing in the late 1970s, William Catton and Riley Dunlap, early environmental sociologists, wrote an oft-cited paper that argued that virtually all sociological theories were anthropocentric; that is, they view human society as the center of the natural world, with humans controlling and using the environment without regard for the natural resource–based limits to social growth. They termed this sociological worldview the "**human exemptionalism paradigm**" (HEP). By contrast, they argued for a competing worldview that would critique mainstream sociology's HEP worldview. They called their alternative the "**new ecological paradigm**" (NEP). The NEP started from the assumptions that humans are one of many interdependent species in the global ecosystem and part of a large web of nature, that humans depend on a finite biophysical environment, and that humans cannot stand above ecological laws. The HEP–NEP distinction provided environmental sociology with a way to differentiate itself from mainstream sociology. However, we have yet to see sociology as a discipline fully embrace the NEP worldview, though "the environment" and "environmental issues" have drawn the attention of researchers working in various other sociological subfields with greater frequency over time.

Environmental sociology has by now established itself as a recognized subfield in sociology. The continuation of the environment as a social problem has reinforced this, giving environmental sociologists a relevant role to play in examining the potential paths toward environmental reform and synthesis of the social and ecological systems. On its website, the Environment and Technology section of the American Sociological Association explains the role of environmental sociology in this way:

> Many of society's most pressing problems are no longer just "social." From the maintenance of genetic diversity to the disposal of radioactive wastes, from toxics in the groundwater below us to global warming of the atmosphere above, the challenges of the 21st century are increasingly coming to involve society's relationships with the environment and technologies upon which we all depend. . . . Facing the challenges of the 21st century requires more than sound scientific understanding and technological solutions. Too often missing from the debate is knowledge of the complex social, economic and political relationships that drive society in destructive directions. Environmental Sociology brings together the tools of social sciences and applies them to these key issues of our day. Examining environmental issues in turn is reshaping the field of sociology.

Many of our environmental sociology colleagues in other nations are not organized in the same manner as American sociologists are. Because of this, the interactions between North American environmental sociologists and sociologists throughout the rest of the world have been facilitated by the International Sociological Association's Research Committee on Environment and Society (RC 24), which was formed in 1971 and has seen continued growth (in international meetings) and increased significance among environmental sociologists over time.

Finally, in looking to institutions, there is every reason to believe that environmental sociology will continue to thrive as a subdiscipline. The structures for the continued production of knowledge and dissemination of knowledge and the education of professionals are well established and growing. For instance, there are well-established journals in which environmental sociologists publish. Increasingly, research in environmental sociology is being published in "mainstream" sociological journals. Recent institutional growth in the field is evidenced by the growth in graduate programs dedicated specifically to environmental sociology (students interested in this should explore the Environment and Technology section's website for the most up-to-date list). In fact, environmental sociology is one of the fastest-growing subfields in the discipline today, which is perhaps an indicator of the growing awareness that social system–ecosystem dynamics are severely out of balance. This book will introduce you to the work that environmental sociologists do.

THE LAYOUT OF THE BOOK

This book is divided into four parts as a way of broadly organizing your introduction to the ways in which environmental sociologists think about and study the relationships between social systems and ecosystems. The book begins with a brief introduction to socioenvironmental theory, followed by three sections addressing the social causes, consequences, and responses to environmental disruption. The book concludes by looking at where the sociological study of society–environment interactions might productively focus in coming years and suggests some important questions that remain incompletely answered.

Part 1 of the book introduces you to the variety of theoretical frameworks that environmental sociologists have developed to describe and explain the patterns they have uncovered in the ways that social systems and ecosystems interact. These patterns of interaction range from the micro-level, at which people as social beings encounter and comprehend the natural world, to the macro-level, at which the global economy shapes and is shaped by the constraints of the biosphere. By beginning with a broad overview of socio-environmental theories, we hope to provide you with an opportunity to see how these theories both guide and emerge from the types of analyses you will read in the next three parts of the book.

Part 2 of the book explores the systemic causes of social disruption of ecosystems. The focus here is on the ways in which major social institutions such as governments, corporations, and labor generate and respond to environmental change and interact with each other in regard to environmental conditions. Since science and technology are primary mechanisms through which humans understand and mediate their relationships with ecosystems, an additional focus of Part 2 is the social institutions and processes that shape science and technological innovation. An examination of population dynamics and the ways in which human population change and distribution intersect with ecosystemic processes follows. Part 2 concludes with a look at the critical social and environmental arena of energy. Throughout Part 2, you will be asked to think critically about the social dynamics of power as environmental sociologists recognize that the capacity to determine the nature of social system–ecosystem interactions is not distributed equally throughout society.

In Part 3 of the book, the focus is on the consequences of environmental disruption for social systems. That is, where Part 2 looks at how and why society changes the environment, this next part of the book looks at how the environment changes society. The disorganization of ecosystems produced by social systems affects those social systems in a wide variety of ways. Those social impacts of human-induced environmental change do not affect all people equally or in the same ways. Therefore, you will find that a primary focus of Part 3 is on issues of social inequality in terms of who bears the costs of environmental disruption (and who reaps the benefits), from local through global levels of distribution. In particular, the concepts of "environmental justice" and "environmental health" are introduced and further explored through specific analyses of food production and consumption systems, "natural" disasters, and global climate change. Paralleling what you will have read in Part 2, your reading of Part 3 will help you to see that, just as the power to determine the ways in which social systems and ecosystems interact is unevenly distributed throughout society, so is the power to avoid, deny, or deal with the results of these interactions.

Part 4, the final part of the book, examines the ways in which society has responded to human-induced environmental disruption. Much of the focus here is on how and why communities, social movements, and nongovern-mental organizations have mobilized to address a wide variety of environmental concerns. This type of citizen mobilization has emerged all over the world, at the local, regional, national, and transnational levels, with great variation in the environmental issues focused on and the strategies employed. Part 4 exposes you to this rich variety of social response to problems arising from the ways that social system–ecosystem relations are currently organized. Part 4 also introduces you to "sustainable development," a concept intended to guide efforts toward reorganizing the relationships between social systems and ecosystems in ways that produce fewer environmental disruptions and greater social benefits. We conclude with a brief discussion of the future of environmental sociology; raise some questions that remain to be fully answered about the social causes, consequences, and responses to environmental problems; and suggest some areas of focus for the further sociological study of social system–ecosystem relations. In the spirit of engaging students in an area we find intellectually stimulating and vitally important to the future, we hope that you might take on researching and answering these questions to advance the state of the subdiscipline and improve the prospects for our socioenvironmental future.

CHANGES TO THE SECOND EDITION

The four-part layout of the book is identical to the first edition of the book. The main changes to the second edition are as follows:

- The lesson in the first edition titled, "Climate Change: Why the Old Approaches Aren't Working" has been replaced with a lesson titled, "Normalizing the Unthinkable: Climate Denial and Everyday Life" (Lesson 15).

- Two brand-new lessons have been added: one on energy and one on food. These are titled "Energy, Society, and the Environment" (Lesson 9) and "Producing and Consuming Food: Justice and Sustainability in a Globalized World?" (Lesson 12)

- Key terms and concepts are now bolded at first use within the text, with definitions provided in a glossary/index at the end of the book.

- Those of you who are good at math will note that the addition of two lessons should result in a book called Twenty-Two Lessons in Environmental Sociology. To ensure continuity with the first edition, we decided not to call this chapter (the introduction) a lesson, nor are we calling the conclusion a lesson. Therefore, the numbers of some of the lessons have changed from the first to the second edition, but the order remains the same.

- Finally, all of the authors updated the data and examples in their chapters. Many of the chapters are significantly revised. The main themes, however, remain the same.

We hope you find these changes to be useful. Instructors have indicated to us what has worked for them in the first edition and we have attempted to revise based on the needs of the subdiscipline.

Finally, we would like to thank the formal reviewers who provided many helpful suggestions regarding revisions for the second edition:

- Eric Bonds, University of Mary Washington
- Laura K. Chambers, Jacksonville University
- Michael Haedicke, Drake University
- Denise Kall, St. Ambrose University
- Stefano Longo, North Carolina State University
- Amy Lubitow, Portland State University
- Aaron Peeks, Elon University

We are also grateful to our colleagues and students who have used the book and offered useful feedback, suggestions, and encouragement. We hope that *Twenty Lessons in Environmental Sociology* continues to be a valuable tool in supporting their efforts to teach and to learn.

SOURCES

Buttel, Frederick H. 2003. "Environmental Sociology and the Explanation of Environmental Reform." *Organization & Environment* 16:306–344.

Catton, William R., and Riley E. Dunlap. 1978. "Environmental Sociology: A New Paradigm." *American Sociologist* 13:41–49.

Foster, John Bellamy. 1999. "Marx's Theory of Metabolic Rift: Classical Foundations for Environmental Sociology." *American Journal of Sociology* 105(2):366–405.

Schnaiberg, Allan. 1980. *The Environment: From Surplus to Scarcity.* New York: Oxford University Press.

Part 1

THEORY

The Social Construction of Nature
Of Computers, Butterflies, Dogs, and Trucks

Stella M. Čapek

Student using public Wi-Fi in newly constructed urban greenspace, Brooklyn, New York. Photo by Ken Gould.

Environmental sociology is a wide-ranging field that includes a variety of theories and methodological approaches. If you did this for a living, you might find yourself studying topics as seemingly different as the environmental movement (local and global), public opinion, natural resource use, social impacts of technology, inequality and environmental justice, and constructions of nature and gender. Or you might study the economics and politics of environmental policy, sustainable community design, cultural meanings attached to food, or particular issues such as climate change, deforestation, and population—and that is only a partial list. But regardless of the topic, the job of theory in environmental sociology is to make social structure visible—that is, to identify the stable, persistent, often hidden patterns of social relationships that become established over time. And social relationships are only the beginning of the story, since *environmental* sociology is about understanding the two-way relationship between society and

13

the environment. Theory is like any other process that makes hidden things visible; just as ultraviolet light reveals striking color patterns that are there all along but invisible to the naked eye, sociological theories throw a certain kind of (analytical) light on society to illuminate social and environmental connections that are not immediately obvious.

One way to look at social structure is to see it as invisible "strings" that link individuals to social groups and to the environment in a patterned way. Why are these relationships so invisible in the first place? Some are taken for granted and are simply not thought about, while others are masked by power relationships. Still others are extremely complex, making it difficult to discern a pattern. Environmental sociology offers theoretical models that make key relationships more visible and allow us to understand better what holds them in place. By making structures visible, theories also offer us the opportunity to make more conscious choices about participating in or changing these patterns. Without understanding how they work, and who and what is attached to them (including ourselves), conscious choice is impossible.

In the following discussion, we will consider several snapshot images that will invite us to apply theories from environmental sociology. Because theory can often seem abstract, I want us to imagine actual bodies in actual places—our own bodies, or those of others. In fact, whether we are considering the globalization of environmental problems or the background levels of chemicals in our bloodstreams, our research questions and theories always connect to real people in specific situations. The three scenes that I will ask us to consider are these: a person throwing a can out of the window of a speeding truck; a person sitting at the keyboard of a computer, making a fast connection on the Internet; and a person physically dismantling a computer that has been "thrown away" in the United States and exported to an "e-waste processing center" in another country. Although these snapshots are only three out of many possibilities, they offer an excellent opportunity to connect structures across time and space and to learn about the insights and creative uses of environmental sociology.

I will draw on several theories from environmental sociology. They are all related, even though they address very different scales of human action, from individual and small group (micro) behavior to "big picture" (macro) patterns like globalization and shifting ideas about time and space. First, I will discuss a micro-level concept, "naturework," that comes out of symbolic interactionist theory. Symbolic interactionism focuses on how human beings and social groups symbolically communicate and acquire a sense of identity through social interaction. Naturework looks at how human beings construct ideas about nature and their relationship to it. Then, I will "zoom out" to theories of globalization and modernization that explore how space and time are being experienced in new ways by human beings. The context for these structures is a global capitalist system shaped by a "treadmill" logic, a social structure that continues to churn out ideas, material arrangements, and identities that have enormous implications for the environment. All of these theories shed light on the snapshot scenes we will consider—the truck, the computer, the people who have a relationship to these technologies, and even creatures like butterflies and dogs. They will show how small, cumulative actions ripple outward into the global ecosystems of the planet, and how important it is to keep nature "in the picture" as we make social decisions.

NATUREWORK AND ITS USES: OF TRUCKS AND BUTTERFLIES

Scene One: A truck zooms down the freeway, the window rolls down, an arm appears, and fingers reach out to toss a can from the moving vehicle. The can sails through the air and lands along the edge of the highway with a small crash. Maybe it's a beer bottle or a cigarette butt. Or an entire ashtray full of cigarette butts. Whatever it is, it lands on the side of the road as the truck quickly disappears over the horizon. The object becomes part of a jagged mosaic of broken glass shards, cigarettes, cans, miscellaneous objects considered trash, and—as I once learned doing a highway cleanup—wings from migrating butterflies that can't compete with the cars speeding down the highway. The delicately beautiful but damaged butterfly wings are a small, well-kept secret in a roadside no man's land that stretches for miles.

What can an environmental sociologist do with this scene, and how can she or he use theory to create new angles of vision on it? I choose this particular act—what we call in this society "littering"—because it seems to be a very simple, *unthinking* act. But of course, this unthinking act would be *unthinkable* under a different set of social circumstances, in another time or place. Sociology in general, and environmental sociology in particular, suggests that the simplest act is not simple at all and is rarely individual or private—it is part of a network of actions and social relationships that have consequences for other people and for the environment.

Gary Alan Fine has coined a useful term, "**naturework,**" that refers to how we constantly work to transform "nature" into culture, filtering it through the screen of social meanings that we have learned. To a social constructionist like Fine, there is no such thing as "raw" nature. For example, when we look at a tree, we notice some things about it and not others. While nature, or the tree, does in fact exist, what is more important, he would argue, is that we inevitably construct an image of what the tree is and behave toward it accordingly. Fine points out that "being 'in nature' implies being in culture" since culture influences how we see the tree. When we transform nature into culture, we create consequences for individuals as well as social policy.

Symbolic interactionists point out that human beings are constantly at work, negotiating meaning and constructing reality. For example, we invent (or someone else invents) terms like "wilderness," "Mother Nature," "desert," "human being," "freeway," and "climate change." Some of these terms are more contested than others, but all represent a human interpretation of what "nature" is "doing." Likewise, we invent words for what animals are "saying" and teach them to children; for example, in English, a dog says "bow wow!" while in Czech, the same dog (according to human translators) says "haf haf!" Language is part of a broader task of classifying and making sense of things, and in fact, much of naturework has to do with creating and maintaining borders between categories. For example, where is the line drawn between humans and (other) animals? (If we didn't care about this line, we wouldn't insult people by calling them "animals.") What kind of line exists between humans and the technologies that we invent? Between nature and "civilization"? What kind of nature is "good" or "bad," dangerous or safe? Do we include nature inside the boundaries of our skin, or do we see it as exclusively outside us?

These kinds of boundary questions generate others that are even more specific. For example, how do you (or I) feel about particular animals? Should they be hunted? Protected? Pets? Food? What about the human body? Should you shave the hair off of certain parts of your body? Should you mask the odors of nature? Should you apply cosmetics to distinguish yourself from or to signal your connection with nature? Do you think of nature as female (as in "Mother Nature")? Do you know the names of the trees, the birds, the rivers? Does the sight of a tree or a sunset make you glad? When you go camping (if you go camping), do you take many things with you? Do you carry a cell phone? When you walk or drive, are you plugged into your own private music system and personal theme music? Are you a "frequent flyer"? When you travel, do you take photographs? A few? Many? Do you have allergies and see nature as an attacker or a nuisance? Is your model of the "American Dream" a detached single-family home with a lawn? Do you know where your trash goes? All of these small, often unthinking decisions represent naturework and result in a particular relationship with the ecosystem and a specific set of outcomes. A symbolic interactionist would point out that although naturework might seem more obvious when we interpret big events like hurricanes, most naturework happens on a daily basis and is enacted through the seemingly insignificant details of our lives. It doesn't *feel* like work because the categories that we use to understand the world appear normal to us and, in many cases, emotionally and morally reassuring.

Let's go back to the truck, the highway, the arm, and the flying can. How might the concept of naturework help us to interpret this situation? In fact, many things have to be in place for the can to be tossed out the window. First, one has to feel separated from the place where the can will fall. If this piece of earth is considered just "dirt" or empty space at the edge of a highway, not an alive organic material that interacts with us at every moment, it is easy to see it as a kind of trash receptacle or sponge to absorb waste. This is also not likely to be a place where one's loved ones live. Second, one has to assume that he or she is not accountable for the act of "trashing." Speeding down the highway, it is easy to leave behind any thought of consequence or accountability and to assume that no one will care, or at least no one will know who threw the can (notice that this also implies that we are accountable at most to another human being—perhaps a police officer—rather than the ecosystem or the Earth's biosphere). Third, in not giving this action much thought, one has to assume it is fairly trivial (as the word "littering" suggests). No thought is given to cumulative impacts because "nature" will clean it up, there is plenty of space in the trash can, or there are better things to worry about on a given day. All of these assumptions add up to one conclusion: *It doesn't matter.*

The idea that it doesn't matter is supported by social patterns that encourage a certain kind of naturework. Let's look at this more closely. A person driving down the highway in a fast-moving vehicle is likely to feel quite (unrealistically) separated from what is outside, including nature in the form of landscape and weather. U.S. culture, or very specific groups in that culture, invented the idea that cars and trucks are a good way to get around, that their average replacement time should be about 3 years, that they are better than public transportation, that they are an important marker of status, that speed is to be valued, that the Earth is just material that we drive on and use for our own purposes, and that throwing a can out the window represents freedom. The common piece of naturework in all of these constructions is the view that we are separate from the natural world and have the power to control it or ignore it. William Catton and Riley Dunlap, in a classic article on the models, or paradigms, that we use to interpret our relationship to the ecosystem, call this view the "human exemptionalist paradigm" (HEP) (see Introduction and Lesson 2). Instead of seeing ourselves as part of the ecological system of the planet (or what they called NEP, a "new ecological paradigm"), we see ourselves as apart from it, in a controlling position that is enhanced by our technology. A banner that I saw displayed at a local Toyota dealer could be a poster for the HEP worldview: Next to an image of a speeding car are the words "Hear the atmosphere scream as you tear it in half." The ad sells the idea that the domination of nature (especially through speed and technology) is an attractive and highly desirable experience. One need not look far to find many messages like this in contemporary societies like that of the United States.

But what if the Earth were considered sacred, or if, as scientist Donella Meadows and others have argued, we are in fact participants in a partnered dance with nature? What if invisible strings linked the hand to the can that is thrown and the strings lingered in place, reminding us of consequences? What if ecological thinking were so prevalent that it would be impossible to "litter"? Sociologists Michael Bell and Michael Carolan point out that at present in the United States if a person does not consciously go out of his or her way to take environmentally beneficial actions, by default the status quo results in environmental harm. A different set of default arrangements, a different design, could support ecological sustainability. Under those conditions—and this is Bell and Carolan's point—even unthinking acts would be more likely to produce environmental benefits. For example, if more sustainable materials were designed into the front end of the manufacturing process, it would be far easier to recycle materials. "Green architect" William McDonough, for example, discusses a "cradle to cradle" concept, where a product reaches the end of its life cycle only to be "born" into a new use. Urban and environmental sociologist Harvey Molotch reminds us that "How we desire, produce, and discard the durables [i.e., the material objects] of existence helps form who we are, how we connect to one another, and what we do to the earth."

Let's explore the "desire" piece of the formula. A key point to remember is that while we are busy constructing the meaning of the world and our own identities through naturework, others are busily attempting to construct our identities for us. For example, the advertising industry, an essential feature of contemporary global capitalism, works around the clock to construct us primarily as "consumers" always in need of a newer, more "cutting-edge" product (see Lesson 5). The social psychology of capitalism depends on us experiencing a kind of "halo effect" around an item we desire, a halo that quickly begins to fade as soon as we possess the item and our attention moves to a new object (think about how this works in your own experience when you buy things). The social and economic (and political) relationships of capitalism depend on intense competition and a drive to increase profits. This pattern is built around a kind of "**treadmill**" logic, as Allan Schnaiberg and others have pointed out; individuals and corporations run in place faster and faster in an effort to keep up in the (now global) game of competition (see Lesson 2). The treadmill creates a voracious appetite for natural resources as people are persuaded to "toss" older products. This may include tossing a can out of the window or getting rid of a truck or a computer after a few years, to replace it with the latest model. It is not considered too important to know where things go after they leave our hands. What is important is the desire for the new object.

The advertising industry fuels our desires by specializing in a particular kind of naturework: It attracts buyers by invoking a love of nature but sells products that often disconnect us from nature. In the multibillion-dollar cosmetics industry, for example, the "natural look" not only carries a large price tag but sells a fabricated image of perfection. "Natural skin" enhanced by cosmetics is billed as fresh and flawless, while nature itself includes many flaws and irregularities (and much more variety). Similarly, local organic apples are likely to contain many more blemishes but more freshness and diversity (and significantly fewer dangerous pesticides) than their mass-produced relatives available at national grocery store chains and based on monoculture and industrialized agriculture (see Lesson 12). "Natural" cosmetics often contain unsafe products that arguably do some violence to the environment and to the body that wears them. From name-brand undergarments billed as the "natural woman's" look to cosmetics that disguise what nature has given, it is a simulacrum, or false imitation, of nature that is being sold, not nature itself. In fact, "real" nature is not considered particularly attractive. This should not be surprising since the advertising industry has to be interested only in what can be captured and converted into a commodity and sold, and nature "in the raw" eludes capture.

If we shift our attention from cosmetics to ads for vehicles, we also find nature in the picture. A desire for the pure, untouched, and wide-open landscape is a staple feature of most television ads for cars, trucks, jeeps, sport-utility vehicles, and off-road vehicles. But in this case nature is seen as a place to "get away from it all" and/or a place that is waiting to be conquered by human technology. Nature is in fact a backdrop or a stage set for the enactment of key cultural fantasies about "freedom" and "domination" and "individualism." Since the vehicle conquers nature by representing the freedom to go anywhere and since, if the vehicle and others like it truly do go anywhere, there will soon be no pristine environment, the ad is selling pure paradox. Just as importantly, it sells the idea that the purchase of an expensive product is the admission ticket to this ego-enhancing performance.

But suppose that one's own naturework leans in the direction of ecological sustainability (see Lesson 20) and one wishes to step off the "treadmill" by becoming disinterested in consuming new products. Sociologist Zygmunt Bauman argues that this person is the true outsider, the deviant in a consumption-based society. To be socially accepted or even understandable to one's neighbors, a person needs to revel in the seduction of ever-new and identity-expanding choices offered by consumer goods, whether these are the latest models of cars, adventure tourism "packages," cosmetics, or a multitude of other possibilities. How true is this? Bauman is right that this has been the mainstream script for many years in countries like the United States. But the acceptance or rejection of this notion depends on time, place, situation, awareness, and socioeconomic position. The theories of environmental sociology can help us consider under what conditions ecologically sustainable actions become more or less possible. They can also teach us about what stands in the way of sustainable actions and solutions—from naturework to the treadmill logic of global capitalism to what Bell and Carolan call "technological somnambulism," the tendency to unquestioningly accept the use of and spread of new technologies.

Consider this example: Because of a history of strong labor unions, Sweden has had a law that supports the right of workers to discuss the implications of a new technology before it is introduced into the workplace. But at my college, such decisions are administratively made at the top. A new photocopying machine undercut previously successful efforts to use recycled paper because the paper tended to jam in the new machine, causing extra work for administrative assistants. The paper was phased out, and no one had a chance to talk about it at all. "Nature" became a threat to efficiency and was removed. But as more colleges and institutions become interested in how they contribute to a sustainable "ecological footprint," the possibility arises for more democratic discussions, better research into design, and a clearer grasp of the cost–benefit balance that comes with any new technology.

Since technologies always have complex (and often unanticipated) impacts on society and the environment, environmental sociology can play a key role in identifying impacts that are not immediately obvious (see Lesson 7). For example, it can help us to identify the range of "stakeholders" who will be helped and/or harmed by a particular technology, and it can offer a systematic way to evaluate the "goods" and "bads" for social groups (and for nature, or the ecosystem, an often-forgotten stakeholder). For example, I benefit from a feature on the new photocopier that allows me to be a "remote user," printing two-sided (good for the environment!) copies from my office. That new possibility represents a positive and exciting aspect of innovation. But the machine doesn't use recycled paper, and if it breaks down, my colleagues and I can't fix it ourselves by undoing a paper jam, as we could with the previous model—we have to call our Information Technology division and hope that someone is "home." So when we look at a new technology ("smart" phones, for example), we always need to ask for whom it is beneficial and why. The difficult challenge is to arrive at an overall picture of costs and benefits. That would require many groups with different kinds of knowledge and experience to be part of a democratic discussion. The theories of environmental sociology produce models and research findings that contribute to a "big-picture" understanding of any technology, as well as the naturework through which we see it.

Today, we have growing evidence that the mainstream script based on "conquering" nature is fraying around the edges, under pressure from the realities of climate change and impending oil scarcity, as well as movements for social and environmental justice. When I find myself looking at yet another advertising banner at the local car dealer with a picture of a truck and the words "It's a big, tough truck. What's not to like?" I think about how many of my students and colleagues would make a list of "what's not to like" quite different from what they thought even a year ago. Certainly, Ford and General Motors have discovered that suddenly there is much "not to like" about their large, fuel-inefficient vehicles. Many of my students now find the image of the lone vehicle presented as a powerful object of desire conquering an empty landscape (is it Alaska? Montana? New Mexico?) to be laughable, even ridiculous. Many of them would like bike paths, public transportation, and fuel efficiency. But to arrive at critique and to construct fresh choices, a person needs to have thought about it and to become aware of the many uses of naturework.

OF TIME, SPACE, AND COMPUTERS

Scene Two: Somebody sits with his or her fingers on a computer keyboard, looking at an electronic screen offering the promise of instant global communication. Not long ago Time *magazine celebrated this hypothetical person by selecting her or him as "Person of the Year." The magazine's cover contained the image of a partially reflective metal-like computer screen that "you" are invited to look into. The accompanying message is that you, the person with fingers on the keyboard, are Person of the Year because, in a world democratized and decentralized by the Internet, you have tremendous power and influence. Like the truck's passenger in Scene One—but even more so—"you" have the freedom to go anywhere, fast. But unlike the passenger in the truck, you aren't tossing anything out of the window. Or are you?*

Clearly, *Time* magazine's editors decided that in the United States use of the Internet was so widespread that the computer (and its imagined connection to "you") deserved a place on the cover, instead of the usual choice of one influential person. The accompanying article claims that the ability to use the Internet represents the end of top-down authority and the rise of democratic freedom to shape the world. It also celebrates "community and collaboration on a scale never seen before." A very empowered "you" sits in front of the screen, reveling in your historically new choices.

What would an environmental sociologist notice about this image and what it presupposes? First, he or she would notice that this is an image aimed only at those who have access to this technology. Second, the sociologist would take a hard look at the idea that access to the Internet makes you free from top-down authority and constraint. On the one hand, cell phones and social media have contributed significantly to social change movements around the world (for example, what came to be known as the "Arab Spring"). On the other hand, while there are significant opportunities to gather and share information in ways previously unavailable (and unimaginable), spyware on many websites and restricted access to information in the wake of 9/11 are only two examples that undermine the assumption that the Internet represents total freedom. And an *environmental* sociologist would inquire about connections to and disconnections from the environment that accompany the person sitting at the computer screen.

We could begin, once again, with the concept of "naturework." Where is nature in this picture? Unless "you" are looking at a virtual image of nature on the screen, the environment seems to be conspicuous by its absence. The computer is most likely indoors—although a new technological advantage is ever-increasing portability, so you may have taken your laptop (or your "smart" phone, or some even newer technology, a great example of the "treadmill" of production!) to a park. You are probably looking intently at the screen for extended periods of time, and you are probably in a sedentary posture. Nature is present in the form of your body, and your actions are shaping that body (your eyes, your posture, your health). Nature is also present in the materials that make up the room you are sitting in (the built environment) or in trees in the park—but if you are looking at the computer screen, you are less apt to notice your surrounding environment. Chances are that you are also ignoring your *internal* environment that is sending signals about eye strain, hunger, brain overload, and bad posture. All of this adds up to a separation from your immediate environment, a version of what sociologist Anthony Giddens calls "disembedding." Let's consider how the ideas of Giddens and some other scholars of modernity might help us analyze the relationship between the computer, the person, and the natural environment.

Social theorist Giddens claims that a new aspect of human experience in "late modern" societies is the way that time and space are rearranged to "connect presence and absence." Because of an increasingly globalized and interconnected world and because of the development of electronic communication and spaces (like cyberspace) that appear not to be connected to actual places, human beings experience what Giddens calls "disembedding" and "distanciation." **Disembedding** refers to social relations being "lifted out" of their local contexts and restructured across time and space. In other words, global economies and electronic communication networks connect us to physically absent people in places that are geographically remote from us (China, perhaps, or a friend in another city). This way of relating to people and places at a distance, or **distanciation**, comes to be a normal and expected part of our social organization and interactions.

New technologies harness the wonder of new understandings of nature, including how to make space and time work differently (up to a point). The problem is that these technologies are offered as if there were no strings attached—like the car sitting in a pristine landscape, the computer or cell phone suggests limitless freedom and no drawbacks. But there are limits of a very real kind. Giddens points out that relationships at a distance depend entirely on trust—trust that unseen people are who they claim to be and trust in "expert systems," such as those who set up and maintain the electronic networks (or the Information Technology experts who maintain the photocopier for me, the "remote user").

There are other kinds of limits that interfere with our ability to understand the bigger picture. Giddens argues, for example, that the new arrangement of space and time "tears space away from place." Notice the violence of the metaphor—this new development not only breaks the historical relationship between humans and physical places, but there is some roughness to the break. Giddens' metaphor suggests ragged edges and torn roots. And there is an additional twist—our local places are becoming harder to know and understand because they are, Giddens says, penetrated and reshaped by distant global influences. This makes it more difficult to clearly understand our relationship to the environment since what is visible locally may be deceptive. Radiation and invisible toxic pollution affect us whether we see them or not and can be disguised in the most beautiful landscape.

Time is also experienced in a radically new way in modern societies. Social relationships are increasingly separated from a natural calendar of seasons and cycles of day and night. We produce materials such as nuclear waste whose impact reaches far into a future whose time-scale we cannot even imagine. The expanding possibility of instantaneous global communication has reshaped expectations about how time "works." Speed is highly valued, from raising speed limits on highways to faster Internet connections and instant messaging. However, an environmental sociologist can easily make the argument that rising speeds make it more difficult to pay attention to one's local environment, whether a person is in a truck driving down a freeway or sitting at a computer keyboard, intently concentrating on the Internet "highway." Add a cell phone to this mix of speed and attention and the sense of absence from the local environment increases exponentially (as car accident statistics show quite clearly). Although many people pride themselves on their ability to multitask, studies show that it often doesn't work very well in terms of work quality, personal health, and consequences for social relationships. People report not having enough time to pay attention to everything from family to politics to their own mental health (think about how this works for you—do you have enough time?).

A feature of the new time–space structure described by Giddens and others is that it blurs the boundaries between many formerly separate categories of experience. Sociologist George Ritzer—best known for studying the global spread of "McDonaldization" and new forms of consumption— draws on Jean Baudrillard's concept of "implosion" to describe these new combinations of time and space. **Implosion** refers to one phenomenon collapsing, or contracting, into another. One example is the merging of the categories of home and shopping. In an electronically networked world, one does not need to leave one's home to go shopping, and if one desires, one can shop in the middle of the night at an online "cyberstore." Who is minding the cyberstore, and where is he or she located? We usually don't know. Even money is not required, just a credit card (with a promise of payment or growing debt in the future). Thus, home/store, local/global, and future/present collapse into one ambiguous category.

As Ritzer and others point out, such implosions represent ever-new opportunities for selling goods and promoting consumption, a feature that goes hand in hand with the expanding treadmill of global capitalism. Speeded-up experiences of time and access to new, "disembedded" electronic spaces erase earlier limits to consumption. Ritzer calls this a "reenchantment of the world," a process that draws in new consumers through ever more "spectacular" opportunities to consume. Meanwhile, just as these implosions create new connections, they create disconnections, particularly from local people and natural environments. The fact that distant or virtual spaces appear more real and compelling than our immediate environment can create a disturbing gap in our understanding of the environmental consequences of our behavior. It is no accident that, although advertisements for computers and cell phones still sell fantasies related to freedom, power, and individualism, the theme of nature and desire for nature appears to have dropped out of the picture. The seductive magic of a computer or a cell phone permits its user to leap across space and time, a thrilling possibility. But this possibility is embedded in a system that persuades "consumers" to use up resources even faster, producing more waste as they pursue the latest upgrade. Although we may assume that our key relationships are no longer with the physical places that surround us (including nature, in a local and specific way), we still have a relationship with our local environment. Even if—especially if— that relationship is neglected, there are ecological consequences.

THE TRUCK AND THE COMPUTER REVISITED: TOSSING NATURE OUT THE WINDOW?

Putting together some ideas from the theories we have considered, we can look at the similarities and differences between the truck and the computer.

Both are, we could say, fast-moving vehicles, although the computer is connected to fast motion in cyberspace. The truck speeding through the landscape is already altering the human experience of time and space, leaving places behind and focusing attention inside the vehicle or on the road ahead. But the computer screen is a gateway into a virtual world where time and space are compressed and recombined, making the disconnection from the natural environment even more striking. Both vehicles are attractive because they allow the "driver" to rush toward certain things (freedom?) and away from others (boredom? stultifying locations and relationships? limits?). Both involve the consumption of items that enhance the identity of the consumer. The truck is connected to a certain lifestyle that is linked to other consumption items (some of which are used up and tossed out of the window on the way). The computer is likewise connected to a lifestyle that is attractive to its "driver." Does he or she also use things up and toss them away while speeding through cyberspace? If so, what are they, and where do they land?

To answer such questions we need, once again, to look for nature and environment in the picture. Leaving aside the interesting debate about where nature ends and technology begins (a discussion well worth having but probably not now), we can see that the truck is driving through an actual place, even if the landscape is seen only through windows or in a rear-view mirror. The computer seems to have nothing to do with nature at all. But a closer look at both scenes will reveal naturework that creates separation and (illusory) control. The natural environment is as physically real as ever but has become less visible because of social organization and technology. So, for example our computers connect us to the coal, oil and gas, and nuclear power industries that charge them and to large data centers that make our quick searches and downloads possible by emitting greenhouse gases. Invented cyber-landscapes like "The Cloud" offer us "places" to store data beyond our individual laptops and devices. What could be wrong with a cloud, gently hovering over us, speeding up our searches, and keeping our data safe? (Google [2010] brags that "an 18-wheel truck could run over your laptop and all your data would still safely reside on the web, accessible from any Internet-connected computer, anywhere in the world.") A great idea, except that clouds of data add up to clouds of greenhouse gases. Yet, we often feel removed from the more distant landscapes that enable our technologies—disputed landscapes like the Fukushima nuclear reactor disaster, the BP oil spill, the Tar Sands pipeline connecting the United States and Canada, and hydrofracking sites.

We said earlier that it is the job of social and environmental theory to make relationships visible. If we return to the image of the invisible strings connecting people to each other (and to their technological inventions) and if we follow the strings back to the hands that put together the computer and the hands that will someday dismantle it, it will be impossible to ignore the ecological impact of the production, distribution, consumption, and disposal of computers, especially when multiplied by the number of users. No matter how liberated from place or from nature a person feels, the reality is that the computer was manufactured from Earth elements and goes back to the Earth and that there are tangible material consequences at each end of the production process (see Lesson 7). These include components that are poisonous to human beings and other life forms. There is a real cost—medical, social, and political—to ignoring these matters. Yet, quite often no more thought is given to throwing away an older model of computer than is given to throwing the can out of the truck. With a growing mountain of obsolete equipment and the message that throwing things away is necessary and even pleasing, it is clear that something big is going out the window—the idea of nature as a visible or significant presence and an enormous amount of material that can do environmental harm. And so we arrive at our third and last snapshot.

Scene Three: A young boy (or girl) picks through a heap of discarded electronic equipment from the United States. The actual place may be southern China or Delhi, India (we know this because of research conducted by environmental sociologists). We can begin to imagine this girl or boy (or man or woman) at a low tech "e-waste processing center," a place where people with few other choices manually harvest this highly toxic electronic waste for salvageable materials. The pay is low, and there are no protections in place for their bodies or for the surrounding environment.

We can only begin to imagine this scene because most computer users in the United States and in many other places have never seen it. It is disturbing to imagine it and to think that in some way we participate in it. Although from a distance the computer production process appears to be a clean and "high-tech" operation, at both the assembling and disassembling ends it is hazardous and farmed out to low-wage assembly line–style factories in developing nations. Instead of a can being thrown to the edge of a U.S. highway, electronic toxic waste is landing in places that are globally "at the edge of the highway" as Western nations (and even more so multinational corporations) speed by in pursuit of economic growth and political power. The "tearing away" from place first evident in the truck scene now has global dimensions. The difference is that globalization extends the arc of the object being disposed of and expands its geographical reach. Like the butterfly wings at the edge of the highway, the export of toxic components has been a well-kept secret. And that is the latest challenge for theorists in environmental sociology—to make these global structures plainly visible so that we can see and so that we can act.

CONCLUDING THOUGHTS: OF NATURE AND DOGS

Although this discussion has included only a small slice of what environmental sociologists do with theory, it reflects the wide range of interests and levels of analysis that are characteristic of the field. From naturework to shifting arrangements of time and space in the context of global capitalism, it offers tools for understanding the connection between our individual identities, nature, and broad patterns that are reshaping the context of our human experience and generating new kinds of relationships.

At the same time, we can notice that there is creative resistance to these patterns, some of which is also expressed through technology—for example, one might be using the computer to research social change and to connect with organizations working for ecological sustainability. There are many groups around the world working for environmental justice and for safeguards that would change Scene Three, for example, by making it more visible to the people in Scene Two, or by working to organize the people in Scene Three for better alternatives (see Lessons 10, 16, and 18). When environmental sociologists produce theories and research to document and analyze relationships between society and environment, they contribute to the possibility of real social change.

Here is a closing thought and one last image. My friend and colleague Elaine lives in a rural area over in the next town, in a self-designed house that reflects her fondness for stained glass art and large dogs. On her way to work, some of the dogs run alongside her truck for a little while, then turn around and go home before she hits the main road. But one morning, after an ice storm, the story line changed. She had to drive very slowly on the slippery unpaved road leading from her house. Because the truck couldn't "outrun" her most enthusiastic dog, he jumped in the back of her truck, rode to the university, and entertained himself by barking at passersby for much of the day. We don't know whether he *really* said "bow wow!" or "haf haf!" but we know that he attracted a lot of attention as an element of "nature" out of place.

I remember this story for several reasons. I like to think about how that dog insisted on connecting time and space and refused to be left behind in the "home" world while my friend went to "work" (he didn't appreciate distanciation). He brings to mind the many things we think we can outrun, including our impacts on the environment. Like the barking dog, fossil fuel scarcity and climate change are reminders of ecological actualities that we cannot continue to outrun. In our speeded-up world, you could say that our road is getting slippery and there are plenty of signs that we need to slow down and take an immediate, careful, and radical look at our actions and at our connections to the environment.

I propose that it would be even more appropriate to see social theory as the barking dog in this picture, shaking up our usual routines and reminding us that we are engaged in a dialog with the environment, whether we want to see it or not. It is our social structures that are blocking our view of everything from tiny damaged butterfly wings to global flows of hazardous waste. If we accept the invitation from environmental sociology, we will be connecting the invisible strings that link our hands with the things that we throw away, looking to see where they land, questioning relationships of power and desire, and moving toward a better design for socioecological relationships.

SOURCES

Bauman, Zygmunt. 1997. *Postmodernity and Its Discontents*. New York: New York University Press.

Bell, Michael Mayerfeld, and Michael S. Carolan. 2004. *An Invitation to Environmental Sociology*. Thousand Oaks, CA: Pine Forge.

Catton, William R., and Riley E. Dunlap. 1980. "A New Ecological Paradigm for Post-Exuberant Sociology." *American Behavioral Scientist* 24:15–47.

Fine, Gary Alan. 1998. *Morel Tales: The Culture of Mushrooming*. Cambridge, MA: Harvard University Press.

Giddens, Anthony. 1990. *The Consequences of Modernity*. Stanford, CA: Stanford University Press.

McDonough, William. 2002. *Cradle to Cradle: Remaking the Way We Make Things*. Minneapolis, MN: Sagebrush Educational Resources.

Meadows, Donella. 2004. "Dancing with Systems." *The Systems Thinker* 13(2):2–6.

Molotch, Harvey. 2003. *Where Stuff Comes From: How Toasters, Toilets, Cars, Computers, and Many Other Things Come to Be as They Are*. New York: Routledge.

Ritzer, George. 1999. *Enchanting a Disenchanted World: Revolutionizing the Means of Consumption*. Thousand Oaks, CA: Pine Forge.

Schnaiberg, Allan, and Kenneth Alan Gould. 1994. *Environment and Society: The Enduring Conflict*. New York: St. Martin's.

Smith, Ted, David A. Sonnenfeld, and David Naguib Pellow, eds. 2006. *Challenging the Chip: Labor Rights and Environmental Justice in the Global Electronics Industry*. Philadelphia, PA: Temple University Press.

2

Theories in Environmental Sociology

Luiz C. Barbosa

Discarded television on shore of Hudson River, Staatsburg, New York.
Photo by Ken Gould.

A good place to begin a discussion of sociological theories of the environment is by providing a definition of what **theory** is. There are several definitions in the literature. A definition that I use in my own courses is by sociologist Jonathan Turner. In his book *The Structure of Sociological Theory, Fifth Edition* (1991) he states that "Theory is a 'story' about how and why events in the universe occur." This is a simple but useful way of understanding what theories are. Theories are indeed stories or narratives about how things work. Turner also points out that sociologists do not agree on what kind of stories sociology as a discipline should develop; that is, they do not agree on what procedures should be used in developing explanations, the knowledge that can be developed and accepted, and so on. Because of this lack of consensus, the discipline has some vastly different stories or narratives about how the social world is organized. However, this is not a feature unique to sociology; competing explanations about phenomena are characteristic of intellectual pursuits.

There are a couple of ideas that could be added to Turner's notion of theory as a story. First, sociological theories differ from commonsensical interpretations of events in the sense that they are intellectually guided stories. This means that sociologists use the tools of reason or logic and empirical evidence to build theories. This is different from the assumptions people make about the world based on values, religion, and their own experiences or interpretations. These commonsensical explanations often contradict themselves. This is not to claim that sociological theories lack imperfections. However, social scientists use logical reasoning in an attempt to make different parts of a theory fit together coherently. Theory is a web of interrelated concepts or ideas linked together by logical statements about the relationships among them. For example, Karl Marx (1818–1883) argued that changes in the substructure of society (the economic base) lead to changes in the superstructure of society (its culture, politics, religion, etc.). He also argued that there are links between ideology and political life and between these and religion. His theory contains a web of relationships in which one concept affects another and so on. Another example is the relationship between consumption and environmental degradation in the field of environmental sociology. One can connect the concept of consumption with many other variables or ideas, such as culture, advertising, ideology, wealth, and boredom. *Theorizing assumes the world has order and that events do not happen randomly. It is about searching for cause-and-effect relationships.*

Having a theory about whatever phenomenon one wants to explain can be beneficial for several reasons:

- A theory can provide guidance for investigation.
- A theory can make people think in broader terms than the immediate relationships being investigated.
- One can build on an existing framework provided by a theory; that is, one can add new concepts or ideas to the general framework of the theory.
- A theory can help us generate hypotheses about relationships between concepts.

However, having a theory can also present problems. For example, it can:

- blind us to ideas or relationships not covered by the theory;
- lead us to think at the wrong level of analysis for the problem(s) being investigated; and make us exclude possible causes.

Theories are good only if empirical evidence mounts in their support. If they are not able to withstand empirical evidence, they should be either modified or entirely discarded. Unfortunately, this does not always happen. Once a community of scholars subscribes to a theory, they sometimes attempt to prevent it from falling—a phenomenon that happens in all sciences.

For example, for a long time theories based on the skeleton of Piltdown man, or *Eoanthropus dawsoni*, discovered in 1912 prevailed in British archeology. Piltdown man was believed to be the missing link between human beings and other apes. British archeologists were reluctant to accept theories and evidence that contradicted prevailing explanations. Eventually, the skeleton of Piltdown man was proven to be a fake. Power relationships, prestige, and time and effort spent in research influence a theory's longevity or survival; for example, the fact that Piltdown man was "British" certainly kept the theory alive. However, theories eventually fall when there is little or no evidence to support them, when better theories emerge, or when there is too much contradicting evidence against them, as was the case with Piltdown man.

One important issue to keep in mind when evaluating a theory is background information and context. Issues of race, ethnicity, class, gender, and sexual orientation can affect the composition of a theory and its acceptance. For example, discrimination in academic life meant sociological theories dealing with women and minorities were generally disregarded until the 1960s. Furthermore, the background of the theorist matters. For example, the first sociological theories dealing with African American communities were written by whites and depicted African American communities as pathological versions of the white community. They were written at a time when few African Americans found jobs in academia. Even though sociological works written by African Americans such as William E. B. DuBois (1868–1963) and Oliver Cox (1901–1974) existed, they were relegated to marginal status. Another issue to keep in mind is timing or time period. Sociologists do not exist in a vacuum. They are part of the social matrix of their time; that is, they are affected by history and the social institutions that surround them. As these change, arising issues lead sociologists to reflect and theorize about their world. As described below, environmental sociology itself is a product of a very specific period of time.

Whole courses are taught in sociological theory. The philosophical controversies alone make it a fascinating field of study. Keep in mind that the above explanation is an oversimplification for the sake of discussion. However, one can draw on these ideas when evaluating sociological theories in the field of environmental sociology. The theories below should be thought of as competing "stories" or "narratives" about the relationship between human societies and the environment.

THE ENVIRONMENT AND CLASSICAL SOCIOLOGY

The first theories in sociology were influenced by two main events in history: the Enlightenment and the Industrial Revolution. These events were associated with a great deal of optimism about human beings and human societies. Enlightenment scholars believed human beings were endowed with reason and could think for themselves; thus, they did not need the prescribed thinking and behaviors dictated by religious dogma. These scholars also believed human beings could be perfected given the right social conditions and institutions. They thought that, using reason and science, "natural laws" would be uncovered and this would lead to control of nature and to progress. They believed nature could be subdued. An exception to this optimistic view was the work of Thomas Robert Malthus (1766–1834) (see Lesson 8). In his 1798 *Essay on the Principle of Population*, Malthus argued that while population grew geometrically (2, 4, 16, 32 . . .), the amount of land put under cultivation and food output grew arithmetically (1, 2, 3, 4 . . .); thus, people would eventually run out of food. According to him, the future of the human species was one of devastation caused by famines, pestilence, and wars. Despite Malthus' views, the intellectual mood of the time remained one of great optimism. Innovations brought about through science during the Industrial Revolution further legitimized ideas of progress. Indeed, in the course of a brief period of history human beings accomplished marvelous things. It seemed that, by understanding the laws of nature, human beings were no longer controlled by them.

Sociological theories that emerged in the 19th century focused on understanding the forces that held society together and the forces that led to its transformation, the questions of order and change. There was much concern with social problems brought about by industrialization and modernization in general. The environment was a marginal concept in these theories. The first sociologists were mostly concerned with social institutions and processes and their impact on society as a whole and on people. For example, Émile Durkheim (1858–1917) argued that social phenomena are social facts; they are real in their manifestations. In the same fashion as electricity and gravity are invisible to us but we are able to feel their manifestations, social phenomena such as morality and the collective consciousness, which are nonmaterial and invisible, affect us through their coercive powers—they affect the way we think, feel, and behave. For example, most Americans would feel embarrassed being naked in a public place such as a shopping mall, a feeling that is a byproduct of socialization and a manifestation of the collective consciousness within us. In other societies the norm is just the opposite: In many Amazonian indigenous villages, people walk around with few or no clothes. Durkheim proposed that social facts should be explained through other social facts. In his view, psychological, biological, environmental, and other factors do not satisfactorily explain sociological phenomena. For example, in his famous book *Suicide* (1897) he showed how a decision that appears so personal or "psychological" as taking one's own life has sociological causes, for example the attachments an individual has to social groups. Durkheim's methodology was very influential in establishing what contemporary sociologists call "social constructions" (for example, institutions, culture, and social relationships) as the focus of study in sociology; a clear line was drawn between these social constructions and the material environment, as if human beings and their societies were above the laws of nature. As described below, it was not until the 1970s that the environment became a topic of serious investigation in the discipline.

The lack of attention to the environment has had special consequences in the fields of social change and development, which grew in importance in sociology and other social sciences in the 1950s and 1960s. Theories in these fields have been more than just theories. They have been prescriptions for social change and development, which are often adopted as policy by international organizations and governments—for example, to help poor countries rise from poverty. Theories in the field of development in particular have disregarded environmental consequences in their prescriptions for countries to rise economically. They have often described the environment in terms of raw materials and resources. While Marxist and neoliberal (market-based) theories proposed different means to achieve development, socialism versus free markets, both intellectual camps had indifference for nature in common. The concern with environmentally sustainable development would not enter the field of development until the late 1980s, largely after the publication of the report by the Bruntland Commission titled *Our Common Future*, which brought the concept of sustainable development to the forefront (see Lesson 20).

THE BIRTH OF ENVIRONMENTAL SOCIOLOGY

The emergence of the field of environmental sociology reflects the preoccupation with the state of the environment in the United States in the 1960s and early 1970s. The publication of Rachel Carson's *Silent Spring* in 1962 spearheaded the modern environmentalist movement by raising public awareness about the impact of pesticides on the environment. Issues such as nuclear energy, toxic waste, and pollution were also brought to the center of attention and stirred protest. The introduction of Earth Day in 1970 and the United Nations Conference on Environment and Development in Stockholm in 1972 largely reflected social concerns over these issues. However, the field of environmental sociology would not take off until the late 1970s. Prior to that, interest in environmental issues in the discipline was limited to the field of urban sociology and its attempt to apply ecological models to describe the layout of cities. This "human ecology" was especially prominent at the University of Chicago in the 1920s with the works of sociologists such as Robert E. Park (1864–1944). A series of journal articles by William Catton and Riley Dunlap in the late 1970s and early 1980s was essential in launching the new field of environmental sociology. In these articles, these scholars argued that all theories in sociology were alike in their shared assumption of human exceptionalism from the laws of nature. As noted in the Introduction to this book, they called this prevailing paradigm or model the "human exceptionalism paradigm" (HEP)—which was later changed to "human exemptionalism paradigm" (also HEP). They argued that HEP was based on the assumption that due to culture, technology, language, and elaborate social organizations human beings are exempt from ecological principles and are able to bend environmental limitations. HEP places social and cultural factors as the main determinants of human affairs, a view that, as described above, was highly influenced by scholars such as Durkheim. Catton and Dunlap proposed a "new ecological paradigm" (NEP) for sociology, and the other social sciences for that matter. Even though they acknowledged some of the exceptional characteristics human beings possess, they argued that our species is only one species among many others in the web of life. NEP posits that human affairs are affected by an intricate set of causal relationships within nature. Like all other species on Earth, ours also depends on a finite biosphere for survival. Human inventiveness can temporarily extend carrying capacity limits, but ecological laws cannot be repealed. While NEP was a step in the right direction, it should be kept in mind that it is largely a critique of lack of concern for the environment in sociology. While it suggests directions for the discipline, it is not a theory.

While the works of Catton and Dunlap were important in the development of environmental sociology, developments in ecology and in the environmentalist movement prior to the late 1970s were equally important. Efforts to make ecology "sociological" came before efforts to make sociology "environmental." In the early 1960s, Murray Bookchin (1921–2006) introduced "social ecology" as an alternative to views held by ecologists, who identified ecological problems solely with the preservation of wildlife and wilderness. Bookchin argued that present ecological problems arise from deep-seated social problems; unless these are solved, ecological problems will persist. That is, for him ecological problems cannot be separated from sociological problems. This observation makes a great deal of sense to me as someone who grew up in Brazil. In Rio de Janeiro, where I am from, the growth of slums or *favelas* often begins when squatters invade public lands or forests. As slums grow, the forests that surround the area begin to disappear. Bookchin viewed social inequality as the ultimate cause of ecological problems. He saw hierarchical mentality and class relationships prevalent in society as giving rise to the very idea of dominating the natural world. Social ecology calls for abolition of hierarchy and for the reconstruction of society along ecological lines. This would first entail the elimination of private property, which is the main cause of inequality in society. In the new society, property would be held communally.

The rise of **ecofeminism** in the environmentalist movement of the early 1970s was also an important development in the rise of environmental sociology. It specifically associated one form of inequality with environmental destruction: patriarchy or male dominance. The publication of Rosemary Ruether's *New Woman, NewEarth* in 1975 established the foundations for this brand of environmentalism. In this book she argued there can be no liberation for women and no solution to the ecological crisis without elimination of all forms of exploitation. Ruether argues that eliminating hierarchy is the first step toward construction of an ecological society. This has become a *raison d'être* for ecofeminism.

Another influence in the development of environmental sociology was **deep ecology**. In 1972 at the Third World Futures conference in Bucharest, Norwegian philosopher Arne Naess presented a paper in which he laid out the differences between "shallow" and "deep" ecologies. According to him, the former is primarily concerned with resource depletion and usefulness of the Earth for human beings, while the latter is concerned with the intrinsic value of the Earth—its diversity and richness. Naess later developed some basic principles for deep ecology, which are summarized below:

- Harmony with nature;
- Biospherical egalitarianism or species equality, which means that other species should be able not only to survive but to thrive;
- Material objects should serve bigger objectives such as self-actualization, not consumption for the sake of consumption;
- Awareness of the limits of our planet's resources;
- Use of environmentally appropriate technologies;
- Emphasis on recycling, and
- Emphasis on bioregions and recognition of human differences.

Naess's ideas were popularized in the United States especially through the works of sociologist Bill Devall and philosopher George Sessions. Their book *Deep Ecology: Living as if Nature Mattered* became a classic in the ecological literature. In addition to adopting Naess's basic principles, this book emphasizes spirituality. The authors argue in favor of Eastern and Native American religious philosophies, which they view as promoting harmony with nature relative to the beliefs in Judeo-Christian religions. For example, Native American cultures see elements of the environment as sacred, while Christianity preaches that humans were given domain over the entire Earth by God.

The rise of deep ecology has led to an enduring debate with social ecology, which was largely spearheaded by Murray Bookchin until his death in 2006. Bookchin argued against the "mysticism" of deep ecology. This is illustrated by an essay he wrote titled "Social Ecology Versus Deep Ecology: A Challenge for the Ecology Movement." In this essay he stated that "The greatest differences . . . within the so-called ecology movement are between a vague, formless, often self-contradictory, and invertebrate thing called deep ecology and a long-developing, coherent, and socially oriented body of ideas that can best be called social ecology." He called deep ecology a mixture of "Hollywood and Disneyland, spiced with homilies from Taoism, Buddhism, spiritualism, reborn Christianity, and in some cases eco-fascism." For Bookchin, the biggest allies of social ecology are rational thought and science.

Sociologists would respond to philosophical debates in ecology, developments in the environmentalist movement, and Catton and Dunlap's call for adoption of NEP with new theoretical insights that together created a new and exciting field of study within the discipline. It is ironic that while criticizing the "human exemptionalism" of the classical tradition in sociology, the new theories they developed share a background with the classical tradition, what environmental sociologist Frederick Buttel calls an "ontological kinship." That is, theories in environmental sociology largely built on basic concepts already in existence in the discipline. Below are some of these theories. The list is not comprehensive; it includes only those theories believed to be the most important in the field. They are grouped together into categories that broadly reflect their intellectual or ideological orientations. Be warned that not everyone will agree with this classification. You should think of the text below as a "story" or narrative about the theories being explained, a story about stories so to speak. One important issue that I would like you to keep in mind when reading my account is the philosophical debate about the environmental sustainability of capitalism. Some of the theories—for example, treadmill of production and ecological modernization theory—have a definite stand on this issue, while others are more ambiguous. I think the question of system sustainability is of central importance for solutions to pressing problems such as climate change (see Lesson 15).

NEO-MARXIST POLITICAL-ECONOMY THEORIES

The emphasis of Marxist theory in sociology has been on the class conflict that originates out of competition for the economic spoils or resources of society. In capitalist society, the bourgeoisie, the capitalist class, owns the means of production—that is, the factories, tools, etc.—and the proletariat, the workers, sell their labor. For Karl Marx, those who have wealth have everything else in society: power, prestige, and influence. For him, capitalism benefits the elites and alienates the proletariat, who are paid low wages for hard, mechanical work that lacks creativity. He believed the bourgeoisie was able to maintain power and the status quo through control of the means of production, violence, and ideological indoctrination (brainwashing), the latter by manipulating the means of communication and the belief system in general (e.g., through religion). Marx also saw capitalism as a system that needs to perpetually reproduce itself or expand in order to thrive; that is, growth is imperative in capitalism. However, this systemic requirement leads to the crisis of overproduction. Saturation of the economy forces capitalists to look for new ways to invigorate it—for example, by introducing new technologies and products, through conquest of new markets, and so forth. Marx believed that capitalism, like all the previous modes of production, contained the seeds of its own destruction. Each successive crisis of overproduction would make future crises increasingly more difficult for the bourgeoisie to manage; for example, new markets would end, and eventually the system would collapse. Under the leadership of the proletariat, revolution would take place and eventually a new mode of production would arise, socialism. This would be an intermediary stage, which eventually would culminate in communism.

While Marx appears to ignore the intrinsic value of nature when he asserts that raw materials are given to us *gratis* (for free) by nature and that it is labor that gives them value by transforming them into goods or commodities, he did introduce the notion of "**metabolic rift**," a notion that adds to our understanding of environmental issues. The context behind this concept is Marx's description of the transfer of soil nutrients when food produced in the countryside is sold in cities. The soils of the farms in the countryside were robbed of the nutrients that decaying natural fibers, waste, and so on contribute to their regenerative capacities. The organic matter that would refertilize the soils in the countryside became instead the waste and pollution of cities.

Neo-Marxist models build on Marx's notion of conflict in capitalist society while downplaying or rejecting other aspects of his theory. These models are not limited to class analysis (for example, bourgeoisie vs. proletariat) but include a whole range of other conflicts such as gender, ethnic, racial, political, environmental, and so on. These approaches also tend to reject the notion that the proletariat is at the forefront of a socialist revolution that is about to happen.

Ecological Marxism

There are different varieties of **ecological Marxism**. We already described the work of Murray Bookchin on social ecology above. His work is very representative of the main premises of this theoretical perspective. His claim that in order to understand environmental problems we need to seek their source in the system of inequality human beings have created is a fundamental principle in ecological Marxism. This principle has led to important research efforts in the field (e.g., understanding the health consequences to poor communities and communities of color that result from their being targeted disproportionately as dumping sites for toxic waste and other forms of pollution; see Lesson 10). In addition to inequality, ecological Marxism emphasizes the contradictions that exist in capitalism. For example, one of the most significant contributions in this area is James O'Connor's argument that capitalism undermines the factors that sustain it, such as human labor and the environment. He argues that in addition to the contradiction between capital and labor characteristic of the system, the first contradiction of capitalism, there is a second contradiction between these two factors and nature—both capital and labor depend on the exploitation of the environment. Similar to the first contradiction of the system, the second contradiction can also induce crisis. A good example of this is climate change and the costs associated with it. As the problem deepens, it will very likely have an adverse impact on capitalism and may even affect its ability to function at all in some places. Hurricanes Katrina and Sandy and Typhoon Haiyan (which hit the Philippines in 2013) exemplify the potential seriousness of this problem. Just imagine if more hurricanes and typhoons of their magnitude would hit populated areas on a regular basis (see Lesson 14). The costs would be astronomical and most likely would shake the system. Other conditions associated with global warming, such as rising sea levels, will also generate tremendous costs and create crises throughout the world.

An intellectually stimulating work in the ecological Marxist tradition is John Bellamy Foster's use and expansion of Marx's concept of metabolic rift to understand the current global environmental crisis. He argues that capitalism has created an ecological rift between human beings and nature that can be fixed only by introducing a society that embraces "a new communal metabolism encompassing all of the humanity and the earth." The exploitation of nature to fuel the current system of capitalism benefits primarily the rich.

Ecological Marxism has a journal, *Capitalism, Nature, Socialism,* which has been very influential in the field of environmental sociology.

Treadmill of Production

Treadmill of production theory has its origins in the publication of Allan Schnaiberg's *The Environment: From Surplus to Scarcity* in 1980. It is one of the most enduring theories in the field of environmental sociology. In *The Environment*, Schnaiberg (1939–2009) argues that human societies depend on flows of energy from nature and thus are not exempt from the two basic laws of thermodynamics. The first law is that of conservation of matter and energy, which states that matter and energy cannot be created or destroyed; they can only be transformed. The second law is that of entropy, which states that all energy transformations are degradations that change energy from more to fewer forms. Human social organization gives the impression that we are above these laws; our economic, social, cultural, and other systems obfuscate the fact that we ultimately depend on nature and that the laws of thermodynamics cannot be repealed. Even though it is often ignored, human beings exist within the environmental matrix of the biosphere like any other species on Earth. Our ingenuity has given us more flexibility but has not exempted us from the forces of nature.

Human beings have maintained an increasingly damaging relationship with the environment since the times we were primarily "biological consumers," as hunters and gatherers. As the economies of human societies became more complex, they began to exercise additional pressure on the environment through processes of interchange involving withdrawals and additions. *Withdrawals* are raw materials we take from nature in order to transform them into objects either for "use value" (utility or function) or for "exchange value" (market value), or both. *Additions* are what we return to the environment (for example, pollution and garbage). These cycles of withdrawal and addition can destabilize biospherical systems. Industrialization meant our environmental impact would increase. Machines could produce more quickly, and new technologies were more energy- and chemical-intensive.

This meant that industry took more from the environment (withdrawals) and returned more toxic elements (additions) (see Lessons 4 and 11).

The aim of the treadmill of production is profit for capitalists and investors. The system has to continuously produce and grow in order to generate profit. One way to maximize profit has been to invest in new technologies capable of replacing human labor (see Lesson 7). To amortize the fixed and operating costs of new technologies, industrial production had to be increased, which raised the volume of production waste and the toxicity of wastes. What is ironic about this process is that workers have helped sow the seeds of their own degradation. By generating profits with their work, they have allowed for higher investments in labor-saving technologies, which have replaced them. Influenced by the corporate-framed ideology of modernization, growing world competitiveness, and free trade, workers have been indoctrinated to accept automation and the transfer of jobs overseas (see Lessons 4 and 17). They had to acquiesce to a situation created by corporations that pushed for free trade and established subsidiaries abroad.

Following a neo-Marxist line of thinking, the treadmill of production theory argues that the social institutions of modern industrial society are intertwined and supportive of the treadmill of production. These institutions help "lubricate" the treadmill. For example, the welfare state allocates a significant share of the surplus generated by economic expansion to safety-net mechanisms such as workers' compensation or disability, unemployment insurance, and so on, which help maintain workers loyal to the system. The state promotes growth, which is viewed as necessary for the stability and health of society. When sectors of the economy such as housing stop growing, government officials usually take steps to stimulate them (for example, by lowering interest rates). Labor unions are also supportive of the treadmill since growth generally means jobs for workers—even though with globalization jobs may actually be created in different parts of the world. Education is another social institution that helps maintain the system, by educating future professionals. The family is yet another example. Its function as an agent of socialization has made it the target of marketers. Through television and other media, families are encouraged to shop. Our lives have become so intertwined with the treadmill of production that shopping sometimes is defined as a civic duty. For example, people were encouraged to shop after the tragic events of September 11, not only as a sign of defiance to terrorists but also to keep the economy moving.

Perhaps the most controversial claim made by scholars who subscribe to the treadmill of production concerns the environmentalist movement and environmental efforts such as recycling. Due to its reformist nature, the environmentalist movement is viewed as ineffective. Despite its efforts since the 1960s, environmental degradation continues. The leverage acquired by environmentalists does not begin to compare with the power of those in charge of the treadmill of production; the latter have vast amounts of economic resources they can use to direct the system, while environmentalists have to struggle to amass resources. Treadmill of production scholars argue that efforts such as recycling provide the illusion that people can maintain their consumption lifestyles if they do "their part" to compensate for their consumption patterns, when in reality their lifestyles—or the lifestyle of their societies—are unsustainable in the long run.

Critics of the treadmill of production theory argue against its materialist approach and point to the importance of other factors, such as culture, in creating and solving environmental problems. They believe that changes in cultural practices, such as changes in consumption habits, can lead to improved environmental conditions (see Lesson 12). Some are also uncomfortable with what they view as the "pessimism" or lack of "hope" in the approach. They argue that the theory disempowers those willing to take small steps to ameliorate environmental conditions, for instance through recycling and other programs. They think these small steps are more appealing to the public than radical systemic changes. As we shall see below, some critics argue that what modern societies need is not a radical change of economic systems but more and better technologies.

World-System Theory

World-system theory is built on neo-Marxist ideas and thus has a heavy emphasis on economic relationships. It emerged largely as a reaction to neoliberal theories of development, especially modernization theory, in the debate about the causes of development and underdevelopment. Modernization theory scholars such as Walt Whitman Rostow (1916–2003) argued that the "traditional" values of Third World societies were largely responsible for their underdevelopment. These societies were described as rigid, undemocratic, unscientific, uneducated, and in need of modernization, which meant capitalism, political reform, and Westernization of values. This theory became the darling of international organizations in the 1950s and 1960s. World-system theory emerged largely as a reaction to this blame-the-victim approach. It emphasized the history of colonialism as the main cause of the underdevelopment of the Third World. Thus, like many of the theories discussed in this lesson, it was not originally devised as a theory about the environment. However, scholars have used it to explain environmental issues and have generated some very interesting insights, especially about global environmental problems. In my opinion, it has a great deal of potential in helping us understand the current global environmental crisis.

As proposed by sociologist Immanuel Wallerstein, world-system theory argues that the capitalist world economy has its roots in the period of time he termed "the long sixteenth century," from 1450 to 1640. With maritime voyages, the European economy began to expand and colonialism was set in motion. By the 19th century Europe had, with a few exceptions, engulfed all corners of the world. The nature of this emerging economy was capitalist since its main goal was trade and profit. Its spread would create a global division of labor with Western Europe at its center or "core" and the colonies at its "periphery"—the United States and later Japan joined the core in the

20th century. The relationship between the core and the periphery has been one of exploitation; the core has exploited the periphery for raw materials, labor, and as a market—and more recently as a dumping ground for toxic waste such as electronic waste (e-waste), for example, in Asia and West Africa (see Lesson 3). In between these two zones lies the semiperiphery, a category consisting of countries that declined from the core or managed to rise from the periphery—for example, South Korea, Brazil, and Mexico. In addition to proposing this global stratification system, the theory argues that the capitalist world economy is characterized by economic and political cycles. Economic cycles can be of short duration, such as a short recession, or long-term trends (*"longue durée"*), which can last decades or centuries. Political cycles are characterized by cycles of hegemony (dominance) in which one country leads the core and thus exerts an enormous amount of influence in shaping the system as a whole. Wallerstein argues that three countries have been hegemonic since the rise of this economy in "the long sixteenth century": the United Provinces in the 17th century, the United Kingdom in the 19th century, and the United States in the 20th century. Each shaped the system according to its needs.

An important feature of the theory is that capitalism has led to increasing rationalization and commodification. **Rationalization** is a complicated process of social change that involves the demystification of the world by replacing tradition, emotions, religious dogma, etc., with impersonal bureaucratic institutions and science. **Commodification** means the transformation of anything, including human beings, into goods or commodities that can be sold in the market; a market exchange value is attached to them. It involves economic as well as social mechanisms. A good example of this is land. Land for the native peoples of the Americas was held communally. The capitalism Europeans introduced to the region required land to be commodified; thus, it became private property that could be marketed. Rhinoceros horns are another example of the social-economic elements of commodification. Rhinoceros are threatened by extinction because people are willing to pay large sums of money for their horns, which are highly valued in some cultures as an aphrodisiac or for traditional medicines. Note that rhinoceros horns are made of the same substance as human fingernails, keratin. Another important feature of the theory is dominance. In his book *Historical Capitalism with Capitalist Civilization*, Wallerstein argues that capitalism is controlled by a new kind of human being in history, *Homo economicus*, who shapes the rules of the system in the pursuit of profit. The rest of us have to follow these rules. For example, we have to understand basic principles of economics in order to survive. To put this to a test, just try to obtain goods, including food, from a store without having money or some form of acceptable payment. The United States is a capitalist society, where one cannot survive very well without a job and access to currency. While this is basic knowledge, we do not think about it until we are confronted with unfortunate situations such as unemployment.

The pioneering work that applied world-system theory to the understanding of environmental issues was Stephen Bunker's *Underdeveloping the*

Amazon. In this book Bunker argued that the sale of natural resources from the Third World to the First World (for example, minerals and forest resources) represented a permanent loss for the former—a process similar to Marx's metabolic rift. This loss of irreplaceable resources eventually created underdevelopment in the areas being exploited, not development. Once the resources were exhausted, these areas plunged into cycles of economic instability and poverty. For Bunker, this trade in natural resources meant irreplaceable transfers of assets from the periphery to the core.

Bunker's work made people think about the global links involved in deforestation and other environmental problems. For environmental world-system theorists like me interested in Amazonia, the message was clear: Some of the major environmental problems of our time need to be understood in relation to the dynamics of an evolving world system. Global inequalities involving core, semiperipheral, and peripheral zones are directly linked to environmental degradation and should not be ignored. For example, many of the environmental problems in the periphery and semiperiphery are associated or intertwined with the populations of the core. Consumption in the core has been associated with deforestation, strip mining, pollution, and toxic contamination. Every time someone buys furniture made of mahogany, there is a good chance that he or she is contributing to deforestation in places such as Amazonia. There is also the issue of excessive consumption in the core relative to its population size of less than 18% of the global population. Problems such as climate change are heavily associated with overconsumption by these countries. The semiperiphery is also implicated. In attempting to catch up with the core, some of these countries have literally razed their environments—for example, cutting their forests for timber, agriculture, and mining. Some have also harmed their poorest citizens by allowing them to be exposed to the toxic e-waste exported by the rich countries. Government leaders in these countries are often guided by ideologies of predatory development, such as "Develop 50 years in 5." The intensity of development in the semiperiphery has led to high levels of environmental degradation. As a matter of fact, world-system researchers, such as Thomas Burns and his colleagues, have noticed that degradation is more intense in the semiperiphery than in the core and the periphery. Environmental degradation is limited in the periphery by lack of development, and intense environmentalism in the core has led to passage of strict environmental laws. On the other hand, semiperipheral countries sacrifice their environments for the sake of development. In countries such as Thailand and China people have to wear surgical masks due to heavy air pollution.

An environmentally important world-systemic concept is the **commodity chain.** According to world-system scholars Terence K. Hopkins and Immanuel Wallerstein, a commodity chain is "a network of labor and production processes whose end result is a finished commodity" made for sale in the marketplace. A chain is composed of "boxes" or nodes in the production process that are spread both nationally and internationally. Commodity chains have linked the world economy together throughout its history.

With the age of colonialism, demand in the core for tropical goods such as sugar, cocoa, coffee, tobacco, and so on linked different aspects of production in the periphery to the markets of Europe. In the contemporary, globalized world, the "boxes" or nodes are spread throughout the world. For example, raw materials such as cotton are produced in one country, textiles in another, and the garments in yet another; that is, the nodes are located transnationally.

The knowledge of how commodity chains work has become a major weapon for environmentalists and human rights organizations. They have pressured corporations with consumer boycotts if they disregard the environment and/or human rights (see Lesson 12). For example, acting as watchdogs or "guardians" over the Amazon rain forest, environmentalist organizations such as Friends of the Earth and Greenpeace have successfully applied pressure on Nike, Adidas, and Timberland to stop buying leather produced from cattle raised in illegally deforested areas of the Brazilian Amazon region. They also have pressured the Brazilian subsidiary of Walmart and the supermarket chain Carrefour to stop buying beef produced in these areas of Amazonia or risk consumer boycotts in Brazil and abroad.

Despite its potential to help us understand the dynamics of the global environmental crisis, world-system theory remains largely underutilized. Some scholars find the categorization of countries into core, periphery, and semiperiphery limiting. Even though these have been extended to include new categories such as the semicore and several subcategories of periphery, this has failed to attract large numbers. It is difficult for a theory based on economic relationships and advocating radical change to compete with new theories that are based on cultural explanations and that are reformist. Contemporary sociologists tend to gravitate to explanations that are based on "the social construction of reality" rather than to what they view as "economic determinism." Unfortunately, one cannot understand some of the critical environmental issues of our time without a dispassionate examination of the economic foundations of our society and our world.

NEOLIBERAL THEORIES

The underlying ideas of neoliberalism can be traced to classical economics, especially to the works of Adam Smith (1723–1790). Smith proposed that commercial society, what we now call "capitalist society," was fundamentally different from previous forms because commerce played such an essential role in its composition. He argued that, unlike previous societal forms, commercial society needed less government, not more. Government would be relegated few functions, such as protection against foreign enemies, utilities (sewage, water, etc.), and, above all, protection of private property. Government should also act to prevent monopolies, which thwart competition.

Smith believed that instead of government interference these societies should be regulated by market forces, by the "invisible hand of the market." Competition in a market economy would benefit everyone and would keep the system in synchrony. Merchants who sold at high prices would be outcompeted by those who sold at lower prices, inefficient companies would be replaced by more efficient ones, and so on. Competition would also lead to creativity as individuals would search for new products to sell. For Smith, the pursuit of gain was the most basic of human drives and individuals should be left alone to satisfy it. In the end, the whole society would benefit from individual effort.

Smith was one of several classical economists. However, his ideas, more than those of any other scholar, established the foundations of (economic) liberal thought. In neoliberal thinking, the market continues to be viewed as the best mechanism to achieve important societal goals, such as development and eradication of poverty. Theories about the environment that follow this philosophical view also rely on market mechanisms. Their basic assumption is that consumers make rational choices and they will choose, if properly educated, environmentally friendly goods. They also argue that competition will lead corporations to adopt environmentally friendly technologies once a few of their competitors adopt them.

Ecological Modernization Theory

We can think of **ecological modernization theory** as an antithesis to treadmill of production theory. Its beginnings are associated with the works of European scholars such as Joseph Huber, Martin Jänicke, Arthur Mol, and Gert Spaargaren. The theory is based on the premise that capitalism is a system flexible enough to transition to environmentally "sustainable capitalism." In order for this transition to take place, the theory encourages modern industrial societies to undergo additional modernization and "**superindustrialization**." That is, instead of retreating to a world of simplicity, as suggested by radical environmentalists, what modern industrial societies need is to use better and environmentally friendly technologies as a means of dealing with environmental problems. The theory also relies on the notion of "reflexive modernization." *Reflexivity* involves the individual and society constantly reexamining their own circumstances—beliefs, social practices, etc.—in light of new information or knowledge. At the institutional level, this means that institutions such as government and corporations would use knowledge about the environment and new technologies to change social conduct and institutional arrangements. Transformation of state environmental policy is central in this institutional development. However, while the stewardship of the process would start in government, it would be transferred to the market, which is viewed as a more efficient mechanism for solving problems than the state. This would advance and accelerate the ecological transformation process due to competition, availability of investment capital, and so on.

The state would continue to play a vital role in managing the environment. It would provide the infrastructure and incentives for the adoption of environmentally sound policies and technologies and create the right conditions for self-regulation.

Like its predecessor, modernization theory, ecological modernization theory has been embraced by international organizations. One way of looking at its acceptance by these organizations is that the theory provides "practical" or "realistic" solutions to current environmental problems. For example, think of the potential of environmentally friendly buildings and of entire sustainable eco-communities or cities. When better technologies are employed, they indeed produce results such as less pollution and more energy efficiency. However, acceptance also reflects the theory's neoliberal stance, which is in line with the capitalist ideology that prevails in many international organizations. Its emphasis is on reforming or modernizing the system rather than radically challenging it.

Ecological modernization theory has become a popular approach in environmental sociology, presenting the strongest challenge to the supremacy treadmill of production theory has maintained in the field since the 1980s. Some of its main ideas have also been reincarnated in arguments to transform capitalism into **natural capitalism**.

Natural Capitalism

In *Natural Capitalism: Creating the Next Industrial Revolution*, authors Paul Hawken, Amory Lovins, and L. Hunter Lovins propose a similar thesis to the one advanced by ecological modernization theory about the role of technology, government, and the market in solving environmental problems. For these scholars, the next industrial revolution will be a response to changing patterns of scarcity, which will create tough conditions but also opportunities for adaptable companies. They propose four basic changes conducive to transition to natural capitalism:

- *Radically increase the productivity of resource use.* Fundamental changes in technology and design can lead to substantial savings.
- *Shift to biologically inspired production (biomimicry) with closed loops, no waste, and no toxicity.* Natural capitalism seeks to eliminate waste altogether.
- *Shift the business model away from the making and selling of "things" to providing the service that the "thing" delivers.* The natural capitalism model delivers value as a continuous flow of services.
- *Reinvest in natural and human capital.* Any good capitalist reinvests in productive capital.

The message of both of the above theories is clear: Capitalism is adaptable enough to be "greened," and the market is the best mechanism to generate concrete environmental solutions. For proponents of these theories, one does not throw the baby out with the bath water. Capitalism has generated high levels of prosperity and lifestyle sophistication for the developed countries, and it should not be replaced with systems based on less sophisticated technologies or with some form of ecosocialism. These theories assume that consumers will make the rational or correct choice of products once they are provided with environmentally friendly alternatives. For critics, capitalism has created the major environmental problems of our time, and it cannot be tamed. In order for the system to thrive, it needs growth and expansion; in turn, this means utilization of natural resources and some form of waste. They also criticize the "**technofix**" solutions proposed by scholars who subscribe to modernization theory and similar theories. They argue that technology cannot fix all environmental problems and that it can also create new ones (see Lessons 7 and 13). They state that in the end these theories do not address overconsumption and the long-term environmental sustainability of the capitalist system.

SECOND MODERNITY AND RISK SOCIETY THEORIES

The two last theories that I would like to discuss are **second modernity theory** and its offshoot, **risk society theory**. Even though modernization is a central theme in both of these theories, they are treated separately from ecological modernization theory and natural capitalism in this lesson because their ideological underpinnings are different. Second modernization and risk society theories are heavily influenced by Weberian ideas of rationalization. German scholar Max Weber (1864–1920) proposed that rationalization was increasing in the modern world through the diffusion or spread of bureaucratic institutions, science, and capitalist principles in general. For example, Weber argued that science was "disenchanting" the world by exposing how things really work; that is, science provides rational explanations as opposed to "enchanting" or magical ones based on the supernatural. For Weber, this process of rationalization creates the "irrationalitatsproblem" or irrationality problem, which was his way of describing how too much rationality can create irrational consequences. For instance, the efficiency of rational institutions has made the world more impersonal and thus colder. Weber is famous for writing that modern societies were becoming "iron cages" of bureaucratic rules from which individuals could not escape.

Second Modernity Theory

Second modernity scholars focus on the crisis of modern societies caused by a range of factors, such as declining faith in the political system, deindustrialization caused by globalization, shifts in labor markets, loss of trust in science, cultural changes, and too much individualism and rationalization in Western societies. German sociologist Ulrich Beck and British sociologist Anthony Giddens have been the most influential scholars in the development of this theory. Beck's sociology captures transformations in modern society as people react to problems created by rational institutions. According to him, this new age, the beginning of "second modernity," is characterized by a high degree of uncertainty as people have lost faith in rational institutions such as government and science; we have realized that these are part of the problem. Giddens' sociology has similar themes. For him, modern societies have entered a stage of "high" or "late" modernity, which is highly related to globalization. Giddens opposes the notion proposed by some scholars that modern societies have become "postmodern." He believes changes taking place in the West are part of the process of modernization itself, not "post-modernization." People's values and even self-identity in these societies are being transformed by globalization, which he views as a process of Westernization catapulted by the expansion of modernization from the West to other parts of the world. From his perspective, modern societies are undergoing a process of transformation caused by self-evaluation or "reflexivity." People in these societies are questioning the old order and establishing new social and institutional practices. Part of this reflexivity includes ways to better relate to the natural environment.

Risk Society Theory

A theory that grows out of Ulrich Beck's second modernity theory is risk society. Beck proposes the idea that modern societies are characterized by risk taking. For Beck, risk is a systematic way of dealing with the hazards and insecurities induced and introduced by modernization itself. Modern societies differ from other forms of society in the sense that risks are created by decisions, instead of naturally occurring hazards such as famines, floods, and so on, which plague other societies. Modern societies take deliberate risks. For people in these societies, risk is endemic. They rely on scientific knowledge, weighing the probabilities of risk. However, most people do not fully understand this type of knowledge. According to Beck, as knowledge and technology race ahead, people are left behind, panting in ignorance, increasingly unable to understand and control the machines on which they depend. People's lack of knowledge leads to the mystification of science, to which scientists also contribute with their robes, institutions, etc. People rely on scientists for interpretations of scientific information. This reliance is sometimes problematic. Beck argues that scientists have made errors and are often blind about risk. For him, science weighs the distribution of risks and errors, which are often created by science itself (see Lesson 6). A good illustration of this is nuclear power. It has been made accessible as a result of scientific investigation. Nuclear power plants are built and run with consideration of risks or the probability of accidents. Scientists have weighed the risks and have told the public it is a safe form of energy (see Lesson 9).

Beck suggests that a problem faced by modern societies is the loss of faith in the institutions of modernity such as science, business, and politics. These institutions were supposed to guarantee rationality and security, but they failed. People no longer trust them. However, they are forced to rely on these institutions' expert systems for vital information. Major nuclear accidents such as Three Mile Island, Chernobyl, and Fukushima have made people realize the enormous destructive power of modern technologies. They have become reluctant to accept new technologies even when told they are safe. They feel they cannot trust the information since public officials, scientists, and corporate leaders might make mistakes or lie. The case of genetically modified foods is illustrative of this situation. People fear this type of food even though they have been assured that risks such as allergies have been studied and proven to be small. Environmentalists are also concerned about genetically altered organisms such as genetically modified salmon being released into the environment (see Lesson 12). Whole societies are reluctant to accept these risks. For example, there are severe restrictions imposed on genetically modified foods in the European Union and Japan.

Beck also argues that modern societies have experienced the collapse of collective or group-specific sources of meaning. This simply means that people in these societies are not under intense pressure to conform to social norms as in the past or in other types of society. While this allows them the freedom to choose, it also creates problems. Choice means trying untested possibilities, which means taking risks. Since collective meanings are no longer strong in modern societies, individuals and institutions need to engage in constant evaluations of their choices, a process Beck calls "reflexive modernization." For him, Western modernization is in the process of destroying itself. In its place a "reflexive modern society" is emerging based on the constant reappraisal and reevaluation of values and priorities as technologies change. Risk society scholars generally argue that "reflexivity" is the key element in uncovering solutions to the problems faced by modern societies, including environmental ones. This requires people, social institutions, and society in general to apply existing knowledge to reevaluate personal and institutional practices as well as risk. They argue that science itself needs to undergo a process of "reflexive scientization;" that is, it must turn its skepticism toward evaluating and criticizing itself.

The risk society concept is quite useful in terms of making us understand the costs and benefits of risk taking and why people are reluctant to accept certain strategies or technologies due to fear of the consequences. The notion of reflexivity also directs us to using available knowledge to evaluate our actions and policies in the pursuit of an environmentally conscious and friendly society. This is good. However, we need to be cognizant that reflexivity also involves the inclusion of different points of view. In 2006, Anthony Giddens published an article in an online version of the British newspaper the *Guardian* in which he claims the environmentalist movement should be "ditched." In this article, he argued that climate change is finally at the center of public attention and the "debate should not be left in the hands of those hostile to science and technology." He has also claimed in more recent essays and interviews that further initiatives on climate change should be left to scientists; he sees the political tactics of the environmentalist movement, "the greens," as potentially harmful at this stage of climate change negotiations. Thus, he proposes the exclusion of the very activists who have fought the toughest battles for the preservation of the environment. His statements are ironic because science has been criticized for being part of the problem. Don't we need different voices in finding solutions? Giddens' argument to ditch the movement appears to be a case of "reflexivity" relying solely on what is perceived as "rational," which according to Beck's argument was a main cause of the problem in the first place.

FINAL THOUGHTS

The above theories often provide competing explanations about the relationship between human societies and the environment. However, they also complement each other. It does not matter if one subscribes to treadmill of production theory or modernization theory; risk is an important problem that people in the contemporary world face. It should be an issue of major consideration in any theory dealing with industrialization and the environment. Also, one cannot fully understand environmental degradation without taking into account the global stratification system. Treadmill of production scholars, for example, would have much to gain by integrating elements of world-system theory into their own theory. In recent years they have addressed issues pertaining to the "Global South" versus the "Global North," but this, in my opinion, has not been enough. World-system theory offers a more developed explanation of stratification that would bring theoretical refinement on this issue to treadmill of production theory. World-systems theory would also benefit by borrowing ideas from treadmill of production theory since both production and consumption are major defining factors in the contemporary world.

   As the effects of climate change become a reality, environmental sociologists will need to improve their theoretical models, combine them, and/or develop new ones. Climate change will likely create social issues that current theories do not address (see Lesson 15). For example, what will happen to the populations of low-lying countries with rising sea levels? How will this add to existing problems such as immigration and poverty? What will happen to political relationships between developing and developed countries with climate change? Will rich countries intervene when developing countries cut their forests or pollute the environment? We will need theories that address issues such as these. Unfortunately, the field of environmental sociology is likely to grow in importance by necessity as the global environmental situation is likely to get worse rather than better.

SOURCES

Barbosa, Luiz C. 1993. 'The "Greening" of the Ecopolitics of the World-System: Amazonia and Changes in the Ecopolitics of Brazil.' *Journal of Political and Military Sociology* 21:107–134.

Barbosa, Luiz C. 2009. "Change by Necessity: Ecological Limits to Capitalism, Climate Change, and Obstacles to Transition to an Environmentally Sustainable Economy." Available at SSRN: http://ssrn.com/abstract=1458114 or http://dx.doi.org/10.2139/ssrn.1458114.

Beck, Ulrich. 1992. *Risk Society: Towards a New Modernity.* Thousand Oaks, CA: Sage.

Bookchin, Murray. 1985. "Social Ecology Versus Deep Ecology: A Challenge for the Ecology Movement." *Green Perspective* 4–5.

Bookchin, Murray. 1991. *The Ecology of Freedom: The Emergence and Dissolution of Hierarchy,* rev. ed. Montreal, Canada: Black Rose Books.

Bookchin, Murray. 1995. *The Philosophy of Ecology: Essays on Dialectical Naturalism.* Montreal, Canada: Black Rose Books.

Bunker, Stephen G. 1988. *Underdeveloping the Amazon.* Chicago: University of Chicago Press.

Burns, Thomas J., Eward L. Kick, and Byron L. Davis. 2003. "Theorizing and Rethinking Linkages Between the Natural Environment and the Modern World-System: Deforestation in the Late 20th Century." *Journal of World Systems Research* 9:357–390.

Buttel, Frederick. 1996. "Environmental and Resource Sociology: Theoretical Issues and Opportunities for Synthesis." *Rural Sociology* 61(1):56–75.

Buttel, Frederick. 2000. "Ecological Modernization as Social Theory." *Geoforum* 31:57–65.

Catton, William R., and Riley E. Dunlap. 1978. "Environmental Sociology: A New Paradigm." *American Sociologist* 13:41–49.

Devall, Bill, and George G. Sessions. 1985. *Deep Ecology.* Salt Lake City, UT: Peregrine Smith Books.

Foster, John Bellamy. 2009. *The Ecological Revolution: Making Peace with the Planet.* New York: Monthly Review Press.

Giddens, Anthony. 2006. "We Should Ditch the Green Movement." *Guardian Unlimited.*

Gould, Kenneth A., David N. Pellow, and Allan Schnaiberg. 2004. "Interrogating the Treadmill of Production: Everything You Wanted to Know About the Treadmill but Were Afraid to Ask." *Organization & Environment* 17:296–316.

Hawken, Paul, Amory Lovins, and L. Hunter Lovins. 1999. *Natural Capitalism: Creating the Next Industrial Revolution.* Boston: Little, Brown and Co.

Hopkins, Terrence, K. and Immanuel Wallersteinl. 1994. "Commodity Chains: Construct and Research." In Gary Gereffi and Miguel Korzeniewicz, eds. *Commodity Chains and Global Capitalism,* pp. 17–50. Westport, CT: Praeger.

Malthus, Robert Thomas. 1798. *Essay on the Principle of Population as It Affects the Future Improvement of Society, with Remarks on the Speculations of Mr. Godwin, Mr. Condorcet, and Other Writers,* 1st ed. London: J. Johnson. Retrieved February 13, 2007 (http://www.econlib.org/library/Malthus/malPop.html).

Mol, Arthur P. J. 2001. *Globalization and Environmental Reform: The Ecological Modernization of the Global Economy.* Cambridge, MA: MIT Press.

Naess, Arne. 1973. "The Shallow and the Deep Long Range Ecology Movements: A Summary." *Inquiry* (Oslo), Volume 16.

O'Connor, James R. 1973. *The Fiscal Crisis of the State*. Palgrave Macmillan.

Ruether, Rosemary Radford. 1975. *New Woman, New Earth: Sexist Ideologies and Human Liberation*. New York: Seabury Press.

Schnaiberg, Allan. 1980. *The Environment: From Surplus to Scarcity*. New York: Oxford University Press.

Turner, Jonathan. 1991. *The Structure of Sociological Theory*. Belmont, CA: Wadsworth.

Wallerstein, Immanuel. 1996. *Historical Capitalism with Capitalist Civilization*. London, UK: Verso.

World Commission on Environment and Development. 1987. *Our Common Future*. New York: Oxford University Press.

SYSTEMIC CAUSES OF ENVIRONMENTAL DISRUPTION

3

The State and Policy
Imperialism, Exclusion, and Ecological Violence as State Policy

David Naguib Pellow

"No Dumping" sign on shore of New York Harbor, Brooklyn, New York.
Photo by Ken Gould.

When most people think of the state and policy in relation to the environment, specific environmental policies such as the Clean Air Act or the Endangered Species Act or the Environmental Protection Agency may come to mind. However, what I'd like to do in this lesson is to explore the role of the U.S. nation-state as an institution that embraces and advances the institutional practices of **imperialism**, **environmental racism**, and **ecological violence**. In other words, rather than looking at environmental policy as an add-on to the business of the state, this lesson considers the more fundamental orientation, role, function, ideology, and goals of the state as policy and how that leads to troubling environmental outcomes. Doing so allows us to make important connections across various dimensions of state

53

practices and guards against narrow interpretations of environmental policy. Drawing on theories of the state, environment, and social inequality, the lesson explores how this dynamic emerged in history and then applies it to several cases. We therefore recast or reconsider state imperialist policy as environmental policy, rather than examining practices that are formally defined as environmental.

THE NATION-STATE AS AN ENGINE OF PROFIT AND ENVIRONMENTAL HARM

Perhaps the most enduring academic view of the state (that is, the government and its various administrative arms, agencies, and structures) is that of **pluralism**. The concept of a pluralist state is closely associated with the writings of Alexis de Tocqueville and Robert Dahl. The pluralist idea is that politics in a democracy is a process in which various associations (for example, trade unions, business groups, faith-based organizations, and activist organizations) engage in a competition for access to state resources and governmental influence. In contrast to a context in which the state is an autocratic authority, pluralism involves groups sharing power with the state, thus avoiding dominance by government or by any single interest group. Interest groups and associations strive to influence state policymaking through this process, thus allowing citizens multiple venues for voicing their concerns and gaining access to the political system. In practice, however, the political process in the United States is often less pluralist than we might hope. The theoretical perspectives presented below reflect this more critical view of power and social change with a focus on environmental concerns.

The Treadmill of Production

Sociologists Allan Schnaiberg and Kenneth Gould developed a theoretical framework that captures the dynamics of how market forces and political institutions interact to produce ecological disorganization while creating wealth and power for a minority of persons and lower wages and considerably less power for the majority. This "treadmill of production" is a system in which we can observe the increasing accumulation of wealth and investments into capital-intensive technologies, rising social inequalities, and greater ecological "withdrawals" (extraction of ecosystem materials) and "additions" (pollution), all of which are encouraged and facilitated by the nation-state. The treadmill is a model that describes and explains how capitalist societies have become deeply antiecological and antihumanist (see Lesson 2).

While the litany of ecologically destructive practices associated with the treadmill is familiar (polluted air, land, and watersheds, for example), the social costs are less apparent in the popular imagination. One of the best ways to increase profits is to not only ignore polluting processes but to reduce labor costs. Many businesses do this by introducing computer automation, cutting wages, downsizing employment rolls, and reducing workers' benefits. As a result, we witness increasing levels of economic inequality and instability nationally and globally. Some indicators include the following: the number of temporary workers has increased dramatically in the last two decades, the richest 85 people on the planet possess as much wealth (property, assets, stocks) as do the poorest 3.5 billion, 1% of the population of the United States possesses around 40% of the wealth in that country, 20% owns 80% of the wealth, and real wages have declined precipitously since the early 1970s. What all of this leads to is a workforce where a growing percentage of people are non-unionized, hold temporary jobs, receive low wages, and are at risk of experiencing high levels of under- and unemployment. By contrast, at the other end of the spectrum, we see a smaller elite class of white-collar "knowledge workers" with higher pay, higher education levels, higher social status, greater career mobility options, and safer jobs. Furthermore, we have greater pollution levels, social instability, social conflict, and pressures on the state to take up the slack for people who have been downsized and have little or no childcare or healthcare benefits. The state has, of course, been offering billions of dollars in subsidies to corporations in hopes of encouraging such organizations to remain within the national borders and therefore has fewer funds to pay out to citizens/consumers/workers in social benefits. Furthermore, as the ideology of economic growth at all costs remains a dominant theme in this nation, there is less political will or sympathy for downsized workers and declining public support for labor union demands for better working conditions.

According to Schnaiberg and Gould, the modern treadmill of production really grew in scope beginning in the post-World War II era. This was a time when wages were rising for most workers and a new era of prosperity was ushered in by an alliance among industry, labor unions, and the state. The post-1945 political economy was largely held together by an implicit contract. Private capital's need for a reliable labor force aided in the development of strong trade unions that could collectively bargain for wage increases and safer working conditions. Workers' need for jobs and their general satisfaction with unprecedented material gains led to a "no strike" pledge with management. The state played its part by strengthening public education in order to produce a higher-quality labor force, while also expanding consumer credit to make sure that domestic demand for goods kept pace with the increase in production. Overall, these were good economic times.

But as economic globalization intensified, industry and government began to tighten their belts. As early as the 1960s in the United States, the treadmill had already begun to undergo significant changes from its post-1945 structure. With increasing international competition, investors and managers became concerned about the existing pact between management and labor, which ensured a relatively high wage for workers as employees accommodated the treadmill by maintaining the peace between unions and companies. As global economic competition heated up, industry felt the need to cut costs in order to remain solvent and/or to continue offering high rates of return to investors and shareholders. They did this by weakening the labor movement, reducing workers' wages, and downsizing many positions in firms. Those actions—combined with the movement of companies to lower-cost regions of the country or to other nations—created massive unemployment in urban areas and a national crisis in the form of chronic economic downturns during the 1970s–1990s (see Lesson 4). Before and during this time we also saw an exponential increase in the use of chemicals and toxins in industrial production (with a weak environmental regulatory system), producing widespread ecological harm in many urban and rural areas across the nation. So in many urban areas we now have extensive unemployment, hundreds of square miles of abandoned factories, and toxic waste sites. Ecological disruption and social disruption exist side by side and go hand in hand: These dynamics form the essence of the treadmill of production. The treadmill of production produces and reinforces social and economic inequalities locally, nationally, and globally.

Environmental Justice Studies

A related and growing field of scholarly inquiry—environmental justice studies—focuses on a subset of concerns associated with the impacts of the treadmill of production. Environmental justice studies emphasize the unequal outcomes of market-based and state economic and environmental policy-making on people of color, indigenous populations, and the working class or poor. The major concern of scholars in this field is the problem of environmental inequality—that is, when a population suffers a high burden of environmental harm and is excluded from environmental decisions affecting its communities (see Lesson 10). More often than not, such populations include those groups on society's political, economic, and cultural margins. Research on environmental inequality dates back to the 1970s, when scholars were reporting significant correlations between socioeconomic status and air pollution in U.S. urban centers. Hence, for more than four decades we have had quantitative and empirical evidence of social disparities in the distribution of pollution in the United States. Beginning in the 1980s, researchers focused more directly on the links between pollution and race via studies of the proximity of hazardous waste sites to communities of color. This research demonstrated that, in many cases, race was the best predictor of where hazardous waste sites would be located in the United States, prompting the use of the term **environmental racism** to characterize these disparities. Scholars and activists working on this problem frequently embrace the idea of environmental justice, which is a goal or a vision in which no community is unfairly burdened with environmental harms and where social justice and ecological sustainability prevail. Unfortunately, many societies are structured along intensely unequal social relations and heavily invested in toxic and chemical-intensive technologies, so environmental justice will likely remain an elusive goal for some time.

The Risk Society

Another theoretical framework I would like you to consider is German social theorist Ulrich Beck's idea of the "**risk society**." The risk society is marked by a fundamental transformation in the relationship among industry, the state, civil society, and the environment. That is, at this point in history (which some scholars refer to as "late modernity"), we witness an exponential increase in the production and use of hazardous chemical substances. These practices emanate from the state and industry to civil society through production, consumption, and disposal practices, elevating the level of social and physical risk to scales never before imagined. For more than three decades, the United States has been the world's leading producer and exporter of toxic waste, with an estimated 500 million tons. In the late 1980s and 1990s the United States was producing more than one ton of hazardous waste for every child, woman, and man in the nation. What this means is that the very existence of the modern U.S. nation-state is made possible by the production of toxins—chemical poisons—that permeate every social institution, human body, and the **nonhuman** world. To be modern, then, is associated with a degree of manipulation of the human and nonhuman worlds that puts them both at great risk. To be modern also appears to require the subjugation and control over certain populations designated as "others," those less than fully deserving of citizenship, as a way of ameliorating the worst impacts of such a system on the privileged. These two tendencies—the manipulation of the human and more-than-human worlds—are linked through the benefits that toxic systems of production produce for the privileged and the imposition of the costs of that process on people and nonhuman natures deemed less valuable and therefore expendable. In a sense, then, Beck and Schnaiberg and Gould come together to offer a broader theory of environmental inequality from which we can more effectively analyze the role of the state as a contributor to ecological and social violence.

In his classic book *Imagined Communities: Reflections on the Origin and Spread of Nationalism*, Benedict Anderson proposes the following definition of a nation: "an imagined political community . . . and imagined as both inherently limited and sovereign." The nation is imagined because, while members of this community cannot know or meet everyone inside its borders, in our minds we each live in and share this community. The very idea of a nation-state is rooted in *sovereignty*—the ability of a nation's citizens to self-govern and to determine their own fate without interference from others. This is important because very often a powerful nation's practices prohibit another nation from self-governance, and this is frequently done in order to gain access to valuable ecological resources, in addition to consumer and labor markets.

While the U.S. nation-state clearly embraces the agenda and logic of capitalism, this also has broader social impacts and roots. Ultimately, this is because states—as nations—are inherently exclusionary constructions; they write certain people and social categories out of power, belonging, and citizenship, while including others. For example, states reflect historic and ongoing gender ideologies and interests. Leading feminist legal theorist Catherine MacKinnon describes the state (for example, police, military, and legal institutions) as gendered insofar as it has a predominantly male orientation, meaning that not only do men constitute the majority of people in positions of authority within the state, but the state generally works to protect men's interests. The state as a gendered institution is revealed in its relationship to nonhuman natures as well. No doubt drawing from biblical roots that encourage humans to dominate the Earth and men to dominate women, the U.S. and European Union states engage nonhuman natures through ideologies and practices of domination. Specifically, in her groundbreaking book *The Sexual Contract,* Carole Pateman contends that Western European nation-states were founded on a "sexual contract," which sought the exclusion of women from public spheres of power. Environmental historian Carolyn Merchant links that exclusion to the ways in which Western cultures imagine and behave toward nonhuman natures, in what Jim Mason calls "**dominionism**." Geographer David Harvey would agree. In his writings he argues that the idea that people were meant to dominate nature—emerging from the Enlightenment period—is only half right. He contends that the domination of nature thesis is not so much about dominating or controlling the environment or nonhuman nature as it is a means through which the domination of humans by other humans is accomplished. Thus, historically, the rich rule the poor, men control women, and powerful nations rule over weaker nations; and this is accomplished through the resources and power ultimately derived from human exploitation of ecosystems.

My point here is to locate the state's treatment of people in the same ideological, discursive, and structural space as the state's relationship to nonhuman nature. For example, the field of environmental justice studies maintains that the exploitation of people and the exploitation of the environment are linked. Thus, when the environmental integrity of working-class neighborhoods, indigenous lands, and communities of color is harmed by state and corporate practices, this also results in harm done to public health and the social well-being of the persons living in these spaces (see Lesson 10).

Building on Carole Pateman's writings, Charles Mills argues that the U.S. nation-state constitutes a "racial contract" in that it reflects the fact that European Americans founded this nation, at least partially, through acts of violently controlling and excluding Africans and Native Americans. Drawing on Hobbes' notion of the body politic as a leviathan, Mills asks, if we take the nation as a body metaphor seriously, what about those parts of the national body that are viewed as surplus, as waste? His answer is that they can be discarded like any other form of waste. Mills argues that some populations— such as African Americans—constitute such waste, or "black trash," and are therefore viewed as socially and politically disposable. If these bodies and their communities are viewed as a form of social contamination, it might also make sense that society's physical waste would be co-located among these bodies, communities, and spaces. If the people themselves are viewed as dirty, filthy, and disposable, then environmental racism and injustice (via the location of polluting factories or waste dumps in these communities) are perfectly rational state practices. Thus, the state excludes certain populations from power and meaningful citizenship, and this practice intersects conveniently and reinforces the treadmill of production by placing the least desirable persons in the least desirable spaces. For example, sociologists Robert Bullard, Paul Mohai, Robin Saha, and Beverly Wright reported in a 2007 study titled *Toxic Wastes and Race at Twenty*:

- In 2000, the majority of persons in neighborhoods hosting hazardous facilities are people of color (host neighborhoods are defined as communities within 1.8 miles of a facility). People of color are 56% of the population in these neighborhoods, as compared to non-host areas, where people of color are 30%.
- Those neighborhoods hosting clusters of several hazardous facilities have higher percentages of people of color than communities without such clusters (69% vs. 51%). Those areas containing clusters of facilities also contain populations experiencing high poverty rates.
- Not only do racial disparities in hazardous facility siting still exist, they have actually *intensified* over time, resulting in greater environmental inequalities today than reported in 1987. That is, in many parts of the nation, African Americans, Hispanics/Latinos, and Asian Americans/ Pacific Islanders are more concentrated in neighborhoods hosting hazardous facilities than they were 20 years earlier.

What much of this implies, then, is that the U.S. state does not operate based on pluralist principles of governance. Rather, the U.S. state (like any other state) largely exists to further the interests of some groups over others. This practice extends beyond the U.S. border into other nations, producing unequal relations between the United States and peoples around the globe. Another way of thinking about this is to define it as imperialism. *Imperialism* is best characterized as a system of foreign power in which another culture, people, and way of life penetrate, transform, and come to define a colonized society. In the next sections, I discuss the role of U.S. imperialism in relation to other peoples of the Americas and the world and how it produces environmental harm. The point here is to frame these practices as a key dimension of the *de facto* environmental policy regime of the U.S. state.

U.S. IMPERIALISM

The Monroe Doctrine is one of the most important factors in the development of U.S. imperialism in the 19th century. On December 2, 1823, President James Monroe declared the Americas off-limits to any new European colonization. Latin American leaders initially hailed this new policy as a protective mechanism, until they realized that the United States would soon turn the doctrine into its opposite: Latin America, especially the Caribbean basin, was turned into a virtual U.S. sphere of influence. Politicians and media leaders used the doctrine to develop the idea of "America for the Americans." Simón Bolívar, remembered by many people as the great liberator of many South American nations, would soon declare that the United States seemed destined to torment the Americas in the name of freedom. Many Latin American leaders and environmental activists (especially indigenous leaders) argue that the United States pursues a similar agenda to this day, with continued proclamations of bringing democracy and freedom to nations around the world. This underscores an unresolved tension in U.S. history and present-day politics: the contradiction between our ideals of freedom and our predilection for conquest. And that propensity for conquest is driven not only by a desire for consumer markets and cheap labor but also by a thirst for access to ecological wealth in the global South.

A short while later, a more powerful ideological proposition was put forth on the public agenda, which took the Monroe Doctrine much further. This was Manifest Destiny, the ideology of racial and cultural superiority that guided the United States westward across the continent into Mexican territory, south into Central America and the Caribbean, across the Pacific, and beyond. There was a strong religious component to this concept, which embraced the domination of allegedly inferior peoples and the United States' right to do whatever it wished with their lands and ecosystems. Writing in support of the annexation of Texas during July 1845, politician John O'Sullivan coined the phrase "Manifest Destiny" to describe American expansionism:

> Yes, we are the nation of progress, of individual freedom, of universal enfranchisement. This is our high destiny, and in nature's eternal, inevitable decree of cause and effect we must accomplish it. All this will be our future history, to establish on earth the moral dignity and salvation of man—the immutable truth and beneficence of God. For this blessed mission to the nations of the world, which are shut out from the life-giving light of truth, has America been chosen; and her high example shall smite unto death the tyranny of kings, hierarchs, and oligarchs, and carry the glad tidings of peace and good will where myriads now endure an existence scarcely more enviable than that of beasts of the field.

O'Sullivan's phrase was adopted by Republican congressman Robert Winthrop and others in their work to mobilize for war against Mexico and the takeover of that nation's northern territories. Following O'Sullivan's ideas, God had entrusted the United States with "the development of the great experiment of liberty and federated self-government." Even the great poet Walt Whitman found the white man's burden appealing: "We want to see our country and its rule far-reaching only inasmuch as it will take off the shackles that prevent men the even chance of being happy and good." Before the decade ended, the United States had conquered the entire Southwest and forced Mexico to accede to the Treaty of Guadalupe Hidalgo, signed in 1848.

Some scholars contend that the expansionist tendencies we saw in the 1830s and 1840s continue through today with free-trade agreements and proxy wars the U.S. military and corporations are waging in the Americas. For nearly two centuries we have seen a massive and intensified transfer of ecological and economic wealth from south of the border north to the United States, from what Uruguayan author Eduardo Galeano calls "the open veins of Latin America." As a result, some observers and critics like Galeano believe the United States is the most economically privileged nation on the planet, in large part thanks to the extraction of copper from Chile; hardwoods from Brazil; oil from Mexico, Venezuela, and Ecuador; tin from Bolivia; bananas from Guatemala, Costa Rica, and Honduras; sugar from Cuba; and beef from Argentina. This arrangement—which some scholars call imperialist—has not alleviated poverty in Latin America, and the ecological toll from this resource extraction is extraordinary, including deforestation, oil spills, air pollution, soil erosion, species extinction, and the harm associated with countless tons of herbicides and pesticides that U.S.-based agencies and corporations send to be sprayed on crops, watersheds, and agricultural workers' bodies in the region. Women, children, migrant farm workers, and poor populations suffer especially great burdens from pesticides (see Lesson 11). Not surprisingly, indigenous peoples do as well. For example, Plan Colombia (a Colombian U.S. economic and military aid project designed to fight both anti-government Colombian rebels and the cocaine trade that included the aerial spraying of tons of pesticides on coca and poppy plants in Colombia) disproportionately impacts indigenous people's land and health in that nation, violating their right to a clean environment as is customary under international law. The Foundation for Advancements in Science and Education recently concluded that U.S. chemical manufacturers regularly sell tons of pesticides that are banned in the United States (because of their highly toxic content) to Latin American nations, where they are in widespread use in agriculture.

The process set into motion with the Monroe Doctrine and Manifest Destiny continued far beyond Latin America to Asia and elsewhere. At the same time the U.S. empire was going global, there was a domestic expansion into Native American territories as well.

U.S. Federal Policies and Treaty Making

The same year the Monroe Doctrine came into being, another, a much older ideology of domination was being refashioned. In 1823, Supreme Court Chief Justice John Marshall reinterpreted the "doctrine of discovery," an idea that European explorers and nations employed for centuries. The decision in the U.S. Supreme Court's *Johnson v. McIntosh* case resulted in what has been called the Marshall Doctrine, which concluded that the right of native peoples to their lands is diminished and that the sovereignty of the discoverers (read "Europeans") was inherently superior to that of indigenous peoples. Some scholars argue that this was a creative interpretation of the original doctrine of discovery laid out in a series of papal bulls begun by Pope Innocent IV in the 13th century and evolving over the years so that by the early 17th century it had become a core part of international law, or what is referred to as the "law of nations." These legal norms allowed Europeans to acquire land in foreign places only if it was uninhabited or if native peoples gave or sold the land by consent. This meant that Europeans were thus expected to enter into treaty making with native peoples around the world, which recognized their sovereignty; and the British, for example, generally did so. So Justice Marshall's doctrine was important because it represented a major shift in policy that departed from what was considered international law at the time. Marshall pushed even further in what are called the "Cherokee opinions" of the early 1830s (the Supreme Court decisions in *Cherokee Nation v. Georgia*, 1831, and *Worcester v. Georgia*, 1832), seeking to strengthen the logic of the *McIntosh* decision, given that it was not likely to withstand international legal scrutiny. Thus, he developed the thesis that native peoples within North America constituted nations since they inhabited territories and were ruled by governments with the capacity to engage in commerce and treaty making. However, Marshall maintained—drawing on the ideas contained in the *McIntosh* decision—that native nations were a "peculiar type" of nation that were "domestic" to and "dependent upon" the United States. Hence, native nations enjoyed a subordinate sovereignty vis-à-vis the United States. In other words, this was nothing less than a relationship enjoyed by an empire with its colonies. The implication of these legal decisions was that ecological materials such as land, minerals, forests, fish, buffalo, and water within Native American territories were legally constructed as available for the taking if the U.S. government deemed it necessary. One example of this policy was the Dawes Severalty Act of 1887, through which the federal government began "registering" Indians and forcing them to live on lands that were subdivided into small, individual private property lots. The aim was to "civilize" Native Americans by encouraging them to embrace the notion of private property while drastically reducing their land base, liberating "surplus" lands for white settlers, private companies, and the federal government. While much of this land was dedicated to homesteading (for white families who settled in the West), much of it was ultimately used to create the first national parks and national forests in the United States, which Ansel Adams became famous for photographing, often excluding evidence of native peoples from such vistas. Some estimates are that the Dawes Act resulted in the removal of two thirds of the land (around 150 million acres) that native peoples previously occupied. A 1928 congressional study—the Miriam Report—concluded that these policies left "an overwhelming majority of the Indians . . . poor, even extremely poor." Native peoples were relegated to lands that the federal government believed to be of little economic value, with few mineral and other natural resources.

Other native peoples challenged the Dawes Act in the courts, but in the 1903 *Lone Wolf v. Hitchcock* case, the Supreme Court extended federal power to argue that the U.S. government possessed a right to selectively abide by treaties it had made with native nations. This was the final consolidation of the Marshall Doctrine and led to a formal disempowerment of native nations.

One of the great ironies of the Dawes Act was that much of the land base to which Native Americans were relegated eventually was determined to be among the most well-endowed, ecologically rich areas on the planet. It is estimated that two thirds of all uranium deposits in the United States, one fourth of the nation's sulfur coal, and one fifth of oil and natural gas reserves are on (or beneath) Native American reservation lands. Moreover, reservation lands are also rich in metals and minerals such as gold, iron, molybdenum, copper, iron, zinc, nickel, and bauxite. Thus, the unequal relationship between the U.S. government and tribal governments—as developed in the *McIntosh, Cherokee,* and *Lone Wolf* cases—made possible the transfer of such environmental wealth from Native America to the United States of America. The controversial Bureau of Indian Affairs was the agency that supervised this effort and, unfortunately, often failed to ensure the protection of ecosystems during and after extractive projects. One outcome of these state policies is that, particularly on reservations where uranium mining has occurred, the extent of radioactive contamination is considerable. Socially and economically, another more visible outcome of this history is that native communities are among the poorest in the hemisphere, with a range of public and mental health problems that have been at epidemic levels for many years. Native American Studies scholars such as Paula Gunn Allen, Ward Churchill, Andrea Smith, David Stannard, Haunani-Kay Trask, Waziyatawin, and others reveal that unemployment, alcoholism, domestic violence, rape, suicide, and numerous other social ills are abnormally high in many Native American communities, and each of these scholars attributes those outcomes to the effects of U.S. imperialism.

The Struggle Goes On

The practices of imperialism, environmental racism, and ecological violence continue today, within and beyond U.S. borders. At the time of this writing, at least 10 indigenous nations in North America are teaming up with environmentalists in the United States and Canada to oppose the extraction, processing, and transport of tar sands oil. There are at least three multibillion-dollar pipeline projects in various stages of development that companies like TransCanada Corporation (the company behind the Keystone XL pipeline), Enbridge Inc., and Kinder Morgan Energy Partners are championing. Indigenous peoples and their allies (among them scholar-activists like Bill McKibben) are concerned that tar sands extraction will enable the consumption of an enormous volume of fossil fuels, thus contributing massive amounts of carbon emissions to the Earth's atmosphere and accelerating climate change. The Alberta tar sands contain the second largest oil deposit in the world—something the Canadian and U.S. governments and corporations are desperate to tap. Tar sands projects require the use of large amounts of water and dangerous chemicals and have already devastated the Athabasca

River delta and watershed in Alberta, including deforestation of the boreal forests, open pit mining, drainage of water systems, proliferation of toxic chemicals, habitat and biodiversity disruption, and damage to the indigenous Dene, Cree, and Métis First Nations' cultural life ways. Activist groups like the Indigenous Environmental Network have mobilized people throughout North America to oppose these projects and to support Native peoples and environmental justice.

Native Hawaiians, or *Kanaka Maoli*, live in a state that hosts more federal hazardous waste sites than any other U.S. state. Many of these sites were created through polluting activities carried out by the U.S. military, which has compromised and, in some cases, destroyed native land and fisheries. Between 1964 and 1973, the U.S. Navy released 4.8 million gallons of radioactive waste into Pearl Harbor from its submarines. The Navy also dumped more than 2,000 55-gallon steel drums of solid radioactive waste off the shoreline, posing a major threat to ocean life. Similar dynamics characterize the Clark and Subic U.S. military bases in the Philippines and many others elsewhere. The U.S. military is one of the world's greatest sources of pollution and, with more than 700 bases around the planet, one of the leading purveyors of institutional violence. These examples also suggest that U.S. state practices often tend to steer clear of pluralism and remain largely antidemocratic and unilateralist.

What is to be done? One of the first things we should acknowledge is that many of us reap significant benefits from these policies, including the comforts of cheap gas, electronic gadgets, heating and air conditioning, and other material privileges that are unearned yet the result of unfortunate state and corporate policies that harm people and ecosystems all around us. Perhaps that is one reason why we find it difficult or unappealing to confront these issues. But facing the fact that our way of life is linked to appalling conditions elsewhere can also be empowering because we can begin to build relationships of solidarity and cooperation for a better world with people whom we never knew we had a connection.

CONCLUSION

This lesson considers the historical and ongoing actions of the U.S. nation-state as imperial practices that routinely produce environmental harm and social inequality. Offering a sampling of theories of environment–society relationships, social inequality, and state formation, I argue that in order to better understand how contemporary U.S. policies result in environmental racism and inequality, one must consider the historical, legal, economic, and cultural roots and evolution of the U.S. nation-state itself. Such an exploration suggests that the United States remains an imperial presence in the Americas and globally, and this has dire consequences for any effort to produce social and environmental justice here or elsewhere. In this way, we might locate the deeper origins of the environmental state and, in turn, think through a different set of questions that might achieve reform or trans-formation of those practices. For example, instead of seeking only to strengthen regulation of polluting industries in poor neighborhoods and communities of color, one might also push for a greater democratization of the state and industry. Specifically, communities struggling for environmental justice would likely benefit from a stronger civil society base that involves strengthening the capacity of nongovernmental organizations, neighborhood groups, and workers' organizations to negotiate more ecologically sustain-able and socially progressive institutional policies domestically and abroad.

Today, environmental justice and human rights movements are merging as a global force for social change and democratization. Activists in Europe, the Americas, Africa, and Asia are collaborating to challenge socially and ecologically harmful state and corporate policies around hydroelectric power, incineration, and mineral extraction, for example, while offering alternatives for sustainability and social justice (see Lesson 18). Articulating a vision of global justice and human rights, the Principles of Environmental Justice—drafted at the First National People of Color Environmental Leadership Summit in Washington, D.C., in 1991—contain a number of key demands along this vein. For example, the first principle calls for the "right to be free from ecological destruction"; the second principle calls for the right to be "free from any form of discrimination or bias"; the fourth principle invokes the "fundamental right to clean air, land, water, and food"; the fifth principle affirms the "fundamental right to political, economic, cultural and environ-mental self-determination of all peoples"; the eighth principle cites the right "to a safe and healthy work environment"; and the tenth principle contends that governmental acts of environmental injustice are violations of inter-national law and of "the Universal Declaration On Human Rights, and the United Nations Convention on Genocide." Taken separately and together, these principles speak impressively to a body of international law and human rights that has been in development for several decades. More importantly, in order for these principles to become reality, states and corporations would have to undergo dramatic transformations that would embrace transparency, power sharing, and democracy as standard operating procedure. The work of activists in the environmental justice and human rights movements reveals sophisticated efforts at combating global environmental inequalities through the engagement of a range of institutions, thus developing an emerging form of global citizenship and, by extension, a burgeoning transnational public sphere that might ultimately lead to greater democratization of our global society.

And yet, troubling questions remain as to whether all of that effort will ever be enough. That is, what if, as some philosophers contend, the very essence of a modern nation-state is the embodiment of authoritarianism em-ployed to define certain groups as unworthy or only partially worthy of inclusion and recognition as members of the polity? In other words, accord-ing to this idea, integral to the modern nation-state are the ideologies and practices of racism, classism, heterosexuality, patriarchy, and dominionism. If that is so, then it would make sense that scholars begin thinking about solutions to social and environmental crises in ways that move beyond the state altogether. I believe this is a topic that environmental sociologists will be debating in the years ahead.

SOURCES

Anderson, Benedict. 1991. *Imagined Communities: Reflections on the Origin and Spread of Nationalism*. New York: Verso.

Beck, Ulrich. 1992. *Risk Society: Towards a New Modernity*. Thousand Oaks, CA: Sage.

Bullard, Robert D., Paul Mohai, Robin Saha, and Beverly Wright. 2007. "Toxic Waste and Race at Twenty, 1987–2007." United Church of Christ.

Churchill, Ward. 2003. *Perversions of Justice: Indigenous Peoples and Anglo-American Law*. San Francisco, CA: City Lights.

Dahl, Robert. 1961. *Who Governs? Democracy and Power in an American City*. New Haven, CT: Yale University Press.

Galeano, Eduardo. 1997. *Open Veins of Latin America: Five Centuries of the Pillage of a Continent*. New York: Monthly Review Press.

Harvey, David. 1997. *Justice, Nature and the Geography of Difference*. Cambridge, MA: Blackwell Publishers.

Hirst, Paul Q., ed. 1994. *The Pluralist Theory of the State: Selected Writings of G. D. H. Cole, J. N. Figgis, and H. J. Laski*. London, UK: Routledge.

MacKinnon, Catherine. 1982. "Feminism, Marxism, Method, and the State." *Signs* 7(Spring):515–544.

Mason, Jim. 2005. *An Unnatural Order: The Roots of Our Destruction of Nature*. San Francisco: City Lights.

Merchant, Carolyn. 1980. *The Death of Nature: Women, Ecology and the Scientific Revolution*. San Francisco: Harper.

Mills, Charles W. 1999. *The Racial Contract*. Ithaca, NY: Cornell University Press.

O'Sullivan, John. 1845. "The Great Nation of Futurity." *The United States Democratic Review* 6(July):426–430.

Pateman, Carole. 1988. *The Sexual Contract*. Palo Alto, CA: Stanford University Press.

Schnaiberg, Allan, and Kenneth Gould. 2000. *Environment and Society: The Enduring Conflict*. Caldwell, NJ: Blackburn Press.

Smith, Andrea. 2005. *Conquest: Sexual Violence and American Indian Genocide*. Cambridge, MA: South End Press.

Smith, Mick. 2011. *Against Ecological Sovereignty: Ethics, Biopolitics, and Saving the Natural World*. Minneapolis: University of Minnesota Press.

Stannard, David. 1992. *American Holocaust: The Conquest of the New World*. New York: Oxford University Press.

Trask, Haunani-Kay. 1999. *From a Native Daughter: Colonialism and Sovereignty in Hawai'i*. Honolulu: University of Hawai'i Press.

Waziyatawin. 2008. *What Does Justice Look Like? The Struggle for Liberation in Dakota Homeland*. St. Paul, MN: Living Justice Press.

4

Labor Productivity and the Environment

Allan Schnaiberg

Fishermen preparing nets, Tonchigue, Ecuador.
Photo by Ken Gould.

THE PROMISE VERSUS THE HISTORY OF PRODUCTIVITY

Conceptualizing Productivity

The essence of productivity is an increase in economic production for each worker employed. In many industrial societies, the argument has increasingly been made that, with increased productivity, new social problems will be solved. In theory, it is argued that higher productivity and **profitability** *permit* more savings and investments in social and environmental programs. In recent decades, even more economic policy has been mobilized to argue that companies and economies without growing productivity are doomed to be displaced by firms and countries where productivity is higher. As international trade has increased and manufacturing has shifted to lower-wage societies, productivity has become labeled as the key component of "competitiveness."

Yet in practice, the historical processes by which productivity gains have actually been achieved give the lie to this argument. Productivity tends to be a solution primarily for investors and some managers (many of them also become some of the downsized workers). For workers, their communities, and the natural world in which they are embedded, this has become one of the most egregious bait-and-switch social policies. The corporate strategy of constant increases in labor productivity is a central element of the treadmill of production (see Lesson 2).

The Perspective of Corporate Investors and Managers

The greater the productivity of an organization, the greater its profitability, according to modern economics. If I am able to raise the amount of production accomplished by each of my workers each day, my costs of production are reduced. I am then able to sell the commodity that my workers made at a somewhat lower price than my competitors and thereby increase my share of the market for this product.

When this happens over some time period, my profits tend to rise, for two reasons: (1) while I may lower my price somewhat, I generally do not lower it as much as my savings on workers' wages, so I increase my profit on every item I sell; (2) as I compete more effectively over my competitors, I make additional profits because of the increased number of items I am selling. The first of these effects is often defined as my *profit margin* per item I sell (revenue minus costs), and the second is my *profit ratio* (total revenue divided by total cost). These processes vary within countries and across the global economy. For the productive company, they are uniformly desirable outcomes; for the less productive, they are often fatal. In modern economic analysis and journalism, as well as modern politics, though, the focus is on the "winners" and not the "losers," in what can be seen as a kind of **economic Darwinism**.

Yet this is a very selective view of "productivity." Productivity typically has negative effects on the social fabric of a society and the ecological sustainability of its natural environment. To understand this, let's first look more realistically at how productivity is increased. Measurement of actual worker productivity is complex since it requires holding constant a variety of efficiency components in production, to separate out the effects of the workers themselves.

Generally, managers fall back on a simplified calculus: If I can do the same job with fewer workers, then workers' productivity has increased. Some of this is achieved by reorganizing production technologies. But it often generates greater pressure on workers to work harder, longer, and with more workplace tension than they faced previously. Managers can unilaterally decide to "downsize" a workforce—that is, to lay off some significant portion of their workers—and have been doing so in Western economies for decades now.

The Perspectives of Workers/Communities

In order for this to increase productivity, the remaining workers must be willing and/or able to compensate for the lost production of those who were downsized. Their *willingness* can be induced by coercive and/or seductive measures: "Work more or we'll fire you," and/or "Work harder and we'll pay you some additional bonus payments." The first is effective where workers have few other job opportunities. However, the coercive strategy carries with it new potential threats of slowdowns, sabotage, and higher worker turnover in response to the rising stress of the workplace (see Lesson 17). The seductive approach is more effective when the firm has more control of its other costs than its competitors. Its effectiveness dwindles when the total of new worker bonus payments begins to approximate the prior payroll levels of the larger workforce.

In addition to their willingness to increase their labor efforts, though, workers must have the *capacity* to do so. Reducing the labor force by only a modest proportion of workers may be designed to increase the workload of the remaining workers. From a managerial perspective, this creates more efficiency and enhances both productivity and profits.

Perspectives on the Environment

Most of the changes in 20th-century production systems after 1945 consisted of some combination of new energy applications and new chemical processes, generating much less labor-intensive forms of production. For instance, corn production changes, as noted below, exemplify this process in agriculture. Rising chemical pollution emerged in both workplaces (including cornfields) and communities (rivers and streams near cornfields). Parallel changes occurred in much manufacturing, where the materials and processes by which products were formed moved away from the hands of workers and into mechanical and electronic machinery (see Lesson 7).

The modern environmental movement in the 1960s arose in great degree in response to new fears of chemical pollution, exemplified by Rachel Carson's book *Silent Spring*, which presented the widespread reproductive effects of DDT, an early and powerful pesticide. In the 1970s, some environmental movement attention moved to shortages of fossil fuels, due to changes in the concentration of oil production overseas and the decline of U.S. production.

More recently, decades of scientific research has affirmed that the use of fossil fuels has increased carbon dioxide and other "greenhouse gases." These have been correlated with rising atmospheric and oceanic temperatures, altering climate and water distribution and threatening even more disruptions of social and economic life, as well as of ecosystems (see Lesson 15). Although the modern environmental movement was initiated in the United States, the aggregate pollution and depletion (of both energy sources and natural habitats) actually rose in the United States during the period of organized environmental movements, and much greater movement resistance has become embedded within European Union societies.

I now outline two major paths by which investors and managers attempt to increase the productivity of their workers.

RAISING PRODUCTIVITY BY CHANGING PRODUCTION TECHNOLOGIES

One major approach is investment in new production technologies, frequently involving more electronic and mechanical equipment, within existing workplaces. This was the essential strategy used by corn growers.

The Case of Corn

One of the most detailed examples is Michael Pollan's history of corn production. Maize was a very old plant in America. It was generally harvested by hand, and even among early cultivators in Latin America, some manual pollination was done to create new varieties of corn. Corn became essentially an industrialized crop in the United States, especially after 1945. Ever-growing levels of fertilizers, pesticides, and herbicides were utilized to increase the yield of corn per acre.

Gradually, corn production has become essentially a plantation operation, with growing sizes of landholdings and replacement of the labor of planting, harvesting, and storing the grain with mechanized equipment. Likewise, with the large capital investments involved, planters wanted more predictable crops, to cover their loans for the new equipment. Additional equipment was purchased to irrigate cornfields. And the demand for high-yield hybrid corn seeds rose as planters sought to further reduce their risks of pests and water shortages.

The scale of capital investment in corn production rose substantially, and the successful planters bought out the land of smaller and "less productive" farmers. In addition, the debt burden for even large landholders became unsustainable, and many abandoned corn production. Overall, there were substantial increases in the levels of corn production. At first blush, this seemed to serve the economic interests of large landholders quite well. There were a number of social and ecological costs, however. As corn production was industrialized, rural labor forces were eliminated, communities contracted, and local enterprises collapsed because of a lack of wage income and consumer spending. As the dependence on rural labor decreased, so did rural populations, as economically displaced farmers and their children left rural areas in search of employment opportunities.

Moreover, agricultural wastes from cornfields increasingly became toxic, and with growing irrigation there was an increased runoff of chemical pesticides and herbicides into local streams and rivers. And the fossil fuel demands per bushel of corn produced rose substantially. From the standpoint of energy efficiency, the energy inputs involved in corn production vastly exceeded the caloric value of the corn produced. Labor efficiency increased, but energy efficiency declined, producing fewer jobs and more fossil fuel demand simultaneously. Production processes generated fewer social benefits and more ecological disruption.

Despite these social and ecological problems, corn production in the United States has increased substantially. While this seemed to reward "productive" corn planters, it also created new cross-pressures on them. The first problem with rising corn production was that there was too limited a market for all the corn produced. One of the hidden vulnerabilities of increased productivity is that more product must be sold. Productive organizations that lack sufficient markets will find their profits reduced eventually, and investors will move their capital elsewhere. Corn planters responded to this challenge in several ways. Paradoxically, as corn surpluses grew and prices fell, corn producers actually increased their acreage and planting, selling more corn at lower prices, to hold on to their equipment and land. This created still more corn surpluses, further dropping prices and threatening the revenues of corn planters.

Two additional strategies were developed. The first was to widen the use of corn, both in foodstuffs and as animal feed. Pollan outlines how grass-fed beef and other food animals became transformed into corn-fed animals. For livestock owners, this eventually led to enclosures for animals since there was no longer any necessity for grazing. The factory cornfield eventually led to the factory farm, with diminished freedom of movement for all livestock (see Lesson 13).

Because this enclosed corn-fed regimen raised the threat of communicable diseases among densely settled animals, corn feeds were reformulated to include antibiotics and other organic chemicals, designed to both reduce disease and hasten the growth of the animals. The end result of this has been an increase in the chemical levels of corn and meat of all kinds, eventually entering into the human food chain and the land and waters near both cornfields and factory farms.

As corn prices dropped further, research into the use of corn as a synthetic food component rose because the price of corn products was competitive with many other natural food sources. Yet even this expansion of the market did not sufficiently cushion the income of corn planters. They began an extensive and successful lobbying campaign to argue for federal price supports for corn. Part of the campaign was to portray corn producers as just "farmers" living in small towns, who needed protection from the vagaries of weather and markets.

In the post-9/11 political climate, moreover, corn producers scored yet another victory. After the crisis of U.S. terrorism, a new drive to increase "energy security" and "energy independence" in the United States was put on the national agenda. One of the most direct and least politicized strategies that emerged was federal support for the vastly expanded production of ethanol, produced from fermented corn. So successful had this been for corn planters that in the decade following federal support, the market for corn was no longer saturated and corn prices began to rise. This means that corn, a "renewable" resource, has became a core element of both food and transportation. The fact that producing corn is energy-inefficient in both domains has been essentially ignored by most analysts. Since that time, problems with ethanol production from corn have led some researchers to search for more energy-efficient (and cost-effective) feedstocks for ethanol, such as saw grasses. Corn prices have also fluctuated.

Is Corn's History Representative of Other Productivity Processes?

The details of productivity changes for corn overlap to a considerable extent with those for other commodities. While it is true that agricultural production entails more uncertainties than factory production, many of the historical processes just outlined hold for many industries. Where the role of human labor has been reduced in the production process, the alternative technology is often a mixture of increased fossil fuel energy and increased application of synthetic chemicals. Waste has always been a byproduct of all manufacturing processes. However, when machines replace human labor, they offer new capacities for managers and investors, but also new challenges. Purchase of new equipment generally entails both capital outlays and debt, and the result is increased managerial pressure to recoup the investment with increased production and sales.

Just as water power replaced some human workers and steam replaced water power, fossil fuels and electricity replaced steam as a driving force of production (see Lesson 7). This was true not only in the actual production machinery but also in the materials used in products. Wood was replaced by metals and metals by plastics and other synthetic materials. Many of these new processes and products entail toxic chemicals in processing or products.

While some new forms of pollution control were added to production systems and some forms of energy efficiency were even achieved, aggregate production and its **ecological externalities** increased. Contemporary environmental regulation has required producers to negotiate some *qualitative* controls over their production systems. However, almost no governments sought to place *quantitative* limits on the volume of production and profits.

Some of this involved direct political struggles between "shareholders" (investors and managers) and "stakeholders" (workers and community residents). But much of this economic expansion was built into the logic of a newly capitalized production apparatus. Once an enterprise laid out financial capital for a new set of production machinery, there was an increasing motive to recoup this investment and raise profits by increasing the volume of production and net revenues. Workers could be downsized—but it was less economically and politically acceptable for managers to downsize newer capital equipment. Indeed, in fields such as information technology, growing capital outlays were increasingly necessary to *sustain* profits, let alone increase them, in the face of growing technological competition.

In part because of this disparity between disinvesting in workers and investing in physical production equipment, ecological pressures on habitats were both directly and indirectly increased. The indirect pressures arose precisely because the ratio of physical capital to workers grew substantially and the capacity of managing physical capital to generate profits outstripped managerial controls of workers. In order for employment to remain stable, workers had to join in efforts to ensure that firms were encouraged to invest still more. This appeared to be the only way in which replacement jobs could be generated. Production had to constantly expand to produce more goods and services just in order to employ the same number of workers.

An earlier form of pressure involved mobilizing the firm's workers to reject the government's environmental regulation (see Lesson 17). This sometimes meant that workers in industrial communities accepted living in a highly toxic environment because their employment seemed dependent on maintaining existing production forces. And government agencies likewise avoided threatening these sources of jobs.

However, the contemporary alliance for new investments and jobs was even more powerful in aligning workers with investors' and managers' interests. Despite this "common front," growth of profits and wealth of the economic elite far outstripped the wages of workers—initially, blue-collar workers and then increasingly middle-class and professional workers. This often led to workers voting for tax reductions for corporations, as well as diminished environmental and public health protection, to help sustain "competitiveness" in the national and global markets. Freudenburg (1991) argued that, in reality, "good" business climate ratings—the classification for business areas in which there are limited environmental regulations and worker protections—actually correlate with worse economic outcomes: The states named as having "bad" business climates (in other words, having environmental regulations and safety protections for workers) actually had better economic performance (growth in jobs and incomes) over subsequent 5- and 10-year periods.

This coalition for productivity and competitiveness also leads to a disjuncture between the rising social needs of displaced and reduced-wage workers, on the one hand, and workers' support for lower taxation of corporations and investors, on the other hand. Moreover, there seems to be diminished community support for mainstream environmental movements. Environmental enforcement can raise the costs of corporations and often requires larger regulatory expenditures by government agencies. In effect, then, one benefit of choreographing rising productivity by investors and managers is that it mutes the voices raised in opposition to the negative social and environmental outcomes.

RELOCATION AND "OUTSOURCING"

Domestic Relocation

The concept of relocation is deceptively simple: If local workers cost too much, firms should find less expensive workers elsewhere. Relocating plants domestically, to areas with less expensive workers, is one major strategy. For some decades after the 1960s, U.S. manufacturers shifted production out of "rustbelt" communities (Eastern, Northern, and Midwestern), where workers were unionized. Plants were shifted to "sunbelt" communities (Southern and Western), where state laws, work shortages, and managerial threats and inducements inhibited worker unions from forming. Industries such as textiles were shifted almost completely from rustbelt states.

Many of the sunbelt communities, in their quest for new employment and tax dollars, simultaneously offered little enforcement of environmental protection or worker safety. This afforded higher rates of productivity for employers since corporate expenses for some raw materials (including water), for much of their waste disposal, and for worker safeguards were lower than they had been in the somewhat more regulated rustbelt communities.

Outsourcing: International Relocation

Outsourcing, or moving production away from Northern industrial economies and into less developed Southern ones, is an extension and substitute for relocation within the country. This has been the most common U.S. pattern of recent decades. This shift has primarily been due to the search for higher productivity and profits, both for less expensive labor and for lowered waste disposal costs. Ironically, whereas some of the earlier movement of capital to less developed areas involved less sophisticated technologies, movement has been accelerated even in the production (and servicing) of high-technology products, such as electronics. While the labor component of total production costs is not small, a large portion of the costs of production involves larger energy and chemical applications to production.

The most notable of these shifts has been in the production of silicon computer chips, the ultimate in high-value products. Part of the movement of "silicon" from Silicon Valley in California appears to have been the highly toxic production processes and the growing concerns of local environmental groups and worker organizations.

Much of the investment in less developed countries—ranging from China to Mexico—involves heightened workplace pollution and local air and water pollution. In each case, the host government has colluded with foreign investors, trading these social and ecological costs to provide more job opportunities (often for displaced agricultural workers) and higher tax revenues. These interests coalesce with those of investors in countries like the United States who are seeking greater returns on their investments (directly tied in the modern economy to higher productivity and profits).

In the United States, domestic relocation meant moving away from union-ized workers. As union membership declined in the United States, the very investment strategy that had lowered union resistance also permitted a global search for new production locations for investors. Historically, in ad-dition to union resistance, this centrifugal tendency had been restrained by the friction of space, the complexities of communications, and the unpre-dictable systems of national control over foreign investors.

With the rise of electronic communications, rapid airplane travel, and the increasing global pressures to "free up markets," many of these frictions were reduced. A faster pace of technological research and development made previous investments depreciate much faster (and were often accelerated with **depreciation allowances** in taxes paid to the government). Indeed, the pace of increased capitalization of production and the rise of large profits and corporate mergers made many such costs relatively small in the face of new opportunities for investment and profits.

Ecologically, this search for less expensive workers and workplace locations expanded the range of habitats that were becoming disrupted to make room for factories, mines, and natural resource processing facilities. New workers often lived in the midst of corporate structures that seemed modern and communities that were among the most despoiled in modern human history.

Both China and Mexico exemplify such recent trends, although Mexico was far more directly pressured by foreign investors. The health and eco-logical costs are substantial in both countries. Acceptance of these conditions by both workers and their governments supports the productivity-based model of "competitiveness."

Among the most recent of these processes is the outsourcing of white-collar service work—built around the availability of both more powerful computers and advanced telecommunications systems. The direct effect of these new office systems on the environment is primarily in energy intensi-fication of overseas service work. However, the rising toxic problems of both computer chip production and computer scrapping may also predict other health hazards for humans and habitats.

CONCLUSION

Increased labor productivity has become a standard economic indicator for the U.S. economy. When productivity "falters," alarms are raised that the United States will no longer remain "competitive" with its global trading partners.

The harsh reality is that manufacturing is basically no longer carried out in the United States, and agriculture offers a limited range of jobs (and many of those are reserved for low-wage undocumented workers). Labor unions have been largely downsized, along with their previous members. Major unions today have grown in the service sector because U.S. investors have moved their capital abroad (see Lesson 17).

Yet communities and workers still fantasize about the return of the factory, and every domestic and foreign manufacturer is encouraged to relocate to a U.S. community. Communities and their populations seeking jobs are willing to subsidize private producers and often to ignore local ecological degradation to attract new investors.

Labor productivity has largely been achieved by investors and managers, and only a small group of workers has benefited from it. In the process, a substantial human and environmental toll has been paid. Despite the associated social and ecological costs, increasing labor productivity remains a central goal of corporations and a key strategy of states in pursuing economic growth and global competitiveness.

SOURCES

Freudenburg, William R. 1991. "A 'Good Business Climate' as Bad Economic News?" *Society and Natural Resources* 3(Spring):313–331.

Gould, Kenneth A., David N. Pellow, and Allan Schnaiberg. 2008. *The Treadmill of Production: Injustice and Unsustainability in the Global Economy.* Boulder, CO: Paradigm Publishers.

Pellow, David N., and Lisa Sun-Hee Park. 2002. *The Silicon Valley of Dreams: Environmental Injustice, Immigrant Workers, and the High-Tech Global Economy.* New York: New York University Press.

Pollan, Michael. 2006. *The Omnivore's Dilemma: A Natural History of Four Meals.* New York: Penguin.

Smith, Ted, David A. Sonnenfeld, and David N. Pellow, eds. 2006. *Challenging the Chip: Labor Rights and Environmental Justice in the Global Electronics Industry.* Philadelphia, PA: Temple University Press.

5

Corporate Power
The Role of the Global Media in Shaping What We Know About the Environment

Elizabeth H. Campbell

The Apple store on the "Magnificent Mile," Chicago, Illinois.
Photo by Ken Gould.

In pursuit of privileging corporate actors in the global market, **transnational corporation** (TNC) elites have been increasingly successful in lobbying international organizations, such as the World Trade Organization (WTO), for increased freedoms on the movement of capital, technology, and goods and services. The WTO, established in 1995, is the main governing organization of the multilateral trading system, staffed by unelected bureaucrats, whose proceedings are held in secret, thereby denying public participation. TNCs, with the consent of global organizations and through binding regional and global trade agreements, undermine the efforts of individual governments to regulate TNCs within their borders.

Take, for example, Chapter 11 of the 1994 North American Free Trade Agreement (NAFTA), negotiated to promote the free flow of goods and services among the United States, Canada, and Mexico. This provision was supposedly written to protect investors if foreign governments tried to seize their property, but corporations have stretched NAFTA's Chapter 11 to undermine environmental decisions and the decisions of local communities. In California a billion-dollar case was filed against the United States because of an effort by the state government to protect the health of its citizens through the enactment of an environmental protection law that banned the chemical methyl tertiary-butyl ether (MTBE). This gasoline additive, found to cause cancer in laboratory animals, infiltrated 30 public water systems and another 10,000 groundwater sites. University of California scientists were commissioned to assess the problem, and their study warned that the state was placing its water resources at risk. On March 25, 1999, California's governor ordered that MTBE be phased out of all gasoline sold in the state.

In response, Methanex, a Canadian company that is the world's largest producer of the key ingredient in MTBE, claimed under Chapter 11 of NAFTA that its market share, and therefore its future profits, were being expropriated by the governor's action. The company argued that it must be allowed to sell the product in California or be paid $970 million in compensation. While NAFTA may protect corporate investors like Methanex, it does not protect ordinary people who may become ill from the contaminated water (see Lesson 11) or taxpayers who will pay the bill if the secret tribunal decides in favor of such companies. NAFTA makes no provisions for a full appeal to U.S. courts and sets no caps on the amount of damages that can be awarded a corporation. This is an example of a foreign corporation invoking regional trade agreements that trump state laws aimed at protecting the health and environment of its people.

Motivated largely by profit margin, TNCs increasingly operate with little public accountability. How did this happen? Why did the American public agree to a shift in power from local people and states to unaccountable, unelected international institutions and TNCs? How did the public endorse job insecurity and outsourcing (see Lesson 17), lower wages, downsizing of the welfare state, decline in social services, and a rollback of environmental protection standards? Like all industries, the media industry is now both global in scope and largely owned by a handful of TNCs. This lesson examines the rise and influence of corporate power in the global media industry and its impact in shaping what we know or don't know about social and environmental issues.

THE NEED FOR DIVERSITY OF VIEWS IN A DEMOCRACY

The largest media giants have achieved unprecedented success in writing the media laws and regulations in favor of their own corporations and against the interests of the public. Their concentrated power permits them to become one of the largest factors in socializing each generation about politics, the environment, and personal values. Today's media **conglomerates** have almost total power to set the agenda for what will and will not be discussed in mainstream newspapers and magazines and on TV and radio.

As a result, environmental issues are often debated in such ways to ensure that corporations are never pointed out as a cause or source of environmental degradation.

Debate on global warming is a classic example (see Lesson 15). For well over a decade the debate about global warming, driven by corporate interests and crafted by powerful think tanks and public relations (PR) firms, has largely centered on whether or not it is a problem. People generally do not favor action on issues when arguments appear to be "balanced" on both sides and there is clear doubt. Corporations and the institutions representing them play a key role in providing the media with "credible experts" who are normally not climate scientists but who nonetheless confidently dispute scientific claims of global warming. By disproportionately saturating the global media with these so-called experts, they offer enough manufactured doubt to ensure that governments take no initiative to act.

Powerful **think tanks** in Washington, D.C., that have enormous influence in shaping the debate, such as the CATO Institute, the Heritage Foundation, and the Competitive Enterprise Institute, use scare tactics by asserting that cuts in energy consumption would hurt the world's workers, the struggling poor, and the elderly. Further, they argue that renewable energy sources like solar and wind are not only expensive but also environmentally damaging. These think tanks use emotive arguments and fear tactics to bash environmentalists and environmental issues, rather than engaging with them on a more reasoned, substantive basis. Moreover, such think tanks promote the views of a few scientists who disagree with the vast majority of climate scientists that warming is a consequence of the increasing levels of greenhouse gases in the atmosphere, much of which stems from the burning of nonrenewable energy resources like coal, gas, and oil. Widespread public concern over this issue is not translating into government action, in part because the issue cannot be seriously debated and better understood in the mainstream media. The corporate media works hard to avoid larger questions of power and institutional reform by instead focusing on controversial scientific reports and discrediting individual advocates.

By reducing complex issues like climate change to simplistic special interest–driven sound bites about whether or not it really exists, citizens consuming the media become incapable of understanding and acting on real debate and questioning and instead prefer easy answers, quick fixes, and easy-to-grasp phrases. Audiences thus grow apathetic, cynical, and quiescent about media presentations of environmental issues, which has resulted in an increasingly widespread lack of interest in engaging in them. For example, although atmospheric levels of carbon dioxide reached the watershed record level of 400 parts per million in 2013, U.S. public interest in the issue of climate change has dramatically declined since 2008. Democracy, however, demands an informed, active, and involved citizenry in order to ensure that the majority of voices and interests are well represented. As seen from the example of MTBE and Methanex, foreign corporations are primarily concerned with making profits and have little to no regard for the way in which their business activities disrupt local environments. It is only local citizens and governments—and not absentee corporate landlords—that know best when the air they breathe, the water they drink, and the food they consume is contaminated; thus, such persons are best situated to respond to the problem. A well-informed citizenry that is exposed to all angles and interests in a substantive issue is more motivated and better equipped to engage in the political decision-making process. The more citizens who engage in the democratic process to ensure their interests are protected through the enactment of environmental and labor laws, the stronger the democratic system becomes. A democracy beholden only to corporate interests will never pursue a path toward social and environmental sustainability.

THE RISE OF TRANSNATIONAL CORPORATIONS

Historically, the corporation was a public institution created by the government to serve public interests. Early American corporations could only be created through special charters granted by state legislatures. These charters limited what corporations could do, for how long, and how much they could accumulate. In legal theory, corporations were classified as concessions or grants of the government. They were political creations, over which the state exerted great regulation and control. In the United States, corporations were required by law to serve the public interest. If corporate actions were found to violate the public interest, states reserved the right to revoke their charter and dissolve the corporation. The initial creation of private finance was to aid in the expansion of state colonial and imperial interest as well as to help in war efforts between empires. As corporations increased their wealth and therefore their political power, laws that initially tried to manage them were relaxed.

By the mid-19th century corporations became increasingly privatized in both law and ideology. That is, they were beholden no longer to public officials but rather to private citizens who invested in them. As a result, their power and influence in the public greatly expanded. Many legal and cultural justifications for public accountability were stripped away. Corporations were reinvented as natural manifestations of free exchange among individuals, separate from the state. The public charter system basically collapsed, and the right of state legislatures to regulate corporations was eliminated.

Relying on the Fourteenth Amendment, added to the Constitution in 1868 to protect the rights of freed slaves following the Civil War, the U.S. Supreme Court ruled in the 1886 *Santa Clara County vs. Southern Pacific Railroad* decision that a private corporation is a "natural person" under the U.S. Constitution. That decision granted corporations the same rights and protection extended to persons by the Bill of Rights, including the right to free speech. Corporations were thus given the same "rights" to influence the government in their own interests as were extended to individual citizens, paving the way for corporations to use their wealth to dominate public thought and discourse. Corporations, as "persons," were thus free to lobby legislatures, use the mass media, and construct a public image that they believed would best serve their interests.

Prior to the 1886 Supreme Court ruling, only humans were "endowed by their creator with certain inalienable rights." Today, corporations can claim rights instead of just privileges. In terms of politics, it was once a felony for corporations to give money to politicians and political parties. By claiming the human right of free speech, corporations expanded that to mean the unlimited right to put corporate money into politics. This corporate right was reaffirmed and expanded by the Supreme Court in 2010 in its ruling in the *Citizens United vs. Federal Election Commission* case. Today, corporations largely control the U.S. political parties and individual politicians. In terms of business, state and local communities once had stronger laws that protected and encouraged local entrepreneurs and local businesses. Today, by invoking "discrimination" under the Fourteenth Amendment, many of these laws have been abolished. Local and regional economies are less able to protect themselves from predatory TNCs that have no long-term investment in the local communities. The Fourteenth Amendment has also been invoked by corporations to defend their right to privacy. In doing so, TNCs have been successful in ensuring that federal regulatory agencies do not investigate them for crimes and do not gain access to environmental information crucial to protecting public health. Finally, as natural persons, corporations successfully lobbied states to change corporate charter laws to eliminate "public good" provisions from charters, to allow for multiple purposes, and to exist forever.

DEFINING CHARACTERISTICS OF CORPORATIONS

From this "right" of the corporation, corporate interests have been increasingly equated with the human interest: Consumption is happiness. Through advertising, marketing, and control of information, corporations are able to create desires, invent needs, and foster traditions that encourage unquestioned consumption. Product advertisement is a multi-billion-dollar industry. Corporations today spend over half as much per capita on advertising than the world spends on education. Those who control the mass media control the core culture.

Unlike that of other entities, corporate influence is better situated to penetrate all aspects of social, cultural, and political life through a wide variety of means. In addition to their power to influence the public through advertising and through the control and influence of the mainstream media, corporations have exceptional influence on public policy. This can range from financing large parts of elections to creating corporate-funded think tanks and "grassroots" front groups to represent industry interests in the name of concerned citizens. PR firms have become adept at creating the impression of grassroots support for corporate causes so as to convince politicians to oppose environmental reforms. The names of the corporate front groups are carefully chosen to mask the real interests behind them. For example, prior to disbanding in 2002, the Global Climate Coalition (GCC), a coalition of 50 U.S. trade associations and private companies representing oil, gas, coal, automobile, and chemical interests, aimed to cast doubt on the severity of the problems associated with global warming and instead created confusion by magnifying uncertainties. The GCC was formed in 1989 following the hot summer of 1988, when global warming briefly emerged as a lead story in the news media. GCC's efforts helped to squelch media attention and policy action on climate change for over a decade.

Today, there is a common set of shared beliefs, values, and assumptions of how corporations operate. Corporations are largely understood to be private, sovereign enterprises. There is a fundamental belief in the separation between the public and the private. Sustained economic growth is viewed as the sole path toward human progress. In order to maximize this growth, the preferred environment is the "free" market economy. The assumption is that privatization—or a corporate-controlled economy—removes inefficiencies in the public sector, allowing more goods to be brought to more people faster.

The largest TNCs penetrate every single country. They exceed most governments in size and power and define the policy agendas of states and international bodies, such as the WTO and increasingly the United Nations (UN). All TNCs are motivated by profit above and beyond any other interest, such as environmental integrity or social equity. TNCs are extremely mobile. They are able to transcend state boundaries with little difficulty. Detached from people and place, TNC owners are easily able to hire and fire employees at will. Employees of TNCs are therefore expendable, a trend that contributes to rising job insecurity (see Lesson 17). There is no longer a commitment to the local community since TNCs belong to the global marketplace. This is dangerous as it is the local community that is best situated to detect and respond appropriately to environmental issues. Absentee ownership is a key defining feature of today's TNCs. Most are monopolistic and discourage competition. This is evidenced by the fact that 70% of world trade is controlled by just 500 corporations. A mere 1% of all TNCs own half the total stock of direct foreign investment. With unmatched political and economic resources, the main goal for corporations today continues to be their struggle to wholly liberate themselves from the burden of public social and environmental accountability yet, at the same time, lobby Congress for greater subsidies to pursue their interests (see Lessons 12 and 13).

CORPORATE WELFARE

Each year the U.S. Congress pays out tens of billions of dollars to American corporations in the form of direct subsidies and tax breaks (see Lesson 3).

In fiscal year 2012 these subsidies totaled nearly $100 billion. Corporate welfare costs more than four times as much as welfare to the poor. TNCs thus collect more government handouts than all of the nation's poor people combined. One of the largest recipients of corporate welfare are weapons contractors like General Electric (GE)—also a global media conglomerate that owned and operated NBC Universal until March 2013. One way contractors get subsidies is by mandating that military aid given to foreign countries be used to buy American weapons. Each year this program results in the transfer of tens of billions of U.S. taxpayer dollars to U.S. weapons merchants. The most successful U.S. industries would not be competitive internationally if the federal government had not developed their basic technology with taxpayers' money through programs like the Advanced Technology Program and then given it away to private corporations (see Lesson 7).

In addition to providing jet engines for military aircraft, GE makes nuclear reactor missile propulsion systems and delivery vehicles for nuclear weapons. It has designed more than 90 nuclear power plants in over 10 countries. Between 1946 and 1965, GE made plutonium for the U.S. military at Hanford Nuclear Reservation, a massive 570-square-mile facility in Washington. One of the worst incidents during GE's tenure at Hanford was a calculated experiment in which radioactive particles containing more than 500 times the radiation of the Three Mile Island accident, when nuclear reactors suffered a partial meltdown, were deliberately released into the air. The toxic and radioactive legacy left behind at Hanford is staggering. Thousands of citizens living downwind continue to suffer from cancer and other chronic illnesses. Today, GE continues to sell nuclear technology abroad, with no acknowledgment of the complex and persistent environmental damage caused by radioactive material In addition to penetrating the global ecosystem and food chain, nuclear waste is a global problem with no sustainable solutions.

In 2012 GE spent over $21 million lobbying the U.S. Congress to craft legislation that would benefit its company and garner contracts. In recent elections it has shelled out over $4 million in campaign contributions. This work paid off as it was awarded over $3 billion in federal contracts in fiscal year 2010. GE also featured in the top 10 corporate recipients of U.S. government subsidies, totaling tens of millions of dollars. GE garnered direct subsidies from the government despite over 25 proven instances of fraud, waste, and abuse in handling government contracts. Some of this negligence includes violations of polychlorinated biphenyl (PCB) regulations, violations of California's pesticide registration requirements, emission violations, violations of Florida's and New York's hazardous waste laws, and violation of the Clean Air and Clean Water Acts. Indeed, GE is no friend of the environment. GE has lobbied hard to overturn the U.S. Superfund Law of 1980, which allows the government to hold polluters responsible for cleaning up their toxic chemicals. GE argued instead that it was unconstitutional for the Environmental Protection Agency (EPA) to force the company to pay for the cleanup of the Hudson River in New York, where GE dumped carcinogenic

PCBs for over three decades. Given GE's history and its control over the global media, it should be no surprise that complex environmental issues were not presented or thoroughly debated on NBC or its countless subsidiaries.

In addition to foreign-policy spending and research and development that funds corporate technology, corporations benefit from other public projects. Corporations are able to use the public infrastructure, such as transportation and communication. They benefit greatly from the public investment in education: Today's students are tomorrow's workforce. Corporations also benefit from publicly funded environmental cleanups, such as the Hanford Nuclear Reservation. Up until the late 20th century, corporations freely disposed of their toxic industrial waste into rivers, waterways, and neighborhoods. The multi-billion-dollar healthcare and long-term environmental costs of this waste have largely been absorbed by the taxpayers since corporations use their influence in Congress to ensure they will not be held accountable and their influence in the media to ensure the public is not informed.

In addition to benefiting from these public institutions, corporations are increasingly privatizing these historically public institutions as well. Education, healthcare, security, policing, detention, corrections facilities, public lands, public water, and public airways are increasingly being privatized. This means that TNCs are currently attempting to monopolize, for example, control of world water systems and supplies. Several years ago the World Bank, one of the world's largest lenders and sources of development assistance, adopted a policy of water privatization and full-cost water pricing in poor, developing countries (see Lesson 18). In the United States, city water systems have now been contracted to corporations like Bechtel Group, Inc., a corporation with a long history of environmental abuses, to upgrade. Privatization of public resources means that democratically elected governments sign away their control over domestic water supplies by participating in trade treaties like NAFTA and the WTO, where TNCs are granted unprecedented rights to public resources.

The powers to educate, jail, rehabilitate, care for the poor, and manage nature itself are all being entrusted to corporations, which have no accountability to the public. As these functions are sold off, the government itself is transformed, if not dismantled, into an institution of private enterprise, where ordinary citizens have no voice. TNCs are considered individual citizens under the law and are dependent upon public money for their own growth and expansion, but they are not accountable to the public. As more public lands and institutions are privatized by TNCs, as TNC profit margins trump all other interests, and as the public is increasingly squeezed out of the decision-making arena, there has been comparatively little media attention directed at this seismic social change. The following sections thus examine more closely the role of the corporation in the global media and how it shapes our knowledge and decisions on a wide variety of issues.

THE HISTORY OF CORPORATE GLOBAL MEDIA

We are increasingly inundated with information, but what do we know? How do we know it? And what don't we know? We quickly tire of sound bites, sensationalized stories, and buzz words—but often before we even begin to understand the complexity behind the attention-grabbing head- lines. Like all industries, the media are also becoming increasingly global in the age of the connected international corporate system. It currently serves two main functions. First, the global media plays a central economic role for non-media firms by facilitating their business interests. This is done by pro- viding advertising outlets to facilitate corporate expansion into new markets, new countries, and new regions. Second, the global media's news and enter- tainment provide an informational and ideological environment that helps to sustain the political, economic, and moral basis for marketing goods and for having a dominant free-market agenda. The media are central to con- vincing us that American-style democracy and the free-market economy are the only paths toward "freedom."

The role of the media in our society can only be understood in a political and economic context. That is, who owns and controls the media, and for what purposes, has always been a political issue. Until the 20th century, media were largely local and national. Today, in the same way that corpora- tions have become increasingly global in nature, so too have the media. The owners and producers of media no longer have only their national interests in mind but rather the interests of making profits on a global scale. As the global capitalist system continued to develop, communication was central to expanding commercial interests.

The first form of global media was wire-based international news agen- cies such as Reuters and eventually the Associated Press. These entities pro- duced news and then sold it to local and national newspaper publishers. By the 1850s there were about four main commercial news agencies that had established a cartel, dividing the entire world market for news production and distribution. These were European—Germans, French, British, and eventually Americans. Since the very beginning of global media, dating back to at least the mid-19th century, global news services have been oriented to the needs and interests of the wealthy nations that provide their revenue. These news agencies sold news content to their own nations as well as colo- nized nations, which could not support their own global news services.

The emergence and ascension of the TNC laid the groundwork for the rise of the global media. The film industry and then radio broadcasting were two of the first forms of global media. By 1914, 85% of the world film audience was watching American films. The experience with these media elevated the importance of control of media and telecommunications systems in general as a powerful political tool. By the end of World War II, through the use of global media, the United States was able to assert its global dominance as a hegemonic power or world leader.

Along with its policies of opening markets throughout the world for trade, the United States also advocated for the "free flow of information." In theory, the idea that news, information, ideas, and opinions have unrestricted movement across political boundaries is largely positive. In practice, however, the "free flow of information" has instead meant that U.S.-based TNCs are able to operate globally, across borders, with minimal oversight, fewer checks and balances, and fewer contending voices. While the American-dominated global media wanted free access to news and information markets, they were not necessarily interested in freedom of information and diversity of opinions and perspectives, critical aspects of a flourishing and sustainable democracy. The post-World War II era was thus characterized by a shift away from public-owned national and local media toward commercially owned global media. While public media are funded largely by public tax dollars, private media are funded by corporate advertisers selling increased consumption.

With the spread of English global news media came increased commercial marketing—that is, more commercials and advertising—and the consolidation of formerly distinct media industries such as film, music, publishing, and broadcasting. By the 1970s, the beginning of economic "free"-market rule on a global scale, the trajectory and nature of the global media system were clear: It was largely a profit-driven system dominated by TNCs based in highly industrialized capitalist nations, especially the United States. State deregulation of private industries, a decline in the social welfare state, and privatization of state-run companies and services—the defining characteristics of economic globalization—greatly facilitated the expansion of TNCs and hence the increasing growth and consolidation of global media.

An example of state **deregulation** of private industries includes the infamous 1994 Republican Party "Contract with America," heavily influenced by corporate-sponsored think tanks that encouraged measures aimed at repealing existing environmental regulations, preventing new ones, and disabling the authorities that enforce environmental regulations. Think tanks and congressional representatives alike argued that the cost of federal regulations to the economy totaled billions of dollars annually. These unsubstantiated concerns were manifested in several pieces of legislation that sought to override the mandates of the Clean Air Act, the Clean Water Act, the Safe Drinking Water Act, and the Endangered Species Act, among others.

Contrary to the fact that TNC interests are outwardly against governmental regulation, the TNC-dominated system of economic globalization has been a political choice that has nonetheless been aided by governments. After all, it is states that are signatories to various international trade agreements that facilitate the growth and expansion of TNC interests. Today, the system of free-market liberalism rests upon the widespread acceptance of a global corporate ideology. This ideology has played an important role in rationalizing and sanctifying unequal relations of power. It helps explain why the Enron scandal—perhaps the largest corporate scandal in history—quickly disappeared, while Hollywood drama continues to receive ongoing prime-time coverage. It also helps to explain why the media has focused primarily on the drama of National Security Agency whistleblower Edward Snowden's asylum-seeking adventure, and not on the complicity of communications TNCs like AT&T, Google, Microsoft, and Apple in giving the spy agency information about you without your knowledge and consent. The ideology that the free-market economy is actually free and that what is good for corporations is good for the people—acting through the global media—is today a powerful form of social control.

CORE ELEMENTS OF THE GLOBAL MEDIA CORPORATE IDEOLOGY

There are two core elements of the new global media corporate ideology. The first element is the idea that markets allocate resources efficiently and should provide the means of organizing economic and perhaps all human life. It is dominated by a strong belief in privatization—reducing public control and increasing corporate control, thereby increasing profit margins. The second element is that freedom is often equated with the absence of any state business regulations. Political freedom is something different, and it is often subservient to economic freedom. In other words, the idea is that economic freedom leads to and guarantees political freedom. Media are, however, not free at all. Instead, it tends to regard corporate domination as natural and benevolent. The media preach both overtly and covertly the virtues of commercialism and the market. Today's global media have no social, moral, or political obligations beyond the pursuit of profit.

Concentrated wealth and power, on the one hand, and dire poverty, hunger, famine, and landlessness, on the other, cannot exist outside of systemic propaganda in modern democracies. There are several essential ingredients or news filters that constitute the propaganda model. These elements interact with and reinforce one another. The raw material of news must pass through these filters in order to be printed or aired. The elite domination of the media and the marginalization of competing voices that results from the operation of these filters occur so naturally that media employees believe they are interpreting the news "objectively."

SIZE, OWNERSHIP, AND PROFIT ORIENTATION

In the United States, the bulk of the news, commentary, and daily entertainment are controlled by only six firms that are among the world's largest corporations: Comcast/NBC Universal, 21st Century Fox/News Corp, The Walt Disney Company, CBS Corporation/Viacom, Time Warner, and Sony Corporation of America (in comparison, in the mid-1980s there were some 50 corporate owners of the media). These corporations have more annual revenue than the next 20 combined. Together these six corporations own newspapers, magazines, book publishing houses, movie and TV production studios, Internet services, and record labels. They also own the national delivery systems for the programming they control or lease, such as broadcast networks and cable. Moreover, they increasingly own the delivery mechanisms into each American home or office as well, such as telephone company lines, cable systems, and satellite dishes.

The process of increased ownership over all aspects of media production and distribution is called vertical integration (see Lesson 13). Vertical integration is a defining characteristic of TNCs and is defined as the control over a total process—from the raw material (news) to fabrication (fashioning it into a newspaper or broadcast network) to sales. Vertical integration allows for price control and monopoly. If there are only six corporations controlling the bulk of the information and these corporations are largely interested in selling their specific agenda and self-interest (free-market ideology), it means that, despite more information, there is less and less diversity in its content; hence, it becomes less democratic.

These six corporations constitute a private ministry of information and culture. Through their ascendance to power, they have successfully implemented a system of tiers. At the top are leading news sources such as the *New York Times* and CNN, from which the local papers and broadcast networks, situated at the bottom, get their national and international news; therefore, there is a single perspective being portrayed from the global to the national to the local level. While it is expressed in different media and by different actors, the message stems from the same source. The directors of these companies are usually businesspeople interested less in the quality of the product and more in the size of the profit margin. If, for example, information about the personal lives of Hollywood film stars attracts a large audience base, this will be the sole determining factor in shifting media resources to cover this information. Profit-driven media are further entrenched by the fact that it is banks and other institutional investors who are large owners of media stock. Again, profit margin is the single most defining factor in what constitutes news, not moral, political, or social obligations to keep the public informed of key issues relating to their health and well-being.

Since these companies are extremely diverse and own everything from radio to newspapers and from theme parks to online entertainment services, the corporate media owners have big stakes in policy decisions. In other words, it is less likely for these corporate owners to encourage their reporters to investigate environmental problems linked to corporations. Take, for example, the story that "the cloud," that magical place where we are now encouraged to store our digital music, photos, documents, and other data, is in reality a growing source of greenhouse gas emissions (see Lesson 1). Perhaps you have not been made aware of this issue by the corporations that own the data centers generating the emissions, as well as the news media you rely on for information. "The cloud" relies on an expanding series of enormous data centers that are in continuous operation and require a tremendous amount of electricity. Some of them draw as much power as 180,000 households and can be seen from space. The electricity that powers the data centers is most commonly generated from the burning of fossil fuels (see Lesson 9). Since the data centers cannot be allowed to fail in a power outage, they are often backed up by large diesel-fueled generators. What appears to you as a clean, efficient, and reliable **post-industrial**, dematerialized, data storage and retrieval system is actually a coal-powered collection of very material storage facilities warehoused in a variety of locations here on Earth. Storing data in "the cloud" increases greenhouse gas emissions and accelerates global climate change, but that story has not been widely told in the corporate media.

THE ROLE OF ADVERTISING

The media are required to conform to advertisers' wishes. Political discrimination is therefore structured into advertising allocations. Only those with money can buy space. Those with the most money are TNCs, which also share the same ideology and agenda of the promotion of free-market capitalism. Advertisers choose selectively among programs on the basis of their own principles. Large corporate advertisers on television will rarely sponsor programs that engage in serious criticism of corporate activities. Other institutional voices, perspectives, and ideas are systemically denied opportunities to access the global media as they do not bring to bear the same resources needed to purchase space to sell their ideas. Such examples include local organic farming cooperatives, environmental sustainability projects, alternative energy sources, endangered species issues, conservation issues, and anti-fracking initiatives.

In addition, the global media's attempt to attract larger audiences (in order to secure more profits) means that there is increased competition for advertising. Advertisers are also primarily interested in profit margins and thus wish to advertise their products in places where they can reach the largest audiences. Again, if the largest audiences can be formed most quickly and most easily through the tactics of shock value, crude vulgarity, sex, violence, and celebrity gossip, then there is an incentive for the global media to focus superficial attention on these stories rather than on in-depth coverage of complex social, economic, environmental, and political issues that shape our quality of life.

This has led to the phenomenon best described as "infotainment" and "advertorials." These terms depict how "news" has become mostly entertainment information and how editorial commentary is largely driven by the special interests of advertising companies. Morning and evening news programs today largely consist of analyses of the previous evening's television shows, particularly the so-called reality-based TV programs. Guests largely include celebrities, design and fashion experts, pop culture specialists, and musicians. This has led to the deterioration of the quality of news, which has now been reorganized largely to serve corporate ambitions and no longer includes the independent, diverse public information on which democracy depends. Simply debating whether the news has a liberal or conservative bias is a distraction from corporate control and dominance of the global media.

GLOBAL MEDIA SOURCES

As the global media corporations continue to be concerned mostly with profit margin, there has been a dramatic reduction in the number of field reporters and overseas bureaus. Investing in sustained, in-depth, field-based investigation and reporting is expensive. Most of these positions and bureaus have been cut. Parts of American news production have been outsourced to countries like India with huge concentrations of inexpensive labor. Another cost-saving technique has been the increasing reliance on "official sources" for important political and economic information. The global media increasingly turns to information provided by the government, businesses, and other "experts" as the key source for important stories on a wide variety of issues. Institutions like the Pentagon, the U.S. State Department, and corporate entities have the resources available to provide media organizations with information via press statements, speeches, forthcoming reports, scheduled press conferences, and photo opportunities.

These large bureaucracies of the powerful subsidize the mass media and gain special access by their contribution to reducing the media's costs of acquiring the raw materials necessary to produce the news. The large entities that provide this subsidy become "routine" and "authoritative" news sources with privileged access to the global media. Free speech is thus directly tied to one's wealth. Media power is political power, and only the wealthiest are able to fully access it. Those institutions or entities without entire departments dedicated to PR are often unable to access the global media to express their concerns or offer their own reports on key issues. This has contributed to a narrowness of the news, a lack of rich debate, and a general decline in the diversity of perspectives portrayed in the news. If most reporters turn to the same sources for authoritative positions on issues, there is little room for widespread debate; hence, it is easy to conclude that the news is objective. Moreover, as journalists increasingly rely on corporate and governmental entities as the sole source of their information, they often become more reluctant to challenge these sources so as not to damage their established relationships and ongoing access to these sources.

VIOLATING THE CORPORATE AGENDA

Since the media carries the free-market agenda, when it criticizes or diverges from the agenda, corporate-sponsored institutional monitors harass and put extreme pressure on the media to toe the line. Whenever the media does not adopt the official corporate or governmental position on an issue, these monitors will systemically attack the media for careless reporting, unfounded claims, and other violations. As mentioned above, the best example of this is the issue of global warming. Instead of engaging this issue thoroughly to examine different options of addressing the root causes, each new scientific report or global treaty has been met by harsh, well-organized, PR-driven, corporate backlash that seeks to discredit the individual authors and the reports themselves (see Lesson 15).

These tactics reach back to the beginning of the modern environmental movement with the 1962 publication of Rachel Carson's book *Silent Spring*, which detailed the environmental destruction that DDT and other dangerous toxins caused and subsequently helped to raise awareness about environmental destruction (see Lesson 16). In response, the agrichemical industry doubled its PR budget and distributed thousands of book reviews trashing *Silent Spring*. The Monsanto chemical company published *The Desolate Year*, a parody in which failure to use pesticides caused an insect plague to devastate crops across the United States. Today, entire PR firms exist in part to help corporations distribute propaganda and lobby against environmental protection. U.S. businesses spend an estimated $1 billion a year on the services of anti-environmental PR professionals who help wage their battles in the global media.

The threat of these attacks serves to condition the media to expect trouble—and cost increases—for violating the corporate agenda. In return, the media respects these power holders and rarely questions their ulterior motives. Self-censorship thus occurs without the need for an officially stated policy to deter the media from covering certain topics. Genuine political variety in the media is thus absent. One outlet may have a more conservative or liberal tilt, but their news sources, criteria for selection of issues, and corporate sponsors are largely the same. The same companies that fund anti-environmental campaigns and movements also pour money into mainstream environmental organizations. This tactic helps ensure that the environmental organizations see corporations as partners and not as enemies. As the old saying goes, "Don't bite the hand that feeds you." It also allows corporations to buy a green image that is worth millions in the consumer marketplace. Moreover, by maintaining close relationships with environmental organizations, corporations are better able to understand environmental organizations' key critiques. In doing so, corporations can shape their PR campaigns directly around environmental organizations' agendas. The media TNCs have little interest in telling you where your old TV, laptop, tablet, and smart phone go, or whose land, water, air, and bodies are poisoned in the process.

GLOBAL MEDIA EVASION

While it is clear that the global media focuses largely on pursuing a free-market agenda that encourages consumption and acceptance of official positions on a wide variety of political, economic, environmental, and social issues, equally important is what the media fails to focus upon. A great example is garbage, a key social and environmental issue of the 21st century. What happens to the household, corporate, chemical, restaurant, industrial, and toxic waste generated each and every day? Most of the public has absolutely no idea since it is largely ignored by the global media, yet it is a defining feature of modern industrial societies. Of course, the millions of metric tons of garbage and the long-term social and environmental impacts of landfills and incinerators are important issues currently affecting millions of people's lives—though not those of key power holders; thus, it becomes a nonissue.

Because it focuses on style and process over content, the media focuses its attention on things like a spokesperson's wardrobe, word choice, and presentation skills rather than the content of his or her argument or statement. Moreover, by offering "two sides of the story," the media fails to look at the multiple sides and angles to any story. In any given issue, there is not simply a "pro" and an "anti" position but rather a wide range of views and opinions. These voices are all shored up into either the "for" or the "against" camp. This is certainly clear with environmental issues: One must choose to be either an "environmentalist" or an "anti-environmentalist" when in fact some individuals and groups support some reforms and conservation efforts but have concerns about others.

For instance, the issue of hydraulic fracturing for natural gas extraction (fracking) is often simplified in the news media as those who are in favor or against it. A more complete examination might put the single issue into a broader framework that examines energy production and consumption and various priorities and goals of either reinforcing or changing these habits (see Lesson 9). Because the media isolates complex issues such as energy into a single issue of fracking in a specific region, the public fails to understand the relationships and connections between global energy production and consumption. In other words, "both sides of the story" are never the complete story.

In addition, complex issues like energy, while often reported upon, are never explained by the media. Dependence on nonrenewable fossil fuels, corporate control over these resources, and the violence created by their withdrawal are rarely examined. News articles seek to "report" on real-time events but rarely provide a context in which the public might be better able to understand them. Extremely complex social, political, economic, and environmental processes are reduced to fragmented and unconnected factoids. This type of reporting fails to associate social and environmental problems with the socioeconomic forces that created them. Most of the public is thus left with the impression that energy consumption, corporate power, the war on terrorism, and toxic waste are completely distinct, unrelated issues. It is clear that the rise of global commercial media coincides with a decline in public-owned media and public affairs news stories. Crowd-sourced, Internet-based news sources suffer from low levels of social credibility, and limited resources to support investigative journalism.

CONCLUSION: CORPORATE MEDIA POWER
IN THE WIRELESS FUTURE

Today, the single most valuable piece of property worth owning are the radio frequencies of the electromagnetic spectrum over which an increasing amount of communication and commercial activity is broadcast in the era of wireless communications. Personal computers, tablets, wireless Internet, smart phones, radios, and television all rely on the radio frequencies of the spectrum to send and receive messages, pictures, audio, and other data. In an era where more and more of daily communications are in cyberspace, access to the airwaves is critical.

Those who can pay will, of course, be connected, but it is unclear about the millions of people who cannot afford access. If the flow of human communications is controlled by global media companies and governments increasingly have little influence, to whom will citizens turn to ensure that a diversity of social, political, environmental, and economic views are expressed—especially when they may differ from those of the corporate owners? Moreover, when companies like Time Warner and Disney own the channels of communication as well as much of the content that flows through them, what mechanisms will be put in place to ensure that a diversity of voices and perspectives is nourished?

In addition, these companies control the channels of communication and have demonstrated a willingness to exploit the personal data of individuals floating through cyberspace. What safeguards will be put in place to protect citizens? When citizens' very right to communicate with one another is no longer ensured or secured by the government but is controlled by global media conglomerates, how will citizens access the important information, news, and analysis needed to make informed decisions about critical social and environmental issues? In cyberspace, you don't just watch the media TNCs, they watch you, and they report your activities to the government that could regulate them. The control of information is a critical issue in the attention given to, and the social response to, environmental problems.

SOURCES

Bagdikian, Ben. 2004. *The New Media Monopoly*. Boston, MA: Beacon.

Beder, Sharon. 1998. *Global Spin*. White River Junction, VT: Chelsea Green.

Cook, Gary. 2012. *How Clean Is Your Cloud?* Greenpeace.

Derber, Charles. 1998. *Corporation Nation*. New York: St. Martin's Griffin.

Gould, Kenneth A., David N. Pellow, and Allan Schnaiberg. 2008. *The Treadmill of Production: Injustice and Unsustainability in the Global Economy*. Boulder, CO: Paradigm

Herman, Edward, and Noam Chomsky. 2002. *Manufacturing Consent: The Political Economy of the Mass Media*. New York: Pantheon.

Herman, Edward, and Robert McChesney. 1997. *The Global Media*. New York: Continuum.

Korten, David. 2001. *When Corporations Rule the World*. Bloomfield, CT: Kumarian.

McChesney, Robert, and Victor Pickard. 2011. *Will the Last Reporter Please Turn Out the Lights: The Collapse of Journalism and What Can Be Done to Fix It*. New York: The New Press.

McCright, Aaron M., and Riley Dunlap. 2000. "Challenging global warming as a social problem: An analysis of the conservative movement's counter-claims." *Social Problems* 47(4):499–522.

McMichael, Philip. 2011. *Development and Social Change: A Global Perspective*. Thousand Oaks, CA: Sage Publications.

Moyers, Bill. 2002. "Trading Democracy." *NOW*, PBS, February 1, 2002.

Stauber, John, and Sheldon Rampton. 1995. *Toxic Sludge Is Good for You*. Monroe, ME: Common Courage Press.

Zepezauer, Mark, and Arthur Naiman. 1996. *Take the Rich Off Welfare*. Tucson, AZ: Odonian.

6

The Science of Nature and the Nature of Science

Richard York

In vitro orchid propagation, Santa Marianita, Ecuador.
Photo by Tammy Lewis.

On July 16, 1945, the detonation of the first atomic bomb—Trinity—lighted the skies near Alamogordo, New Mexico. It was the product of the Manhattan Project, which had started with a small group of researchers in 1939 but by 1945 had become the greatest scientific undertaking in history. How large the explosion would be was not known with certainty beforehand. Of course, there was the concern that it would be a dud and produce no explosion at all. However, some of the scientists on the project thought it might be big enough to incinerate the entire state of New Mexico. In fact, there was some concern that the explosion could ignite the atmosphere, thereby destroying virtually all life on Earth. In the actual event, it produced a 20-kiloton explosion, far greater than any bomb had ever produced before but, fortunately, not sufficient to engulf the Earth. Nearly seven decades later, we still live with the dark legacy of this explosion and the many thousands—most much bigger—that followed it. Science had unlocked the secrets of the atom, and those secrets gave humanity the power to destroy itself.

Some of the greatest minds in history, the architects of this marvel of science, including the enigmatic genius J. Robert Oppenheimer who had led the development of the mighty weapon, subsequently came to have some regrets about what they had unleashed on the world. In an interview two decades after the Trinity test, Oppenheimer recalled the following:

> We knew the world would not be the same. A few people laughed, a few people cried, most people were silent. I remembered the line from the Hindu scripture, the Bhagavad-Gita. Vishnu is trying to persuade the Prince that he should do his duty and to impress him takes on his multi-armed form and says, "Now, I am become Death, the destroyer of worlds." I suppose we all thought that, one way or another.

In their creation of the atomic bomb, the scientists of the Manhattan Project had demonstrated, more forcefully than ever had been done before, both the enlightening power of science to gain knowledge of the world and the horror that the scientific establishment can foist upon humanity and nature.

If we are to understand the world in which we live and to bring about a sustainable and just society, we must grapple with both of these aspects of science: its power and its horror. From its foundation, the field of environmental sociology has taken a realist stance about environmental problems—they are indeed real, not just a socially constructed perception (see Lesson 1)—and, thus, has always had a commitment to learning from the natural sciences, which study the ecosystems and natural resources upon which all societies depend. However, environmental sociologists have also always recognized the role that science, particularly in its contribution to technological development, has played in generating the modern environmental crisis. Thus, questions about the role of science in society have been central to the field of environmental sociology.

Most environmental sociologists would probably agree to a large extent that we must be simultaneously appreciative and skeptical of science. If we are to understand the human interaction with the natural environment and to overcome the environmental problems we face, we must follow a fine line between two extremes: on the one hand, the rejection of science and, on the other, the uncritical valorization of the scientific establishment. Here, I present an examination of the tension between these two extremes and discuss some of the ways environmental sociology has engaged the science question.

Before going any further, however, we must first answer the following question: What is "science"? Unfortunately, there is no single widely accepted answer, which is in part due to the multifaceted meaning of the term. To help us gain some understanding of the topic, I will make a distinction between two different aspects of science. One I will call "the **logic of science**" and the other I will call "the **establishment of science**." The basic argument I will make is that we need to understand, appreciate, and have a commitment to the former while being critical of the latter.

By "the logic of science" I mean the philosophy of knowledge that underlies the scientific enterprise, informing its methods and theories. Science developed from the fusion of empirical and rational philosophies of knowledge, with particular emphasis on the former. Both of these philosophies can be traced back to the ancient Greeks in the Western tradition (with parallels in other cultures), but their modern versions emerged in the 17th century. Francis Bacon (1561–1626) is often identified as a key figure who initiated the scientific revolution, with his argument that we should reject the long-established medieval practice of looking for truth in texts and, rather, seek knowledge from an examination of the natural world. This is the fundamental claim of **empiricism**: All true knowledge comes from our senses—sight, hearing, taste, touch, and smell—not from ungrounded speculation or divine revelation. Thus, perhaps the most central feature of a scientific approach to knowledge is that it relies on observation of the world of our experiences. Furthermore, it seeks explanations of the features of the empirical world grounded in conditions of the world itself, not in realms inaccessible to our senses, such as those invoked by mysticism and religion.

The scientific project also incorporated insights from rationalism, an intellectual tradition dating back to some of the greatest scholars of antiquity, such as Pythagoras and Plato, which was revitalized in the early modern era by René Descartes (1596–1650). Descartes and other rationalists were interested in how knowledge could be gained without reliance on the senses since they considered the senses to be easily fooled. In a thought experiment, Descartes wondered what knowledge we could be certain of if our senses were systematically fooled by, for example, demons that wished to trick us. The modern version of this thought experiment is well presented in a movie with which perhaps many of you are familiar: *The Matrix*. In *The Matrix* the world that nearly all humans experience is an illusion generated in their minds by a computer. Although they perceive it as real, they are in fact kept in pods from birth to death, never actually experiencing the real world, which was largely destroyed in a war between humans and the machines they created. The key question for the rationalist, then, is this: If we live in such a world where our senses cannot be relied upon to give us accurate information, how can we have a sure foundation for knowledge?

Due to these types of concerns, rationalists prefer to base knowledge on what can be logically deduced from a parsimonious set of assumptions that is not based on sensory experience. This is best exemplified in the field of mathematics, where theorems are proven strictly by logical inference from a minimal number of axioms ("self-evident" propositions) without reliance on observational evidence. Rationalism is concerned with what the logical consequences are of a given set of propositions. In combining these two philosophies of knowledge, rationalism and empiricism, the logic of science can be described as an approach to gaining knowledge about the world based on the rational analysis of empirical evidence. Thus, empiricism grounds rationalism in the world of our senses, while rationalism tempers empiricism by teaching us to be skeptical of the reliability of the observational evidence available to us. Now, as I will discuss, this should not be taken to mean that scientific analysis in practice has always or even typically adhered to the strictures of rationalism and empiricism, but rational empiricism is at the core of science, at least in its ideal form.

All claims about the existence of environmental problems or an environmental crisis have embedded in them an assertion about the condition of an objective external world. If we are to understand this objective world, we need a methodological program that allows us to gain definite knowledge of it. The scientific philosophy outlined above provides the basis of a methodological program that can help us to understand the material world in which we live. Since efforts aimed at understanding the environmental crises of modernity and the role humans play in them are fundamentally concerned with the constituency of the natural world, the environmental social sciences cannot divorce themselves from the natural sciences. Following a scientific approach, if we want to have real knowledge of the natural environment, we must rely on empirical evidence about that environment, not ideological, spiritual, or other non-empirical arguments.

Now, it should be apparent to you that this discussion leaves out some very important issues. What does science have to tell us about ethical questions? After all, many of our most pressing concerns about the environment, as well as in other realms, are about what is right or wrong, not what is true or false. For example, the question of whether we *ought* to allow the killing of whales is at base a value question: Do whales (and other creatures for that matter) have moral worth? This is not the same as the questions of what the current population sizes are of various species of whales (or other creatures) and whether certain practices (for example, industrial whaling vessels prowling the world's oceans) are likely to drive whales to extinction. Indeed, some people even profess indifference to the extinction of many species. Considered in this light, it is clear that many of the hottest environmental debates are founded on both factual and ethical questions: (1) What are the effects of human activities on the natural environment? (2) Are the consequences of human activity good or bad, desirable or undesirable? The simple fact of the matter is that the logic of science can help us to address the first question but is mute with regard to the second. Thus, we see that there is an important scope condition to scientific inquiry. Scientific analysis can address questions of fact (that is, empirical questions) but it can provide no particular guidance about questions of right and wrong (that is, ethical questions). This is not to say that science does not raise serious ethical issues—a point to which I will return shortly.

While there is considerable virtue in the logic of science, when we turn to the "establishment of science" we find much about which to be critical. By the "establishment of science" I mean the actual practice of science; the social, economic, political, and cultural institutions which support it; the research centers (universities, transnational corporations, and national laboratories) where scientists work; and of course the scientists themselves. Whereas the logic of science is a philosophy of knowledge, the establishment of science is an actual socially situated set of institutions. Thus, the establishment of science must be assessed by examining how it really operates in society and what its consequences have been for nature and humanity, not by recourse to abstract philosophical reasoning. Since science is pursued by humans, it is intrinsically a social phenomenon and, thus, cannot be seen as a free-floating institution disembodied from other human endeavors. Although the scientific community does support the ideal of objectivity, in practice scientists are not free of the biases and prejudices; social, cultural, and economic pressures; psychological quirks; and emotional states common to all humans. Science has never been carried out on an ethereal plane, where cool, clear minds pluck unsullied truth from nature. Thus, scientific findings and theories may reflect to some degree the social milieu in which they were formed.

The scientific institutions of our time have their origins in the emergence of "modernity"—the period following the Renaissance in Europe, when feudalism was replaced by capitalism and industrialism, beginning roughly in the 17th century. Science through most of its history has been dominated by members of the social elite, and scientists have often sought to further the interests of those in power by engineering weapons of war, developing technologies aimed at aiding global economic imperialism, and accelerating the exploitation of natural resources and laborers for profit by capitalists (see Lesson 7). Thus, it is necessary to recognize that the modern scientific establishment from its start was not aimed simply at the goal of understanding the world in which we live but was intimately linked to existing power structures and typically focused on achieving ends dictated by the ruling class.

This link between the scientific establishment and those in power remains clear in the contemporary world. As highlighted at the beginning of this lesson, it is a matter of no small importance that so much of scientific effort has been directed at developing weapons. A very substantial share of the research that took place over the 20th century in physics, chemistry, and to a lesser extent biology—from work on rocketry and explosives to work on poison gases and deadly microbes—was done at the behest of, and with funding from, military interests. Furthermore, another substantial share of research effort is driven by raw financial interests, where corporations seek to increase profits by developing technologies of production and new products for the market, without particular regard for human well-being, environmental sustainability, or the lives of other creatures (see Lesson 4). For example, a considerable amount of experimentation on nonhuman animals is done merely to develop new consumer goods, such as cosmetics, that causes much animal suffering and does little to enhance human quality of life, for the sole purpose of generating greater profits for corporations. Similarly, the development of genetically modified organisms (GMOs) is to a large extent driven by the desire of large corporations to increase profits since products stemming from genetic engineering (for example, GM crops, pharmaceuticals) may potentially have vast markets. In this, the corporations pushing such technologies do not have it in their interest to highlight the potential social and environmental costs associated with GMOs since the profits will flow to the corporations while the costs will be shared with society as a whole.

Science and scientists cannot be seen as disinterested parties seeking truth for its own sake. This is not to say that individual scientists are not typically honest and well-meaning. Furthermore, while it has often served the interests of the ruling class, the scientific community has also brought to light the impacts of societies on the natural environment, such as in its analyses of global warming, ozone depletion, and escalating rates of species extinction. However, it is necessary to recognize that the structure of the scientific establishment, particularly in its connections to the ruling class, cannot be relied upon to serve the interests of the mass of humanity or of the other creatures with which we share the Earth. Due to the nature of the scientific establishment, environmental sociologists and other scholars must continually engage in a critique of science. However, it is also necessary that in this critique we not lose sight of the importance of studying the natural and social world in a rational manner so that we can understand the processes that generate environmental and social crises.

The outright rejection of the logic and methods of science because of the environmental and social problems generated in the modern world by technology is fraught with danger. In fact, generating skepticism toward science at times has been a key tactic of powerful interests seeking to subvert environmental protection. Most notably, the fossil fuel industry has waged a tireless campaign to discredit the science demonstrating the emerging crisis of human-generated climate change—where the scientific consensus is clear in its assertion that human activities are contributing to global warming—in much the same way that the tobacco industry sought to misrepresent scientific findings about the health effects of smoking (see Lessons 5, 9, and 15). The assault on climate science and scientific research more generally was particularly severe under the presidency of George W. Bush, which took every opportunity to undermine global warming research and particularly the presentation of that research to the public. The Bush administration, for example, sought to cut funding for scientific research that highlighted environmental problems, censored government scientists, and intimidated other scientists who conducted research and presented findings that contradicted the administration's political positions.

In light of these various considerations, environmental sociology has generally engaged the science question in a nuanced way. Environmental sociologists have examined how scientific claims about the environment are produced, contested, and presented to the public. Here, the main questions have been about how the environment is perceived by society and how some perceived conditions and changes in the environment come to be identified as "problems." These debates focus on the extent to which social (and scientific) perceptions of the environment are "socially constructed"—that is to say, perceptions are created in the social realm through discourse—rather than being reflections of the real external natural world.

As I have already mentioned, taking a strong social constructionist position undermines the entire field of environmental sociology because it in effect denies that there is an environment independent of human perception of it, or at least that we can have reliable knowledge of the natural world. However, milder forms of social constructionism have proved valuable in helping us to understand the social and political processes through which scientific and other claims are shaped and manipulated by social actors and how these social processes often can create public perceptions of the environment that are distinctly at variance with objective environmental conditions (see Lesson 1).

Researchers have focused on how the environmental movement and other social actors present information about the environment and make the case that human modifications of the environment are problematic. It is clear that environmental writers, such as Rachel Carson and Aldo Leopold, and the larger environmental movement, including national organizations such as the Sierra Club and grassroots environmentalists such as Earth First!, played key roles in increasing public awareness of the human effects on the environment, emphasizing some environmental conditions more than others (see Lesson 16). Thus, public environmental concern did not simply come from a diffuse and general public awareness of the environmental effects of modern societies but was generated by the concerted efforts of a variety of social actors. The environmental movement plays a key role in both disseminating and interpreting scientific knowledge about the ecological consequences of human actions and questioning the wisdom of such actions. Similarly, other social actors, such as conservative think tanks, have worked to deny the existence of environmental crises and to "deproblematize" human-generated environmental change (see Lesson 5). These actors frequently question whether environmentalists are correct in their identification of human effects on the environment and/or portray human-induced change as beneficial rather than detrimental.

In these types of debates, scientific claims are of central importance because they often serve as the starting point for the creation of socially salient ideas about what is happening in the environment, and the validity and interpretation of the science is highly contested. For example, claims about global warming have been challenged by conservatives, particularly in the United States, despite the scientific consensus, with industry-funded anti-environmental groups claiming variously that humans are not affecting the environment or that global warming will in fact be good (or at least neutral) for societies. Similarly, the science of genetic engineering has been at the center of heated controversy over the development and use of GMOs, with various activist organizations questioning the safety of GMOs for human health and the environment and biotechnology firms and their allies denying the existence of any serious risks.

Recognizing the social influences on scientific findings is clearly important since research agendas are often determined by those with the resources to fund research, rather than stemming from disinterested consideration of the intellectual merits of various topics. Although empirical evidence is a central part of answering questions about the natural world, data do not speak for themselves. Rather, what data are collected and how they are collected, analyzed, and interpreted are not independent of the social context of research. For example, timber companies are unlikely to fund research that demonstrates the detrimental environmental consequences of logging, and, unsurprisingly, scientists funded by timber interests are unlikely to design studies that highlight such consequences.

These issues are not limited to research done by corporations but also play out in universities and colleges, since many researchers who are not employed by corporations still receive funding from corporate sources. The influence of corporations on university research has become more intense as governments have cut funding to public institutions, increasingly pushing universities to seek private sources of funding. Furthermore, public universities, still being partially dependent on government support and concerned about cuts to their funding, are subject to political pressures from elected officials who are often sympathetic to corporate interests. For these reasons, a variety of scientists, from foresters to geneticists, even if scrupulous and fair-minded, are often limited in the type of research they can do and present. Thus, with good reason, many sociologists do not accept scientific findings uncritically and often take into consideration in their evaluation of factual assertions whose interests are served by various research programs.

In a similar manner, environmental sociology has analyzed the growing variety of technologically generated risks in modernity. Much of the debate in this area centers on the extent to which the "experts," primarily scientists, can be relied on to fairly assess the risks associated with new technologies. For example, who should decide whether or not to build nuclear power plants or allow the use of GMOs? Do scientists know better than laypeople whether or not the potential benefits of such technologies outweigh their potential costs? Although at first glance it may seem that scientists are the best candidates for making such decisions since they have specialized knowledge about the technologies to be considered, on further consideration the issue appears to be much more complex.

Since scientists depend on empirical evidence to make their assessments, when data are absent they do not necessarily have greater insight than laypeople. In the case of many technologies, such as GM crops, questions are often about the long-term consequences of large-scale use, and this cannot be assessed with high certainty for new technologies that have been tested over only limited time periods in a restricted number of settings. For example, scientists did not foresee the threat that chlorofluorocarbons represented to the ozone layer until after they came into widespread use. And, as I noted at the start of this lesson, there was considerable uncertainty about how large of an explosion the first atomic bomb would yield, despite the fact that it was studied by many of the greatest scientific minds in the world. (Did the scientists and military bureaucrats have the right to make the decision to conduct the Trinity test, despite the potential consequences for all of humanity and nature?) Scientific methods are good at assessing risk when there are sufficient data but have only limited potential to give reliable assessments in the absence of such data.

Since the potential costs and benefits of new technologies are not evenly distributed across society, issues of justice and fairness are central to risk assessment, and these are not entirely reducible to empirical questions. After all, in making calculations about risk by estimating the potential costs and benefits of new technologies, is an economic measure (such as dollars) the most appropriate, or should the life of humans and other creatures be assessed with a different metric? Clearly, there are ethical questions to be considered that will not yield to scientific analysis.

Furthermore, it is increasingly the case that scientists have financial stakes, beyond simply the funding of their research, in the technologies they advocate and, thus, commonly have a conflict of interest when asked to assess whether the benefits of new technologies are likely to outweigh the risks. For example, many geneticists hold patents for gene-based technologies and/or own shares of companies that stand to profit from biotechnology applications. Thus, the extent to which such scientists can be relied upon for an objective evaluation of technological risks is quite dubious. Clearly, questions about how scientific knowledge should be applied and how decisions are made about which risks are worth taking are matters of no trivial importance. Environmental sociology, then, has studied how the public has sought to democratize science, as well as how the social elite has often sought to insulate decisions about technological applications and scientific ethics from public scrutiny.

I have touched on only some of the complex issues that environmental sociologists face in engaging science. There are three key points to take from this lesson. First, environmental sociologists, by necessity, generally take a realist stance toward environmental problems. That is to say, they recognize that concern for the environment is in substantial part due to real changes occurring in the natural world, not merely because of cultural changes in values, beliefs, and perceptions. Thus, environmental sociology is dependent on a scientific approach to understanding the human–environment interaction, where knowledge is sought through rational investigation of empirical evidence. Second, and existing in some degree of tension with the first point, environmental sociologists also recognize that social perceptions of the environment are affected by political, economic, and social processes, where those in power often manipulate, subvert, deny, or obfuscate scientific knowledge to further their own interests. Therefore, it is necessary to situate scientific knowledge in its social context. Third, environmental sociologists recognize that the effects of science on the environment have been double-edged. On the one hand, the logic of science has allowed for a growing understanding of the natural world and how humans have affected the biosphere. This rational knowledge allows for the recognition of environmental problems and an emerging understanding of what needs to be done to address them. On the other hand, science has given humans unprecedented power to manipulate nature, and this has contributed to a growing suite of technologies that generate new and greater threats to ecosystems and disrupt the metabolic exchange between society and the environment. Environmental sociology grapples with these many facets of science in an effort to understand society and nature. It is to be hoped that such understanding will help us to bring about a just and sustainable world.

SOURCES

Beck, Ulrich. 1992. *Risk Society: Towards a New Modernity*. Newbury Park, CA: Sage.

Burningham, Kate. 1998. "A Noisy Road or Nosy Resident? A Demonstration of the Utility of Social Constructionism for Analysing Environmental Problems." *Sociological Review* 46(3):536–563.

Conner, Clifford D. 2005. *A People's History of Science: Miners, Midwives, and "Low Mechanicks."* New York: Nation Books.

Ehrlich, Paul E., and Anne H. Ehrlich. 1996. *The Betrayal of Science and Reason: How Anti-Environmental Rhetoric Threatens Our Future*. Washington, D.C.: Island Press.

Else, Jon H. (Director and Producer). 1980. *The Day After Trinity*. (Film). Pyramid Films.

Gould, Stephen Jay. 2003. *The Hedgehog, the Fox, and the Magister's Pox: Mending the Gap Between Science and the Humanities*. New York: Harmony Books.

Levins, Richard, and Richard C. Lewontin. 1985. *The Dialectical Biologist*. Cambridge, MA: Harvard University Press.

McCright, Aaron, and Riley E. Dunlap. 2000. "Challenging Global Warming as a Social Problem: An Analysis of the Conservative Movement's Counter-Claims." *Social Problems* 47(4):499–523.

Merchant, Carolyn. 1980. *Death of Nature: Women, Ecology, and the Scientific Revolution*. San Francisco, CA: Harper.

Mooney, Chris. 2005. *The Republican War on Science*. New York: Basic Books.

Rhodes, Richard. 1987. *The Making of the Atomic Bomb*. New York: Simon & Schuster.

Rosa, Eugene A. 1998. "Meta-Theoretical Foundations of Post-Normal Risk." *Journal of Risk Analysis* 1:15–44.

Yearly, Steven. 2002. "The Social Construction of Environmental Problems: A Theoretical Review and Some Not-Very-Herculean Labors." In Riley E. Dunlap, Frederick H. Buttel, Peter Dickens, and August Gijswijt, eds. *Sociological Theory and the Environment: Classical Foundations, Contemporary Insights*, pp. 274–285. New York: Rowman & Littlefield.

York, Richard, and Brett Clark. 2006. "Marxism, Positivism, and Scientific Sociology: Social Gravity and Historicity." *Sociological Quarterly* 47(3):425–450.

York, Richard, and Brett Clark. 2010. "Critical Materialism: Science, Technology, and Environmental Sustainability." *Sociological Inquiry* 80(3): 475–499.

7

Technological Change and the Environment

Kenneth A. Gould

Mushroom cloud/skull statue memorializing the site of the first controlled nuclear reaction, across from new nanotechnology facilities at the University of Chicago, Chicago, Illinois.

Photo by Ken Gould.

One of the primary ways that human societies mediate their relationship with the natural world is through the development and use of technology. Societies use technology to overcome the obstacles to surviving and thriving that they perceive in nature and to modify the natural world in ways that meet certain human needs and desires. The social creation of new technologies transforms both societies and the natural world upon which human societies depend. Therefore, in order for us to understand the dynamic relationship between social systems and ecosystems, we need to understand the role played by technology in shaping that relationship.

WHAT IS TECHNOLOGY?

So what is technology? In simplest terms, technology is how we make "stuff" and do "stuff." In order to make certain kinds of stuff and do certain kinds of stuff, we organize and reorganize social relations and nature. And technological change is most commonly produced by social actors and institutions. It doesn't fall from the sky, and it doesn't emerge in some predetermined path of linear progress. Specific social groups (corporations, governments, and other forms of social organization) make it their business to move technological change in specific directions and for specific purposes. For instance, take a look at the classroom when you go back to class to discuss this lesson. A classroom is, in part, a technology for making or doing stuff. In this case, the stuff to be made is educated people and the stuff to be done is education. The classroom is organized, created, and maintained by a social institution (your college). Manifest in your classroom are both social relations (the relationships between people) and relations between the social system and the ecosystem. Is your classroom organized with chairs in a circle or with all the seats facing a central point? The physical organization of the classroom (the technology of education, if you will) tells you much about the social relations within it, as well as the social expectations. With seats in a circle, you expect to have to talk to others in the room quite a bit. With the chairs facing a central point, you expect to be spoken to and for you to speak much less, and then perhaps only to the person occupying the central point of focus (the lectern). In a circle, you expect social relations to be more egalitarian, with each participant playing a more equal role. With chairs facing a central point, you expect social relations to be more hierarchical and authoritarian, with a single power holder (your professor) commanding most of the attention.

What you can see by looking at the physical structure of your classroom is an indication of the social structure of the classroom. That is, the way that the technology of education (your classroom) is organized both reflects and determines social relations. The same is true of any technology for doing and making anything. The technology itself—a computer, a factory, a hog farm, a television, a smart phone, or a nuclear weapon—manifests specific social relations. Technology consists of both physical, tangible "things" and the social relations they imply. No technology is separable from its social relations, even though those relations are intangible and take a little more work to actually "see."

You will have missed the early part of your class thinking about the ways in which the physical parts of the technology of education reflect and determine the social relation parts of the technology of education, instead of paying attention to what's being said. That's okay; you can get notes from the person next to you. Now think about the relationship to nature manifest in the classroom. What is all the stuff in the classroom made from? Your notebook, made from trees. Your seat, made from plastic, made from oil. Maybe some aluminum made from bauxite here and there. All of the physical things in your classroom have their origins in nature and have been transformed, through technologies (social relations and physical hardware), into something else to meet human goals.

You probably have electricity in your classroom too, to power lights, computers, projectors, etc. That means that your classroom is physically hard-wired to some technology for transforming some natural element or process into electricity. Look at the electrical sockets in your classroom. You could follow the wires from those sockets all the way back to the cogenerator, power dam, coal-burning power plant, nuclear reactor, photovoltaic cells, or wind turbine that has been constructed to convert natural resources or processes to meet human goals (see Lesson 9). Perhaps the socket leads to a coal-fired power plant that burns coal mined in some region quite distant from your own. People there are busy transforming nature in their location in order to allow you to have lighting so you and your professor can produce education in your location. And that electricity is probably transmitted through copper wires, made somewhere off-campus, from copper mined in yet another distant community by still other people. In all likelihood, there aren't coal or copper mines on your campus. So your classroom and you are connected to other parts of the country and the world, using natural resources from distant ecosystems.

Your classroom, and any other technology you use or are a part of, connects you to a variety of relationships with the natural world, both immediate and far removed. And the technologies for converting natural resources into other stuff (electricity, books, seats, etc.) also connect you to other sets of social relations, with people you may never know or see, who mine coal and copper or work in factories producing wires or wood pulp for paper.

So technology is a series of entanglements with social systems and ecosystems, close and far, obvious and hidden. Your smart phone, your pen, your computer—all represent a series of relationships between you and others and between you and the natural world. Those relationships are not random. They reflect the social origins of the technologies, the goals of those who designed the technologies, the interests of those who require or request you to use the technologies, and the ways in which society has been organized to use and change nature.

TECHNOLOGICAL CHANGE

Social scientists who study technology and technological change have used a variety of schema to identify various phases or periods in the development of technology. You have probably heard some of these eras of specific techno-logical applications described with terms such as "the bronze age" or "the iron age." Note that the materials used signify these eras of technology. Lewis

Mumford, in his classic work *Technics and Civilization*, identified three distinct eras of modern technological development: "paleotechnic," "eotechnic," and "neotechnic." The paleotechnic phase was typified by the use of wood as the primary material and the use of moving water and wind as the primary energy sources. The eotechnic phase was typified by the use of iron as the primary material and the use of coal to generate steam as the primary energy source. The neotechnic phase, he argued, was typified by the use of steel as the primary material and the use of electricity. Here again, the elements of nature, modified through human intervention, are central to our categories of technological phase. The ways human societies use and transform nature are key to our understanding of what various technologies are.

We can categorize different technological eras in various ways, by changes they produce in society and nature, both large and small. For our purposes here, let's look at two very large, very broad, and very transformative eras of technological change, both of which completely revolutionized the ways that human societies are organized and the ways that those societies relate to, modify, and rely upon nature. These two periods of technological transition were so transformative of society and the natural world that they have been viewed by most as revolutionary: the agricultural revolution and the Industrial Revolution.

The Agricultural Revolution

The realization that by planting seeds of desirable plants, people could transform ecosystems to make them produce large volumes of preferred food crops radically changed the relationship between human societies and nature. Prior to the technology of agriculture, human societies were primarily organized for a hunting and gathering survival strategy. In order to get the food they required, groups of people collected the plants and other foods they found in nature. This meant that, as local plant and animal stocks were depleted, people had to migrate to other areas in search of food. They developed patterns of migration that followed the seasonal availability of food plants and the seasonal migration of other animals (which also followed seasonal patterns of the availability of food and water). The technology of agriculture changed all that, allowing humans to modify their local ecosystems to meet their food needs, rather than modifying their societies (through migration) to meet local ecosystem conditions.

In a real sense, the power balance between environment and society was shifted toward greater human agency and greater ecosystem malleability. Humans cleared portions of local ecosystems of their naturally occurring plants, animals, and habitats and replaced them with increasingly vast fields of human-selected species of plants. This large-scale transformation of land from natural ecosystems to farm fields has continued ever since as prairies, savannas, and forests are cleared. Plants were selected for attributes most desired by humans (food and textiles), and that selection began to replace the process of natural selection in the evolution of certain species. A similar process occurred with the domestication of animals used for meat, dairy, and textiles. Animals were taken from the wild and raised and reproduced to serve human needs (see Lesson 13). Pastures were cleared, ecosystems transformed, and species gradually modified to serve human goals.

With settled agriculture, human populations could remain in a single location, modifying the environment to facilitate settlement. Settlement allowed for the building of permanent structures, rather than the portable or disposable shelters logically necessary for societies of nomads. Settlement also allowed for the accumulation of material possessions. Keeping material possessions to a minimum makes good sense if you'll have to move them from place to place all the time (something that anyone who has ever moved quickly realizes). If you can plan to be in a locale indefinitely, you can begin to fill your permanent structures with "stuff," thus creating an incentive for the production of more material things. So, in a real sense, the technology of agriculture is what began the process of human societies constructing permanent houses and filling them with material possessions.

The successes of agriculture also led to the creation of what sociologists call a **"labor surplus."** Where soils were fertile and water was available, agriculture was very successful and large quantities of food could be produced by fewer and fewer people. This process of increasing yields and decreasing demand for human labor has continued so that now, in countries like the United States, vast food surpluses are produced with a very small percentage of the population engaged in actual primary food production. But even very early in the process, fertile regions allowed for growing numbers of people to eat, without themselves being engaged in food production. With large populations permanently settled in a single location without survival-oriented work to do (food collection or production), other activities and new ways of organizing people in more complex ways emerged. Along with permanent houses, permanent ritual sites, large-scale irrigation works to support agriculture, and other engineering projects requiring vast amounts of human labor were organized. Pyramids, temples, aqueducts, and astronomical observatories were constructed by harnessing surplus labor (often involuntarily). How the Egyptian pyramids were built is no mystery: The answer is agriculture. It is worth noting that much of this large-scale construction was organized to support agricultural success and expansion physically (irrigation works), to appeal to nature through religion for adequate rain and fertility (temples), and to track seasonal changes to determine appropriate planting and harvest schedules (astronomical observatories).

Supporting larger populations in one place required more complex social organization in governance and the production and distribution of a wider variety of goods and services. Labor surpluses also allowed for the creation of standing armies, and agricultural expansion increased the value of transforming and taking more land, especially in fertile areas. With hunting less important to survival but conflict over access to arable land more important, the primary goal of weapons technology turned from killing other animals to killing humans. Agricultural societies gave rise to the first central state authorities, commanding standing armies and controlling access to land and the distribution of food. While we may think of ourselves as living in industrial or even postindustrial societies, it is easy to see that many features of both human social organizations and their relationship to ecosystems actually stem from the radical social system and ecosystem shifts that came with the technology of agriculture.

The Industrial Revolution

The discipline of sociology was initially developed by people attempting to understand the vast transformations of social organization that emerged in the 19th century with the rise of industrialization. While the great agricultural civilizations emerged primarily in Asia, Africa, and Latin America, the first great industrial civilizations emerged in Europe. European social analysts like Marx, Weber, and Durkheim established the scientific study of societies and social change in efforts to understand the new patterns of social relations generated by the emergence of industrial production. The Industrial Revolution produced the second great technological transformation of the relationship between social systems and ecosystems, although, as noted in the Introduction to this book, the ecosystemic aspect of change was not of particular interest to early sociologists. The industrialization of production generated a vast array of social changes, far too numerous to address at length here. Among these, however, it is worth noting the creation of new classes (such as those Marx termed the "proletariat," or industrial working class, and the "bourgeoisie," the capitalist class) and the formation of industrial cities (London being the first city to reach 1 million in population since the fall of Rome).

In terms of the society–environment relationship, industrialization ushered in societal dependence on enormous inputs of nonrenewable resources, particularly fossil fuels. Industrial civilization was, and remains, predicated on nearly limitless supplies of relatively cheap and portable nonrenewable energy inputs (see Lesson 9). It was the capacity to convert coal into steam, and thus energy, on an ever-increasing scale that gave industrial society its form and its trajectory. Our current society can be thought of as one designed specifically to thrive in, and to survive off of, endless increases in energy inputs. Those conditions appeared to be sustainable at the dawn of the industrial era, when the exhaustion of necessary resources appeared unlikely. In the current era, it is the foreseeable end to increasing supplies of such energy, and the environmental impacts of using that energy (see Lesson 9), that are causing many to consider the need to wholly reorient the path of human society to what some are conceptualizing as a "post-fossil fuel society".

The technological changes that coalesced into the Industrial Revolution were intended primarily to vastly increase humans' ability to produce an increasing range of synthetic products, from textiles to machines themselves.

Just as the agricultural revolution made the large-scale production of food possible, the Industrial Revolution made the large-scale production of other goods possible. And just as agriculture required the growing transformation of natural ecosystems into farm fields, industry required the growing conversion of elements of ecosystems (trees, coal, metals, etc.) into natural resource inputs in the production of products. Of course, as industrial production expanded and new markets for new products were expanded to meet the increased supply, the pace and scale of the extraction of natural resources and their conversion to products increased, with two major results.

First, ecosystems and habitats, at first locally and later globally, were pillaged to meet the needs of industry for raw materials. We can think of these as ecosystem "withdrawals." These withdrawals would eventually lead to socially generated problems of natural resource depletion such as deforestation and oil scarcity. Second, the capacity of industry to produce on increasingly vast scales resulted in the world being increasingly full of social products and byproducts. The products, although useful for a time, eventually find their way into dumps, landfills, the oceans, and incinerators. The byproducts tend to be returned to ecosystems as industrial air-, water-, and land-based emissions. In addition, many of the products create byproducts themselves in the course of their use, such as cars producing air emissions, discarded batteries, and used motor oil. We can think of these socially created artificial elements injected by industrial societies back into ecosystems as ecological "additions." These new additions to nature would quickly give rise to problems of environmental pollution (such as pesticide toxicity and greenhouse gases). The Industrial Revolution is therefore most notable in terms of the social system–ecosystem interaction for increasing the social capacity for, and rate of, conversion of natural resources into products and byproducts. The result has been wholesale disruption of local and global ecosystems that natural scientists have only just begun to comprehend.

In giving rise to the modern city, the new industrial technologies also quickly gave rise to the familiar socioenvironmental problems that are part of urban landscapes: urban smog and resulting respiratory disease, the accumulation of trash and the difficulty of disposing of it in a safe and hygienic manner, the contamination of freshwater supplies and the threat of waterborne illness, and the social inequities in exposure to these urban environmental hazards (see Lesson 10). These environmental hazards were, and are, compounded with other key features of the urban social environment, such as inadequate housing, congested infrastructure, and lack of healthcare, housing, employment, and justice. In addition, the urban environment cut off large portions of the human population from direct daily contact with natural environments, which had been a key fact of human existence since the dawn of the species. This disconnection from nature would lead many in "modern industrial society," including sociologists (see the Introduction to this book), to conclude that society was no longer dependent on nature and that the two could be thought of as separate concerns.

THE TECHNOLOGICAL TRAJECTORY

As you can see, both the revolutions in agricultural technology and industrial technology completely transformed the relationship between social systems and ecosystems. In the broadest sense, the greatest change that emerged from each was an enormous increase in the incentive and capacity to adjust natural systems to meet social needs, rather than adjusting social systems to meet naturally occurring ecosystem realities. In this process, the human capacity for technological innovation, our ability to develop new techniques to transform the natural world, has been key. As social systems now come to realize the dramatic negative social implications of their vast transformation of ecosystems, it is important to ask: Where is our technological trajectory headed? Why? Who or what determines the path of technological innovation? And how might we choose a path of technological innovation that resolves some of the conflict between social systems and ecosystem?

Social Institutions and Technological Decision Making

Social institutions pursuing specific social goals largely control the progress and direction of technological change. These institutions exert substantial control over the research and development process in numerous ways, including influence on educational institutions, research facilities, research and development funding, and the distribution of profits derived from outcomes. At each point of the research and development process, these social institutions are able to influence the agendas of scientists and engineers and, thus, the trajectory of technological innovation. There is no "runaway technology," as some environmentalists have argued. Nor is there a clear "natural evolution" of technological direction, as most might assume. The direction of scientific and technological research and development is a result of human intentionality and decision making (see Lesson 6). As a result, the history and current direction of technological research and development reflect the power and the political and economic interests of the social institutions that control the process.

The main social institutions guiding the technological research and development agendas are universities, states, and corporations. Each of these institutions has specific interests, which are reflected in their agendas for scientific research and technological innovation and which thus shape the social system–ecosystem interactions that the rest of the world inherits. Universities have historically been viewed as the institutions with the greatest dedication to the "objective" pursuit of scientific truths and as being somewhat independent of political and economic pressures. In universities, it was often the scientists and engineers who set the research and development agendas, and they were largely immune from the influence of the political and economic goals and rewards stemming from states and corporations. However, as the costs of research and development increased and public funding for universities declined, states and corporations gained greater influence over the agendas and goals of science and technology workers within universities. As a result, the interests of states and corporations ripple through the university system and reduce the capacity of these formerly more autonomous institutions to chart a distinct technological research and development direction.

Governments are the primary source of funding for basic scientific research. **Basic science** seeks to explain natural phenomena and forms the knowledge base that supports engineering. The knowledge base upon which **applied science** will be built is thus influenced by the ways that state decision makers prioritize certain paths of inquiry and distribute funding for it. The goals of states in funding basic science are fairly clear. First, states fund basic science and some applied research and development to enhance their military power. Since governments are the market for weapons systems, they have a vested interest in making sure that the creation of ever-more-powerful military technology is a major thrust of technological innovation. As a result, the pursuit of more effective military systems has become one of the dominant goals—if not *the* dominant goal—of the technology research and development agenda of our species. The enormous amount of funding offered by the state for military research and development directs the human technological trajectory toward destructive ends while sapping funding from quality of life–enhancing research along other paths of human inquiry (such as health, environmental protection and remediation, renewable energy, etc.). Since military technology is particularly environmentally destructive, energy-inefficient, and natural resource–intensive, it has a significant negative impact on the nature of social system interactions with ecosystems.

The other goal of states in sponsoring research and development is the pursuit of global "economic competitiveness." By using tax revenues to subsidize the research and development agendas of corporations based within their borders, states try to boost their gross domestic products. Increasing the economic power of the country increases the relative power of a state, giving it greater influence over the global arenas in which it competes with other states. Because of this, increasing the economic power of the state becomes a technological goal in its own right, along with increasing the military power of the state. And those two goals are intertwined in a military–industrial complex because the greater tax revenues gained through successful international economic competition make more funding available to support military research and development, and greater military power facilitates greater access to the global natural resources, waste sinks, markets, and labor pools needed for economic growth (see Lesson 3).

The interests of corporations in technological research and development are somewhat less complex than those of states. Corporations pursue technological innovation to enhance **profitability**. Corporations are the leading institutional source of funding for technological innovation and the primary employers of engineers. As a result, the goals of corporations have greater influence over the human technological trajectory than those of any other social institution. Corporations use the government subsidy of basic research as the basis for their applied research (see Lesson 6) that produces profit-enhancing products to be sold to states (military hardware), other corporations (including labor-replacing technologies), and individual consumers (consumer goods). Lines of research that will lead to products that may produce social or ecological benefits but do not promise to generate profits are not funded and not pursued. Corporate profitability is then, in some sense, the ultimate criterion for determining much of the human technological trajectory. Given that technology is such a big factor in shaping the relationship between social systems and ecosystems, we can see that corporate interests have come to be a major—if not *the* major—factor in determining how social systems and ecosystems will interact (see Lesson 5).

The goal of corporate profitability influences the direction of technological innovation in other ways. Corporate profitability sets much of the research agendas of scientists both within the firm and within the university. By sponsoring university research, corporations create a system of incentives and disincentives for the pursuit of various lines of scientific inquiry and engineering development. By providing the laboratories in which research and development are conducted, corporations control the scientific and engineering infrastructure of society. By offering shared profit incentives with educational institutions and university researchers, corporations influence the direction of higher education. The nature and structure of scientific and engineering education tend to reflect the social agendas of the institutions that fund it. Corporations have also been known to overtly and covertly squelch lines of scientific investigation that may threaten the goal of corporate profitability, as we have seen in research on the health effects of tobacco, the ecological threats from pesticides, the environmental impacts of acid rain, the health and ecological impacts of genetically modified organisms, and the contribution of carbon dioxide emissions to global climate change (see Lessons 5, 11 and 15).

SCIENCE, TECHNOLOGICAL INNOVATION, AND POWER

The trajectory of technological innovation is greatly influenced by a relatively small number of decision makers in governments and corporations who establish research priorities, provide research facilities, and determine the distribution of funding. The result is a global technological infrastructure, system, and direction that reflects the interests of a privileged few and pursues those interests despite the many obvious negative consequences for social system–ecosystem dynamics. The fact that the bulk of technological decisions are made in corporate boardrooms and opaque government institutions shields technological innovation agendas from democratic processes. Although the outcomes of research and development decisions often become obvious to the public at large, the decision-making processes that ultimately lead to these outcomes are generally unavailable for public input and public influence. We all must live with the technological consequences in terms of the products that are and are not available, the technologies that do and do not exist, the employment opportunities that are created and destroyed, and the public health and ecological impacts that are generated, but we are generally denied a role in determining those consequences.

For example, you may not even be aware that one of the leading areas of technological research and development investment right now is **nanotechnology**. Nanotechnology is the engineering of matter on an atomic and molecular scale to produce new materials and technologies with at least one dimension sized from 1 to 100 nanometers. Nanotechnology allows for the creation of a myriad of new materials not found in nature, and the production of microscopic machines. Although you may not be aware that governments, transnational corporations, and universities are already heavily invested in nanotechnology, you may already have nanomaterials in your body. A wide range of cosmetics, sunblocks, and athletic wear includes nanoparticles, literally tiny particles of unknown (at least to us) materials. Nanoparticles can pass through your skin, enter your bloodstream, and cross the blood–brain barrier. We don't know what the health effects of nanoparticles are because there has been little investment in doing that research. The lucrative research in nanotechnology is in creating new nano products and getting them to market quickly. You might prefer for the research on the public health and environmental impacts of nanoparticles to have happened long before you started rubbing them into your skin. But since that is not profitable research, you would need a way to influence the research and development agenda before new products and processes are developed.

Democratic input into research agendas is quite limited. What often passes for democratic controls on technology are mechanisms for "public consultation" arranged after new technologies are created. These public consultations are often organized by the very institutions that sponsor technological research and whose interest is to gain public acceptance for the innovations. These public forums are designed primarily to reduce public fears, which are viewed by those who have a vested interest in technology as irrational (see Lesson 11). You have already been told that it is irrational to fear microwave radiation from smart phones and not to worry about the health effects of genetically modified organisms; you will soon be told not to fear the nanoparticles entering your body. Research on the social and ecological implications of technology is often highly politicized (see Lessons 6 and 14) and commonly intended to boost the chances for public acceptance of existing and new technologies. This makes it difficult for people to reach informed conclusions about the costs and benefits of technological change.

The Myth of "Progress"

Another factor that keeps the general public from participating in science and technology decision making is the myth of "progress," a set of ideological constructs promoted by the institutions that control the research and development process. Most people tend to think that research takes a natural course determined by free inquiry and the evolution of ideas and that technologies are routed along a linear progression where one development automatically follows from another. That is, people are led to believe that there is in fact no institutional agency in the technological trajectory and that what little human agency exists is in the hands of individual experts pursuing either public good or private gain. The ideology of capitalism argues that the pursuit of private gain naturally leads to the common good. The combination of the myth of technological neutrality and the ideology of capitalist ethics produces complacency in regard to research and development on the part of the public. This complacency serves the interests of the institutions that do have agency in determining the societal technological path and the social system–ecosystem relations that go with it. People tend to ask "what will they think of next?" rather than telling technology-producing institutions what they should be working on next.

While it is true that democratic citizenries could demand and exert greater influence over the research that states support, the ideological power of objective science (see Lesson 6), technological neutrality, and capitalist ethics keep this possibility from entering the public consciousness. Science and technology decision making has, for the most part, been organized out of politics. The result is that powerful individuals and institutions are left to use the human technological capacity in pursuit of their own interests largely unchecked by the majority. In no other arena are the long-term consequences for human society and the environment as great and the political discussion so muted. Conflicts do emerge from time to time (on nuclear technology, genetic technology, etc.), but even then the political discourse largely revolves around a ban on the implementation of a specific technology rather than a quest for democratic control over the processes that generate technology. Should our social institutions invest in renewable energy research or military drones? Should science education promote genetic engineering or sustainable organic agriculture? Should engineers be working on more energy-efficient transportation infrastructure or the next iPhone upgrade? Should scientists spend more time and effort investigating the environmental and public health impacts of nanoparticles or developing new nanotechnology-based consumer products? If you knew that your cosmetics contained nanoparticles, whose health effects are unknown and unstudied, you might want some say in that decision. Rather than waiting passively to receive the next "big thing" from technology producers, perhaps we should be actively participating in deciding what "big things" they ought to start working on.

The Democratization of Technological Innovation

If we are to seriously pursue a more environmentally sound relationship between social systems and ecosystems, we may find it useful to make the technological innovation processes subject to democratic controls. The potential social and ecological impacts of technologies must be assessed by informed publics, under conditions in which citizens are empowered to determine the goals of research and development, the prioritization and funding of that research, and the manner in which technologies will be implemented or prohibited. This input needs to occur at the earliest stages of the innovation process, determining the purpose of basic lines of inquiry in order to use our scientific and technological capacity to maximize democratically determined social and environmental benefits. That would be a very different model than the one in place currently, in which institutions produce and implement technologies without public input and then the public must overtly object to negative social and ecological consequences once they appear (see Lessons 11 and 12). After-the-fact protests and control efforts in which the public expresses opposition to prior technological decisions are certainly less than optimal for democratic governance and the creation of a technological trajectory that serves social and environmental goals. A sustainable social system–ecosystem dynamic requires a new technological revolution, not just in what technologies are created, but in how society organizes and directs the innovation process.

SOURCES

Beder, Sharon. 1997. *Global Spin: The Corporate Assault on Environmentalism*. White River Junction, VT: Chelsea Green.

Gedicks, Al. 2001. *Resource Rebels: Native Challenges to Mining and Oil Corporations*. Cambridge, MA: South End Press.

Gould, Kenneth A. 2006. "Promoting Sustainability." In Judith Blau and Keri E. Iyall Smith, eds. *Public Sociologies Reader*, pp. 213–230. New York: Rowman & Littlefield.

Gould, Kenneth A. 2007. "The Ecological Costs of Militarization." *Peace Review* 19(3):331–334.

Gould, Kenneth A., David N. Pellow, and Allan Schnaiberg. 2008. *The Treadmill of Production: Injustice and Unsustainability in the Global Economy*. Boulder, CO: Paradigm.

Hess, David J. 2007. *Alternative Pathways in Science and Industry: Activism, Innovation, and the Environment in an Era of Globalization*. Cambridge, MA: MIT Press.

Lukes, Steven. 1974. *Power: A Radical View*. London, UK: Macmillan.

Maclurcan, Donald, and Natalia Radywyl, eds. 2012. *Nanotechnology and Global Sustainability*. New York: CRC Press.

Mumford, Lewis. 1934. *Technics and Civilization*. New York: Harcourt Brace Jovanovich.

Noble, David F. 1977. *America by Design: Science, Technology, and the Rise of Corporate Capitalism*. New York: Alfred A. Knopf.

Nye, David E. 1996. *American Technological Sublime*. Cambridge, MA: MIT Press.

Schnaiberg, Allan. 1980. *The Environment: From Surplus to Scarcity*. New York: Oxford University Press.

White, Geoffrey, ed. 2000. *Campus Inc*. Albany, NY: Prometheus Books.

8

Population, Demography, and the Environment

Diane C. Bates

Strollers parked at Disneyworld, Orlando, Florida.
Photo by Ken Gould.

The world's human population as of January 3, 2014 at 2:44 p.m. (EDT) was 7,138,177,229, with more than one person added every ten seconds. Social scientists have long debated how human population affects environmental quality; population growth is frequently cited as a leading cause of environmental degradation. Understanding human population dynamics goes well beyond merely counting the number of people in a location. For example, outmigration from rural areas changes how households use agricultural land; middle-class out-migration from urban areas can create an environment hostile to public health by leaving abandoned and vacant properties in poor communities. The age and class composition of a population predict what sorts of environmental and health threats are likely to emerge from risks present in a given location. The stability and resources of a population affect its ability to respond to and recover from environmental threats. Social theory on the relationship between population and the environment has historically focused exclusively on growth, but understanding how populations change over time is important for all students of the environment. Moreover, people experience population change at the local level rather than on the national scales more typical of demographers and social theorists. For example, residents of the Northeastern rustbelt may note how three decades of uneven population decline have left neighborhoods with vacant buildings, overgrown lots, and abandoned factories. Likewise, residents of the suburban sunbelt cannot help but observe how more and more people keep moving into the area and converting open space into residential subdivisions, office parks, and shopping centers. This chapter ties together these local experiences with the larger study of the interaction between human populations and our environment. It first defines several key terms in understanding population dynamics, then proceeds to a discussion of the main controversies in population theory. It closes with a nuanced analysis of an empirical case study that highlights how population growth in the South American country of Ecuador has variable effects on the nation's forest resources.

Population refers to the number of people living in a specific geographical area at a specific point in time. **Demography** is the discipline in the social sciences that studies the characteristics of human populations, including how they change. In the United States, the Census Bureau compiles the most comprehensive demographic data, including the decennial census and the annual American Community Survey. Census Bureau data represent the highest-quality demographic data available on a national scale and can be accessed freely at its website (www.census.gov). At the international level, the United Nations Statistics Division compiles census and other statistical information from member nations and publishes them annually in the *Demographic Yearbook* as well as making some of these data available on its website (www .unstats.un.org). Some of the most important demographic variables include population density, population growth rates, birth and death rates, and migration. **Population density** indicates the average number of people who live in a specified area unit, usually a square mile or square kilometer. **Population growth** measures changes in population over time by taking a population at one time and adding all the births and immigrants who arrive before a later time, while subtracting the deaths and emigrants. Rates are calculated by dividing the number of births/deaths/immigrants/emigrants for every 1,000 people in a given population. Although it does not distinguish between natural change (births and deaths) and migration, a crude population growth estimate can be calculated by dividing the population at a later time by the population at an earlier time. Likewise, simple population growth rates can be calculated by subtracting an earlier population from a later population, and then dividing by the earlier population.

In addition to counting the number of people in a population, demographers typically collect and publish data on the characteristics of populations, such as age and gender composition, consumption levels, and subpopulations, such as racial or ethnic groups. Unfortunately, the relationship between population change and environmental quality is not as straightforward or easy to define as demographic variables. Indeed, the relationship between human population growth and the environment has been the subject of social theory and social investigation for centuries.

MALTHUS, SOCIAL DARWINISM, AND MORAL CONTROL

Victorian-era social theorist Thomas Malthus famously proposed a relationship between environmental quality and population growth (see Lesson 2). His *Essay on the Principle of Population* (first published in 1798) asserted that, without restraint, human population growth would eventually exceed the production of food, resulting in a massive crash in population. Specifically, he posited that human population growth increased exponentially; two people in generation 1 produced two children (generation 1 population = 2); each of those two people produced two children in generation 2 (population = 2 × 2 = 4); each one of those four people produced two children in generation 3 (population = 4 × 2 = 8); and so on. Based on his assessment of food production in Europe, Malthus reasoned that the production of food would increase only in an arithmetic or linear fashion, such that the increase between generations would be constant. Given these projections, Malthus warned that if humans did not control their own population growth, then a combination of war, disease, and especially famine would control population anyway. In part due to his own devout faith, Malthus believed that humans were unlike other animals in their capacity to exert moral control over their behavior. He therefore indicated that the most ethical course of action would be to limit human population growth, beginning with the working classes of European cities, whose lack of moral control (in his view) created large families that the poor could not feed on their own. This conclusion resonated with the era's Victorian elites in its emphasis on restraint of sexual impulses, moral condemnation of the poor, and opposition to charity designed to improve the situation of the poor, since feeding the poor would only prolong the inevitable misery and population crash.

Herbert Spencer, a founding theorist in sociology, echoed Malthus in his writings about the moral superiority of the elite, although his work also naturalized social hierarchy (Spencer 1972). According to Spencer, human society was evolutionary and progressed from less to more complexity. Spencer, like Malthus, believed that moral human individuals and groups demonstrate higher levels of progress and that these traits could be passed to the next generation. Over time, more evolved groups would come to dominate weaker groups; Spencer described this as the "survival of the fittest." In his view, the moral superiority of the European (and especially British) elite reflected its evolutionary position, and this subsequently explained and legitimated European geographical expansion and subjugation of African, Asian, and Native American human groups.

Malthus and Spencer both influenced the theory of Charles Darwin, who explained that plants, animals, and even humans evolved in a process of competition for survival. Darwin's *The Origin of Species* (published in 1859) asserted that environmental stressors gave a reproductive advantage to individuals and species that adapted best to them; more of their offspring would survive into the next generation. This reproductive advantage (that is, natural selection) will become more pronounced in subsequent generations such that entire species evolve to become progressively more suited to their environment. Darwin's evolutionary theory revolutionized scientific thought and reduced human exceptionalist arguments, including those advanced by Malthus. Ironically, Spencer's ideas were so well integrated into Darwinian theory that they are now sometimes referred to as "social Darwinism." **Social Darwinism**, like Malthusian theory, posits that the relationship between humans and their environment has a "natural" evolutionary course but that this course can be overcome through social action, particularly restraint on population growth among those groups considered less evolved.

MODERNIZATION: THE DEMOGRAPHIC TRANSITION, THE GREEN REVOLUTION, AND NEO-MALTHUSIANISM

Following two world wars and the decline of the European global empires, Malthusian and social Darwinist thought reemerged in modernization theory, at least inasmuch as population policies assumed a connection between uncontrolled birth rates and food production. **Modernization theory** attempted to explain global inequality as a result of different levels of economic and cultural progress rather than as a set of innate, inherited, or moral characteristics. European domination could be explained because Africans, Asians, and Native Americans did not have the science, technology, or economic knowledge of Europeans. In a postcolonial context, European and North American knowledge would be shared with "less developed countries" in order to shepherd them into a more rationalized modernity. In terms of population dynamics, two particular elements of modernization theory stand out: the extension of modern agriculture known as the "green revolution" and the emphasis on birth control, particularly in order to achieve the so-called demographic transition.

The **green revolution** refers to a series of technological innovations to the production of food crops that were designed to increase productivity; more food could support more people. In general, these technologies reflected the system of agriculture that had been most productive in North America, particularly systems that produced single crops (*monocropping*). The green revolution introduced and/or expanded the use of mechanized tools (for example, irrigation, tractors, threshers), chemical fertilizers, and chemical pesticides in all regions of the globe. Another central technology for the green revolution was the development and introduction of high-yield varieties (HYVs) of rice, corn (maize), wheat, and other staple crops. HYVs typically produced more edible grain, while allowing plants to grow faster in more marginal environments and withstand the use of chemical fertilizers and pesticides. Agricultural scientists used advanced genetics and biotechnology to create HYV crops in international laboratories, such as the International Maize and Wheat Improvement Center in Mexico and the International Rice Research Institute in the Philippines. Green revolution technologies greatly increased food production worldwide; for example, world rice production more than tripled from 147 million metric tons in 1961 at the onset of the green revolution to over 463 million metric tons in 2012.

Unfortunately, the green revolution created additional and distinctly modern problems (see Lesson 12). Monocrop systems, especially HYVs, typically required higher levels of chemical input (fertilizers and pesticides) than traditional agriculture. Consequently, world fertilizer consumption grew faster than crop production: from 31 million tons in 1961 to over 239 million tons in 2012. Chemical additions to agricultural crops have since been linked to salinization and a decrease in biodiversity among beneficial species and in neighboring nonagricultural lands. The high water demands of mechanized, industrial agriculture have also led to an extension of irrigation systems that has significantly and negatively altered freshwater resources, most dramatically in central Asia's Aral Sea, which has lost more than half of its volume and geographical area since the 1960s. Green revolution technologies raised the cost of production substantially by requiring the purchase of HYV seeds (which were often infertile, so seeds had to be purchased each season), chemical inputs, farm machinery, and irrigated water. The increased cost of production meant that over the long term the green revolution has favored larger producers over smaller ones and small producers have been progressively squeezed out of production of basic grains. Moreover, HYVs are typically grown in fields of single crops at a scale appropriate for mechanized agriculture, as opposed to traditional agriculture, which was tended by human workers and contained a greater variety of plant species, including nonfood species used for livestock or fiber. These changes led to massive displacement of the rural labor force and nutritional deficiencies for many small farmers in countries as different as Mexico and India. Unable to compete in agriculture, many of these small producers and agricultural workers have relocated to cities, which have expanded spectacularly since the 1950s in all regions of the globe.

While the green revolution unquestionably increased food production (albeit with social and environmental costs), advocates of modernization also held that a modern society would have low birth and death rates and, thus, low population growth rates. A **demographic transition** would occur when low growth rates were achieved through controlled fertility and low death rates were achieved through modern healthcare and sanitation. According to this model, in premodern societies, birth and death rates were both high but population growth remained small because the deaths more or less cancelled out the births. However, as sanitation, nutrition, and healthcare improved with modernization, life expectancies increased and death rates declined (especially infant mortality rates). Because of the cultural lag following technological change, birth rates remain high and population growth increases dramatically. Only when family planning norms adjust downward to account for longer life expectancies and higher survival rates among children will population growth slow and stabilize, indicating that a demographic transition to a modern society has occurred.

The demographic transition model is based on the historical experience of European and North American societies but has been expanded to include Asian nations such as Japan, South Korea, and Taiwan. Less developed nations in Asia, Africa, and the Americas did see their death rates decline significantly in the postcolonial period, while their birth rates remained at traditionally high levels. Consequently, population growth in less developed regions of the world expanded dramatically in the latter half of the twentieth century: Africa's population more than quadrupled in these 50 years, Latin America's more than tripled, while Asia's and Oceania's more than doubled (see Table 8-1). Even regions where the demographic transition had allegedly occurred increased their population, with North America nearly doubling its population and Europe adding a third of its population. Note, however, that these are raw population figures and do not distinguish between births and increases due to immigration, which accounts for significant proportions of the increases in both Western Europe and North America.

Population pyramids are often used to display the explosive population growth that occurs before a demographic transition. These graphs present national populations by age and sex (that is, the age and sex structures of the population) as a means for distinguishing between countries that have already made the demographic transition and those that have not. Figure 8-1 depicts population pyramids for Kenya, China, and Germany to highlight these different stages. Kenya's population pyramid in 2012 looks like a pyramid, in which the largest categories of the population are children (0–14 years); this portends a future baby boom as these young people enter their prime childbearing years (15–29). In contrast, China's population pyramid displays a population evidently in the early stages of a demographic transition: The top half of this graph looks like a pyramid, with the largest proportion of people past their prime childbearing years (ages 40–49). However, the graph tapers in age categories

Table 8-1 Population and Population Growth in Selected Regions, 1950–2000

	Population 1950 (millions)	Population 1980 (millions)	Population 2000 (millions)	Percent Change
Africa	250	483	1022	408%
Asia	1,403	2,638	4,164	297%
Europe	547	693	738	135%
Latin America and the Caribbean	167	362	590	353%
North America	172	255	345	201%
Oceania	13	23	27	207%

Source: Population Division of the Department of Economic and Social Affairs of the United Nations Secretariat 2010: Table 1.

below these ages, indicating that people are having fewer children. Finally, the pyramid for Germany exhibits characteristics of a population that has undergone a demographic transition, as evidenced by the relatively equal distribution among age categories. In fact, Germany's age structure reveals an aging population, with almost equal proportions of older and younger people.

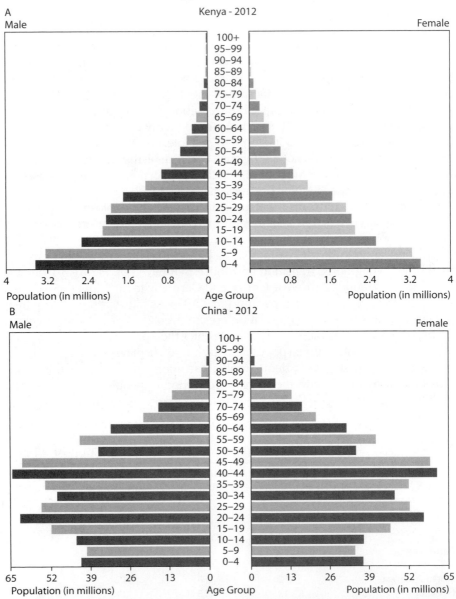

Figure 8–1 A–C Population pyramids for Kenya **(A)**, China **(B)**, and Germany **(C)**.

Source: U.S. Census Bureau, International Data Base 2012.

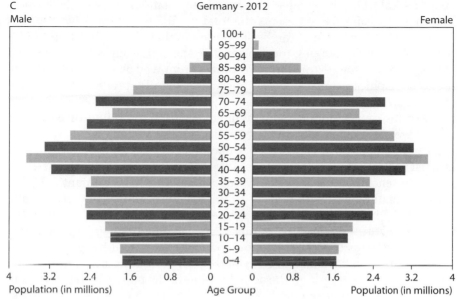

Figure 8–1 A–C (*Continued*)

Because rates of growth are highest in the poorest regions of the world, neo-Malthusian arguments emerged in the late 1960s calling for control of population and conservation of resources. Paul Ehrlich's *The Population Bomb* (1968) attempted to avoid the elitist trappings of Malthus by proposing an equation that measured environmental impact through a combination of population, affluence, and technology ($I = P \times A \times T$). Population (P) reflects the number of people, affluence (A) indicates the level of consumption by those people, and technology (T) reflects the type of technology used by those people. Environmental impact (I) thus varies not only by raw numbers of people but also by their consumption and waste patterns, sometimes now measured as their "**ecological footprint**," or the amount of land necessary to sustain consumption and absorb wastes. Based on higher consumption levels and use of more environmentally damaging technologies, the average North American individual is estimated to have over five times the ecological impact of an African (see Table 8-2). Neo-Malthusians have also expanded on Malthus' attention to food supply to include references to the carrying capacity of a

Table 8–2 Ecological Footprint in Hectares per Person

Africa	1.4 ha
Asia	1.8 ha
Europe	4.7 ha
Latin America and the Caribbean	2.6 ha
North America	7.9 ha

Source: Ewing, Moore, et al., 2010.

geographical unit (for example, an ecosystem, a nation, or the entire planet). The **carrying capacity** represents the total population of any given species (for example, humans) that can be supported in that geographical unit without permanently damaging the ecological systems that support that species. Damages come from extraction of resources from well as pollution added to that geographical unit. Neo-Malthusians generally predict that, unless changes are made in terms of all components of the $I = P \times A \times T$ equation, the carrying capacity of the planet will be reached and famine, disease, war, and, at worst, complete global ecosystemic collapse will follow.

Responding to these concerns, population policy became an integral part of most nations' development plans. The West has reviled China's one-child policy for encouraging sex-selective abortions and female infanticide, but China's population growth rate has dropped significantly, from 1.9 annually in 1955 to 0.7 in 2005 (see Table 8-3; also review the age structure in Fig. 8-1B). Unable to institute a policy like China's, India sent mobile sterilization teams into its rural areas to reduce its population growth rate, although these successful programs have also been criticized for sterilizing men and women based on quotas rather than the actual wishes of the people being sterilized. Funding from European and North American sources allowed for greater distribution of birth control and family planning technologies to developing countries in the 1960s and 1970s but came under increasing pressure from parties as disparate as the Roman Catholic Church, the U.S. government, and Muslim clerics, who argued against women's access to birth control and abortion. Even this debate could not stifle the excitement surrounding the United Nations Population and Development Conference in Cairo in 1994, where the links between controlling population growth and sustainable development were made explicit (see Lesson 20). In addition to their focus on population control, the UN's Decade of the Woman, from 1985 to 1995, highlighted women's education, economic security, and health as a means for reducing birth and infant mortality rates. Women in Development programs rely on the assumption that women who have opportunities outside of motherhood and who can depend on the survival of their children will have fewer children. Whether due to this global effort or to other changes in the global social system, population growth rates have slowed somewhat since the 1980s (see Table 8-3).

Table 8-3 Annual Population Growth Rates, 1955–2005 (selected countries)

	1955	1965	1975	1985	1995	2005
China	1.9	2.1	2.2	1.4	1.1	0.7
India	2.0	2.3	2.2	2.1	1.9	1.6
Kenya	2.8	3.2	3.6	3.8	3.0	2.2
Mexico	2.7	3.1	3.2	2.2	1.9	1.3
United States	1.6	1.4	0.9	1.0	1.1	1.0
Italy	0.6	0.8	0.6	0.1	0.2	0.1

Source: United Nations Statistics Division 2007.

POPULATION AS A STRAW DOLL:
MARX, FAMINE, AND XENOPHOBIA

Karl Marx called Malthus' 1798 *Essay* a "lampoon" that was popularized entirely because it legitimated the partisan interests of the English elite. Apart from this ideological component, Malthus was criticized by contemporaries and later social theorists for methodological weaknesses, notably his assumption of linear, arithmetic growth rates in food production, which apparently had no empirical foundation and was rendered inaccurate by the green revolution. Likewise, modernization theories involving food production and population dynamics have shown empirical and ideological weaknesses.

The main critiques of Malthusian, neo-Malthusian, and modernization theories about population growth point to the lack of discussion about the distribution of people and resources. A neo-Marxist critique of Malthus has been cogently and convincingly argued elsewhere by John Bellamy Foster. Foster has also drawn from Marx's work to call attention to the importance of population in terms of concentration in cities, where people have become dependent on industrial agriculture to produce food and organic waste is disposed in landfills instead of returned to agriculture. The "**metabolic rift**" that has developed between human food production and waste has overburdened rural natural systems by irrigation, fertilizer, and pesticide contamination and created pollution and health risks in urban areas. Given the rural population displacement and urban growth associated with the green revolution, this metabolic rift has created massive pollution problems in all regions of the world.

Critics also point to the lack of distributive concerns by neo-Malthusians. Responding directly to the assumptions of modernization theory, Amartya Sen's life work has sought to emphasize how the famines and poverty in places like sub-Saharan Africa and South Asia reflect the inhumane distribution of resources rather than any absolute shortage of food. Sen describes a world where the powerful use food as a weapon and famines reveal more about local and global inequalities than about food production. A well-known example of this from history involves the Irish potato famine; between 1845 and 1851, nearly 1 million Irish died of starvation or starvation-related illnesses and another million emigrated to escape the famine, while the English continued to grow and export tons of wheat from manor lands in Ireland. In contemporary times, the persistent violence in the Sudan has forced hundreds of thousands (if not millions) of small farmers to abandon their agricultural land and flee to refugee camps. Stripped of their ability to produce their own food, these refugees rely on food aid shipments. However, the delivery of these shipments is controlled by warlords who demand loyalty from the refugees and camp personnel. These examples demonstrate Sen's key concern that famines represent less of a shortage of food or (as neo-Malthusians may suggest) population exceeding its ecological carrying capacity than a manifestation of vast power differences between groups of people. When people interpret famines as examples of a population exceeding its carrying capacity, they ignore the human agents that cause famines and blame the victims for their own misery.

Apart from famines, local and global inequality directly determines how much food is available to people. A considerable portion of agricultural land worldwide is dedicated to export and luxury crops rather than basic food crops; often, these crops occupy the most productive agricultural land. I personally have seen extensive tea plantations in Kenya, coconut plantations in northeast Brazil (see Fig. 8-2), banana plantations in Guatemala, citrus plantations in Mexico, strawberry plantations in Florida, and artichoke plantations in California, while the workers on these plantations may suffer from basic health and malnutrition problems. Moreover, immense rangelands as well as oceans of grain (such as corn in the American Midwest and soy in the Brazilian south) feed cattle instead of humans (see Lesson 4). Only more affluent consumers include meats, especially beef, in their staple diets. Since the 1980s, poorer nations have experienced strong economic pressure to continue to produce luxury and export crops as these represent some of the few means to generate hard currency used to repay national debts and eventually expand local markets, social services, and infrastructure. However, world trade has generally seen a decline in the value of agricultural exports relative to manufacturing and high-tech exports; countries that rely on agricultural production for foreign exchange (like Ecuador, which sells flowers and bananas) guarantee themselves a subordinate position in the global hierarchy.

A focus on population growth in the Global South may also reflect social fears in the Global North more than real population concerns. Increased immigration from the Global South to the Global North has contributed to

Figure 8–2 Coconut plantation in northeastern Brazil.
Source: Diane C. Bates.

xenophobic, ideological beliefs about population growth in poorer countries, particularly where immigrant newcomers are socially distant from natives, as with northern Africans in the Paris suburbs, Latin Americans in the U.S. border states, South Asians in the north of England, and Asians in Australia. Workers in the Global South (agricultural and otherwise) are aware of the limits to advancement in their local economies and increasingly migrate to North America, Europe, East Asia, and the Middle East in search of better-paid work. This process of migration, in fact, has contributed greatly to the population growth rates in the Global North, where some countries (such as Germany and Italy) would register negative population growth rates were it not for immigration. Regardless of the relative size of these groups and the economic importance of immigrants in their host countries, many see the influx of newcomers as a population "problem" couched in environmental language as strain on local resources in receiving countries and an effect of "overpopulation" in sending countries. Nativism has bubbled up all over the Global North. Sociologists Lisa Sun-Hee Park and David Naguib Pellow examine this process in detail in their case study of Aspen, Colorado (2011). Wealthy Aspenites passed local ordinances against immigration from Latin America, with the logic that increased immigration threatened the regional environment. Without reflecting on their own consumption of extravagant second homes and recreational skiing, Aspenites were able to scapegoat immigrants as the true threat to nature, and to link this to national nativist narratives widespread among large North American environmental organizations. U.S. environmental groups like the Sierra Club and Zero Population Growth have expressed neo-Malthusian concerns about population; without attention to the social complexity behind population dynamics indicated above, they risk reproducing elitist and xenophobic agendas.

POPULATION AND TROPICAL FORESTS IN ECUADOR: A DEMOGRAPHIC CASE STUDY

This final section uses a case study to explore the complex relationship between population growth and tropical deforestation in the South American nation of Ecuador. Ecuador stretches from the Pacific coast over the Andes and into the upper reaches of the Amazon basin, containing about 14.6 million inhabitants. North–south mountain chains divide the small country into three distinct social and environmental regions: the Pacific coast, the Andean highlands and valleys (the Sierra), and the Amazonian lowlands (the Oriente). Prior to European contact, most of the population in what is now Ecuador lived in the temperate Andean highlands and valleys, where they were able to take advantage of how altitude created small variations in climate. These microclimates allowed pre-Columbian farmers to produce a wide variety of agricultural products, ranging from tropical fruits like the papaya to temperate staples like potatoes. The rich volcanic soils of the Sierra allowed for relatively intensive agriculture and relatively dense populations. In contrast, nearly impenetrable tropical rain forests flanked the Andes in the west (the coastal region) and the east (the Oriente). These forests prevented the expansion of agriculture from the Andes because the terrain was difficult to traverse, fast-moving rivers prevented navigation, and Andean migrants faced both tropical diseases and hostile indigenous people in the lowlands.

European colonization dramatically changed the relationship of people to Ecuador's forests, starting trends that continue into current times. The Spanish created plantation-like manor farms (*latifundia*) in the richest and most productive Sierra land, while obliging the indigenous highland people to perform labor and assimilate to Spanish customs. Because the best land was occupied by plantations, subsistence farmers planted their fields further onto steep mountainsides, contributing to alpine deforestation and erosion. Today, valley lands remain concentrated in large farms that produce commercial goods, such as dairy products and cut flowers. On the Pacific coast, the Spanish recognized the protected harbor at Guayaquil and the nearby stands of tropical timber suitable for shipbuilding. As the port city of Guayaquil grew, the Spanish also cleared forests for plantations of cacao, from which chocolate is derived, and later bananas, which remain Ecuador's most important agricultural export crop today. In order to attract labor from the Sierra, coastal plantation owners set aside nearby land for workers and their families. The growth of export-oriented plantations and associated urban economies has attracted many people from the Andean region, and more Ecuadorians now live in coastal provinces than in the Sierra. Only in the Oriente, with its poor access to population centers in the Sierra and worse access to the international trade networks offered through Pacific ports, have forests remained largely intact. This situation changed only since the latter half of the 20th century after oil was discovered, providing an incentive and funds to build roads deep into the northern Oriente. The Ecuadorian government in the 1950s and 1960s also used oil revenues to develop colonization programs that made land available to poor farmers who were willing to migrate to remote coastal and Oriente forests to develop new agricultural land.

The relationship between population growth and deforestation in Ecuador appears to be a fairly simple one: As population grew, forests were removed from the country's landscape (Fig. 8-3). However, Figure 8-3 obscures a more complex relationship between the use of forest resources and human activities. The coastal population has grown most, although the Oriente surpassed the Sierra in regional population early in the 21st century (Fig. 8-4). Over 76% of forests on the coast have been cleared, leaving only about 2 million hectares, while just over a quarter (26%) of the Oriente has been deforested and over 7 million hectares remain; two thirds of the forests in the Sierra have already vanished, with only 3 million hectares remaining. A simplistic, neo-Malthusian explanation of these data would predict the following: Population growth has declined in the Sierra relative to the Oriente and the coast, so pressure on forests will decrease in the Andes. Population growth will eliminate

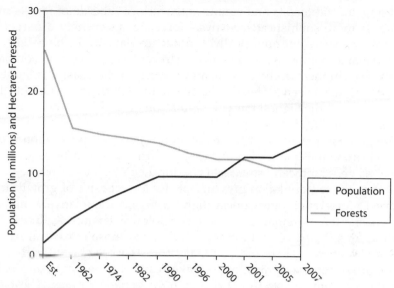

Figure 8–3 Ecuadorian population and forests over time.

Note: Original population estimate is based on 1889; original forest cover was estimated by the Food and Agriculture Organization of the United Nations (2001:120–122). Because comparable dates were not available for forest cover and population estimates, data are smoothed by adding or subtracting average annual increases or decreases between known data points.

Sources: Minnesota Population Center 2007; Central Intelligence Agency 2007; Food and Agriculture Organization of the United Nations 2001, 2005.

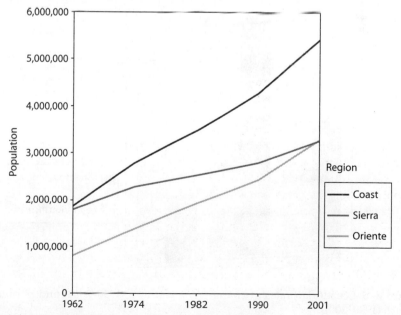

Figure 8–4 Population growth in Ecuador by region.

Source: Minnesota Population Center 2007.

remaining coastal forests and significantly reduce the size of forests in the Oriente. A more sophisticated analysis forecasts an entirely different outcome that is borne out empirically. Limited to data from the most recent years available, Figure 8-5 shows that in recent years rates of population growth were highest in the Oriente and lowest on the coast, while rates of deforestation have been highest in the Sierra and lowest in the Oriente. How can an area with the highest rates of population growth have the lowest rates of deforestation?

The simple answer is that the relationship between population growth and environmental quality is not the same from place to place, even in a country as geographically small as Ecuador. Ecuador's coast has seen high levels of absolute population growth but the lowest rates of growth in the country. Deforestation rates appear high but reflect the relatively small size of the coastal forests remaining in 1996. Sociologist Thomas K. Rudel classified Ecuador's Pacific coastal forests as similar to those in Central America and the Caribbean, where most primary forests were cleared early in the process of European colonization to make way for export agriculture, leaving only remnant forests in relatively inaccessible locations. The coastal economy today remains centered around export-oriented agriculture but with large urban centers and tourist zones. Deforestation still occurs when

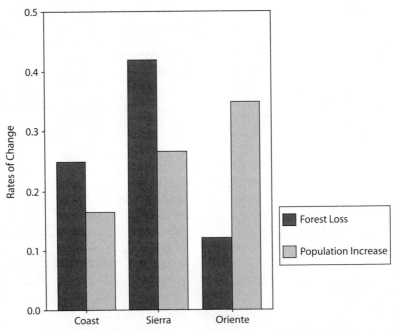

Figure 8–5 Ecuadorian rates of change of forest loss (1996–2000) and population growth (1990–2001).

Sources: Minnesota Population Center 2007; Food and Agriculture Organization of the United Nations 2005.

small farmers clear marginal forests to meet urban demand for food or create shrimp ponds in mangrove forests; however, plantations replaced most of the region's forests generations ago, and urban residents increasingly consume food produced elsewhere. The remnant forests that still exist are now located only in those areas most inhospitable to agricultural expansion; thus, the actual threat of population growth on remaining coastal forests is limited. Rudel even suggests that places like Ecuador's coast are excellent for promoting ecotourism (see Lesson 20) and environmentally certified agricultural products because urban and international consumers and tourists can exert great pressure on the quality of goods they purchase and relatively few locals depend directly on the forest for their livelihoods.

In contrast, Ecuador's Amazonian region shows relatively high rates of population growth but relatively low rates of deforestation, although these figures are also somewhat distorted by the region's relatively small population and large forest in 1996. Most of the Amazon basin was too remote and inaccessible to be converted to plantation crops; distance continues to limit the profitability of farms except along main transportation corridors. As is true elsewhere in the Amazon basin, these geographical obstacles have also concentrated populations in cities, while rural areas face chronic shortages of labor. Urban population growth, measured either absolutely or as a rate, affects forest conversion in two ways. The demand for agricultural products in Amazonian cities has led to forest clearing on transportation corridors and has encouraged land-extensive ranching adjacent to these corridors. Since the region's fast-growing cities absorb excess labor, farmers utilize land-extensive, rather than labor-intensive, strategies to make their farms productive. After initial clearing, small-scale cattle ranching requires little human labor, which can often be performed by women and children. In this way, a single household can clear and maintain farms of 100 hectares or more, with intensive agricultural activities concentrated nearest the transportation corridors and ranching beyond. Dramatic as this sort of deforestation may appear from roads, little deforestation occurs outside these corridors. As a consequence, inaccessibility will likely continue to protect large blocks of Amazonian forest, as demonstrated by the relatively low rates of deforestation displayed in Figure 8-5. Ecuador has also established indigenous reserves and national parks in the less populous regions of the Oriente, which may provide the institutional infrastructure necessary to protect these large forests over time.

Positive environmental outcomes seem less likely in the Sierra, which has seen the highest rates of deforestation recently and only moderate rates of population growth (see Figs. 8-4 and 8-5). Pre-Columbian and plantation agriculture had converted most valley and gently sloped land to agriculture long ago, leaving only remnant alpine forests. Temperate climates in Andean valleys and tenuous access to coastal ports limited the development of export-oriented agriculture, although greenhouses for cut flowers have provided some access to global markets in the past two decades. Most deforestation in the Sierra today reflects the removal of forests upslope from the region's growing cities, where poor migrants clear land to provide housing, fuel, and subsistence for their families and sell whatever surplus they may produce. In this case, population growth has a direct effect on forest cover: More people trying to live in and from these forests leads to more degradation. Thus, although population growth in the Sierra has been slow when compared to the coast and the Oriente, this growth has had a direct negative effect on the region's forests. The loss of remnant forest buffers in the mountains that cradle Ecuador's cities creates additional environmental problems for these cities, including erosion, degradation of water sources, and poorer air quality. Forest conservation and management in this context are hampered by the increasing numbers of squatters, their inability to meet their immediate needs except by extracting short-term gains from the forest, and the absence of control over access to these forests. In the Sierra, even slow population growth will likely have major negative effects on the region's environment.

This foray into Ecuador's forests underscores the complexity of the relationship between human populations and the nonhuman environment. At the regional level, human populations can expand while creating the conditions for environmental protection (as in Amazonian parks) or conservation (as with coastal ecotourism). However, growth in the number of people who are directly dependent on the environment (like squatters in the Sierra) does tend to degrade the local environment. Ecuador also demonstrates that the relationship between food production and population growth makes no sense on national and subnational scales; global food commodity chains and urban markets have freed human populations from their local food sources. Plantations in the Sierra and coastal regions have removed the best land from production of food for local populations, while small farmers in Amazonia clear forests mainly for urban markets. Both situations transfer the reason for food production from supporting human populations to supporting human economies. Consumer preferences for greener products may thus have a greater effect on environmental quality than population control. Finally, demographic trends are best understood within their social and historical contexts. Slow population growth in the Sierra does more damage to that region's forests than faster population growth in the coastal and Amazonian regions. To understand this situation requires more than a statistical representation of population growth; a sociological and historical perspective illuminates the patterns of resource use and inequality that shape this relationship.

CONCLUSION

Ecuador represents a tiny fraction of the world's growing human population, but sociologists must consider population dynamics and the demographic profiles of affected communities, whether considering environmental issues on a local, national, or global scale. How many people live in an area, their characteristics, and how that population changes in time determine how they interact with their environment. We don't yet understand the full implications of 7 billion people for the global ecosystem, but with more people, rising levels of consumption, and more damaging technologies, global environmental problems such as climate change and atmospheric ozone thinning point toward more serious concerns for the future. Moreover, the uneven distribution of resources, ranging from food to stop famines to political power to compel remediation of contaminated sites, underscores the importance of understanding not just population growth but contextualized demography as an element in environmental sociology.

SOURCES

Central Intelligence Agency. 2007. *The World Factbook*. Retrieved June 28, 2007. (http://www.cia.gov/library/publications/the-world-factbook/).

Darwin, Charles. 1909. *The Origin of Species*. New York: P. F. Collier and Son.

Ehrlich, Paul R. 1968. *The Population Bomb*. New York: Ballantine Books.

Ewing, B., D. Moore, S. Goldfinger, A. Ourster, A. Reed, and M. Wackernagel. 2010. *The Ecological Footprint Atlas 2010*. Oakland, CA: Global Footprint Network.

Food and Agricultural Organization of the United Nations. 2001. *Estudo de la Información Forestal en Ecuador*. Santiago, Chile: United Nations.

Food and Agricultural Organization of the United Nations. 2005 *Global Forest Resources Assessment*. Retrieved July 8, 2007. (http://www.fao.org/forestry/site/32089/en/ecu).

Foster, John Bellamy. 1999. "Marx's Theory of the Metabolic Rift: Classical Foundations for Environmental Sociology." *American Journal of Sociology* 105(2):366–405.

Foster, John Bellamy. 2002. *Ecology Against Capitalism*. New York: Monthly Review Press.

International Rice Research Institute. 2007. *Atlas of Rice and World Rice Statistics*. Retrieved April 21, 2007. (http://www.irri.org/science/ricestat/index.asp).

Malthus, T. R. 1914. *An Essay on Population*. New York: E. P. Dutton.

Marx, Karl. 1865. "On Proudhon: Letter to J. B. Schweizer." Retrieved January 18, 2007. (http://www.marxists.org/archive/marx/works/).

Marx, Karl. 1906. *Capital: A Critique of Political Economy*. New York: Modern Library.

Minnesota Population Center. 2007. *Integrated Public Use Microdata Series—International: Version 3.0*. Minneapolis, MN: University of Minnesota.

Park, Lisa Sun-Hee, and David Naguib Pellow. 2011. *The Slums of Aspen: Immigrants Vs. the Environment in America's Eden*. New York: New York University Press.

Population Division of the Department of Economic and Social Affairs of the United Nations Secretariat. 2007. *World Population Prospects: The 2006 Revision*. New York: United Nations.

Rudel, Thomas K. 2005. *Tropical Forests: Regional Paths of Destruction and Regeneration in the Late Twentieth Century*. New York: Columbia University Press.

Sen, Amartya. 1981. *Poverty and Famines: An Essay on Entitlement and Deprivation*. New York: Oxford University Press.

Spencer, Herbert. 1972. *On Social Evolution: Selected Writings,* edited by J. D. Y. Peel. Chicago, IL: University of Chicago Press.

United Nations Statistics Division. 2010. *Demographic Yearbook 2009-2010.* Retrieved January 23, 2014. (http://unstats.un.org/unsd/demographic/products/dyb/dyb2009-2010.htm).

United States Census Bureau. 2012. "International Data Base: Population Pyramids." January 23, 2014. (http://www.census.gov/population/international/data/idb/informationGateway.php).

United States Census Bureau. 2013. "World Population Clock." January 23, 2014. (http://www.census.gov/main/www/popclock.html).

Vandermeer, John, and Ivette Perfecto. 1995. *Breakfast of Biodiversity: The Truth About Rainforest Destruction.* Oakland, CA: Food First Books.

9

Energy, Society, and the Environment

Shannon Elizabeth Bell

The Flamingo hotel and casino on the Las Vegas Strip, Las Vegas, Nevada.
Photo by Ken Gould.

"The essential problem is not just that we are tapping the *wrong* energy sources (though we are), or that we are wasteful and inefficient (though we are), but that we are *overpowered*, and we are *overpowering* nature . . . The only reasonable path forward is to find ways to use *less* energy."
—Richard Heinberg, *Energy: Overdevelopment and the Delusion of Endless Growth*, p. 3

What is energy? Energy is not something that we can easily describe or directly observe, but it is central to everything taking place in our natural world. Physicists define energy as "the ability to do work," and thanks to the tremendous technological innovations that our world has seen over the past two centuries, humankind has become increasingly successful at using the energy stored in fossil fuels, vegetation, wind, water, and sunlight to "do work" for us. However, many of the energy technologies we use have also come at very serious costs to our environment.

While a sociology of energy was recognized and described more than 35 years ago by Rosa, Machlis, and Keating (1988), it was not until the urgency of climate change became clear that energy became a topic of such critical importance to environmental sociologists, for energy production is the largest contributor to the generation of global warming–causing greenhouse gasses (see Lesson 15). Environmental sociologists ask questions about how human behavior affects the environment *and* how the environment affects people and societies. Some questions we might ask about energy include: What are the social, environmental, and public health consequences of energy production? Which communities are most likely to bear the burden of pollution from energy production? Why do some communities protest the pollution while others do not? What strategies do corporations involved in the energy sector use to acquire political power? How have some groups successfully fought for cleaner energy solutions in their communities? And what societal changes need to be made in order to reduce the amount of energy we use? As you continue to read, I encourage you to jot down other sociological questions that come to mind.

In this lesson, we will examine the interactions between energy, society, and the environment by first exploring global energy consumption patterns. Then, we will consider the major sources of energy and the social and environmental costs associated with these sources. Finally, we will contemplate the hope for change. A major goal of this chapter is to encourage reflection on the true costs associated with our energy consumption habits. As Butler and Wuerthner (2012) and others have argued, we do not simply have a fossil fuel problem; rather, we have an energy problem. We are an overpowered society, and if serious changes are not made to our energy consumption patterns, we have no hope of halting this runaway train of climate change and environmental health devastation.

GLOBAL ENERGY CONSUMPTION PATTERNS

Over the past two centuries, worldwide energy consumption has risen at an alarming rate. Population growth certainly has a lot to do with this increase in energy consumption; the world's population is about seven times larger than it was right before the Industrial Revolution (see Lesson 8). However, as Butler and Wuerthner (2012) point out, we are not using seven times as much energy as we were 250 years ago—we are using *30 times* as much energy. Even within the past 60 years, the increases in energy use have been staggering: Our world has gone from producing 375 billion kilowatt-hours of energy in 1951 to 4,106 billion kilowatt-hours of energy in 2011.

As shown in Figure 9–1, of the energy that was consumed throughout the world in 2011, 87% was generated from fossil fuels, including oil (33%), coal (30%), and natural gas (24%).

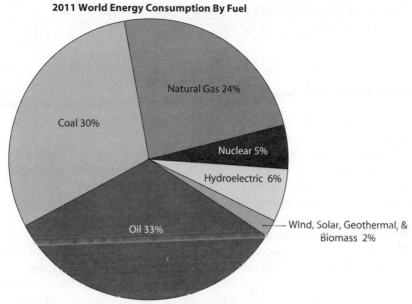

2011 World Energy Consumption By Fuel

Natural Gas 24%

Coal 30%

Nuclear 5%

Hydroelectric 6%

Oil 33%

Wind, Solar, Geothermal, & Biomass 2%

Figure 9–1 World energy consumption by fuel.
Source: BP Statistical Review of World Energy 2012.

In 2011, the United States consumed 97.262 Quadrillion BTU of energy, making it the second leading consumer of energy in the world, second only to China, which has more than four times the population of the United States (EIA, 2013a). The United States has 5 percent of the world's population but consumes 19 percent of the total energy (EIA, n.d.). Butler and Wuerthner (2012) estimate that on average, each person living in the United States uses the power of approximately 150 "energy slaves," meaning that if all the power that we use were supplied by human labor, it would require 150 people working around the clock every day in order to provide it. Take a moment to consider all of the ways that you use energy in your daily routine. As a student, you probably use a computer on a daily—possibly hourly—basis. Do you have a smart phone? How and where do you wash your clothes? Do you drive a car? Or ride a bus? Do you ever fly on an airplane to visit family or friends or to go on vacation? How do you keep your food cold? Do you cook your food? Do you turn lights on in your home when it is dark outside? Do you heat your home in the winter? Do you cool it with fans or air conditioning (or both) in the summer? Most Americans are consuming energy—and large amounts of it—throughout most (if not all) hours of the day.

As energy production increases, so does ecological degradation, threats to public health, and losses in biodiversity. In the following sections, we will examine the major sources of energy used throughout the world and the social and environmental costs associated with these sources.

SOCIAL, ENVIRONMENTAL, AND PUBLIC HEALTH COSTS OF THE MAJOR SOURCES OF ENERGY

Oil (Petroleum)

As Butler and Wuerthner (2012) have noted, oil is "the lubricant of modern civilization." It is refined into many different products, such as gasoline, diesel fuel, heating oil, jet fuel, propane, as well as asphalt and road oil. We are dependent on oil, not just for energy production, but also for many of the products we use on a daily basis, like plastics and various chemicals. Thirty-three percent of world energy consumption is from oil, and 61.5% of all the oil used throughout the world is in the transportation sector.

In recent years there has been much talk about "peak oil"—the year when the global rate of oil extraction will reach its highest point and will then start to decline. The response to declining oil supplies in conventional geological formations has been to seek out increasingly remote and difficult-to-access sources of oil in tar sands and shale oil deposits, and to drill ultra-deep-water wells tens of thousands of feet below the ocean floor. As the easy-to-reach oil reserves become depleted, we are entering what Michael Klare calls "the era of extreme energy." The consequences of this quest for "extreme energy" include a tremendous amount of ecosystem destruction and an increased risk of environmental disasters like the BP *Deepwater Horizon* oil spill of 2010, during which an estimated 210 million gallons of oil gushed from a well on the ocean floor in the Gulf of Mexico and caused unimaginable and far-reaching devastation to sea life, wetlands, and coastal communities.

While the United States has about 5% of the global population, it is responsible for 25% of the world's annual oil consumption. According to the Union of Concerned Scientists, more than 95% of the energy used for transportation in the United States comes from oil. The electric car is touted as one major way to reduce our dependence on oil. But where does electricity come from? In the following sections, we will take a closer look at the primary sources of energy used to fuel the electric sector and examine the ecological and public health costs associated with these sources.

Electric Power in the United States

In terms of electricity consumption, the United States ranks number one in the world, at 3,866.4 billion kilowatt-hours consumed in 2010. Figure 9–2 shows the net electricity generated in the United States in 2012 by energy source. Coal provided 37.4% of the electricity produced in the United States, followed by natural gas (30.4%), and nuclear (19.0%). Renewable energy sources (including hydroelectric, wind, geothermal, biomass, and solar) accounted for 12.1% of electricity.

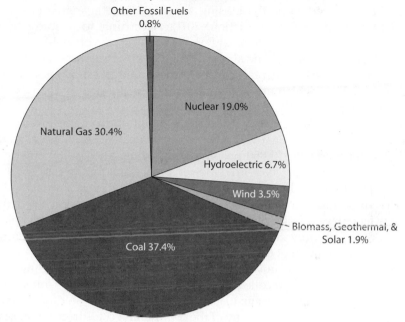

U.S. Net Electricity Generation 2012

Figure 9–2 U.S. net electricity generation, 2012.
Source: EIA 2013b.

Coal

James Hansen (2012, p. 61), renowned climate scientist and former director of NASA's Goddard Institute for Space Studies, has called coal "the single greatest threat to civilization and all life on our planet." In 2010, coal-fired power plants were responsible for close to 45% of global carbon dioxide emissions from energy consumption, which was an increase from 42% in 2006. This trend is not likely to end anytime soon; by 2035, world carbon dioxide emissions from coal are projected to increase by 68.1% over 2005 levels. Coal has a higher carbon content that other fossil fuels; thus, burning coal leads to the emission of more carbon dioxide per unit of electricity generated than any other fossil fuel. Further, the mining and processing of coal typically leads to the release of methane, which is trapped in natural deposits and is more than 20 times more potent a greenhouse gas than carbon dioxide. Thus, coal is a leading (and growing) cause of global climate change. For this reason, James Hansen (2012, p. 62) asserts that "[a] moratorium on coal-fired power plants is by far the most important action that needs to be pursued" to help mitigate climate change.

In addition to the considerable role that burning coal plays in hastening climate change, it is also responsible for tremendous costs to public health.

Emitting 386,000 tons of toxic air pollution each year, U.S. coal-fired power plants are estimated to be the leading source of toxic air emissions in the nation (American Lung Association, 2011). According to a study by the Environmental Protection Agency (EPA), the smokestacks of coal-fired power plants release 67 different toxic air pollutants, 55 of which are known neurotoxins that cause developmental damage to the brains and nervous systems of children and 24 of which are known, probable, or possible human carcinogens. Furthermore, Physicians for Social Responsibility (2009) estimates that every year in the United States, fine particle pollution from coal-fired power plants is responsible for nearly 23,600 premature deaths, 38,200 heart attacks, 554,000 asthma attacks, 21,850 hospital admissions, and 26,000 emergency room visits. In addition, coal-fired power plants are the largest source of mercury pollution in the nation; such plants emitted more than 65% of all mercury air pollution in 2005. In December 2011, the EPA passed new federal limits on mercury emissions from existing and future coal-fired power plants; however, this will only curtail future mercury emissions and does nothing about the accumulation of emissions that have already taken place.

Does your college or university burn coal on campus? According to the Sierra Club, more than 60 colleges and universities across the United States operate coal-fired boilers on site to generate heat and hot water for the buildings on their campuses. Like many of the commercial coal-fired power plants in the United States, these smaller-scale plants are older facilities that have been **grandfathered** in under Clean Air Act regulations, which means that they are legally emitting large quantities of toxic pollutants that modern power plants are not permitted to release. The Sierra Club's Beyond Coal Campaign (www.sierraclub.org/coal) has been working with communities and student environmental organizations across the country to retire coal-fired plants and replace them with cleaner energy solutions. Is there a student chapter of the Sierra Club's Beyond Coal Campaign at your college or university?

While the environmental and public health costs associated with burning coal are immense, the coal industry also causes great ecological and social harm before this fossil fuel is ever burned. Throughout the entire lifecycle of coal—including mining, processing, washing, transportation, burning, and waste disposal—workers and local residents are imperiled by industry practices (Bell, 2013). Huge swaths of land are decimated by surface mines in coal-mining areas, leading to disastrous floods and ecosystem destruction. More than 1 million acres and 500 mountains in Central Appalachia have been destroyed by **mountaintop removal (MTR) mining,** which is a form of surface mining that blows mountain ranges apart to unearth thin seams of coal for extraction by gargantuan draglines. Public health researchers Michael Hendryx, Melissa Ahern, and their colleagues have conducted numerous studies about the health impacts of living close to MTR mining operations. These studies have found that communities near MTR sites suffer elevated rates of cancer, mortality from chronic cardiovascular disease, and birth defects. In addition, these communities experience greater poverty and mortality disparities and have a poorer health-related quality of life than non-MTR communities.

After coal is mined, it must be cleaned and crushed in processing plants to remove the noncombustible materials like sulfur. Coal dust from processing plants covers nearby towns, causing respiratory distress and asthma among local residents and making it impossible to enjoy the outdoors for any length of time. Toxic **slurry** from the "washing" of coal accumulates in enormous open impoundments and in underground injection sites, sometimes leaching into the aquifer and contaminating well water with toxic metals and chemicals used in the coal-washing process (see http://www.WVPhotovoice .org/Big-Coal-River-Problems.html for "photostories" created by women living in a community affected by coal-slurry contamination. These women were part of an eight-month Photovoice project that I conducted in five coal-mining communities).

After the coal is burned, the ash that is left behind, called **coal combustion waste** (CCW), must also be dealt with. CCW contains all of the heavy metals present in coal, but in a more concentrated (toxic) form. CCW is most often stored as a liquid in impoundments next to the coal-fired power plants from which it came. These impoundments have been known to fail, like the coal ash disaster that occurred in December 2008 in Kingston, Tennessee, when a dike ruptured, releasing 1.1 billion gallons of toxic waste into the Emory River, contaminating the water and land.

But what about clean coal? "Clean coal" is a term with no clear-cut definition. As Fitzgerald (2012) explains, the concept of "clean coal" first appeared in the 1980s to refer to technologies designed to reduce sulfur dioxide and nitrogen oxide that were implemented in coal-fired power plants built after the passage of the Clean Air Act. Then, in the 2000s, when concerns about climate change were on the rise, the phrase "clean coal" began to be used by industry groups to "brand" **carbon capture and sequestration** (CCS) technologies that were being developed to reduce carbon emissions. In CCS, carbon dioxide waste from power plants and other point sources is captured and then transported to an underground storage site, where it is deposited so it will not enter the atmosphere. Still others within the coal industry use "clean coal" to simply refer to any coal-burning technology that is in any way an improvement over previous technologies. As Goodell (2012, p. 149) asserts, "'Clean coal' is not an actual invention, a physical thing—it is an advertising slogan. Like 'fat-free doughnuts' or 'interest-free loans,' 'clean coal' is a phrase that embodies the faith that there is an easy answer for every hard question in America today."

Whether it's accurate to call it "clean coal" or not, the possibility that CCS could have a large impact on carbon dioxide emissions is widely contested, and there are numerous concerns about the safety of such technologies. While some small-scale CCS demonstrations have been enacted, even CCS proponents admit that we are likely at least 20 years away from mainstream use of these technologies. Moreover, according to a study out of the Massachusetts Institute of Technology (MIT), the efficiency that would be lost from implementing CCS would actually require that 27% *more* coal be burned in order to generate the same amount of electricity as a conventional coal plant.

Environmental justice activists (see Lesson 10) fighting irresponsible mining practices in Central Appalachia vehemently assert there can be "no such thing as clean coal." They argue that even if there were a way to sequester most of the carbon dioxide from coal-fired power plants, the coal extraction process, described above, causes so much pollution and harm to coal-mining communities that coal can never truly be "clean." As activist Lorelei Scarboro told me during our interview for my (2013) book, "I believe in 'carbon sequestration': it's *already* sequestered, leave it there!"

Natural Gas

While coal-fired power plants have long been the dominant source of electricity across the world, natural gas is quickly becoming competitive with coal, particularly in the United States, which has been dubbed the "Saudi Arabia of natural gas." While in 2006 natural gas plants generated just over 20% of the electricity produced in the country, six years later they produced more than 30% of the nation's electricity. This growth in natural gas can be attributed to technological advances in gas extraction and to a regulatory loophole in the Energy Policy Act of 2005 that exempts the natural gas industry from a number of federal environmental laws, including the Safe Drinking Water Act, the Clean Air Act, and the Clean Water Act. These exemptions have made it possible for the industry to use a contentious technology known as **hydraulic fracturing**, or **"fracking,"** in combination with horizontal drilling, to access previously unrecoverable natural gas deposits trapped in shale formations that cover large portions of the United States. Hydraulic fracturing is also used to extract oil from shale formations.

Promoted as a "transition fuel" because of its lower carbon dioxide emissions than coal when burned, industry proponents often argue that natural gas can serve as a bridge between burning coal and generating electricity from renewable energy sources like wind and solar. The idea is that because burning natural gas is less carbon-intensive than coal, switching to natural gas now can mean lower carbon dioxide emissions in the short term while we continue to develop technologies to better harness and use renewable energy sources in the future. However, others argue that building infrastructure to increase our use of natural gas will likely hinder, not help, the transition to renewables. Because we are operating within a capitalist system, the sole purpose of which is to increase profits, companies that have invested in building new natural gas power plants, pipelines, and wells will have no incentive to cease their operations once the technologies for renewable energy advance enough for a "transition" to occur. Many also believe the environmental benefits of using natural gas instead of coal are overstated; a number of scientists argue that hydraulic fracturing releases enough methane "to more than cancel out any green-house gas benefits" that come from burning natural gas rather than coal (Zehner, 2012, p. 141). This assertion is supported by a recent study published in the *Proceedings of the National Academy of Sciences* by Scott M. Miller and colleagues, who found that the United States is actually emitting 50% more methane than previous Environmental Protection Agency estimates suggest, and one of the major sources of this added methane is from the extraction and processing of natural gas.

Many argue that the plentiful and cheap natural gas boom made possible by hydraulic fracturing comes at an incalculable cost to water resources and public health. In fact, internationally recognized ecologist and writer Sandra Steingraber (2012, p. 153) has gone so far as to describe fracking as "the tornado on the horizon that is poised to wreck ongoing efforts to create green economies, local agriculture, investments in renewable energy, and the ability to ride your bike along country roads."

So, what exactly *is* hydraulic fracturing? As noted above, it is a technology used in conjunction with horizontal drilling to extract natural gas from shale formations. A vertical well is first drilled down to the shale layer, which is typically between 6,000 to 10,000 feet beneath the surface. Then, horizontal wells are drilled, extending up to two miles out from the vertical well. After the drilling, the fracturing phase begins. Once reinforced with concrete, explosions are set off in the horizontal well through the use of "perforating guns" in order to create small holes through the casing and concrete into the shale formation. The high-pressure injection of fluids is the next phase in the process. Millions of gallons of fresh water are mixed with a proppant (typically sand) and a proprietary concoction of chemicals. The liquid mixture is injected at an extremely high pressure into the well bore, creating a dense array of fractures in the surrounding rock. The chemicals in the "fracking fluid" serve various purposes: killing bacteria, preventing corrosion and the buildup of deposits in the pipes, and reducing friction so that the solution can travel farther. The proppant in the mixture acts to hold the fractures open once they are created. These induced fractures provide the necessary permeability for the natural gas to migrate out of the pore space of the rock and up through the well so it can then be captured and processed.

What happens to the millions of gallons of chemical-laden fracking fluid after the process is complete? First, it is important to note that not all of the fluid is actually recovered; wastewater retrieval rates can vary anywhere between 10% and 90% in a given well. Secondly, the fluid that returns to the surface (called "produced water" by the industry) brings with it naturally occurring toxic substances, including gasses, liquids, and solids, which are present in underground oil and gas deposits. Benzene is one such naturally occurring toxin that can be transported to the surface via the fracking fluid. Benzene is a deadly chemical that causes damage to the bone marrow and can also cause leukemia. The fracking process can also unearth naturally occurring radioactive materials, such as uranium, thorium, radium, and lead-210, as well as heavy metals and salts.

And then, of course, the wastewater also contains the vast array of chemical additives discussed above. In an effort to identify the possible public health ramifications of these fracking chemicals, Colborn and colleagues (2010) compiled a list of 632 different chemicals used in natural gas operations. Of these 632 chemicals, only 353 were identified by Chemical Abstract Services numbers (thus, these were the only ones they could research). The authors conducted a review of the literature on each of these chemicals to determine the potential health impacts of these substances. They found that 75% have effects on the liver, respiratory system, gastrointestinal system, skin, eyes, and other sensory organs. Over 50% of the chemicals in their study cause chronic and long-term damage to the nervous system, 40% cause damage to the immune system, 46% harm the cardiovascular system and blood, 40% cause kidney damage, and more than 25% can cause cancer and mutations. Thirty-seven percent affect the endocrine system, which acts on a number of organ systems, including the reproductive system. Thus, many of the chemicals in the produced water are extremely harmful to human health (see Lesson 11).

Once the recoverable wastewater is removed from the well, it must go somewhere. While the industry has recently become better about recycling and reusing some of the wastewater for other wells, a large portion of this fluid is injected underground for "permanent" storage. As Horton (2012) found, there is increasing evidence that injecting wastewater underground is causing earthquakes in areas that have not historically experienced seismic activity. Furthermore, there are numerous accounts of surface water contamination from leaking on-site storage ponds or storage tanks, spills, or flood events (see Wilber, 2012 and Korfmacher et al., 2013). While industry denies the claims that wastewater could contaminate aquifers close to hydraulic fracturing sites, according to the EPA, increasing numbers of landowners have found toxic chemicals and other substances linked to natural gas extraction in their drinking water. As Bamberger and Oswald (2012) conclude, contaminated surface water can also enter the food chain through livestock, wildlife, and agricultural products that are consumed by humans.

Another risk associated with hydraulic fracturing is methane contamination of well water. In their study of 60 drinking-water wells in the Marcellus and Utica Shale regions of northeastern Pennsylvania and upstate New York, Osborn and colleagues (2011) found compelling evidence of methane contamination in drinking-water wells within 1 kilometer of "fracked" shale-gas wells. By analyzing the geochemistry of the methane found in the drinking-water wells and comparing it to the methane in the nearby shale-gas wells, the researchers determined that the carbon in the two methane sources had the same isotopic signature, leading them to conclude that the methane in the drinking-water wells did, in fact, migrate from the shale-gas wells. While the health effects of ingesting methane are not well understood, when mixed with air, the gas can become flammable and explosive. You may recall seeing a film clip of tap water being lit on fire. Methane is such a potent gas that it can even make *water* flammable. In addition to its flammable properties, when it is released into a confined space, methane can lead to asphyxiation, due to the fact that it replaces oxygen in the air. Thus, methane contamination of drinking water supplies can pose dangerous risks to local residents.

Nuclear

Recently, the home page of the Nuclear Energy Institute, the main trade group for the nuclear industry, featured a photograph of a white, heterosexual nuclear family happily holding hands in an open field beneath a big blue sky. The text accompanying the photo read, "NUCLEAR. Clean Air Energy." Nuclear energy is promoted as "green" and "clean" because it does not emit carbon dioxide while generating electricity. What nuclear proponents conveniently fail to mention is the fact that the waste from nuclear energy production includes radioactive toxins that remain *deadly* for tens of thousands of years, and that we have no permanent, or even semi-permanent, place to store this lethal waste. Right now in the United States, nuclear waste is stored on site at nuclear plants in chambers that were not designed for long-term storage. Furthermore, while nuclear reactors may not emit carbon dioxide, looking at the entire life-cycle of nuclear energy reveals a different picture of the nuclear industry's carbon footprint. Mining uranium emits greenhouse gasses (both carbon dioxide and methane), and the construction of nuclear plants—built with massive amounts of steel and concrete—produces tremendous amounts of carbon dioxide. When the externalities associated with nuclear energy production are accounted for, it is not accurate to dub this industry "green."

As shown in Figure 9–2, 19% of the electricity in the United States is generated from nuclear power plants. While a higher percentage of some other nations' energy portfolios is produced by nuclear (like France, where 75% of the electricity generated in 2012 was from nuclear power), the United States has more nuclear reactors and produces more electricity from nuclear plants than any other nation. There are currently 104 nuclear reactors operating in 65 power plants located in 31 states in the United States.

To produce electricity in a nuclear reactor, an isotope of either uranium or plutonium is split, which produces energy to heat water into steam, which then turns steam-driven turbine generators that create an electric current. While a tremendous amount of energy can be generated from a very small amount of fuel, the waste products of this process are radioactive and extremely poisonous. The 1979 Three Mile Island disaster (U.S.), the 1986 Chernobyl disaster (Ukraine), and the 2011 Fukushima Daiichi disaster (Japan) are all frightening reminders of the risks associated with nuclear energy production. In each of these events, a partial or complete meltdown of reactors caused radiation to be released into the air and water, producing varying degrees of illness and death among workers and residents in nearby areas.

The Fukushima Daiichi nuclear disaster poses an ongoing threat to Japan, and possibly the world. In March 2011, a 9.0 magnitude earthquake and resulting tsunami knocked out the Fukushima nuclear plant's power, causing the cooling system to fail, which led to the meltdown of three nuclear reactors. Decontamination of the plant and containment of the radioactivity have proven to be extremely difficult. In July 2013, more than two years after the disaster, it was discovered that radioactive water from the damaged reactors was leaking into the Pacific Ocean. The long-term effects and reach of this disaster will not be known for many years.

The effects of radiation exposure depend on the amount and type. Generally, the higher the amount of exposure, the sooner the effects will be seen, and the higher the likelihood of death. Radiation exposure causes DNA damage. This DNA damage can cause cell death, mutations, or cancer. Because radiation can affect genetic structure, that damage can be passed from generation to generation. As noted by Kuletz (1998), this effect is evidenced in the higher rates of birth defects seen among northern Ukrainian children born after the 1986 Chernobyl accident.

Plant workers and emergency personnel who help in the aftermath of a meltdown typically experience the greatest exposure and may suffer from acute radiation sickness. According to Christodouleas and colleagues (2011), bone marrow depression, severe gastrointestinal complications, and radiation dermatitis (burns) are among the major manifestations of radiation sickness. Furthermore, in areas surrounding a nuclear accident, nuclear reactor fallout may cause elevated long-term cancer risks, as well as reproductive failure and, as previously mentioned, birth and genetic defects.

While nuclear meltdowns are disastrous events with long-term consequences for many people, they are relatively rare, given the number of nuclear plants around the world (about 430 of them). However, the risk of such events occurring may increase, given the fact that the United States at present has no permanent disposal site for nuclear waste. Yucca Mountain in Nevada was the proposed site for a long-term geologic repository for spent nuclear fuel; however, this plan was cancelled by the Obama administration in 2009. The Yucca Mountain site was abandoned in large part due to heavy opposition from the state of Nevada and the Shoshone Nation. With no permanent repository, spent nuclear fuel is currently housed in temporary storage facilities at the nuclear power plants where the waste is produced. Those storage sites won't last forever, though, and something will need to be done with all of the radioactive, lethal waste the nuclear industry has produced and will continue to produce into the foreseeable future.

SOCIAL, ENVIRONMENTAL, AND PUBLIC HEALTH COSTS OF RENEWABLE SOURCES OF ENERGY

As shown in Figures 9–1 and 9–2, just over 12% of the electricity in the United States is provided by renewable energy sources, including hydroelectric (6.7%), wind (3.5%), and solar, geothermal, and biomass (which together provide about 1.9% of electricity). Does your university use any sources of renewable energy on campus? Student groups across the nation have been pushing their college and university administrators to make the transition to renewable forms of energy for heating and cooling their campuses. Ball State University in Muncie, Indiana, is one of the leaders in making this transition: in 2009, Ball State broke ground for the construction of the nation's largest ground-source, closed-loop district geothermal energy system. Once completed, the system will replace the university's four aging coal-fired boilers with geothermal energy to heat and cool 45 buildings on the 731-acre campus (see http://cms.bsu.edu/about/geothermal for more information about this exciting project).

As a whole, renewable energy sources tend to be better for the environment *and* better for public health. But can renewable energy save us? The short answer to this question is no, not if we do not find ways to reduce our society's overall demand for energy. In his study of the energy-use patterns of nations across the world over the past 50 years, Richard York (2012) found that the implementation of renewable energy production did *not* replace fossil-fuel use but rather increased the overall amount of energy consumed. The general pattern he found across the nations in his study was that for each unit of total energy use that came from non–fossil-fuel sources, less than one quarter of a unit of fossil-fuel energy use was displaced. This pattern was even more extreme in the case of electricity: For each unit of electricity that was generated by a non–fossil-fuel source, less than one tenth of a unit of fossil-fuel–generated electricity was displaced. Zehner (2012) also found similar results in his research. He terms this phenomenon the "Energy Boomerang Effect" and describes it thusly:

> Alternative-energy production expands energy supplies, placing downward pressure on prices, which spurs demand, entrenches energy-intensive modes of living, and finally brings us right back to where we started: high demand and so-called insufficient supply. In short, we create an energy boomerang—the harder we throw, the harder it will come back to hit us on the head. (p. 172)

In other words, creating more energy creates more consumption.

A related phenomenon, which is associated with energy efficiency, is called the "**Jevons Paradox**." Increasing efficiency has the effect of making a resource less expensive to use, which then can actually cause an *increase* in the consumption of that resource. Thus, while energy efficiency can be an important aspect of decreasing energy use, in some cases it can actually have the opposite effect and increase energy consumption.

In the remainder of this section, I will describe the main sources of renewable energy, including the benefits and drawbacks of each. While there are fewer environmental and public health problems associated with these energy sources (which is the reason for the shorter descriptions), there are still a number of hidden costs associated with renewable energy sources, particularly solar.

Solar

There is a tremendous amount of energy emitted from the sun. Environmentalists, such as the president of the Earth Policy Institute, Lester Brown, often cite the statistic that the amount of solar energy striking the Earth every hour is equivalent to what it would take to power the world for an entire year. However, actually capturing this energy is another story. Based on calculations using the installed costs for existing solar projects in California, Zehner (2012, p. 9) calculates that building enough solar panels to power the planet would cost about $1.4 quadrillion, which is about 100 times the GDP of the United States. Furthermore,

> Mining, smelting, processing, shipping, and fabricating the panels and their associated hardware would yield about 149,100 megatons of CO_2. And everyone would have to move to the desert, otherwise transmission losses would make the plan unworkable. (Zehner, 2012, p. 9)

As Zehner (2012) argues, another hidden cost of solar involves the toxins associated with the construction and disposal of solar photovoltaics. The manufacturing process emits hexafluoroethane (C_2F_6), nitrogen trifluoride (NF_3), and sulfur hexafluoride (SF_6), which are all greenhouse gasses that are more than 10,000 times more potent than carbon dioxide.

As well as emitting extremely potent greenhouse gasses, solar photovoltaics are manufactured using highly toxic materials. A solar panel has a usable lifespan of only about 20 to 25 years, and once that limit has been reached, it must be disposed of. According to Zehner (2012), if the panel is laid to rest in a landfill, the toxic chemicals in the panel can seep into groundwater supplies, or if it is incinerated, the chemicals can contaminate the air and waterways.

Geothermal

While solar panels capture the energy from the sun that hits the Earth's surface, geothermal systems capture the heat from within the Earth's crust by pumping liquid through a series of underground tubes. As in the case of Ball State University, geothermal systems can be used to heat buildings and can also cool them by reversing the process and "sinking" heat into the ground. Smaller-scale geothermal systems constructed for heating and cooling buildings and individual houses can be much more energy efficient than traditional furnace and air conditioner systems. They do, however, require some electricity to pump liquid through the buried tubes. Additionally, these types of systems require that there be a plot of land where the tubing can be buried. Thus, as Zehner (2012) reveals, household geothermal systems tend not to work for more energy-efficient housing designs like multiunit apartments, condominiums, or clustered housing units.

Larger-scale geothermal systems can also be used to produce electric power. Because geothermal is a constant source of energy, it is one of the few renewable energy sources that is considered a good substitute for coal. However, there are limited places where large-scale geothermal plants can be built and be economically viable. As Zehner (2012) points out, they need to be in locations where the Earth's crust is especially hot or where there are naturally occurring hot springs. Drilling deeper to construct engineered geothermal systems in other locations is possible, he notes, but there is a high risk of earthquakes associated with these systems.

Hydroelectricity and Megadams

While industrial-scale hydroelectricity production is a powerful renewable resource with low greenhouse gas emissions, it does have significant ecological and social costs. Habitat fragmentation, changes in flow rates and silt deposits, and loss of water quality are all problems associated with hydroelectric dams that can have serious consequences for vulnerable species (Butler and Wuerthner, 2012). One example Butler and Wuerthner (2012) give is the network of dams constructed on the Columbia River in the Pacific Northwest. These dams impeded the migration of wild salmon and had far-reaching impacts on the health of this species. In addition to the effects on wildlife, throughout the world, dams have displaced millions of indigenous people (see Lesson 19) from their ancestral lands.

Biomass

Referring to a number of different fuels, such as wood, energy crops, construction waste, animal waste, and garbage, biomass is yet another renewable form of energy that some have touted as a "green" solution. However, as with the other forms of energy, there are hidden costs. Biomass burning generates dangerous air pollution. Physician and medical groups have made statements against biomass incinerators, citing numerous health risks. For instance, the American Academy of Family Physicians states, "Current research . . . indicates that the burning of poultry litter and wood wastes . . . leads to increased risk of premature death and serious chronic illness" (Vick, 2011, p. 4). The American Lung Association supports this sentiment, stating, "Burning biomass could lead to significant increases in emissions of nitrogen oxides, particulate matter and sulfur dioxide and have severe impacts on the health of children, older adults, and people with lung diseases" (Vick, 2011, p. 5).

Wind

Wind is arguably one of the most promising, and least harmful, renewable energy sources. However, wind technologies are, unfortunately, also heavily reliant on fossil fuels. As Zehner (2012, p. 42) states, "Wind is renewable. Turbines are not." The unpredictability of wind is also a challenge. To maintain a continual supply of electricity, fossil-fuel plants have to be fired up to fill in the gaps in supply. Thus, it would be more accurate to think of wind as a "hybrid" energy source rather than one that is truly "renewable."

Critics of wind often cite the number of birds that are killed by wind turbines. However, the number of birds killed by wind turbines is actually quite small when compared to other causes of death. As Zehner (2012, p. 39) argues, the estimated 2.3 birds killed each year by one wind turbine (multiplied by 10,000 turbines, that is still only 23,000 birds a year) doesn't even come close to the 4 million birds that are killed from flying into communication towers each year or the "hundreds of millions" that are killed annually by house cats and *windows*!

THE HOPE FOR CHANGE

In the previous sections, I described many of the hidden and not-so-hidden environmental and public health costs of energy production across the major sources. However, I want to clarify that through presenting these costs, I am not implying that we should abandon the push to move toward renewable energy sources. Rather, what I am suggesting is that we also need to be spending a *significant* amount of effort to develop solutions that will *reduce* our overall use of energy. Our current rate of energy consumption is completely unsustainable (see Lesson 20). However, reducing energy consumption does not have to mean reducing our quality of life; to the contrary, it might actually improve it.

A great deal of research (for instance, Rosa, 1997) has established that high levels of energy use, and the associated contribution to carbon dioxide emissions, are *not* closely connected with societal well-being as measured by various objective social conditions, such as the mental and physical health of the general public. In fact, according to the New Economics Foundation, there are quite a number of so-called "less-developed nations" where people live long lives and report high levels of life satisfaction, while also having relatively small ecological footprints. The **"Happy Planet Index" (HPI)**, developed by the New Economics Foundation, is way of measuring the well-being of a nation's citizenry that stands as an alternative to the purely economic measure of GDP (see Lesson 20). The HPI calculates "happy life years" for nations using self-reported life satisfaction levels and life expectancy and dividing that value by the per capita ecological footprint of the nation. According to environmental sociologists Richard York, Christina Ergas, Eugene A. Rosa, and Thomas Dietz (2011), most of the nations with the highest HPI values are in Latin America, with Costa Rica scoring the highest on the HPI. At 114th out of 143 nations, the United States ranks quite low on the Index. Interestingly, between 1990 and 2005, as the ecological footprints of China and India rose, both of these nations experienced declines in their "happy life years." Thus, by extension, decreasing our energy consumption may, in fact, lead to greater happiness.

One example of this within the United States can be seen in the levels of satisfaction among different types of commuters. In a study of individuals in Portland, Oregon, who commuted using different forms of transit (biking, walking, car, and public transportation), Smith (2013) found that those who commuted to work via the "active modes" of biking and walking reported the highest levels of well-being, even after controlling for other factors, such as distance of commute and income. Smith's study reveals an inverse relationship between the amount of energy consumed during one's daily commute and the level of happiness that person experiences with his or her commute.

While individual lifestyle changes can have some impacts on a society's energy consumption levels, given the fact that residential energy usage is just one sector within the energy landscape, larger systemic changes are necessary in order to significantly reduce overall energy consumption. In 2011, the commercial and industrial sectors together consumed 61.6% of the electricity produced in the United States. Take one look at the Las Vegas "Strip" at night, and it is incredibly obvious that commercial businesses waste a lot of electricity—*a lot*. Thus, for any real reductions in energy consumption to occur, change needs to be implemented at a policy level (see Lesson 3).

King (2012, p. 237) argues that there are two main system-level changes that could stop the expansion of energy consumption: (1) instituting a cap on energy generation ("capping the grid") and (2) attaching a price tag to the external costs of energy production, especially carbon emissions. He maintains that by establishing a cap on the energy grid and levying a carbon tax, "the oldest, dirtiest plants would become uneconomic, making way for cleaner generation." This would also address the problem that York (2012) and Zehner (2012) describe, whereby renewable energy does not displace fossil-fuel use but rather expands the overall available energy (which then leads to increased consumption). Through implementing what is essentially a moratorium on the growth of the energy sector, prices would increase due to scarcity, "ushering in the largest conservation and efficiency movement ever seen" (King, 2012, p. 232). In order to protect lower-income and vulnerable populations, a sliding rate scale could be implemented based on income, much in the same way that our income tax system works.

How Do We Get There?

One of the greatest barriers we face is shifting national and international energy policy debates away from asking, "How can we reduce our carbon footprint while still maintaining our overpowered lifestyles?" to the more important question of, "How can we reduce our overall energy demand?" In other words, there needs to be a transformation in the way we are framing how we think about our energy future.

As ordinary citizens, what can we do to contribute to this change in societal mindset? An important first step is to *talk about* this reality with friends, family, neighbors, classmates, and co-workers. Tell them about the environmental and public health consequences of our addiction to an ever-expanding energy supply. And then, importantly, discuss the many ways that quality of life can actually be *increased* by reducing our energy consumption patterns.

Taking it a step further, we can seek out environmental groups (see Lesson 16), such as the Post Carbon Institute (www.postcarbon.org), that are advocating for decreasing overall energy production and consumption, rather than simply increasing renewable energy. Find out what you can do to participate in their advocacy actions and events. Organize a letter-writing campaign to your representatives asking their support for placing a cap on the energy grid. Write a letter to the editor of your local newspaper; organize a teach-in on your college campus; create a Facebook page or Twitter account or use some other social media tool to disseminate the facts about energy consumption and environmental destruction. In all that you do, always remember to talk about possible solutions (some of which were discussed in this chapter).

One very important thing to remember is that, as Zehner (2012) discusses in his book *Green Illusions: The Dirty Secrets of Clean Energy and the Future of Environmentalism*, people are far more receptive to change if they do not feel that they will have to make major sacrifices. One of the most important ways that you can advocate for instituting a cap on the energy grid is by identifying all of the quality-of-life *gains* that could be achieved by powering down our society. For instance, if we had limits on the amount of energy we could use in a given day, we would likely make different choices about what we do with our evenings. Instead of watching television to unwind after work or school, we might instead choose to play outside, garden, make art, ride our bikes, go for a run or a walk, cook, or join a sports team. Furthermore, it is likely that far fewer of us would feel obligated to take our work home with us in the evenings, leaving more time for family, friends, and hobbies. We might also make different decisions about where and how we live. Rather than choosing to live in a suburban community with a 30-minute car commute into work every day, we might instead choose to live in a smaller home within biking or walking distance of work. And, as noted above, there is evidence that people who commute using their own power (walking or biking) enjoy their daily commutes significantly more than those who commute via single-passenger cars. In other words, powering down our lives would likely mean living happier, more socially integrated and physically active lives. That message *really* needs to be heard.

SOURCES

American Lung Association. 2011. *Toxic Air: The Case for Cleaning Up Coal-Fired Power Plants*. Washington, D.C.: American Lung Association. Retrieved April 30, 2013, from http://www.lung.org/assets/documents/healthy-air/toxic-air-report.pdf.

American Petroleum Institute. 2009. *Hydraulic Fracturing Operations—Well Construction and Integrity Guidelines*. API Guidance Document HF1, First Edition. Washington, D.C.: API Publishing Services. Retrieved April 29, 2013, from http://www.shalegas.energy.gov/resources/HF1.pdf.

Bamberger, Michelle, and Robert E. Oswald. 2012. "Impacts of Gas Drilling on Human and Animal Health." *New Solutions: A Journal of Environmental and Occupational Health Policy* 22(1):51–77.

Bell, Shannon Elizabeth. 2013. *Our Roots Run Deep As Ironweed: Appalachian Women and the Fight for Environmental Justice*. Urbana and Chicago: University of Illinois Press.

BP. 2012. *Statistical Review of World Energy*. Retrieved April 27, 2012, from www.bp.com/statisticalreview.

Braun, Yvonne A. 2006. "Large Dams as Development: Restructuring Access to Natural Resources in Lesotho." In Andrew K. Jorgenson and Edward L. Kick, eds. *Globalization and the Environment*, pp. 151–171. Leiden, NL: Brill Press.

Bullis, Kevin. 2009. "Q & A: Steven Chu." *MIT Technology Review*. May 14. Retrieved May 4, 2013, from http://www.technologyreview.com/news/413475/q-a-steven-chu/.

Butler, Tom, and George Wuerthner, eds. 2012. *Energy: Overdevelopment and the Delusion of Endless Growth*. Post Carbon Institute/Watershed Media.

Button, Gregory. 2010. *Disaster Culture: Knowledge and Uncertainty in the Wake of Human and Environmental Catastrophe*. Walnut Creek, CA: Left Coast Press.

Carolan, Michael. 2013. *Society and the Environment: Pragmatic Solutions to Ecological Issues*. Philadelphia, PA: Westview Press.

CDC (Centers for Disease Control and Prevention). 2013. "Facts about Benzene." Emergency Preparedness and Response. Retrieved April 30, 2013, from http://www.bt.cdc.gov/agent/benzene/basics/facts.asp.

Christodouleas, John P., Robert D. Forrest, Christopher G. Ainsley, Zelig Tochner, Stephen M. Hahn, and Eli Glatstein. 2011. "Short-Term and Long-Term Health Risks of Nuclear-Power-Plant Accidents." *New England Journal of Medicine* 364(24):2334–2341.

Colborn, Theo, Carol Kwiatkowski, Kim Schultz, and Mary Bachran. 2010. "Natural Gas Operations from a Public Health Perspective." *Human and Ecological Risk Assessment* 17:1039–1056.

Davies, Lincoln L. 2011. "Beyond Fukushima: Disasters, Nuclear Energy, and Energy Law." *Brigham Young University Law Review* 2011:1937–1989.

EIA (Energy Information Administration). 2011a. "Natural Gas." International Energy Outlook 2011. Retrieved April 26, 2013, from http://www.eia.gov/forecasts/ieo/nat_gas.cfm.

———. 2011b. "Shale gas: Hydraulic fracturing and environmental issues." International Energy Outlook 2011. Retrieved April 29, 2013, from http://www.eia.gov/forecasts/ieo/hei.cfm.

———. 2012a. Annual Energy Review. Table 8.2a. Electricity Net Generation: Total (All Sectors), 1949–2011. Retrieved April 26, 2013, from http://www.eia.gov/totalenergy/data/annual/showtext.cfm?t=ptb0802a.

———. 2012b. "Horizontal drilling boosts Pennsylvania's natural gas production." *Today in Energy*. May 23. Retrieved April 28, 2013, from http://www.eia.gov/todayinenergy/detail.cfm?id=6390.

———. 2012c. Annual Energy Review. Table 8.9 Electricity End Use, 1949–2011. Retrieved May 4, 2013, from http://www.eia.gov/totalenergy/data/annual/index.cfm#electricity.

_____. 2013a. Overview Data for the United States. Retrieved April 26, 2013, from http://www.eia.gov/countries/country-data.cfm?fips=US&trk=m.

_____. 2013b. *April 2013 Monthly Energy Review.* Table 7.2a. Electricity Net Generation: Total (All Sectors). Retrieved April 26, 2013, from http://www.eia.gov/totalenergy/data/monthly/#electricity.

_____. 2013c. "Pennsylvania natural gas production rose 69% in 2012 despite reduced drilling activity." *Today in Energy.* March 21. Retrieved April 27, 2013, from http://www.eia.gov/todayinenergy/detail.cfm?id=10471.

_____. 2013d. "How many nuclear power plants are in the U.S. and where are they located?" Frequently Asked Questions. Retrieved May 3, 2013, from http://www.eia.gov/tools/faqs/faq.cfm?id=207&t=3.

_____. 2013e. "What are the products and uses of petroleum?" Frequently Asked Questions. Retrieved May 4, 2013, from http://www.eia.gov/tools/faqs/faq.cfm?id=41&t=6.

_____. n.d. Total Primary Energy Consumption. International Energy Statistics. Retrieved May 4, 2013, from http://www.eia.gov/cfapps/ipdbproject/IEDIndex3.cfm?tid=44&pid=44&aid=2.

EPA (U.S. Environmental Protection Agency). 1998. "Study of Hazardous Air Pollutant Emissions from Electric Utility Steam Generating Units—Final Report to Congress." February 1998. 453/R-98-004a. Available: http://www.epa.gov/ttncaaa1/t3/reports/eurtc1.pdf.

_____. 2005. "U.S. EPA Toxics Release Inventory Reporting Year 2005 Public Data Release." Section B. http://epa.gov.tri/tridata/tri05.pdfs/eReport.pdf.

_____. 2010. "EPA Releases Results of Pavillion, Wyo. Water Testing." News Release from Region 8. Sept. 1. Retrieved April 30, 2013, from http://yosemite.epa.gov/opa/admpress.nsf/20ed1dfa1751192c8525735900400c30/1b6ae692cfeeab50852577920066afd4!OpenDocument

_____. 2012a. How does electricity affect the environment? Retrieved October 17, 2012, from http://www.epa.gov/cleanenergy/energy-and-you/affect/index.html.

_____. 2012b. "Oil and Gas Production Wastes." Radiation Protection. Retrieved April 30, 2013, from http://www.epa.gov/radiation/tenorm/oilandgas.html.

Federal On-Scene Coordinator. 2011. "Federal On-Scene Coordinator Report on *Deepwater Horizon.*" Retrieved May 4, 2013, from http://www.uscg.mil/foia/docs/dwh/fosc_dwh_report.pdf.

Fitzgerald, Jenrose. 2012. "The Messy Politics of 'Clean Coal': The Shaping of a Contested Term in Appalachia's Energy Debate." *Organization & Environment* 25(4):437–451.

Geredien, Ross. 2009. "Assessing the Extent of Mountaintop Removal in Appalachia: an Analysis using Vector Data." Technical Report for Appalachian Voices, Boone, NC. Retrieved May 20, 2010, at: http://ilovemountains.org/reclamation-fail/mining-extent 2009/Assessing_the_Extent_of_Mountaintop_Removal_in_Appalachia.pdf.

Goodell, Jeff. 2012. "The False Promise of 'Clean' Coal." In Tom Butler and George Wuerthner, eds. *Energy: Overdevelopment and the Delusion of Endless Growth,* pp. 149–150. Post Carbon Institute/Watershed Media.

Hansen, James. 2012. "Coal: The Greatest Threat to Civilization." In Tom Butler and George Wuerthner, eds. *Energy: Overdevelopment and the Delusion of Endless Growth,* p. 61. Post Carbon Institute/Watershed Media.

Horton, S. 2012. "Disposal of Hydrofracking Waste Fluid by Injection into Subsurface Aquifers Triggers Earthquake Swarm in Central Arkansas with Potential for Damaging Earthquake." *Seismological Research Letters* 83(2):250–260.

IAEA (International Atomic Energy Agency). 2013. "Nuclear Share of Electricity Generation in 2012." Power Reactor Information System. Retrieved May 3, 2013, from http://www.iaea.org/PRIS/WorldStatistics/NuclearShareofElectricityGeneration. aspx.

International Energy Agency. 2011. World Energy Outlook 2011: Special Report: Are We Entering the Golden Age of Gas? Paris, France: International Energy Agency.

King, Robert E. 2012. "Cap the Grid." In Tom Butler and George Wuerthner, eds. *Energy: Overdevelopment and the Delusion of Endless Growth*, pp. 235–237. Post Carbon Institute/Watershed Media.

Korfmacher, Katrina Smith, Walter A. Jones, Samantha L. Malone, and Leon F. Vinci. 2013. "Public Health and High Volume Hydraulic Fracturing." *New Solutions: A Journal of Environmental and Occupational Health Policy* 23(1):13–31.

MIT. 2007. "The Future of Coal." Cambridge, MA: Massachusetts Institute of Technology. Retrieved May 2, 2013, from http://web.mit.edu/coal/The_Future_ of_Coal.pdf.

Miller, Scot M., Steven C. Wofsy, Anna M. Michalak, Eric A. Kort, Arlyn E. Andrews, Sebastien C. Biraud, Edward J. Dlugokencky, Janusz Eluszkiewicz, Marc L. Fischer, Greet Janssens-Maenhout, Ben R. Miller, John B. Miller, Stephen A. Montzka, Thomas Nehrkorn, and Colm Sweeney. 2013. "Anthropogenic emissions of methane in the United States." *Proceedings of the National Academy of Sciences.* doi:10.1073/pnas.1314392110.

NEI (Nuclear Energy Institute). 2013a. Home page. Retrieved May 3, 2013, from http://www.nei.org/.

——. 2013b. "Storage of Used Nuclear Fuel." Retrieved May 4, 2013, from http://www.nei.org/Key-Issues/nuclearwastedisposal/Storage-of-Used-Nuclear-Fuel.

NRC (U.S. Nuclear Regulatory Commission). 2012. "High Radiation Doses." Retrieved May 3, 2013, from http://www.nrc.gov/about-nrc/radiation/health-effects/high-rad-doses.html.

Orrego, Juan Pablo. 2012. "The False Solution of Megadams." In Tom Butler and George Wuerthner, eds. *Energy: Overdevelopment and the Delusion of Endless Growth,* pp. 157–159. Post Carbon Institute/Watershed Media.

Osborn, Stephen G., Avner Vengosh, Nathaniel R. Warner, and Robert B. Jackson. 2011. "Methane contamination of drinking water accompanying gas-well drilling and hydraulic fracturing." *Proceedings of the National Academy of Sciences.* 108(20).

Palmer, M. A., E. S. Bernhardt, W. H. Schlesinger, K. N. Eshleman, E. Foufoula-Georgiou, M. S. Hendryx, A. D. Lemly, G. E. Likens, O. L. Loucks, M. E. Power, P. S. White, and P. R. Wilcock. 2010. "Mountaintop Mining Consequences." *Science* 327(5962):148–149.

Physicians for Social Responsibility. 2009. "Coal-Fired Power Plants: Understanding the Health Costs of a Dirty Energy Source." Available: http://www.psr.org/ assets/pdfs/coal-fired-power-plants.pdf.

Rodrigue, Jean-Paul, and Claude Comtois. 2013. Chapter 8 in *The Geography of Transport Systems,* 3rd ed. New York: Routledge.

Rosa, Eugene A. 1997. "Cross National Trends in Fossil Fuel Consumption, Societal Well-Being and Carbon Releases." In Paul C. Stern, Thomas Dietz, Vernon W. Ruttan, Robert H. Socolow, and James L. Sweeney, eds. *Environmentally Significant Consumption: Research Directions,* pp. 100–109. Washington, D.C.: National Academy Press.

Rosa, Eugene A., G. E. Machlis, and K. M. Keating. 1988. "Energy and Society." *Annual Review of Sociology* 146:149–172.

Silicon Valley Toxics Coalition. 2009. "Toward a Just and Sustainable Solar Energy Industry." White Paper. Retrieved May 4, 2013, from http://svtc.org/wp- content/uploads/Silicon_Valley_Toxics_Coalition_-_Toward_a_Just_and_Sust.pdf.

Smith, Oliver. 2013. "Commute Well-Being among Bicycle, Transit, and Car Users in Portland, Oregon." (Poster) Transportation Research Board 92nd Annual Meeting, Washington, D.C. January 14, 2013. Retrieved April 19, 2013, from http://bikeportland.org/wpcontent/uploads/2013/01/TRB_Osmith_55x44.pdf

Solomon, S., D. Qin, M. Manning, Z. Chen, M. Marquis, K. B. Averyt, M. Tignor, and H. L. Miller, eds. 2007. Climate Change 2007: The Physical Science Basis. Contribution of Working Group I to the Fourth Assessment Report of the Intergovernmental Panel on Climate Change. Cambridge, UK, and New York: Cambridge University Press.

Steingraber, Sandra. 2012. "The Whole Fracking Enchilada. In Tom Butler and George Wuerthner, Eds. Energy: Overdevelopment and the Delusion of Endless Growth, pp. 153–154. Post Carbon Institute/Watershed Media.

Union of Concerned Scientists. 2012. "Cars, Trucks, and Oil Use." Retrieved April 26, 2013, from http://www.ucsusa.org/clean_vehicles/why-clean-cars/oil-use/.

Vick, Therese. 2011. "Second Opinion: The Medical Profession Diagnoses Biomass Incineration." Blue Ridge Environmental Defense League. Retrieved May 4, 2013, from http://wiregrass-ace.org/linked/second-opinion.pdf.

Wilber, Tom. 2012. Under the Surface: Fracking, Fortunes, and the Fate of the Marcellus Shale. Ithaca, NY: Cornell University Press.

World Nuclear Association. 2012. "Nuclear Power in the World Today." Retrieved May 4, 2013, from http://www.world-nuclear.org/info/Current-and-Future-Generation/Nuclear-Power-in-the-World-Today/#.UYSYecrmjoA.

York, Richard. 2012. "Do Alternative Energy Sources Displace Fossil Fuels?" Nature Climate Change 2(6):441–443.

York, Richard, Christina Ergas, Eugene A. Rosa, and Thomas Dietz. 2011. "It's a Material World: Trends in Material Extraction in China, India, Indonesia, and Japan." Nature and Culture 6(2):103–122.

Zehner, Ozzie. 2012. Green Illusions: The Dirty Secrets of Clean Energy and the Future of Environmentalism. Lincoln, NE: University of Nebraska Press.

Part 3

SOME SOCIAL CONSEQUENCES
OF ENVIRONMENTAL DISRUPTION

10

Environmental Inequality and Environmental Justice

Michael Mascarenhas

Social movement organization relief center in the Lower Ninth Ward following Hurricane Katrina, New Orleans, Louisiana.

Photo by Ken Gould.

The publication of Rachel Carson's groundbreaking work, *Silent Spring*, in 1962 drew public attention to the widespread chemical contamination of both our environments and bodies. "For the first time in the history of the world," Carson wrote, "every human being is now subjected to contact with dangerous chemicals, from the moment of conception until death" (p. 15). Fifty years later, chemical and other hazardous forms of environmental pollution permeate every aspect of our modern *risk society* (see Lesson 2). Most of us are unaware that we are surrounded by harmful chemicals in our homes, at work, and at play, and that we carry the legacy of our chemical dependence in our bodies.

Consider the following data compiled by Sylvia Tesh in her 2000 book *Uncertain Hazards: Environmental Activists and Scientific Proof*:

Nearly 70,000 chemical products have been introduced since World War II and 1,500 new ones are added each year. Total U.S. production of chemicals amounts to over 300 million tons annually. In 1994, 22,744 facilities released 2.26 billion pounds of listed toxic chemicals into the environment. In 1994 approximately 62 million people . . . lived in countries where air quality levels exceeded the national air quality standards for at least one of the six principal pollutants. In 1995 over 40 million Americans were served by drinking water systems with lead levels exceeding the regulatory action level. By September 1995, a total of 1,374 sites had been listed or proposed for listing [on the Superfund's National Priority List] . . . In addition, EPA had identified 40,094 potentially hazardous waste sites across the nation (p. 4).

As a result of this environmental legacy, low levels of many toxic chemicals are detectable in North Americans no matter what their age. The 2006 report by Environmental Defence on pollution in Canadian families detected 46 chemicals in 13 family members (six adults and seven children). These chemicals included 5 PBDEs (polybrominated diphenyl ethers), 13 PCBs (polychlorinated biphenyls), 5 PFCs (perfluorinated chemicals), 9 organochlorine pesticides, 4 organophosphate insecticide metabolites, 5 PAHs (polycyclic aromatic hydrocarbons), and 5 heavy metals. In total, 38 carcinogens, 23 hormone disruptors, 12 respiratory toxins, 38 reproductive/developmental toxins, and 19 neurotoxins were detected in the study volunteers (Environmental Defence, 2006, p. 59).

These and other sources of environmental disruption have resulted in increased exposure and decreased health for many people. For example, asthma incidence has increased dramatically over the past decade, and the lifetime incidence of breast cancer is now one in eight (Brown, 2007). According to the National Cancer Institute (2012), incidence rates of some cancers are rising, including melanoma of the skin, non-Hodgkin's lymphoma, leukemia, myeloma, childhood cancer, and cancers of the kidney and renal pelvis, thyroid, pancreas, liver and intrahepatic bile duct, testis, and esophagus.

But in addition to the growing concern regarding the amount of pollution in our environment and bodies is the concern of environmental inequity and justice. In other words, how is this pollution distributed throughout society? This chapter introduces the **environmental justice** framework as a theoretical and methodological approach to examining the uneven ways in which pollution and other environmental hazards are distributed among particular social groups, communities, and regions (see also Lesson 14). The chapter pays close attention to the history of the environmental justice movement and debates within this burgeoning social science discipline. Lastly, this chapter also examines the impacts of recent environmental reforms and asks how recent policy changes to environmental laws, regulations, and policies influence environmental inequity and justice.

DEFINING ENVIRONMENTAL JUSTICE

Over the past several decades, public health researchers, activists, and policymakers have devoted a great deal of attention to understanding the social dimensions of environmental injustice: the notion that sources of environmental pollution are unevenly distributed among different social groups or categories. More recently, some scholars and health researchers have begun to explore how recent changes in government policies in the form of deregulation, austerity measures, commonsense policies, and privatization are woven through and shape contemporary environmental injustices. This recent change in governance, often referred to as **neoliberalism**, supports the efficiency of free markets, free trade, and the expansion of private property. Through Canadian examples, this lesson explores the intersection between neoliberalism and environmental justice. Those concerned with environmental injustices have focused their energies on two claims regarding the relationship between environmental pollution and race and class. The first claim posits that racial and ethnic minorities, low-income people, and indigenous peoples are more likely to live close to hazardous environmental facilities and that their communities continue to be the targets for the siting and growth of "dirty industries." The second claim argues that with an increased public awareness regarding the relationship between environmental pollution and health problems—largely born from high-profile cases such as Love Canal, New York; Three Mile Island, Pennsylvania; Woburn, Massachusetts; and Warren County, North Carolina—it has become increasingly difficult to site hazardous or dirty industries in middle-class white communities. It is the premise of the lesson that neoliberalism has contributed to both the political and economic justifications for the siting and growth of dirty industries in minority, indigenous, and low-income communities.

Regarding the uneven distribution of environmental pollution, Sylvia Tesh (2000) wrote, "in 1993 over 40 percent of the Hispanic population, and over 25 percent of the Asian/Pacific population was exposed to poor air quality" (p. 4). Moreover, "Three out of every five Black and Hispanic Americans live in communities with uncontrolled toxic waste sites" (p. 4). In a national-level study using 2000 Census data and the location of commercial hazardous waste facilities, Robert Bullard and his colleagues (2007, p. xi) concluded, "significant racial and socioeconomic disparities persist in the distribution of the nation's commercial hazardous waste facilities." A key finding of their report (2007, p. xi) was that "race continues to be an independent predictor of where hazardous wastes are located," stronger "than income, education and other socioeconomic indicators." Their report (2007, p. xii) concluded, "African Americans, Hispanics/Latinos and Asian Americans/Pacific Islanders alike are disproportionately burdened by hazardous wastes in the U.S."

In her 1998 ethnography *The Tainted Desert: Environmental Ruin in the American West*, Valerie Kuletz wrote that a nuclear landscape encompasses most of the Southwest—"much of New Mexico, Nevada, southeastern California, and parts of Arizona, Utah, Colorado, and Texas. (To the north, in the West, we can also add parts of the state of Washington and Idaho)" (p. 10). This area, she wrote, includes "large land masses for uranium mining and milling, the testing of high-tech weaponry, and waste repositories" (p. 7) that include weapons stockpiles and nuclear production facilities. This region is also "home to the majority of *land-based* American Indians today on the North American continent" (p. 11).

In recent years the rural center that makes up the Sarnia-Windsor-London triangle in southern Ontario expanded the capacity of the region's landfill as well as approved a 4-million-gallon-per-day sewage treatment plant (for the city of London). These new waste industries are in addition to numerous other landfills that dot the countryside; heavy agricultural use, and a highway of electromagnetic towers (and wires) also span this area, not to mention heavy industry, particularly in the Windsor and Sarnia area. It is also home to eight First Nations territories.

I cite these data partly to make the reader aware of the extent of environmental pollution but also to illustrate the numerous environmental conditions that this pollution affects. Environmental justice activists and scholars present a broad concept of the environment in which we live, work, learn, and play. The environment from this perspective is not a people-free biophysical system but rather the ambient and immediate surroundings of everyday life activities and relationships linking people with their immediate environs. These include, but are not limited to, residential environments, working environments, and recreation environments. Turner and Wu (2002, p. 1) described the environment as encompassing "the air people breathe walking down a city or country street, the water drawn from their taps or wells, the chemicals a worker is exposed to in an industrial plant or strawberry field, and the forests people visit to hike, extract mushrooms, and engage in spiritual practice." This conception of the environment links labor and public health, recreation and housing, and culture and history. Furthermore, this understanding of the environment breaks the boundaries between nature and society, work environments and open spaces, and urban and rural places.

The U.S. Environmental Protection Agency (EPA, 2007, p. 1) defines *environmental justice* as follows:

> [t]he fair treatment and meaningful involvement of all people regardless of race, color, national origin, or income with respect to the development, implementation, and enforcement of environmental laws, regulations, and policies.

Environmental inequality (or *environmental injustice*), then, refers to a situation in which a specific group is disproportionately affected by negative environmental conditions brought on by unequal laws, regulations, and policies. A specific form of environmental inequality is the phenomenon of **environmental racism**, or the deliberate targeting of communities of color for toxic waste facilities, the official sanctioning of poisons and pollutants in minority communities, and the systematic exclusion of people of color from leadership roles in decisions regarding the production of environmental conditions that affect their lives and livelihoods.

HISTORY OF ENVIRONMENTAL JUSTICE

Over years of painstaking research and emotionally charged activism, environmental justice scholars have been able to link questions of social justice, equity, rights, and people's quality of life. Originally forged from a synthesis of the civil rights movements, antitoxic and waste campaigns (often referred to as NIMBY or not-in-my-back-yard), and environmentalism, environmental justice has focused on the class and racial inequalities of pollution. The growth of tragic and high-profile cases like Love Canal and Woburn has increased the publicity and power of this largely grassroots movement. A feature-length movie, *A Civil Action*, starring John Travolta, was made about the Woburn case. Furthermore, such publicity later inspired legislation in the United States that identified hazardous waste sites—commonly known as "Superfund sites"—and established a protocol for remediation. In 1994, President Clinton signed Executive Order 12898, charging all federal agencies with integrating environmental justice concerns into their operations.

Beginning in the early 1970s, a substantial body of literature began to emerge in the United States documenting the existence of environmental inequalities among particular social groups, specifically minority, aboriginal, and poor communities In 1982 a major protest was staged in Warren County, North Carolina, over a PCB landfill in a majority African American town. Several hundred protesters (many of them high-profile civil rights activists) were arrested, and the issue of environmental justice was thrust into the national spotlight and onto the political agenda. In 1983, one year after the Warren County protests, the U.S. General Accounting Office conducted a study of several Southern states and found that a disproportionate amount of landfills (about three out of every four) were located near predominantly minority communities. This regional study was followed in 1987 by a national study, *Toxic Wastes and Race in the United States*, by the United Church of Christ Commission on Racial Justice. This groundbreaking study found that race was the most significant factor in determining where waste facilities were located in the United States. Among other findings, the study revealed that three out of five African Americans and Hispanic Americans lived in communities with one or more uncontrolled toxic waste sites and 50% of Asian/Pacific Islander Americans and Native Americans lived in such communities. A follow-up study in 1994 concluded that this trend had worsened. In 1990, sociologist Robert Bullard published his now-classic book *Dumping in Dixie: Race, Class, and Environmental Quality*. This was the first major study of environmental racism that linked hazardous facility siting with historical patterns of segregation in the South. This study was also one of the first to explore the social and psychological impacts of environmental racism on local populations and to analyze the response from local communities against these environmental threats.

In addition to the growing body of research, conferences, such as the Urban Environment Conference in New Orleans in 1983 and the University of Michigan Conference on Race and the Incidence of Environmental Hazards in 1990, brought together researchers from around the nation who were studying racial and socioeconomic disparities in the distribution of environmental contaminants. These conferences were attended by several leading "activist-scholars" who, while working closely with community activists, came together to present and debate their findings and implications. The scientific analyses presented at these and other conferences began to frame the toxics struggle in terms of power, class, and racial inequality.

In February 1994, in an attempt to remedy environmental inequality and injustice, President Clinton established Executive Order 12898. The order required that

> each Federal agency shall make achieving environmental justice part of its mission by identifying and addressing, as appropriate, disproportionately high and adverse human health or environmental effects of its programs, policies, and activities on minority populations, and low-income populations.

This order was clearly aimed to rectify environmental problems that have disproportionately affected minority and low-income populations (O'Neil, 2007). Two decades have passed since the executive order, yet its effect on environmental justice programs such as Superfund is still rather ambiguous. Moreover, scholars and activists continue to examine the various and complex dimensions of environmental hazards and their intersection with race and socioeconomic position; however, this research has also not been without much debate and controversy (see Lesson 6).

DEBATES WITHIN ENVIRONMENTAL JUSTICE

Although the vast majority of studies on environmental justice conclude that racism is the major driving factor, there has been much debate about the degree to which this form of injustice is a function of racial inequalities or socioeconomic position or some combination of the two. This controversy has come to be known as the "race versus class debate." Robert Brulle and David Pellow (2006) argued that this controversy has done much to sharpen the methodological and conceptual approaches to analyzing environmental injustices; however, they also pointed out that many scholars and activists have argued that the debate misses the point and that the production of industrial toxins and their generally unequal distribution deserve to be the main focus of research efforts and political change.

Although research points to a relationship between environmental injustice and social hierarchies, the existence and extent of environmental inequalities and their relationship to race, class, or both are still the subject of much political and empirical debate. For example, in his 2005 meta-analysis of 49 environmental equity studies, Evan Ringquist (2005) found that there was overwhelming evidence of environmental inequities based upon race but little evidence to support the notion that similar inequities exist with respect to economic class. However, Gary Evans and Elyse Kantrowitz (2002, p. 303) documented evidence of an inverse relationship between income and other indices of socioeconomic status with environmental risk factors, "including hazardous wastes and other toxins, ambient and indoor air pollutants, water quality, ambient noise, residential crowding, housing quality, educational facilities, work environments, and neighborhood conditions." The poor, especially the nonwhite poor, Evans and Kantrowitz (p. 304) argued, "are the most likely to be exposed not only to the worst air quality, the most noise, the lowest-quality housing and schools, etc. . . . but also to lower-quality environments on a wide array of multiple dimensions." This exposure to multiple suboptimal physical conditions, rather than any singular environmental exposure, is what makes the relationship between socioeconomic status and health so elusive. These studies highlight the complexity and multiple dimensions of compromised environmental conditions that affect particular groups of people.

More recently, a 2006 report from the United Nations Development Programme echoed a similar finding between poverty and environmental inequality. The group's report, *Beyond Scarcity: Power, Poverty and the Global Water Crisis*, found that the crisis of water and sanitation is, above all, a crisis of the poor throughout the world. The World Bank (1992) has also published statistical data on global air and water pollution. For example, in low-income countries from the 1970s to the late 1980s, the average levels of suspended particulate matter in cities increased by 8% (from 300 to 325 ug/cubic meter of air), while cities in the middle-income countries over the same period of time witnessed improved air quality (from approximately 180 to 150 ug/cubic meter of air).

Brulle and Pellow (2006) pointed to a number of complexities that hamper the establishment of a clear link between environmental inequality and health disparities among certain segments of the population. These complexities include "the lack of appropriate statistical measures, varying individual exposure levels, lengthy incubation periods, confounding influences on health, such as access to health care and individual behaviors" (p. 3.5) that range from diet and exercise to employment and housing conditions. As a result of these complexities, Brulle and Pellow argued that researchers know very little about the ways in which health risks from environmental conditions interrelate with and contribute to health disparities between different social groups and communities.

DIMENSIONS OF THE ENVIRONMENTAL JUSTICE MOVEMENT

Despite these empirical and political challenges, the environmental justice movement has had a significant impact on the direction of environmental policy, research, and activism in the United States and around the world (see Lesson 16). The nature and extent of the movement's impact can be divided into five dimensions, which range from local struggles to more global concerns. A detailed description of the five dimensions of the environmental justice movement was given by David Pellow (2005). The following brief description borrows from Pellow's comprehensive analysis.

Local Struggles

Without a doubt, it is at the local community level where struggles for environmental justice have had the most profound impact. Some examples include the forced closing of large polluting industries. For example, waste incinerators and landfills in Los Angeles and Chicago; power plants in Southgate, Los Angeles, and San Jose, California; and oil refineries as well as metal plating and chrome plating facilities in San Diego and Los Angeles were all forced out of business due, in large part, to local community struggles. Other examples include the prevention of polluting operations being built or expanded. Pellow (2005) pointed out that this is clearly the case in

> the chemical plant proposed by the Shintech corporation near a low-income African American community in Louisiana; securing relocations and home buyouts for residents in polluted communities like Love Canal, New York, Times Beach, Missouri, and Norco, Louisiana; and successfully demanding environmental clean ups of locally unwanted land uses (LULUs) such as the North River Sewage Treatment plant in Harlem, New York (p. 1).

These local struggles have made it extremely difficult for polluting industries to locate or expand incinerators, landfills, and related LULUs anywhere in the nation without much controversy and conflict. The NIMBY discourse has also been strategically employed by opponents of "clean" industries, such as wind and solar energy, as well by opponents of dirty industries.

Institution Building and Cultural Impacts

The environmental justice movement has built up local organizations and regional networks and forged partnerships with preexisting institutions such as churches, schools, neighborhood groups, and cooperatives. While this dimension represents an important piece of the environmental justice movement, maintaining and building environmental institutions or networks that can systematically respond to growing environmental injustices have been difficult in some areas of the country, and many regional networks have often fallen victim to shifts in political ideology or fiscal shortfalls and budgetary cuts. Given this challenge, Pellow (2005) argued, building enduring institutions and sustainable communities may, in fact, be the environmental justice movement's greatest challenge.

On a broader cultural and discursive level, Pellow (2005) wrote,

> the language and discourse of environmental justice have entered the lexicon of public health, corporate responsibility, climate change debates, urban planning, transportation development, and municipal zoning processes in cities around the U.S. where these issues might never have been considered two decades ago (p. 2).

These changes constitute a significant dimension of the environmental justice movement.

Legal Gains and Losses

While few and relatively recent, the litigated cases emerging from environmental justice conflicts have not been successful in changing the systemic and institutional causes that continue to produce and reproduce compromised environs in some communities. Early on, environmental justice activists and attorneys devised a strategy to apply civil rights law to cases of environmental injustice. Again, Pellow (2005) summarized:

> Specifically, they argued that Title VI of the 1964 Civil Rights Act would be applicable to [environmental justice] cases. Title VI prohibits all institutions that receive federal funds from discriminating against persons based on race, color or national origin. Unfortunately, the courts have uniformly refused to prohibit government actions based on Title VI of the Civil Rights Act without direct evidence of discriminatory intent (p. 2).

However, the court's interpretation, while important for highlighting how specific groups are disproportionately affected, assumes that racism and its effects can be isolated, and that the government should be able to "catch it in the act" as it were. The problem with this line of inquiry is the assumption that we agree on what racism is and how it works.

The EPA has also been of little assistance on the legal front. Since 1994, when the EPA began accepting Title VI claims, more than 135 have been filed and none has been formally resolved. Furthermore, Pellow (2005) wrote,

> only one federal agency has thus far cited environmental justice concerns to protect a community in a significant legal case. In May 2001, the Nuclear Regulatory Commission denied a permit for a uranium enrichment plant in Louisiana, based on its findings that environmental justice concerns were not taken into account in that siting proposal (p. 2).

National Environmental Policy

Despite serious challenges for the environmental justice movement in terms of both institution building and legal recourse, the movement has succeeded in affecting environmental policy at both the national and state levels of government. The most prominent among these achievements occurred in 1994 when President Clinton signed Executive Order 12898, charging all federal agencies with integrating environmental justice concerns into their operations. The passage of environmental justice laws or policies in more than 40 states, including California, Massachusetts, Indiana, Tennessee, Rhode Island, and Minnesota, has added to the development of a comprehensive environmental policy regime. However, Pellow (2005) argued that despite these legislative advances, many of these new environmental policies are either very specific (for example, related to brownfields) or too general and diffuse to bring about substantial and long-term environmental equality. In response to this shortcoming, many activists have shifted their focus away from the national and state levels of government back to local communities, "where their work has a more tangible influence and where polluters are more easily monitored (p. 3)."

Globalization and Environmental Justice

The impact of globalization and transnational capitalism and the growth of multilateral and international trade agreements have seriously undermined local government attempts to regulate environmental and public health conditions and, as a result, have connected the local with the global in uneven and unjust ways. Perhaps the most vivid example of globalization and environmental injustice comes from Lawrence Summers, a now-retired chief economist of the World Bank. In his now-infamous memo Summers (1991) argued that the World Bank should encourage the movement of pollution from rich core countries in the **Global North** to poor countries in the **Global South** because the cost of illness associated with pollution would be less in economically marginalized communities. This was because, according to Summers, those in the Global South were likely to earn lower wages than those in the Global North and to have a shorter life span; both would suggest that the economic cost of their illness, in terms of either sick days off or cumulative sickness from working in polluted environs, would be substantially lessened. Summers argued that a clean environment was worth more to people in industrialized states than to those in the Global South, and since the cost of pollution would be less in poor countries, it made perfect economic sense to export "dirty" industries to the Global South.

In other words, "global" environmental problems also bear down disproportionately upon minorities, the poor, and aboriginal peoples. The unequal distribution of environmental "bads" is, of course, compounded by the fact that globally and nationally developed countries and their citizens are the major polluters (see Lesson 19). In response to this trend, environmental justice activists and scholars have engaged in collaborations, resource exchange, networking, and joint action that transgress national boundaries and connect the Global North and South.

NEOLIBERALISM AND HOW IT EXACERBATES ENVIRONMENTAL INJUSTICE

For environmental justice scholars and activists, environmental problems are social problems; the two are often inseparable. This is, according to Andrew Szasz, because "toxic victims are, typically, poor or working people of modest means. [Thus] [t]heir environmental problems are inseparable from their economic condition" (1994, p. 151). As Szasz clearly argued, integrated in demands for clean and healthy communities are larger assertions for "the restructuring of the current relationship between economy and society" (p. 82). More recently, however, sociologists Daniel Faber and Deborah McCarthy (2003) have argued that contemporary environmental governance reform (commonly referred to as "neoliberalism") and contemporary environmental and social injustices (which neoliberalism produces) are different sides of the same coin. In fact, they assert that neoliberalism and contemporary environmental and social injustices "are now so dialectically related (if not essential) to each other as to become part of the same historical process" (p. 45). Understanding the relationship between neoliberalism and environmental justice is an important first step in analyzing the macro institutions that produce uneven development on a daily basis. It is to this relationship that I now turn.

It has been said that neoliberalism is the most powerful ideological and political project in modern global governance reform (see Lesson 3). Yet, despite its familiarity, defining what neoliberalism is and what its social and ecological consequences are has not been an easy task. Part of this difficulty comes from the fact that neoliberalism comes in the form of many different policies such as deregulation, austerity measures, commonsense policies, and privatization, to name a few. And because of this complexity, the social and environmental consequences of neoliberalism remain difficult to quantify and qualify. Furthermore, upon closer inspection of particular neoliberal projects, one is more likely to find one or more features from different types of policies rather than a straightforward implementation of a unified philosophy.

Scholar David Harvey (2003) defines neoliberalism as a theory of political economic practice that posits that humanity's well-being can best be advanced by liberating individual entrepreneurial freedoms and skills. The institutional framework that best facilitates these political and economic practices is characterized by strong private property rights, a self-regulating market, and free trade. The appropriate, and only, role of the government, according to this theory, is to guarantee the proper functioning of such markets. Furthermore, if markets do not exist (in such areas as land, water, education, social security, healthcare, and environmental pollution), then they must be created through state action, if necessary.

Social scientists have highlighted several important components to neoliberal reform over the past 30 years. For example, in Canada neoliberal reform has resulted in sweeping amendments to virtually every provincial statute that dealt with environmental protection or natural resource management. Second, there have been major reductions in the budgets of environmental and natural resources agencies. And finally, there was a dramatic restructuring of the roles and responsibilities of governments and the private sector.

Neoliberal reform has resulted in major changes in the use of industrial, agricultural, and municipal lands. Many rural areas have experienced the growth of large industrial feedlots (see Lesson 13). For example, livestock farms in southwestern Ontario have the highest livestock concentration in the province. Similarly, the density of pig farms is also higher than provincial averages in these areas, the same areas that are also home to seven aboriginal communities. In fact, First Nations communities are located either downstream, downwind, or downgrade of these major industrial agricultural lands, all which were able to dramatically expand their operations with the rolling back of provincial environmental laws and regulations.

In addition to agriculture, energy is another predominant land use activity in southwestern Ontario. This area, particularly the Sarnia River, is referred to by locals as "chemical alley"—arguably Canada's largest concentration of petrochemical industries and associated water and air pollution. Between 1974 and 1986, a total of 32 major spills, as well as 300 minor ones, contributed to approximately 10 tons of pollutants in the St. Clair River. Furthermore, since 1986, the Ministry of the Environment has recorded an average of 100 spills per year. This does not include the significant agricultural runoff of pesticides and fertilizers, as well as other nonpoint pollution sources from nearby livestock producers that enter the watershed and river every year. Furthermore, because the St. Clair River connects Lakes Huron and Erie, it is also a major shipping route; and the necessary dredging of contaminated sediments to permit heavy marine traffic poses yet another serious environmental problem. The St. Clair River is also a source of drinking water for Walpole Island and Aamjiwnaang First Nations.

Neoliberal reform in Ontario has reduced monitoring and reporting requirements for industry and severely impaired the ability of provincial ministries and local agencies to regulate and monitor environmental conditions. As such, the recognition of environmental harm and environmental pollution has become much more difficult. This is particularly true for First Nations communities, which simply do not have the capacity to provide the monitoring technologies and expertise to demonstrate scientifically the relationships between health disparities and environmental inequalities. Neoliberal reform in Ontario has also reduced or eliminated opportunities for public participation in land use decisions, such as environmental problems arising from "normal" farm operations and location of waste disposal sites. These impacts were again disproportionately discriminatory toward First Nations partly because of where they were located—downwind, downgrade, and downstream—but also because of a lack of legitimate opportunities to participate in environmental governance that affects their health and welfare.

Indigenous peoples, like First Nations in Canada, are increasingly becoming the target of the externalized social and environmental costs associated with neoliberal policy reform. This is because indigenous peoples still maintain sovereignty over vast resource streams, many still held in common, such as water, oil, diamonds, forests, and, of course, labor, to name only a few, which are desperately needed for this phase of capitalist expansion. This is still true in spite of a brutal history of colonialism that has devastated many indigenous cultures and lands, leaving only a social and environmental skeleton of its previous wealth. Neoliberalism, then, is a concerted effort by those in power to disconnect, and in some cases remove, indigenous peoples from their resources and land.

Indigenous lands also represent a space, conveniently located on the margins of our spatial consciousness, to cheaply and inconspicuously dump the vast wastes of this phase of capitalist expansion. In an attempt to delineate new frontiers for capitalist expansion, many countries in the Global North have increasingly shifted their focus between external and internal forms of expansion. Individual nation-states of the Global North have differed in their institutional response to the challenges of transnational capitalism. In most cases, Harvey suggested, "some combination of internal motivation and external pressure lies behind such transformations" (2003, p. 154). For example, the United States, the current global "empire," has largely chosen to expand its markets, and its fiscal crisis, to the Global South through the direct use of its military and other coercive powers. However, as Kuletz (1998) clearly pointed out, the United States has also led the way in forms of **internal colonialism**, particularly with regard to its Native Americans. However, other less powerful empires, like Canada and China—nation-states rich in resources yet weak in military power—have exclusively focused on internal colonialism to facilitate this phase of capitalist expansion.

The concept of "internal colonialism," Kuletz wrote, "has been used by political scholars, such as Gramsci, to describe political and economic inequalities between regions in a specific society" (1998, p. 8). Much like colonialism, where the wealth and well-being of "core" countries are augmented at the expense of the "periphery," internal colonialism is based on unfair and unequal exchange relations, like resources for pollution, between the urban and rural spaces. The presence of internal colonialism, Kuletz suggested, where one's existence (in the Global North) is premised on the exploitation and marginalization of others (in the Global South), usually of a different cultural, racial, or class background, argues against the liberal notions of democratic pluralism and freedom. But whereas colonialism was marked by the deliberate and direct use of government to remove and disperse indigenous peoples from traditional territories, this contemporary phase of growth is supported by deregulation, privatization, and free market ideology.

In addition to studying how globalization and neoliberal orthodoxy have affected the health and well-being of aboriginal peoples, environmental justice scholars and activists have studied other social groups that have been, and continue to be, the recipients of this form of institutional discrimination. For example, David Pellow's 2004 historical and ethnographic study *Garbage Wars: The Struggle for Environmental Justice in Chicago* analyzed the historical origins of environmental inequalities in Chicago's communities of color and in workplaces where municipal and industrial solid wastes were collected, processed, and eventually dumped. Pellow's analysis revealed the bitter irony of how recycling facilities—ostensibly built to prevent waste from entering landfills and incinerators in already overburdened neighborhoods—were creating occupational hazards for both workers and communities of the South Side of Chicago (workers and communities that were predominantly immigrant, African American, Latino, and Asian American). "Despite its promises," Pellow pointed out, "recycling was just one more example of environmental inequality, stemming from a long line of waste management practices as old as the local city dump and as old as human civilization" (2004, p. 2).

Another example of environmental justice scholarship has been the analysis of the rapidly growing phenomenon of urban poverty. The United Nations Human Settlements Programme (UN-Habitat) report *The Challenge of the Slums: Global Report on Human Settlements 2003* represented the first truly global audit of urban poverty. This report broke with traditional United Nations circumspection and self-censorship to squarely indict neoliberalism, especially the International Monetary Fund's structural adjustment programs, as the chief cause of the rapid increase in urban poverty. In his 2004 article about the UN report, "Planet of Slums: Urban Involution and the Informal Proletariat," Mike Davis wrote that there may be more than a quarter of a million slums on earth.

The world's highest percentages of slum-dwellers are in Ethiopia (an astonishing 99.4% of the urban population), Chad (also 99.4%), Afghanistan (98.5%), and Nepal (92%). The poorest urban populations, however, are probably in Maputo and Kinshasa, where (according to other sources) two thirds of residents earn less than the cost of their minimum required daily nutrition. In Delhi, planners complain bitterly about "slums within slums" as squatters take over the small open spaces of the peripheral resettlement colonies into which the old urban poor were brutally removed in the mid-1970s. In Cairo and Phnom Penh, recent urban arrivals squat or rent space on rooftops, creating slum cities in the air.

Whereas the classic slum was a decaying inner city, the new slums are more typically located on the edge of urban spatial explosions. This land use pattern, referred to as "slum sprawl," is as much of a problem in the developing world as is suburban sprawl in the rich countries. Davis wrote:

> The urban poor, meanwhile, are everywhere forced to settle on hazardous and otherwise unbuildable terrains—over-steep hillslopes, river banks and flood-plains. Likewise they squat in the deadly shadows of refineries, chemical factories, toxic dumps, or in the margins of railroads and highways. Poverty, as a result, has "constructed" an urban disaster problem of unprecedented frequency and scope, as typified by chronic flooding in Manila, Dhaka and Rio, pipeline conflagrations in Mexico City and Cubatão (Brazil), the Bhopal catastrophe in India, a munitions plant explosion in Lagos, and deadly mudslides in Caracas, La Paz and Tegucigalpa. The disenfranchised communities of the urban poor, in addition, are vulnerable to sudden outbursts of state violence like the infamous 1990 bulldozing of the Maroko beach slum in Lagos ("an eyesore for the neighbouring community of Victoria Island, a fortress for the rich") or the 1995 demolition in freezing weather of the huge squatter town of Zhejiangcun on the edge of Beijing (p. 48).

The urban and working poor, indigenous peoples, and other social groups that have been disadvantaged politically or economically by globalization are among the growing groups of humanity that the neoliberal state is unable and, in some circumstances, unwilling to provide for. If refugees represent such a disquieting element in the order of the modern nation-state, then indigenous peoples represent the resource element of globalization (see Lesson 19). Both groups break the continuity between human and citizen, nativity and nation-ality. Italian philosopher Giorgio Agamben (1998) noted that this discontinuity becomes most evident in moments of crisis where both international humanitarian organizations and individual states prove themselves, despite their solemn invocations of "sacred and inalienable" human rights, absolutely incapable of resolving the problem of a globalized humanity.

ENVIRONMENTAL RACISM AND WHITE PRIVILEGE

Racism and classism—either overt or covert—have clearly played an integral role in the setting and maintenance of these uneven and exploitative land use patterns. "Whether by conscious design or institutional neglect," argued sociologist Robert Bullard, "communities of color in urban ghettos, in rural 'poverty pockets,' or on economically impoverished Native-American reservations face some of the worst environmental devastation in the nation" (1993, p. 27). I suggest that neoliberalism has aided in the legitimacy and effect of this uneven and unjust social and environmental relationship. But a chapter on environmental inequality and environmental racism would not be complete without a discussion on white privilege.

Peggy McIntosh (1988) defined white privilege as unearned race advantage and conferred dominance. This form of racism is particularly powerful and pervasive, in part because we are taught that racism is something that puts others at a disadvantage. However, McIntosh argued, we are not taught to see one of institutional racism's corollary aspects, white privilege, which puts whites at an advantage. The majority of white Canadians and white Americans continue to associate racism with individual malicious intentions, and because racism is associated with hostile and intentional acts, the majority of whites can exonerate themselves from environmental racism. However, while whites may not individually engage in acts of racism, by virtue of the historical application of particular governmental mechanisms and legislative practices, they have been able to accrue unearned social, economic, and environmental privileges at the expense of the health and welfare of First Nations and Native American, Black and Hispanic Americans, Latinos, Asians, and other visible minorities. What distinguishes today's racism from previous racial programs and practices is that neoliberalism is largely seen as a technical and administrative project, not a racial one (Mascarenhas, 2012).

To challenge the dominant discourse of neoliberalism, we need to start asking why whites are not comparably burdened with pollution (Pulido, 2000). For example, instead of asking if an unwanted land use was placed near First Nations land or in a predominantly Hispanic neighborhood, we need to start asking why it is that whites are not comparably burdened with this type of environmental pollution. Only then will we start to envision environmental equity and justice for all.

SOURCES

Agamben, Giorgio. 1998. *Homo Sacer: Sovereign Power and Bare Life*. Stanford, CA: Stanford University Press.

Agyeman, Julian, Robert D. Bullard, and Bob Evans. 2003a. "Joined-up Thinking: Bringing Together Sustainability, Environmental Justice and Equity." In J. Agyeman, R. D. Bullard, and B. Evans, eds. *Just Sustainabilities: Development in an Unequal World*, pp. 1–16. Cambridge, MA: MIT Press.

———, eds. 2003b. *Just Sustainabilities: Development in an Unequal World*. Cambridge, MA: MIT Press.

Brown, P. (2007). *Toxic Exposures: Contested Illness and the Environmental Health Movement*. New York: Columbia University Press.

Brulle, Robert, and David Pellow. 2006. "Environmental Justice: Human Health and Environmental Inequalities." *Annual Review of Public Health* 27:3.1–3.22.

Bullard, Robert D. 1990. *Dumping in Dixie: Race, Class, and Environmental Quality*. Boulder, CO: Westview Press.

——— 1993. *Confronting Environmental Racism*. Boston, MA: South End Press.

——— 1994. *Unequal Protection: Environmental Justice and Communities of Color*. San Francisco, CA: Sierra Club Books.

Bullard, R. D., P. Mohai, R. Saha, & B. Wright (2007). *Toxic Wastes and Race at Twenty 1987–2007. Grassroots Struggles to Dismantle Environmental Racism in the United States*. Cleveland, OH: The United Church of Christ.

Carson, R. (1962). *Silent Spring*. Greenwich, CT: Fawcett Publications, Inc.

Clinton, W. J. (1994). Executive Order 12898. Federal Actions to Address Environmental Justice in Minority Populations and Low-Income Populations: Fed Reg 59:FR7629.

Davis, Mike. 2004. "Planet of Slums: Urban Involution and the Informal Proletariat." *New Left Review* 26:5–34.

Environmental Defence. 2006. *Polluted Children, Toxic Nation. A Report on Pollution in Canadian Families*. Toronto, Ontario: Environmental Defence.

Evans, Gary, and Elyse Kantrowitz. 2002. "Socioeconomic Status and Health: The Potential Role of Environmental Risk Exposure." *Annual Review of Public Health* 23:303–331.

Faber, Daniel, and Deborah McCarthy. 2003. "Neoliberalism, Globalization, and the Struggle for Ecological Democracy: Linking Sustainability and Environmental Justice." In J. Agyeman, R. Bullard, and R. Evans, eds. *Just Sustainabilities: Development in an Unequal World*, pp. 38–63. Cambridge, MA: MIT Press.

Foster, John Bellamy. 1993. " 'Let Them Eat Pollution': Capitalism and the World Economy." *Monthly Review* 44:10–11.

Gedicks, Al. 1994. *The New Resource Wars: Native and Environmental Struggles Against Multinational Corporations*. Montreal, Canada: Black Rose Books.

Getches, David, and David Pellow. 2002. "Beyond Traditional Environmental Justice." In K. Mutz and G. Bryner, eds. *Justice and Natural Resources: Concepts, Strategies, and Applications*, pp. 3–30. Chicago, IL: Island Press.

Hardt, M., and A. Negri. 2001. *Empire: The Crisis of Political Space*. Cambridge, MA: Harvard University Press.

Harvey, David. 2003. *The New Imperialism*. Oxford, UK: Oxford University Press.

Kuletz, Valerie. 1998. *The Tainted Desert: Environmental Ruin in the American West*. New York: Routledge.

Larner, Wendy. 2000. "Neo-liberalism: Policy, Ideology, Governmentality." *Studies in Political Economy* 63:5 25.

Mascarenhas, M. 2012. *Where the Waters Divide Neoliberalism, White Privilege, and Environmental Racism in Canada*. Lanham, MD: Lexington Books.

McIntosh, P. 1988. *White Privilege: Unpacking the Invisible Knapsack* (excerpt from Working Paper #189, "White Privilege and Male Privilege: A Personal Account of Coming To See Correspondence Through Work in Women's Studies"). Wellesley, MA: Wellesley College Center for Research on Women.

National Cancer Institute. 2012. *Cancer Trends Progress Report, 2011/2012 Update*. Retrieved March 26, 2013, from http://progressreport.cancer.gov/highlights.asp

Nue, Dean, and Richard Therrien. 2003. *Accounting for Genocide: Canada's Bureaucratic Assault on Aboriginal People*. New York: Zed Books.

O'Neil, S. G. (2007). Superfund: Evaluating the Impact of Executive Order 12989. *Environmental Health Perspectives* 115:1087–1093.

Pellow, David. 2004. *Garbage Wars: The Struggle for Environmental Justice in Chicago*. Cambridge, MA: MIT Press.

_____ 2005. "The Movement for Environmental Justice in the U.S.: Confronting Challenges and Charting a New Course." *Transatlantic Initiative to Promote Environmental Justice*. Budapest, Hungary, October 27–30, 2005.

Pulido, L. 2000. Rethinking Environmental Racism: White Privilege and Urban Development in Southern California. *Annals of the Association of American Geographers* 90(1):12–40.

Ringquist, Evan. 2005. "Assessing Evidence of Environmental Inequalities: A Meta-Analysis." *Journal of Policy Analysis and Management* 24:223–247.

Summers, Lawrence. 1991. "Office Memorandum from Lawrence M. Summers, Subject: GEP, the World Bank/IMFMIGA." *The World Bank*.

_____ 2000b. "The Rise of the Environmental Justice Paradigm: Injustice Framing and the Social Construction of Environmental Discourses." *American Behavioral Scientist* 43:508–580.

Szasz, Andrew. 1994. *Ecopopulism: Toxic Waste and the Movement for Environmental Justice*. Minneapolis, MN: University of Minneapolis Press.

Szasz, Andrew, and Michael Meuser. 1997. "Environmental Inequalities: Literature Review and Proposals for New Directions in Research and Theory." *Current Sociology* 45:99–120.

Taylor, Dorceta. 2000a. "Introduction." *American Behavioral Scientist* 43:504–507.

Tesh, Sylvia. 2000. *Uncertain Hazards, Environmental Activists and Scientific Proof*. Ithaca, NY: Cornell University Press.

Turner, Robin Lanette, and Diana Pei Wu. 2002. *Environmental Justice and Environmental Racism: An Annotated Bibliography and General Overview, Focusing on U.S. Literature, 1996–2002*. Berkeley, CA: Institute of International Studies, University of California, Berkeley.

UN-Habitat. 2003. *The Challenge of the Slums: Global Report on Human Settlements 2003*. London: Earthscan Publications Ltd.

United Church of Christ Commission on Racial Justice. 1987. *Toxic Wastes and Race in the United States*. New York: United Church of Christ.

United Nations Development Project. 2006. *Beyond Scarcity: Power, Poverty and the Global Water Crisis*. New York: Palgrave Macmillan.

U.S. Environmental Protection Agency. 2007. *Environmental Justice*. Washington, D.C.: U.S. Environmental Protection Agency, http://www.epa.gov/compliance/environmentaljustice/index.html.

World Bank. 1992. *World Development Report*. New York: Oxford University Press.

11

The Sociology of Environmental Health

Sabrina McCormick

Bus exhaust, Quito, Ecuador.
Photo by Tammy Lewis.

When I was eight, I lost almost everything: my room and all the stuff in it—toys, dance costumes, purple barrettes, green tights, sparkly lip gloss. I had to leave them behind when we abandoned our house on Bishop Lake. That summer, a crew had sprayed our house for powder post beetles. Quickly, my mother got sick and dizzy. She had a piece of furniture tested. The crew had illegally sprayed our house with chlordane,

179

a chemical used as a pesticide. Before that year, 3.6 million pounds of chlordane were applied to corn, fruits, lawns, and houses every year. But the initial testing of chlordane that allowed those agricultural applications was not sufficient. Eventually, the U.S. Environmental Protection Agency (EPA) discovered that the chemical can contaminate air, water, and soil and that it causes damage to the nervous and blood systems, lungs, and kidneys. The year before chlordane was sprayed in my room, 1983, regulations were put in place to ban it. That was when I first learned how the environment affects health.

One of the most pressing concerns in any society is the health of its people. Many of the most common yet seemingly mysterious illnesses are clearly caused, at least in part, by exposures in the environment. Although most conceptions of illness causation have focused on the individual for the past hundred years, there is growing concern about environmental causes as more and more people realize that there are direct and intimate relationships between the world around us and our own health. However, healthcare researchers, practitioners, and providers face many obstacles in remedying environmental illness. In this lesson, I describe the field of environmental health and the obstacles that impede better addressing it. I review several landmark cases that have shaped our understanding of environmental illness. To exemplify some of the obstacles to understanding and dealing with environmental illness, I describe illnesses caused by heat waves—a critical issue that demonstrates how environmental conditions affect human health.

SHIFTING TO ENVIRONMENTAL HEALTH

In the early 20th century, healthcare practitioners began to trace illness causation, prevention, and treatment to the individual, rather than the environment in which we live. Seeing the individual as the locus of illness resulted from the rise in *germ theory*—the idea that microorganisms that are transmitted between people are the cause of disease—and from the growing power of polluting industries. *Miasma theories*, which acknowledged environmental contaminants and exposures, fell away as large-scale polluters were released from responsibility for the health effects of their actions. Power, politics, and science got intermixed in medical understanding and treatment (see Lesson 6). These processes reflect how underlying sociological aspects of life get embedded in bodies and health. As such factors shaped our understanding of what causes illness, a new model underlying medical thinking arose in the shape of the **biomedical model.**

E. G. Mishler (1981) described the biomedical model as the unquestioned conceptual model on which medical thinking is based. The model's key assumptions are the doctrine of a specific etiology (the search for causes of disease) and the neutrality of medicine. Generally, biomedical approaches are focused on the individual's role in causing illness, such as diet and lifestyle. This model does not acknowledge the social, political, or economic facets driving the development of medical knowledge. The largest government institutions, the pharmaceutical sector, and major health foundations have provided support for the biomedical approach and have focused little attention on environmental causes of disease. There is only one government institution that has been given the responsibility to address environmental health, the National Institute of Environmental Health Sciences (NIEHS). The NIEHS is one of 21 institutions housed within the National Institutes of Health.

Despite most healthcare and research being based on the biomedical model, concerns about environmental causes of illness have become more common as environmental exposures worsen. The field of environmental health is generally concerned with human exposures to human-made toxins and other harmful exposures in air, food, and water. These exposures are often shaped by social and physical structures. As a result, the field of environmental health also addresses the neighborhoods, schools, and homes in which we live. An individual's or group's racial, ethnic, age, or gender identity shapes experiences in these places and is therefore also of importance in environmental health. For example, asthma rates in inner-city areas have been skyrocketing. These areas are inhabited largely by poor people of color who live adjacent to bus terminals and polluting facilities where air pollution is rife. Recent research has connected this air pollution with asthma rates. This case of environmental illness reflects how race, class, neighborhood, and air interrelate to affect human health (see Lesson 10).

The field of environmental health addresses population-level factors, a broader conception than that encompassed by the biomedical paradigm. An environmental conception of disease demonstrates that the individual-level focus of a biomedical approach ignores broader political and environmental factors that might force polluters to reduce emissions or to face losses by stopping the production of certain products. An environmental framework looks at changes in industrial production practices as the source of changes in health outcomes. In the example of asthma, an environmental framework would bring to light the lack of regulation of small air particles emitted by smokestacks and the need to cut vehicle emissions to protect public health.

In the conception of environmental health, the individual is seen in relationship with the social world. It calls attention to the difference between a focus on sick individuals and one on sick populations. A number of sociological processes play a role in environmental health assessments, such as gender inequality, racial and ethnic identity, social norms and structures, political economy, and environmental justice. An individual risk factor approach seeks to answer the following question: Why are some individuals sick? Conversely, a population-based line of inquiry asks: Why are some groups sick while others are not? Due to the difficulties with conducting research that produces scientifically legitimate answers to these types of questions, innovative methods and topics of study are generally adopted in the environmental paradigm. They include geographic information systems

(GIS) study—or the mapping of geography and human patterns of disease—survey methods, and novel epidemiological and toxicological methods. Collaboration with laypeople can also characterize these research projects.

Concerns about environmental causes of illness arose with the environmental movement and with the environmental justice movement, which focused on how exposures were more extreme for minorities or the poor (see Lesson 16). Today, several health social movements have drawn attention to the role of environmental factors in illness. For example, the environmental breast cancer movement has changed our conception of breast cancer causation from individual-level risk factors like diet, exercise, and alcohol consumption to human-made chemicals and radiation. The movement seeks to overturn an individual-level approach to health by politicizing connections between health, the environment, and industrial production. In other words, they point to the social production of disease. Environmental breast cancer activists claim that the biomedical model of disease prevention, which focuses on genetics and lifestyle, blames women for getting cancer, therefore conveniently removing the responsibility from polluters and government regulators. There are many other movements that attempt to do the same thing. Many of them have arisen because of the most catastrophic and debilitating environmental illnesses today.

TRAGEDIES: MAKING THE CASE
FOR ENVIRONMENTAL HEALTH

The biomedical focus of healthcare has sidelined environmental health, often creating a crisis. Sometimes that crisis is immediate and obvious: There have been catastrophes where thousands of people die overnight. In other cases, these problems grow over years, becoming obvious only to those who feel the brunt of them. Tragedies have often brought environmental health concerns to the attention of policymakers and the public, while other illnesses have slid under the rug.

In the late 1950s in Minamata Bay, Japan, a mysterious illness began to infiltrate local communities, most of which ate fish out of the bay. Neurological symptoms like numbness, slurred speech, and brain damage plagued them. Little explanation ensued until it was discovered that the Chisso Company had been dumping mercury into the bay for 40 years. The company had been producing plastics and chemicals there. When locals became upset about getting sick, the company pressured them to settle for a small amount of compensation while it continued to profit from manufacturing. Many people received nothing. Meanwhile, people in several other locations in the world have gotten what is now called Minamata disease.

In a quiet, rural area in Michigan in the early 1970s, livestock began to drop dead from no known cause. Farmers in the surrounding area got sick. Infected milk was recalled. In a period of months, public health officials discovered that polybrominated biphenols (PBBs), highly toxic chemicals used as flame retardants, had contaminated cattle feed trucked around the state. Public health officials investigated the source of the contamination and claimed it was an individual farmer who had sold this hazardous feed. Pushed by angry communities and farmers, government agencies slowly came to realize that a lack of government responsibility had allowed it and ultimately threatened public health. Eventually, the crisis was contained, but only after a statewide scare.

One warm night in 1984 in the small Indian city of Bhopal, a cloud of gas shot out of a smokestack and formed a plume that shifted and dropped onto the town below. Thousands died. A plant run by Dow Chemical, formerly known as Union Carbide, had leaked methyl isocyanate, an extremely toxic chemical, into the air after an accident in the plant. The company attempted to shirk responsibility, claiming that a worker caused the accident and that only a few deaths resulted. Legal battles ensued for over 20 years. Eventually, some of those who lost loved ones or their livelihoods received compensation. Others never did.

Possibly the most famous case in the United States to ignite attention to environmental illness was the exposure and displacement of communities in Love Canal, New York. In the late 1970s people in the Love Canal area began to mysteriously get ill. Lois Gibbs, a young mother and president of the local homeowners association, began to bring the community together to investigate why. They discovered that their homes and school had been built on the former waste site of Hooker Chemical. The site had been covered up, but toxins had followed the below-ground plume and leached into their basements. Scientific and legal battles began over who was responsible and what had to be done. Without exact scientific evidence about what was causing illness, the residents found it difficult to find Hooker at fault. In 1978, President Carter declared an emergency and evacuated the community. Eventually, the government paid hundreds of families for their losses. This event instigated the Superfund law, which could be used to declare a site toxic and mandate cleanup by the polluters.

These are some of the landmark cases that helped found the field of environmental health. More recently, there have been other tragedies to bring environmental health to light. Possibly the most public tragedy with the most hidden environmental health costs is the World Trade Center disaster. When the World Trade Center was destroyed, the burning buildings polluted the air, releasing human-made toxins that had been hidden in building materials for years. At first, government officials claimed that nearby areas were safe and that residents could return to their homes. Studies since then have shown that firefighters who worked intensively in the area and people who lived there have developed a "World Trade Center cough" and other illnesses. Women have given birth to babies of lower than normal weight. The site has not been safe, despite the assurances from government agencies. New research has found many exposures in the area and some clear associations between airborne pollutants from the disaster and respiratory diseases.

These kinds of severe events are taking place all over the world. In 2007, the illegal practice of shipping toxic waste across borders came to light when a waste site was created to accommodate sulfurous sludge sent from a Dutch company aboard a Panamanian ship to the West African country of Ivory Coast. The open-air site was adjacent to homes in the port city of Abidjan. Soon after the $20,000 fee was paid and the sludge was dropped in the site, members of the community began to develop headaches, skin lesions, and difficulty breathing. Eventually, 15 people died and thousands incurred health problems. Activists arose in the area, and a lawsuit was won against the company, which promised to clean up the site. The long-term impacts on the local environment and community are unclear.

Such tragedies where environmental toxins have threatened public health have been the most obvious cases of environmental illness. They have forced public officials to be more wary of environmental contaminants and the built environment. A crisis often reflects social problems that otherwise go unnoticed. However, if a problem persists long enough, it can be seen in chronic illness as well.

CHRONIC MISHAPS

A number of environmental health concerns have taken years to realize. Often in these cases, a particular group is chronically exposed to an environmental contaminant that eventually leads to illness or disease. Lead poisoning is a perfect example. In the early to mid-20th century, lead became an important ingredient in paint and gasoline. Health studies showed that it was problematic, but a powerful lead industry distracted policymakers from these studies, allowing lead to go unregulated. Over the years, it became clear that air pollution with lead in it was causing severe respiratory problems. Similarly, children exposed to lead paint were acquiring neurological damage (ironically, children were used in advertising campaigns for the paint). As a result, the government required the removal of lead from gasoline and paint. However, the legacy of lead remains in the air and in the homes where it has yet to be removed.

Cancer is of more recent and widespread concern. Cancer is possibly the most contentious and most important environmental health issue facing the United States. One in three Americans will get cancer in their lifetime. The most common cancers are lung, breast, and colon, and the fastest growing in the United States is thyroid cancer. Most attention to prevention of cancer is directed toward diet and exercise. However, a growing body of research shows that there are environmental exposures that cause cancer. For example, pesticides and other chemicals have been linked to heightened cancer rates. There is a great deal of resistance to these studies on the part of both the industries that make chemicals and the pharmaceutical companies that profit from cancer treatments. While diet, exercise, and other factors that individuals can control are important, of growing concern is the lack of protection against carcinogenic exposures on the part of the government.

One group of chronic exposures that may lead to cancer is toxins in personal care products. Makeup, deodorant, lotions, shampoo, and other products are not regulated. As a result, these products often include ingredients for which there are limited health data or that are linked with illness. Daily use of these products adds up, especially for some groups like women who use many more products than men. There is little public awareness about these ingredients, but they may be contributing to a number of different kinds of illness. Some research has shown connections between certain chemicals in these products, like methylparaben, and an increase in cancer incidence. In Europe, some of these ingredients have been banned, but in the United States, they are still legal.

While war causes many immediate deaths, it also causes more long-term health problems that are often ignored. The toxins used in bombs and munitions contaminate both the communities in which the war is waged and the soldiers on the battlefield. One controversial case of this has been Gulf War–related illness. After the Gulf War in the early 1990s, many soldiers came home with strange symptoms, like neurological disorders and fatigue. Over time the term "Gulf War illness" was attached to these disorders. There was little explanation for them, other than exposures to depleted uranium, an ingredient of bombs that American military personnel handled regularly. Meanwhile, populations living in the area where the munitions remained even after the war were exposed.

Environmental illnesses can have a broad range of causes. They can be caused by something you choose to use or exposures that are out of your control. Illness can arise immediately or take years to manifest itself. One individual can face many exposures at once, making it difficult to identify the real cause of illness. Consequently, environmental factors are hard to identify and target. The most tragic cases, where death and deformation result almost immediately, help clarify the relationship between contaminant and illness, but most people do not face such dire circumstances. Therefore, connecting environmental exposures to one's own illnesses is difficult to do. Similarly, "proving" that the environment affects health is also often challenging. The following case study of illness and death caused by heat waves demonstrates that while it might appear obvious that heat makes people sick, politics and conflicting interests can obstruct medical interventions.

DYING OF THE HEAT

Like other tragedies that have forced us to realize that the environment affects health, climate change (see Lesson 15) is having an impact on health around the world. An increasing number of people are projected to die from climate-related illnesses, resulting in one of the greatest public health issues of this century. There are five main types of health concerns regarding climate change: (1) air pollution–related illness, (2) temperature-related illness, (3) vector-borne disease, (4) water- and food-borne disease, and (5) illness or injury from extreme weather events. These changes are both gradual and abrupt, creating immediate catastrophes and public health crises. These problems will vary in extremity depending on the social and physical environment in which people live.

With an increase in global warming, extreme heat events ("heat waves") are already increasing. In the United States, heat- and cold-related illnesses have become a major focus because of their impacts around the country. Extreme heat often causes death, especially in urban areas. An average 400–500 people die of heat-related illness in the United States each year, and this number is projected to rise dramatically with climate change. In fact, more deaths occur due to heat waves than any other natural disaster in the United States. Heat waves lead to poor health in two main ways. Extreme temperature rise leads to heatstroke, while cardiopulmonary problems and respiratory illness are linked to shifts in air pollution concentrations caused by warmer temperatures.

Heat waves affect groups differently based on their race, gender, age, and medical and socioeconomic status. Minority communities and poor people are more seriously affected by heat waves than others. They often lack air conditioning at home or access to cooling facilities. They also often live in urban areas where heat islands are more common due to lack of green space, dark roofing, and other urban characteristics. The elderly in minority communities are particularly at risk: They lack the social networks and ability to gauge how hot they are that can help prevent illness. Some studies also show that women have worse outcomes. Since the elderly are predominantly women and have more difficulty dealing with heat, gender is likely to play a role.

Usually, people living in inner-city areas without access to parks and cooler areas are affected by heat waves much more than those living in suburban or rural areas with access to air conditioning. This raises the question of health inequalities. Health inequalities occur when some populations are disproportionately affected by a particular disease or illness, often because they are poor, have less access to healthcare, or in the case of environmental burdens, have greater exposure to harmful substances. Because heat waves affect minorities in cities more than other groups, environmental justice groups have begun to raise a public outcry about the health impacts of climate change more generally.

Since the 1980s, environmental groups in the United States have addressed climate change; however, only a subset of environmental justice organizations have made health-related issues a priority. These groups have developed a "**climate justice** framework" composed of 10 points. These points focus on the accountability of polluters, the participation of affected people in policymaking, and inclusion of inequalities in planning for climate change health outcomes. These points were used in the "Climate Justice Declaration" that brings together principles from environmental justice and climate activism to emphasize how climate change results in adverse outcomes for the poor and people of color. It shows how related illnesses would be exacerbated by lack of access to healthcare and mitigation measures, disparities in health insurance coverage, and increased susceptibility of inner-city communities and communities of color.

Since the framework was established, groups proposing the climate justice agenda have burgeoned in California, New York, Alaska, Michigan, Illinois, and the United Kingdom. Prestigious academic institutions have also used the framework's language and approach in developing new studies. It has also been used internationally as a way to frame the global burden of greenhouse gas emissions generated by developed nations. More specifically, developing nations will experience the greatest impacts of climate change, while industrialized nations that have contributed the most greenhouse gases historically will have the least impacts. This situation is a central, international climate justice issue. While this discursive innovation and public contention has filtered into national environmental discourse, it is unclear how great an influence it has had in the political arena.

While public concern has grown about the health impacts of climate change and heat waves specifically, less attention has been dedicated to health concerns in policymaking. Policy addressing climate-related health and illness originated in the late 1980s and early 1990s. Initially, only limited attention was given to such concerns. While political developments are still in their infancy, in some areas they are moving quickly to account for rapid, recent climate developments. New reports, policies, and institutions have been generated in order to prepare for and possibly mitigate impending public health crises, but government public health institutions are still unprepared.

The first major federal report that dealt with human health impacts of climate change was produced by the EPA in 1989; it was entitled *The Potential Effects of Global Climate Change*. It drew attention to vector-borne disease and illnesses from extreme weather events and recommended that federal agencies like the Departments of the Interior, Energy, and Health and Human Services, among others, in conjunction with local agencies begin preparations. However, the majority of its focus was on ecosystems, and information regarding human health was limited to descriptions of sensitivities rather than recommendations or projections.

In 1992, the United Nations established the Framework Convention on Climate Change, which called for national governments to conduct risk assessments of health threats posed by global climate change. While the need for public health measures was mentioned, human health was sidelined in the framework. The following year, the Office of Technology Assessment developed a Congressional report entitled *Preparing for an Uncertain Climate*. This document only mentioned that there were possible human health impacts from climate change, especially extreme weather events, and gave almost no attention to the need to prepare for them. The EPA demonstrated greater attention to health concerns in 1997 when it recommended that medical and public health practitioners better educate the public about heat events and that interventions for vulnerable populations be created. In 1998, Congress mandated the creation of the U.S. National Assessment of the Potential Consequences of Climate Variability and Change. It included thousands of stakeholder and scientific participants, eight federal agencies, 20 regional workshops, and assessments of 16 regions. Health concerns were a greater focus than in previous government documents.

Climate-related health policy developments have been shaped by political tensions and normative overtones, resulting in less effective government measures. This is true of government measures to both mitigate and adapt to climate change. Mitigation is the process of reducing greenhouse gases, while adaptation is preparing for its impacts. In order to achieve either type of measure, Congress has been faced with the proposition of enacting legislation. While the Senate has approved climate legislation, it has been thwarted in the House of Representatives. As a result, regional and local climate change mitigation and adaptation initiatives have taken off. In addition, the EPA has been given the responsibility of regulating greenhouse gases as a pollutant under the Clean Air Act. Reducing greenhouse gas emissions both improves local air quality, and also protects the public's health from climate change.

There are measures that can and need to be taken to protect the public's health from temperature rises caused by climate change. However, there are many scientific and political obstacles to making that happen. They are similar to the impediments to protecting the public from other environmental illness. Many American public officials resist acknowledging that heat is increasing because such an admission might result in stricter regulation of the air pollution that causes global warming. In addition, there are medical and scientific factors that make it difficult for policymakers to deal with illnesses caused by heat waves. For example, it is difficult to determine who has died due to the heat as opposed to other illnesses. If an individual had a preexisting heart condition that was worsened by a heat wave, it is difficult to identify if the heat or other heart-related risk factors caused a death. Scientists have difficulty identifying exactly how more extreme heat events will affect cities. Therefore, it is challenging to plan for them. Lack of scientific and medical certainty is an issue that plagues many endeavors to connect the environment with human health. Biomedical research conducted in a lab or in large populations that isolates particular factors or genes is much easier. Therefore, more credibility is often given to that kind of work.

The public health impacts of climate change are just one of the emerging concerns of environmental health specialists. Others include the accumulation of chemicals in the human body, the decreasing availability of clean water and resulting water-borne illnesses, and environmental crimes, such as the illegal trade of ozone-depleting substances and international transport of toxic waste, for which there are few international regulations but that cause many illnesses around the world. These concerns need to be addressed in political and scientific spheres. The field of environmental health has room to grow in substantiating the concerns of social movements, citizens, and policymakers.

BODIES IN THE ENVIRONMENT

Problems with the environment are reflected in our bodies, but acknowledging the environmental causes of illness is controversial. It requires that polluters become more responsible and policymakers less influenced by powerful economic interests. The cases discussed in this lesson demonstrate that making connections between health and the environment is often first achieved by those who suffer environmental illness. For them to gain compensation for their losses and to stop these exposures, public officials must also accept their claims. A key component to this latter process is scientific proof. If an affected community has research that proves an illness is connected to certain exposures, it is much easier to gain the proper treatment and prevention.

A key political principle that may improve environmental health is the **precautionary principle** (PP). Born in Europe and adopted in some local governments in the United States, the PP is regarded as a proactive public health approach that reduces or bans chemicals even in the absence of understanding whether or not they harm human health. Usually, the government uses risk assessment to test how many people will become ill if a chemical is released onto the market. Risk assessment is a type of cost–benefit analysis that uses human lives as a measurement of cost. When a manufacturer generates a new chemical and tests it for harm to human health, the analysis includes a number of human lives that will be lost. The PP takes the opposite approach of arguing for the prevention of lives lost by disallowing products onto the market that cause environmental illness.

Issues of environmental health are local and global. They affect people in the most intimate ways and yet are increasingly caused by global issues. As transnational companies move around the world, often shirking environmental restrictions, communities immediately adjacent to manufacturing facilities, oil refineries, and other plants face harmful exposures. However, toxins and contamination also defy borders: They move through the air and water around the world. As we learn more about them, it becomes all the more plain that communities, states, and nations must collaborate to stop them and prevent the tragic illnesses that have occurred in the past and continue to make us ill.

In my own case, my mother used the legal system to gain compensation for the house that we lost. She also sued for the emotional damages we maintained by losing everything. The company that had illegally sprayed the chemical reimbursed us for a fraction of what had vanished from our lives.

A large company had more power to decide the outcome of my life than we did, as a small family. I experienced the political economy of environmental illness in an obvious way. But all of our lives reflect the social and environmental landscape in which we live. A crisis may bring it to light more clearly, but chronic mishaps also occur over time, sometimes remaining hidden.

SOURCES

Bernard, S. M., J. M. Sarnet, A. Grambsch, K. L. Ebi, and I. Romieu. 2001. "The Potential Impacts of Climate Variability and Change on Air Pollution-Related Health Effects in the United States." *Environmental Health Perspectives* 109(Supplement 12):199–209.

Brown, Phil, and Edwin J. Mikkelsen. 1997. *No Safe Place: Toxic Waste, Leukemia, and Community Action*. Berkeley, CA: University of California Press.

Campbell-Lendrum D., A. Pruss-Ustun, and C. Corvalan. 2003. "How Much Disease Could Climate Change Cause?" In D. Campbell-Lendrum, C. Corvalan, K. L. Ebi, A. K. Githeko, and J. S. Scheraga, eds. *Climate Change and Human Health: Risks and Responses*, pp. 133–158. Geneva, Switzerland: World Health Organization.

Cordova, Robert, Michel Gelobter, Andrew Hoerner, Jennifer R. Love, Ansje Miller, Calanit Saenger, and Disha Zaida. 2006. "Climate Change in California: Health, Economic, and Equity Impacts of Climate Change: A New Report by Redefining Progress." Redefining Progress, accessed on April 4, 2008 (http://www.rprogress.org/publication/2006/CARB_ES_0306.pdf).

Kovats, R. Sari, Diarmid Campbell-Lendrum, and Franziska Matthies. 2005. "Climate Change and Human Health: Estimating Avoidable Deaths and Disease." *Risk Analysis* 25(6):1409–1418.

Mishler, E. G. 1981. *Social Contexts of Health, Illness, and Patient Care*. New York: Cambridge University Press.

Morgan, M. Granger, Robin Cantor, William C. Clark, Ann Fisher, Henry D. Jacoby, Anthony C. Janetos, Ann P. Kinzig, Jerry Melillo, Roger B. Street, and Thomas J. Wilbanks. 2005. "Learning from the U.S. National Assessment of Climate Change Impacts." *Environmental Science and Technology* 39(23):9023–9032.

Pettit, Jethro. 2004. "Climate Justice: A New Social Movement for Atmospheric Rights." *IDS Bulletin* 35(3):102–106.

Tesh, Sylvia. 1988. *Hidden Arguments: Political Ideology and Disease Prevention Policy*. New Brunswick, NJ: Rutgers University Press.

12

Producing and Consuming Food
Justice and Sustainability in a Globalized World?

Jason Konefal and Maki Hatanaka

Grand opening of a White Castle restaurant in front of the Walmart supercenter in Phillipsburg, New Jersey.

Photo by Ken Gould.

Everybody eats! What we eat, where our food comes from, and how our food is produced all affect the environment. However, how many of you have *really* thought about the food that you consume every day? For example, how much do you know about the food you eat prior to its appearance on the shelves of your supermarket? Who produces it, how is it produced, and where? How has what we eat and how it is produced changed over time? To what extent are the production, distribution, and consumption of food sustainable and just?

This lesson addresses these questions using a sociological lens. The first part of this lesson examines the **conventional food and agriculture system**, which is where the vast majority of the world's food is produced. The second section provides an overview of the environmental degradation and social inequities produced by conventional food and agriculture. Next, **alternative**

food and agriculture and the possibilities for a more sustainable and just food and agriculture system are examined. Particular attention is paid to the use of **market-based approaches**, which have become the preferred strategy of many food and environmental movement organizations. In concluding, key questions regarding future potential relationships between food, agriculture, and the environment are presented.

CONVENTIONAL FOOD AND AGRICULTURE

A few generations ago, family farms were the norm in the United States. A huge variety of foods were grown locally. There was a minimum of processed foods. People purchased food from mom-and-pop stores and cooked meals from scratch. Today, the picture is very different. Very few people are farmers. Most food is not grown locally. Global transnational retailers, such as Walmart, have replaced mom-and-pop stores. Increasingly, food is standardized in that it is the same size, shape, color, and taste. There are many more processed foods than fresh foods. Increasingly, cooking is not necessary as food comes already prepared. This section examines the current global, corporate, and industrial character of conventional food and agriculture, and how it came to be (see Lesson 13 for a discussion of livestock production).

From Local to Global

Sociologist Philip McMichael (2009) claims that in much of the world today we have **"food from nowhere."** What does this mean? First, for many people, it means that food just appears at their supermarket, or on their plate at the restaurant. This means that they have little knowledge of where the food they eat comes from, who produces it, or how it was produced. Second, it means that for wealthy people across the world, such things as geography, climate, and seasonality no longer matter in terms of what they eat. In other words, when most Americans go to the supermarket, they expect to find a vast array of food ranging from fresh produce, meat, and seafood, to processed foods, regardless of where they live and the time of year. Lastly, it means that much of the food people eat is not produced anywhere near where it is consumed. For example, the lettuce in your salad may come from California, the tomatoes from Florida, your fish may be from China, and the fruit you eat for dessert may be from Mexico and Chile. It is estimated that the food an American family eats on average travels 4,200 miles to get to the dinner table.

How have people in the Global North, and many urban centers in the Global South, come to have food from nowhere? **Food regime theory** describes and theorizes the globalization of food (McMichael, 2009a). It notes that the globalization of food and agriculture began during the end of European colonization (1870–1914). A key characteristic of colonization was supplying agricultural goods, such as sugar, tobacco, tea, coffee, and cocoa, to the core countries of Europe. Settler colonies, such as the United States, first became part of the world system as producers of wheat and meat, which were staples of the working class in Europe at the time. Following World War II, U.S. policies of "dumping" (i.e., providing free or below-market-price goods) excess grains as food aid furthered the globalization of food and agriculture by making recipient countries dependent on imports of U.S. grains. Most recently, with the implementation of neoliberal free trade policies, many (but not all) barriers to trade were weakened, allowing for the development of transnational agribusiness corporations that control much of food production, processing, and distribution globally.

Today, food and agriculture is truly globalized, with the Global South largely serving as a supermarket for the people of the Global North. Countries such as Brazil, Mexico, Chile, and Thailand are referred to as "new agricultural countries" and specialize in producing high-value, labor-intensive food for consumers across the world. This may include delicate fruits, such as grapes, but also increasingly a variety of processed foods produced by young "factory girls" on assembly lines. For example, Deborah Barndt's study (2008) chronicles the ways that tomato packing and processing, such as making ketchup, are increasingly characterized as women's work in Mexico due to women's *supposedly* obedient and submissive nature, nimble fingers, and cheaper wages. Hence, her research exemplifies the feminization of labor in much of the food processing industry.

From Family to Corporate

Who grows the food you eat? Who turns agricultural products into the foods at your table? Who sells you your food? For most people in the United States, and increasingly the rest of the world, the answer is corporations—and the trend is toward just a small handful of corporations. For example, ConAgra Foods (2013) advertises, "you'll find our food in 97% of America's homes." How did corporations, such as ConAgra Foods, come to control much of food and agriculture? And what does this mean for the kinds of food we eat, how and by whom it is produced?

At the time of the U.S.'s founding, approximately 90% of Americans were farmers. Today, less than 2% of Americans farm for a living and only about 17% live in rural areas. While "family" farms still predominate, they are no longer the stereotypical pastoral family farm, but increasingly large-scale businesses. For example, in 2007, 125,000 farms produced 75% of the entire value of U.S. agricultural production, with the average farm size being 418 acres. Similar trends are also found globally, especially in the Global South, where peasants have progressively lost access to land and natural resources. For example, rural populations decreased by approximately 25% from 1950 to 1997 globally and are projected to continue to decline through at least 2050. Not surprisingly, it is also during this time that there has been an explosion of urban slums across much of the Global South.

Alongside the decline in the number of farmers, the **corporatization of food and agriculture** has dramatically increased. In some instances, large corporations control farming itself, with the most notable examples being the transnational banana and pineapple companies, which own large amounts of land in Central America, Hawaii, and Asia. Today, more prominent is the corporatization of nearly all the other components of food and agriculture besides farming. In other words, large corporations have come to control agricultural inputs (e.g., seeds, fertilizers, and pesticides), processing (e.g., grain elevators and manufactured foods), and retail (e.g., supermarkets and restaurant chains). For example, it is estimated that in the United States, the CR4 (the percentage of the market controlled by the four largest firms) was 83.5% for beef processing, 66% for pork processing, and 58.5% for chicken processing in 2007. Globally, as of 2008, the CR4 was 56% for seeds and 59% for pesticides. Figure 12–1 illustrates how Monsanto, the largest seed company in the world, has expanded its control over the seed sector by buying up competitors. This is generally referred to as **horizontal integration**, which is when a few firms control a particular sector or stage of production.

In addition to fewer corporations controlling each part of agriculture, increasingly it is also the same corporations controlling the different parts of food and agriculture. For example, Monsanto produces and sells not only seeds, but nearly all the inputs farmers need (see Fig. 12–1). And if farmers buy one product from Monsanto, they often have little choice but to also buy the associated products (e.g., pesticides and herbicides). Similarly, Cargill controls nearly the whole meat supply chain, as it is "one of the three major global traders of grain (the major ingredient in animal feed), the second largest animal feed producer, and one of the largest processors of hogs and beef" (Heffernan, 2000, p. 69). Thus, much of food and agriculture has experienced not only significant horizontal integration but also **vertical integration**. Vertical integration is when a firm or set of firms controls multiple stages of production (e.g., inputs, production, and processing). The result is that today, food and agriculture are becoming more corporatized, oligopolistic, and vertically integrated in that just a handful of corporations control nearly every aspect of food, from seed to table.

From Natural to Industrial

We tend to think that food comes from farms. People also are likely to think that farming is based on natural processes. In other words, aided by humans, food is an outcome of nature. For many, food symbolizes nature's abundance and productivity. However, contrary to such assumptions, today most food is produced through industrial processes. In fact, some even argue that much of agriculture has shifted from "**farms to factories.**" What does it mean to say food and agriculture is industrialized? How did it become industrialized?

In short, industrialization means that agriculture relies less on nature and more on inputs. Hence, with some exceptions, such as organics, it is quite likely that your food was produced using significant amounts of chemicals

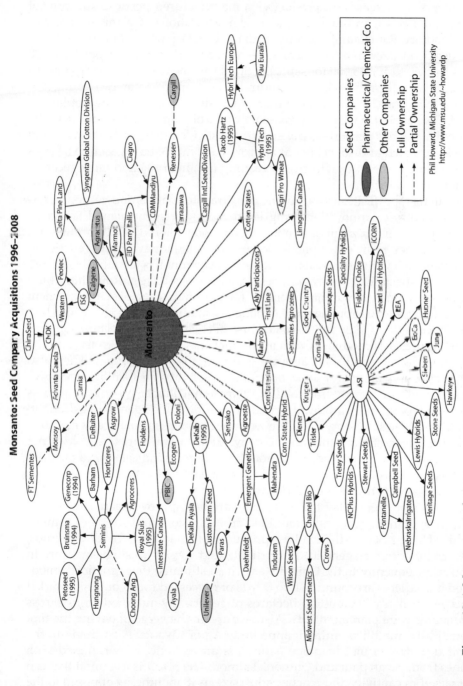

Figure 12-1 Monsanto: seed company acquisitions 1996–2008.

Source: Phil Howard, Michigan State University. http://msu.edu/~howardp.

and contains genetically modified ingredients. Growing food these days involves numerous technologies, including complex machinery and synthetic fertilizers to increase soil productivity, manufactured pesticides to control weeds and pests, and hybrid or genetic modifications of plants to improve productivity. For example, according to the U.S. Department of Agriculture, the use of nitrogen as a fertilizer has increased nearly fivefold, from 2,738,000 tons in 1960 to 12,285,000 tons in 2010. Similarly, the use of pesticides has increased significantly, with agricultural usage approximately tripling between 1980 and 2000, and more than 900 million pounds being applied in 2005. Consequently, today, approximately 62% of planted farm acreage in the United States has pesticides applied, with pesticide use being highest for row crops (e.g., corn and soybeans), at approximately 93%. Lastly, plant varieties have been adapted through cross-breeding (i.e., hybrids) and more recently genetic modification.

Genetic modification is one of the most transformative, and yet controversial, technological innovations in agriculture. In short, genetic modification is when the genes of a plant or animal are somehow altered, often through importing genes from other plants or animals. Plants have been genetically modified for a variety of reasons, but the most common is to make them more resistant to pests (e.g., Bt corn) and resistant to pesticides (e.g., Roundup Ready soybeans). Hence, the primary benefits have been making pest management easier for farmers. Proponents of genetically modified crops also claim that they have higher yields and lessen the use of chemical inputs. Thus, supporters of genetically modified crops argue that they are critical to feeding the growing global population and are good for the environment. They also claim that genetic modification offers the possibility for healthier food (for example, through modifying food to increase nutritional content) as well as greater adaption to environmental conditions (for instance, generating drought-tolerant varieties). Because the U.S. government considers genetically modified varieties substantially equivalent to conventional plant varieties, it does not require that they be labeled, even though recent polls indicate that a majority of Americans would like these foods to be labeled.

The first genetically modified crop variety was approved in the United States in 1996, and today there are 196 varieties approved across 25 crops. The most planted genetically modified crops are corn and soy. For example, in the United States, the leading producer of genetically modified crops, 88% of all corn was genetically modified, and 93% of all soybeans were in 2012. Consequently, in the United States, it is estimated that genetically modified ingredients are found in two thirds of processed foods on supermarket shelves. Globally, 160 million hectares of genetically modified crops across 29 nations were planted in 2011. Also, we are on the verge of having the first genetically modified animal approved: AquaAdvantage Salmon in the United States. AquaAdvantage Salmon is an Atlantic salmon mixed with genes from ocean pout and Chinook salmon. The result is a salmon that can be raised in captivity and reaches adult size in 18 months, as opposed to the three years it takes Atlantic salmon to do so.

While the above technological innovations originated and proliferated in the Global North, they have been increasingly exported to, and have significantly restructured, agriculture in the Global South. Beginning in the 1950s and lasting until the 1970s, there were a series of public and philanthropic initiatives funded by the U.S. government, private foundations, and development agencies (e.g., the World Bank) to export industrialized agricultural technologies and practices to the Global South (e.g., synthetic inputs, machinery, and management practices). This was known as the **green revolution**. Proponents of the green revolution argue that it increased yields and thus improved **food security** throughout much of the Global South. However, some critics contend that instead it has led to food insecurity, changes in diets and associated nutritional deficiencies, further dependence on the Global North and corporations for inputs, and a variety of negative environmental impacts. Currently, analysts such as food policy expert Raj Patel argue that the Global South is experiencing a second green revolution, which entails the diffusion of the latest technological innovations, most notably genetically modified crop varieties. The second green revolution is through private initiatives, largely controlled, as well as aggressively propagated, by corporations. The result is the increasing industrialization of agriculture across the Global South.

CONVENTIONAL FOOD AND AGRICULTURE, THE ENVIRONMENT, AND INJUSTICE

Globalization, corporatization, and industrialization have made food and agriculture highly productive and efficient, but with significant social and environmental costs (see also Lesson 13). For example, have you ever considered the environmental costs of eating grapes in the middle of winter? Have you ever wondered how it is possible to get a Quarter-Pounder with Cheese, fries, and a soda for five dollars? Have you ever thought about the chemicals on or in your food, and the implications of such chemicals for your health, agricultural workers, and the environment? Or, what does it mean for the food you eat, workers, and the environment that an increasingly small number of transnational corporations control nearly all aspects of food and agriculture? Using an environmental sociology lens, this section examines the high environmental and social costs of food and agriculture.

Perhaps most obvious are the effects that the industrialization of food and agriculture has had on the environment. The vast array of chemical inputs used in conventional agriculture pollutes ecosystems and water systems and affects wildlife. For example, nitrogen is a key component of industrial fertilizers. Nitrogen runoff is a leading source of water contamination. In the United States, it is estimated that one third of coastal rivers and bays face nitrogen pollution, with approximately 20% achieving periodic dead zones (e.g., too much oxygen in the water for marine life to survive). Most notable is the annual dead zone where the Mississippi River enters into the Gulf of Mexico, which in 2011 was estimated by the National Oceanic and Atmospheric Administration to encompass 6,765 square miles, which is larger than Connecticut! Pesticides contain a wide assortment of chemicals, including many potential carcinogens, and thus are also a significant source of pollution. According to the U.S. Fish and Wildlife Service, in major rivers and streams pesticides were detected 90% of the time in the water, and in over 80% of sampled fish. Pesticides have also been linked to declines in amphibians and are considered a potential cause of decline in pollinator species (e.g., bees and butterflies).

The production of the agricultural inputs, large-scale farming, processing, and transportation are also all energy-intensive. For example, do you know your **food footprint**? Food footprint is a measurement of how much resources people's diet use and the amount of pollution it produces. If you live in the United States, it is estimated that it takes seven to ten calories of input energy to produce one calorie of food. To put this in perspective, think about it in the following way:

> So if your daily food intake is 2,000 calories, then it took 20,000 calories to grow that food and get it to you. In more familiar units, this means that growing, processing, and delivering the food consumed by a family of four each year requires the equivalent of almost 34,000 kilowatt-hours (kWh) of energy, or more than 930 gallons of gasoline (for comparison, the average U.S. household annually consumes about 10,800 kWh of electricity, or about 1,070 gallons of gasoline). In other words, we use about as much energy to grow our food as to power our homes or fuel our cars. (Starrs, 2005)

Globally, it is estimated that just agriculture—not including the manufacturing of inputs, the processing of crops into final products, and transportation—produces 14% of greenhouses gas emissions. Thus, discussions of how food is produced and what people eat need to be part of the conversation on global climate change (see Lesson 15).

Genetically engineered varieties have also raised numerous environmental concerns. Some claim that scientists and corporations are "playing god" in that they are remaking nature. The problem, opponents argue, is that the consequences of such transformations are largely unknown. Specific concerns include biological pollution, the effects on animals, and the loss of biodiversity. Already, some of the environmental transformations are being seen in the advent of "superweeds" and "superpests." These weeds and pests have evolved to be resistant to the synthetic inputs designed to kill them and thus threaten to undermine the primary benefit of genetically modified varieties. Despite claims to the contrary, significant weed and pest resistance to Roundup Ready varieties of soybeans and their associated herbicide glyphosate are now documented. For example, while estimates vary, the Weed Science Society of America reports that over 14 million acres (5.7 million hectares) are infested with such superweeds.

Such examples illustrate one of the chief concerns regarding the sustainability of industrialized agriculture, namely its treadmill character (see Lesson 2 for an overview of the "treadmill of production"). In short, efforts to increase productivity have led to the use of synthetic inputs and increasing dependence on them. However, while often increasing productivity, such inputs have often led to environmental degradation. The solution has been another round of technological fixes to "correct" the problems produced by the previous technological fixes. However, subsequent technological fixes have tended to generate new sets of environmental concerns, as illustrated by the emergence of superweeds. Ironically, the chief solution to superweeds being advanced by agribusiness is a return to the more toxic pesticides (such as 2,4-D, of which some versions contain dioxins), which genetically modified varieties were supposed to eliminate. At the same time, the increasing cost of inputs continually squeezes out more farmers and thus produces greater consolidation and corporatization of agriculture.

The global character of conventional food and agriculture also has negative impacts on the environment. Most obvious is the energy withdrawals and pollution associated with the transportation of food and agriculture. However, more significant is the ways that the globalization of food and agriculture are affecting ecological limits. Congruent with world-systems theory (see Lesson 2), a key characteristic of the globalization of food and agriculture is unequal ecological exchange. On the one hand, the globalization of food and agriculture displaces ecological limits for the Global North in that it is not constrained by domestic agriculture productivity. Put differently, if Americans had to rely only on domestic land and resources, current ways of producing and consuming food would not be possible. On the other hand, the globalization of food and agriculture shrinks ecological limits for many countries in the Global South, as significant portions of their land and resources (e.g., water) are being used to produce "cash crops" exports for the Global North.

As environmental justice scholars and activists have demonstrated, pollution and environmental degradation are not equally distributed across all people (see Lesson 10). Similar to other environmental issues, conventional food and agriculture is also characterized by significant inequality and injustice. While the chemicals used in conventional food and agriculture affect everyone who eats, farmworkers and neighboring communities are disproportionately affected. Not only is farm work among the lowest paid forms of work; it is also among the most dangerous. For example, pesticide-related illnesses continue to be a significant problem for farmworkers. People living in neighboring communities are also often subjected to pesticides through drift. Furthermore, in many instances, pollution from pesticides and the negative health effects are much greater in the Global South, where more toxic pesticides are often allowed (including ones banned in the United States and other industrialized countries) and regulations on residues and farmworker exposures are either weaker or less strictly enforced. In many instances, dangerous working conditions also extend to food processing, which in the

Global South often resembles other forms of industrialized work, such as garment production (see the "factory girls" example above).

The globalization of conventional food and agriculture is partly based on "accumulation by dispossession," which is the privatization and commodification of formerly public resources or commons (McMichael, 2012). Put differently, what were once largely public goods, such as land, water, and seeds, which nearly all people could access and use, are now increasingly private goods that people need to pay to use. This form of "development," in turn, affects land use patterns, often in ways that heighten environmental degradation (see Lesson 8). For example, having been removed from their historic lands by corporate-driven operations, peasants may seek new land and thus resettle to either more agriculturally marginal land or undeveloped land, such as rainforests in tropical countries. Or, more commonly, as the explosion of slums attests to, they tend to migrate to urban areas in search of work. The result has been the proliferation of shantytowns and a host of associated environmental, social, and health consequences. These include deforestation and increased susceptibility to natural disasters (e.g., the 2010 Haiti earthquake), lack of access to clean water and sewage systems, elevated rates of infectious diseases, high rates of violence and crime, lack of job opportunities, and stigmatization. Genetic technologies have also introduced a new form of accumulation by dispossession in that seeds and genetics are increasingly becoming proprietary and thus no longer part of the global commons. Consequently, "saving seeds" is increasingly no longer possible for many farmers.

While the effects are not as dramatic, the corporatization of food and agriculture has also had negative impacts on communities in industrialized nations. Most notable is how the depopulation of farming in the United States has contributed to rural communities often accepting, and sometimes actively seeking, locally unwanted land uses (LULUs), such as landfills, power plants, and polluting factories, in order to spur economic development. Hence, as farming has become less of an engine of local economic development, rural communities have often been forced to choose between jobs or the environment.

Lastly, the globalization, corporatization, and industrialization of food and agriculture have simultaneously produced societies of abundance and scarcity, often within the same nation. The productivity and efficiency of agriculture, combined with the drive for profitability by corporations, has given rise to ever more processed foods. Compared to unprocessed produce and meat, processed foods tend to offer greater profitability and more opportunity for market differentiation. Consequently, new processed foods are continually showing up on supermarket shelves, and most have high levels of sugar, salt, fat, and cholesterol. Furthermore, those are the food products that the corporations tend to advertise the most. Marion Nestle (2007, p. 22) observes that "nearly 70% of food advertising is for convenience foods, candy and snacks, alcoholic beverages, soft drinks, and desserts, whereas just 2.2% is for fruits, vegetables, grains, or beans." One outcome of the proliferation of processed foods is a global obesity problem. In the United States, some argue that obesity is becoming an "epidemic."

At the same time, the proliferation of processed foods may also be contributing to hunger in the United States. Implicit hunger refers to micronutrient malnutrition caused not necessarily by a shortage of food but rather by access to unhealthy food. Currently, "one in six Americans lives in a household that cannot afford adequate food" according to the International Human Rights Clinic (2013, p. 3). This number has increased by 14 million people since the start of the recent economic recession and includes 17 million children. The notion of **"food desert"** best demonstrates the problem of implicit hunger in America. Food deserts are urban and rural areas where people lack access to affordable fresh and nutritious foods, such as fruits and vegetables. Research indicates that food deserts tend to be found in poor and/or minority areas because it is in these areas that fewer supermarkets are located, and the price of the food tends to be higher as a result of diminished competition. Thus, as the *New York Times* has noted, an "obesity-huger paradox" is found in America in that "the hungriest people in the US today, statistically speaking, may well be not sickly skinny, but excessively fat."

In addition to implicit hunger, there is also explicit hunger. Explicit hunger is when people do not have access to sufficient food. While explicit hunger continues to be a problem in the United States and other industrialized countries, it's a much more serious problem in the Global South. As of 2010, it was estimated that approximately 925 million people globally were hungry, with the vast majority in the Global South. Hunger in the Global South is usually explained in one of two ways. The first is simply that there is not enough food. Hence, solving hunger means producing more food, which means further industrializing agriculture. However, a second explanation contends that hunger is an outcome of an unjust world. Put differently, for many in the Global South, hunger is an outcome of a lack of access to food, mostly because people increasingly cannot afford it. Generally, food prices are outstripping increases in the incomes of people globally. For example, from 2005 to 2008, the World Bank reported that food prices increased 83% globally. This increase was an outcome of drought, which negatively affected production, but also changing diets (e.g., increased consumption of meat globally), financial speculation, and the conversion of agricultural products into biofuels, as opposed to food.

The implications of biofuels merit special attention. In the push to counter their dependencies on fossil fuels, much of the Global North is promoting the development of biofuels, which is fuel derived from agricultural crops. Often biofuels are promoted as a green alternative to fossil fuels, given that they are a renewable resource. Yet, biofuels tend to be made from some of the crops that are the most energy- and chemical-intensive to produce, and thus are among the most environmentally degrading. For example, over 40% of U.S. corn production is now being used for biofuels. Even more problematic are the effects that biofuel production is having on hunger and **food sovereignty**. For example, it is estimated that European companies have "seized five million hectares of farmland—an area the size of Denmark—in developing countries for biofuel production" (Monbiot, 2012, p. 2). Hence, George Monbiot (2012, p. 2) argues that

> Biofuels are the means by which governments in the rich world avoid hard choices. No one has to drive less or make a better car: everything remains the same except the source of fuel. The result is a competition between the world's richest and poorest consumers, a contest between overconsumption and survival.

As exemplified by the development of biofuels, today's globalized, corporatized, and industrialized food and agriculture system is characterized by contradictions, unsustainability, and injustice.

ALTERNATIVE FOOD AND AGRICULTURE

In the last part of this lesson, we introduce some of the movements that strive to counter food safety and quality, environmental, and labor problems associated with the conventional food and agriculture system. These movements, generally referred to as "alternative food and agriculture movements," consist of a variety of stakeholders, including social and/or environmental movement organizations, farmers, consumers, and businesses. Broadly speaking, they share the view that the conventional food and agriculture system is unjust and unsustainable, as it prioritizes the maximization of corporate profits at the expense of food safety and quality, small farmers' livelihoods, cultural diversity, and ecological sustainability.

Alternative food and agriculture movements are characterized by significant diversity in terms of their scale, structure, and tactics. On the one hand, *La Via Campesina* (International Peasant's Movement) is a global grassroots movement that brings together millions of peasants, small (and medium-sized) farmers, female farmers, landless people, indigenous people, and agricultural workers. It strives to return food sovereignty—ranging from the right to use and manage lands, water, seeds, livestock, and biodiversity to the rights to know about how food is produced by whom and where—to producers and consumers. Local food movements, on the other hand, are community-based and thus localized (and regionalized) movements that promote the production and consumption of local food as a means to counter the conventional food and agriculture system. Initiatives such as farmers' markets and community-supported agriculture (CSA) are perhaps the most prominent parts of the local food movement. While quite diverse, alternative food and agriculture movements are tied together through their common goals—that is, the advancement of non–petroleum-dependent and sustainable food systems that are fair and just. Thus, they seek to develop a food system where producers and consumers have voice in the kinds of food produced and how it is produced.

Market-Driven Alternative Food and Agriculture

Of the wide variety of strategies being used by food movements today, market-based tactics have become one of the most prominent. This section addresses why this is the case. Specifically, it examines what market-based approaches are, how they work, and their potential to transform conventional food and agriculture. To begin, consider the following scenario: You go to a nearby supermarket to purchase some carrots. There are two options. At first glance, the carrots look the same—same size, same shape, and same color. However, they are priced differently. One bag of carrots has the store-brand label and costs $2.10. Another bag has the USDA organic label, which means the carrots are produced without the use of synthetic inputs and genetically modified varieties, and costs $3.25. Which do you choose? Do you choose the store-brand carrots because they are less expensive or do you choose the organic carrots because you think they are some combination of tastier, healthier, and better for the environment?

More likely than not you have experienced this scenario, if not with carrots then perhaps another kind of produce, or perhaps even a meat or dairy product. However, have you ever considered the following question: What are the implications of you, an individual consumer, choosing to purchase a particular product? Suppose you purchase the organic carrots. As these carrots were organically grown, this means that they were produced without the use of synthetically manufactured chemical inputs and genetically modified varieties. If you, and enough other consumers, purchase organic carrots, demand for such a product will go up. Greater demand will then lead to supermarkets carrying more organic products and, hence, more farmers growing organic carrots. Thus, through their purchasing practices, consumers can potentially shift food and agriculture toward more just and sustainable forms of production.

From the perspective of movement organizations, consumption is a key site where individuals can exercise their values and politics. This is what Michele Micheletti (2004, p. 114) termed **"political consumerism,"** by which she meant "put[ting] your money where your mouth is." Thus, a key task of movement organizations is educating consumers as to the problems of conventional food and agriculture and the benefits of alternative forms of food and agriculture. Additionally, movement organizations (e.g., Greenpeace) seek to shift demand in the marketplace by pressuring large retailers or branded companies to make commitments to selling or sourcing only alternative products. Thus, Stewart Lockie (2002) describes market-based alternative food and agriculture movements as relying on the "the invisible mouth" (vis-à-vis the market being "the invisible hand"). In other words, movement organizations are using both actual and potential consumer demand as a tool to try to reform food and agriculture.

To distinguish alternative products from conventional products, movement organizations are increasingly relying on standards, certification, and labeling. Specifically, standards have been developed to define alternative production practices (e.g., environmentally sustainable and fair and safe labor conditions), certification is used to ensure that the product complies with the standards, and the product is labeled using a particular logo (e.g., fair trade and organic). In this way, consumers can distinguish alternative products from others on supermarket shelves. Today, alternative food and agriculture standards, certification, and labels are exploding. Prominent examples include organics (sustainable agriculture), Rainforest Alliance (sustainable agriculture and forestry), Marine Stewardship Council (sustainable fisheries), Aquaculture Stewardship Council (sustainable aquaculture), fair trade (equity and justice in international trade), and the Roundtable on Sustainable Palm Oil (sustainable palm oil production). Furthermore, market demand for alternative products is also rapidly growing. For example, according to the Organic Trade Association the organic market in the United States grew by 9.5% overall in 2011 and reached $31.5 billion in sales in 2011. Fair trade food products now encompass coffee, tea, cocoa, honey, bananas, pineapples, mangoes, grapes, nuts and oilseeds, beans and grains, and sugar, among others. The Fair Trade Foundation estimated that retail sales of fair trade products in 2011 reached £1.32bn, a 12% increase from 2010.

How do we interpret the growth in kinds and demand for alternative food and agriculture and assess the impacts of such growth in terms of the production of food? For example, do consumers, social movements, and producers have a greater say in food and agriculture? Is the conventional food and agriculture system becoming more sustainable and just, and/or is it gradually being replaced by a new model? While many proponents of market-based approaches answer "yes" to such questions, viewed through a sociological lens the picture is more complex and contradictory.

A primary reason given for the proliferation of market-based approaches to social change is their congruence with contemporary neoliberalism. As Peter Taylor argues (2005), in using market-based approaches, movement organizations are trying to be "in the market, but not of it." In other words, market forms of activism do not seek to constrain the market, but rather use it to advance specific causes. Consequently, this means that market-based approaches do not challenge the structure and practices of markets; rather, they challenge the kinds of goods that are bought and sold. In fact, in many instances, movement organizations seek to cooperatively work with large corporations. The logic behind this is that given the tremendous influence that large corporations have, if social movements can make them into an ally, significant social change becomes more likely. For example, as Walmart sells more food than anyone else in the United States, getting it to sell and promote alternative products can have huge impacts. Through such efforts, activists hope to "mainstream" alternative products—that is, shift them from niche products consumed by only a small minority of people to everyday products used by the majority of people.

However, there is a burgeoning body of literature that questions if in using market-based approaches, alternative food and agriculture movements are being captured by the market. For example, Julie Guthman's study

(2004) of organic agriculture illustrated how the organic movement was transformed from a largely local, small-scale movement aimed at countering industrialized agriculture to big business. In other words, as the demand for, and the profitability of, organic foods has increased, agribusiness has become heavily involved in the organic sector. In the United States, just two companies control roughly 80% of organic food distribution, and many of the lead corporations in the industrialized food system are also the largest organic companies. For example, General Mills owns such organic brands as Cascadian Farms and Muir Glen, Dean's owns Horizon Organics, Coca-Cola owns Odwalla, and Kellogg owns Kashi. Thus, critics of market-based approaches argue that they lead to a watering down or "conventionalization" of alternative food and agriculture. Put differently, as alternative food and agriculture becomes mainstreamed, its visions and principles often become diluted.

Another concern with market-based approaches to social change is their reliance on political consumerism. As noted above, while some see it as a powerful form of human agency, others are more doubtful. On the one hand, some critics point out that consumers tend to be disorganized and have fewer resources than corporations and thus are at a disadvantage in the marketplace. Others contend that consumption as a form of politics may lead to socially unjust outcomes. For example, at a coffee shop, will you pay $1 more to have fair trade coffee? What if the price gap is greater, perhaps $2 or $3 more? What is your threshold?

Obviously, not all consumers can afford to purchase alternative products. This raises questions as to who gets to participate in the movement, and what kinds of change can be achieved using market-based approaches. In *Shopping Our Way to Safety*, Andrew Szasz (2007) contended that political consumerism is deepening an already class-divided society in that those who can afford to are protecting themselves from risky and dangerous stuff, while the majority of people must suffice on the leftovers. Applied to food, this means that those who can afford to can eat fair trade, ethical, and organic food, while everyone else is stuck with the industrialized food from nowhere. Thus, from this perspective, political consumerism is understood as not changing society per se, but making sustainable, just, high-quality, and safe food into a private right.

CONCLUSION

There is an old saying, "you are what you eat." If this is the case, what kind of person do you think you are? What kind of person would you like to be? What kind of person do you want your children and grandchildren to be in the future?

When we project the future of our food landscape, two scenarios are possible. The first is a continuation of the conventional food and agriculture system. In today's neoliberal world, similar to most other economic activities, transnational corporations largely control food and agriculture. Governments are captured by agribusiness and thus tend to implement business-friendly policies and regulations. Furthermore, agricultural science is increasingly privatized, with agribusiness corporations controlling much of research pertaining to food and agriculture. Hence, under such conditions, the increasing use of biotechnologies and chemical inputs, the lack of labeling of genetically modified foods, continued "fetishism" of the production of food (e.g., not knowing where food comes from and how it is produced), the proliferation of unhealthy foods, and lack of access to food are all likely to continue.

A second scenario would be a more sustainable, just, and healthy food and agriculture system. Thanks to alternative food and agriculture movements, such alternatives exist today, and questions about food, health, justice, and the environment have become public issues. Yet, alternative food and agriculture movements in the United States tend to be driven by middle- to upper-class white consumers who want healthier, more sustainable, and/or socially just food. Furthermore, the use of market-based approaches excludes a significant portion of the population who cannot afford to partake in political consumerism. However, as Allison Alkon and Julian Agyeman (2011) have noted, emerging alongside market-driven food movements are a set of food justice movements by marginalized groups (e.g., poor and people of color) focused on hunger, healthy food, and food sovereignty. Springing up in poor inner-city neighborhoods, in impoverished rural areas, and on Native American reservations, these food justice movements are using collective strategies, such as protests, marches, and public gardens, to transform food deserts into communities with healthy, sustainable, and culturally appropriate food. Thus, similar to the ways that environmental justice movements expanded environmentalism (see Lesson 10), food justice movements may expand food politics to issues of class, race, and ethnicity.

In concluding, this lesson highlights that an increasing number of actors are making efforts, whether they are market-based or not, to contest and change the conventional food and agriculture system, and that you can be part of such efforts. To do so you must understand that your food does not come from nowhere and what you eat tremendously affects people, the environment, and society. We end this lesson by providing a set of questions that need to be engaged if food and agriculture are to become sustainable and just:

- Can corporations coexist with a sustainable and just food and agriculture system? If yes, how?
- Do people need to change how they eat and what they eat?
- Does cooking need to be reinvigorated? If yes, how do we ensure people have time to cook?
- Can the U.S. government be "freed" from agribusiness and used to develop more sustainable and just food and agriculture?
- Can public food and agriculture science be rejuvenated and can it be oriented to meet the needs of the public?

These are big questions. They are questions that sociology can help you think about. And they are questions that require collective action to do anything about.

SOURCES

Adams, Damian C., and Matthew J. Salois. 2010. "Local Versus Organic: A Turn in Consumer Preferences and Willingness-to-Pay." *Renewable Agriculture and Food Systems* 25(4):331–341.

Alkon, Allison H., and Julian Agyeman. 2011. "Introduction: The Food Movement as Polyculture." In A. H. Alkon and J. Agyeman, eds. *Cultivating Food Justice: Race, Class, and Sustainability*, pp. 1–20. Cambridge, MA: MIT Press.

Barndt, Deborah. 2008. "Whose 'Choice'? 'Flexible' Women Workers in the Tomato Food Chain." In C. M. Counihan and P. Van Esterik, eds. *Food and Culture*, pp. 452–466. New York: Routledge.

Benbrook, Charles M. 2012. "Impacts of Genetically Engineered Crops on Pesticide Use in the U.S.—The First Sixteen Years." *Environmental Sciences Europe* 24:1–13.

Blatt, Harvey. 2011. *America's Food: What You Don't Know About What You Eat*. Boston: The MIT Press.

Carolan, Michael. 2012. *The Sociology of Food and Agriculture*. New York: Routledge.

Clausen, Rebecca, and Stefano B. Longo. 2012. "The Tragedy of the Commodity and the Farce of AquaAdvantage Salmon®." *Development and Change* 43(1): 229–251.

ConAgra Foods. 2013. Homepage Accessed at http://www.conagrafoods.com/ on April 1, 2013.

Dolnick, Sam. 2010. (March 12). "The Obesity-Hunger Paradox." *New York Times*. Accessed at http://www.nytimes.com/2010/03/14/nyregion/14hunger.html?src=me on March 30, 2013

Guthman, Julie. 2004. *Agrarian Dreams: The Paradox of Organic Farming in California*. Berkeley: University of California Press.

Heffernan, William D. 2000. "Concentration of Ownership and Control in Agriculture." In F. Magdoff, J. B. Foster, and F. H. Buttel, eds. *Hungry For Profit*, pp. 61–76. New York: Monthly Review Press.

Heffernan, William D., and Mary Hendrickson. 2007. "Concentration of Agricultural Markets." Accessed at http://ccheonline.org/mhendrickson on April 1, 2013.

Holt-Gimenez, Eric, and Raj Patel. 2009. *Food Rebellions! Crisis and the Hunger for Justice*. New York: Food First Books.

Howard, Philip H. 2009. "Visualizing Consolidation in the Global Seed Industry: 1996–2008." *Sustainability* 1:1266–1287.

Howard, Philip. H. 2013. Homepage. Accessed at https://www.msu.edu/~howardp/index.html on April 1, 2013.

International Human Rights Clinic. 2013. *Nourishing Change: Fulfilling the Right to Food in the United States*. New York: NYU School of Law.

James, C. 2011. Global Status of Commercialized Biotech/GM Crops: 2011. *ISAAA Brief* No. 43 (Ithaca, New York: ISSAA).

Lappé, Anna. 2010. *Diet for a Hot Planet: The Climate Crisis at the End of Your Fork and What You Can Do About It*. New York: Bloomsbury USA.

La Via Campesina. 2013. "Organisation: The International Peasant's Voice." Accessed at http://viacampesina.org/en/index.php/organisation-mainmenu-44 on March 28, 2013.

Lockie, Stewart. 2002. "'The Invisible Mouth': Mobilizing 'the Consumer' in Food Production-Consumption Networks." *Sociologia Ruralis* 42(4):278–294.

McMichael, Philip. 2009a. "The World Food Crisis in Historical Perspective." *Monthly Review* 61:Online.

McMichael, Philip. 2009b. "A Food Regime Genealogy." *The Journal of Peasant Studies* 36:139–169.

McMichael, Philip. 2012. *Development and Social Change: A Global Perspective.* Thousand Oaks, CA: Sage.

Micheletti, Michele. 2004. "'Put Your Money where Your Mouth Is!' The Market as an Arena for Politics." In C. Garsten and M. Lindh de Montoya, eds. *Market Matters: Exploring Cultural Processes in the Global Marketplace,* pp. 114–134. New York: Palgrave Macmillan.

Monbiot, George. 2012. (August 12). "Must the Poor Go Hungry Just so the Rich Can Drive."*TheGuardian.* Accessed at http://www.guardian.co.uk/commentisfree/2012/aug/13/poor-hungry-rich-drive-mo-farah-biofuels/print on August 24, 2012.

National Oceanic and Atmospheric Administration (NOAA). 2012. "NOAA: Gulf of Mexico 'Dead Zone' Predictions Feature Uncertainty " Accessed at http://www.noaanews.noaa.gov/stories2012/20120621_deadzone.html on April 1, 2013.

Nestle, Marion. 2007. *Food Politics: How the Food Industry Influences Nutrition and Health.* Berkeley, CA: University of California Press.

Organic Trade Association. 2012. "Organic Trade Association's 2012 Organic Industry Survey Shows Continued Growth." Accessed at http://www.organicnewsroom.com/2012/04/us_consumerdriven_organic_mark.html on April 1, 2013.

Patel, Raj. 2013. "The Long Green Revolution." *The Journal of Peasant Studies* 40:1–63.

Starrs, Thomas. 2005. "The SUV in the Pantry." *SustainableBusiness.com.* Accessed http://www.sustainablebusiness.com/index.cfm/go/news.feature/id/1275 on April 1, 2013.

Szasz, Andrew. 2007. *Shopping Our Way to Safety: How We Changed from Protecting the Environment to Protecting Ourselves.* Minneapolis: University of Minnesota Press.

Taylor, P. 2005. "In the Market but Not of It: Fair Trade Coffee and Forest Stewardship Council Certification as Market-Based Social Change." *World Development* 33(1):129–147.

The Fairtrade Foundation. 2012. "Responsible Capitalism? New Fairtrade Figures Show Business is Changing for Good." Accessed at http://www.fairtrade.org.uk/press_office/press_releases_and_statements/february_2012/responsible_capitalism.aspx on October 8, 2012.

United States Department of Agriculture (USDA). 2007. "2007 Census of Agriculture." Accessed at http://www.agcensus.usda.gov/Publications/2007/Online_Highlights/Fact_Sheets/Farm_Numbers/farm_numbers.pdf on April 1, 2013.

United States Department of Agriculture (USDA). 2012a. "Fertilizer Use and Price."Accessed at http://www.ers.usda.gov/data-products/fertilizer-use-and-price.aspx#26720 on April 1, 2013.

United States Department of Agriculture (USDA). 2012b. "Adoption of Genetically Engineered Crops in the US." Accessed at http://www.ers.usda.gov/data-products/adoption-of-genetically-engineered-crops-in-the-us.aspx on January 7, 2013.

Weber, Christopher L., and Scott H. Matthews. 2008. "Food-Miles and the Relative Climate Impacts of Food Choices in the United States." *Environmental Science and Technology* 42:3508–3513.

13

From Farms to Factories

The Social and Environmental Consequences of Industrial Swine Production in North Carolina

Adam Driscoll and Bob Edwards

Packaged pork and other meat products in supermarket grocery case, New York, New York.

Photo by Ken Gould.

From the Appalachian Mountains in the west to the beaches of the Outer Banks, North Carolina's natural beauty attracts millions of vacationers, retirees, and outdoor enthusiasts each year to enjoy its varied landscapes. The ecological diversity of rural eastern North Carolina's bountiful wetlands, rivers, estuaries, and sounds is no exception. Yet, over the past 30 years these natural resources have come under increasing stress from pollution. When one thinks of industrial polluters, the images that readily come to mind are those of factories belching black smoke into the air or dumping unknown chemicals into a river; rarely is a farm one of the first associations. However, a 1998 Senate Agriculture Committee report estimated that the annual volume of livestock wastes—including pork, poultry, beef, and dairy—in the United States constitutes the largest contributor to the pollution of

America's waterways. In recent decades the agriculture industry has been transformed by the widespread adoption of advanced agricultural technologies that replace family labor. This **industrialization of agriculture** has changed the very nature of farming and replaced environmentally sustainable practices with ecologically destructive ones.

A case in point can be found in the North Carolina pork industry. The traditional pattern of numerous independent farmers raising hogs in small numbers, often to supplement their income from field crops like cotton, tobacco, corn, or soybeans, is all but extinct. Large, **vertically integrated** (the consolidation of multiple stages of production; see Lesson 5) corporations now own the pigs "from birth to bacon" and raise them using advanced, industrial techniques. Anecdotally this is borne out by the absence of pigs at county fairs in eastern North Carolina; showings and competitions among individual farmers and students have virtually disappeared. Gone as well are the benign environmental impacts of traditional pork production, replaced by ones that may best be described as corrosive. This lesson examines the North Carolina case to better understand these profound changes as well as their social and environmental impacts. Furthermore, the changes we describe that characterize North Carolina's hog industry are illustrative of ongoing trends in all animal production, including beef, poultry, and fish.

FROM FARMS TO FACTORIES

Between 1985 and 2000 the North Carolina pork industry changed dramatically in several ways. First, and most obviously, the industry expanded dramatically. However, the fivefold increase in hog population (and wastes generated) rests on more subtle, but consequential, changes in the structure and technology of pork production. This section discusses the growth of the hog industry from 2 million to 10 million head and its concentration onto the coastal plain of eastern North Carolina. Second, we outline the industry restructuring that accompanied this period of dramatic expansion. Third, we describe the **confined animal feeding operation** (CAFO) technology typical of pork and other livestock production nationwide. Finally, we conclude by introducing our concept of **"externalities of scale"** as a tool for explaining how the above changes in the industry combined to transform it into one of the state's worst polluters.

Industry Expansion

Between 1982 and 1992 the North Carolina swine population doubled to reach about 4 million. Production had become **horizontally integrated** (the consolidation of firms occupying the same stage of production) and increasingly utilized capital-intensive CAFO technologies. These industry changes, along with active promotion by the state government, a massive new processing facility, and the growing popularity of pork, set the stage for meteoric expansion

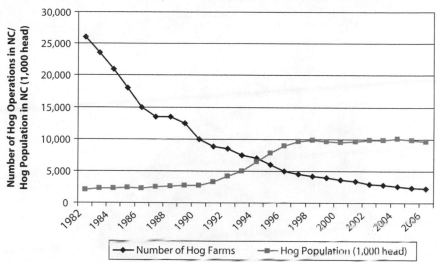

Figure 13-1 The North Carolina hog industry's consolidation and growth from 1982 to 2006. Growth is represented by the state hog population, while consolidation is exhibited in the number of hog farms in the state.

Source: North Carolina Department of Agriculture.

to over 10 million hogs by 1997. Suddenly, North Carolina had more pigs than people, with hogs outnumbering humans by 5 to 1 on the coastal plain and by as much as 50 to 1 in individual counties. Pork surpassed poultry and tobacco as North Carolina's top agricultural commodity. Yet, the number of hog farms declined dramatically over this same period, leaving the state with far fewer, but much larger, hog operations, as shown in Figure 13-1. Overall, these changes catapulted North Carolina to the status of the United States' leading innovator in the expanding and rapidly globalizing pork market.

This explosion in the hog population was accompanied by a simultaneous geographical implosion. In 1982 only one North Carolina county lacked commercial hog farms; by 1997, following the period of intensive growth, approximately 95% of all swine production had concentrated in the eastern counties of the coastal plain, particularly in the southern portion of this region. The top 10 hog-producing counties in the southeastern region of the state accounted for a full 77% of the state's hog population in 2006. Figure 13-2 provides an excellent visual representation of the industry's geographical concentration.

Industry Restructuring

The dramatic expansion of North Carolina's hog industry has been accompanied by equally profound changes in the structure of the industry's ownership. In short, 30-plus years ago thousands of small farmers produced North Carolina's pork. They bought feed from local feedlots and sold pigs to

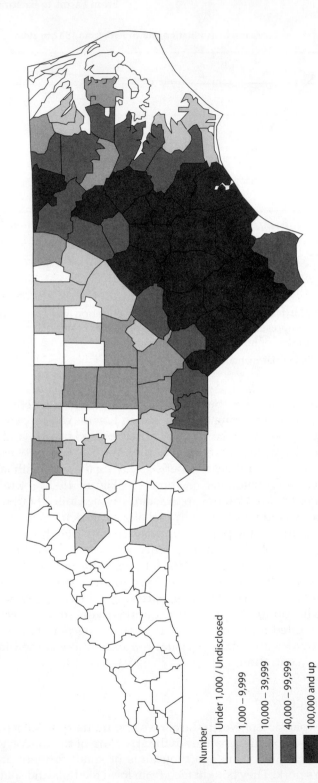

Number

Under 1,000 / Undisclosed

1,000 – 9,999

10,000 – 39,999

40,000 – 99,999

100,000 and up

Figure 13–2 Distribution of swine production in North Carolina by county.

a network of small slaughterhouses, which in turn sold butchered pork to meat wholesalers. Each step along the process consisted of numerous independent businesses. Today, the situation could hardly be more different. Currently, one large multinational corporation, Smithfield Foods, owns outright or exerts contract control over more than 90% of North Carolina's pork industry, from breeding to branded pork products for retail consumption worldwide. This shift has important implications for the consolidation of industry decision making as well as for how the industry is regulated.

The first step of this industry restructuring came in the form of horizontal integration of hog production by corporate "integrators." These large firms replaced the traditional system of numerous independent farmers with one of corporate contract farming, where the integrators own the pigs and farmers are paid a set price for the weight the pigs gain while in their care. The practice of contract hog farming was introduced in 1973 by Wendell Murphy, a former feed mill owner who would go on to become the owner of Murphy Family Farms, Inc., North Carolina's largest and most influential corporate pork integrator. In 1997, Murphy graced the cover of *Forbes* magazine as America's "low-tech" billionaire. The success of Murphy Family Farms rested on the implementation of contract farming and the shift to CAFO-style production.

The contract system enables corporate integrators to determine the exact conditions under which hogs are raised. To meet processor requirements, integrators demand large herds raised with CAFO-style production technologies. This preference led to a "squeezing out" of smaller hog farms, where farmers who did not obtain a contract with a corporate integrator and shift to CAFO-style production could not sell their hogs and were driven out of business (hence the decline in hog farmers from over 25,000 to about 2,300). By about 1995 the process of horizontal integration was complete and the few hog farmers whose businesses had survived were outsourced contractors, essentially renting their land, services, and CAFO to a corporate integrator.

The second step of the restructuring came with the vertical integration of hog production and processing by one multinational firm, Smithfield Foods of Virginia. By 1995, Smithfield was already the nation's largest pork processor and slaughtered over 95% of the hogs raised in North Carolina. In 1998, Smithfield was able to exploit a sustained downturn in pork prices (Fig. 13–3) to expand into the production stage of the hog industry. The price decline caused substantial losses to corporate producers like Murphy Family Farms while creating a windfall for Smithfield. This windfall was used to purchase North Carolina's largest corporate pork producers: Brown's of Carolina (1998), Carroll's Foods (1999), and finally Murphy Family Farms (2000). Vertical integration of domestic pork production and processing was good for Smithfield. In the first *quarter* of 2000, just after its acquisition of Murphy Family Farms, sales totaled $1.4 billion, with quarterly *after-tax* profits of $44.6 million, a 546% increase. Such profits were made possible in part because the costs of waste disposal are paid by the human and ecological communities of eastern North Carolina.

Figure 13–3 National hog prices for the month of December from 1990 to 2001. *Source:* USDA National Agricultural Service.

Confined Animal Feeding Operations

Prior to the industry's explosive growth and restructuring, hog farming was conducted by numerous independent farmers raising hogs in small numbers on pasture or dirt lots. Farms specializing in hog production were rare, with most pigs being raised to supplement a farmer's income from field crops like corn, soybeans, or tobacco. Production techniques varied among traditional farmers, with hogs kept in different sorts of shelters with variable pasture-land available to them. Similarly, feed consisted of a wide range of food sources, from on-farm scraps and crop byproducts to 100% off-farm purchased feed. Hog waste was frequently used as a natural fertilizer for restoring nutrients to fields that grew commercially viable crops on the same farm. The combination of small herd sizes and large accompanying fields led to this form of waste disposal producing no adverse environmental consequences.

Traditional hog farms of this type are all but extinct in North Carolina. Today, nearly all hogs are raised using CAFO technology. CAFOs are frequently dubbed "assembly-line swine" by their critics who want to emphasize that swine CAFOs more closely resemble industrial facilities than the traditional farms just described. Swine CAFOs typically house 2,000 to 5,000 pigs in just a few large buildings, although larger operations exist that produced over a million head each year in a single facility. Contemporary production uses a three-stage process, with a different type of CAFO designed to accommodate each developmental stage. At the first stage of the process are "farrowing" farms, where breeding sows give birth to litters of pigs, which are raised there until weaning at about 15 pounds. "Wean to feeder" facilities are the second stage of the process. Once pigs at these facilities reach about 40 to 50 pounds, they are transferred to a "feeder to finish" facility. They remain at these finishing operations until reaching slaughter weight of about 250 pounds. All three stages, from birth to slaughter, take about 5.5 months.

At all three stages a swine CAFO consists of three essential parts: the hog house, the waste "lagoon," and the sprayfield. Hog houses are long, rectangular buildings with a center aisle and confinement pens along each side. Confinement pens vary in size depending on the stage of development of the pigs. In sow farms, pens typically consist of cramped "gestation crates" occupied by a single breeding sow. In later stages, the confinement pens are designed to accommodate a certain number of animals at the size they will be when they leave that CAFO for the next stage in the process. In other words, when 30 freshly weaned pigs of about 15 pounds each are first put in a confinement pen, they have room to maneuver and fill about one third of the pen. However, by the time they have grown to about 40 to 50 pounds and are ready to be moved to a finishing facility, their increased body mass has filled all the free space in the pen. Thus, on their last day at a given stage of the process, the pigs are so packed in that they cannot move or even lie down. This design is obviously efficient with floor space. It also enables operators to observe and tend to all pigs easily and in small numbers at a time.

Since the animals occupy the confinement pens around the clock, waste disposal is a critical issue. Hog house flooring is made of slats suspended over concrete subflooring. The spaces between each slat are sized so that animal hooves will not fit through them but urine and feces either falls between the slats or is pushed through as it is stepped on by the animals. Periodically, water is flushed along the subfloor to transport the swine excreta out of the hog house. This forms a liquid slurry of feces, urine, water, and anything else that falls through the slats. The slurry is then pumped into an adjacent waste lagoon.

Waste lagoons are open earthen pits 25 to 30 feet deep and several acres in surface area. Newer lagoons have a clay liner, but older lagoons are unlined pits dug directly into the coarse, sandy soil typical of the coastal plain. Swine waste remains in the waste lagoon to process anaerobically and evaporate. The evaporation of waste and its dispersion downwind is a key component of the lagoon–sprayfield waste disposal design. The intention is that the majority of the liquid portion of the swine waste will be dispersed into the atmosphere. The solid waste that remains behind is subject to anaerobic processing, wherein naturally occurring bacteria break the waste material down into its chemical components.

The other key feature of waste disposal practices is the sprayfield. Eventually, lagoons fill up from the mix of slurry and rainwater. As the lagoon level rises, its free board (the amount of space remaining in the lagoon before it overflows) decreases. When waste levels get too high, the slurry is pumped out of the lagoon and sprayed onto an adjacent field. While this system ostensibly mirrors the traditional practice of using hog waste as fertilizer, sprayfields do not grow crops with any market value. The grasses planted on sprayfield crops are chosen for their capacity to rapidly metabolize as much of the nitrogen and phosphorus in swine waste as possible. They can be thought of as giant well-fertilized lawns with little to no commercial value. Sprayfields eliminate swine slurry in three ways. First, some of the waste evaporates during the spraying process. Second, some of it is metabolized into the grass. Third, the rest either soaks into the ground or leaves the sprayfield as runoff.

The last point to emphasize about CAFOs concerns their design and labor requirements. CAFOs are a capital-intensive technology, meaning they are heavily mechanized and automated and require little labor to operate (see Lesson 4). Animals enter a confinement barn pen when they arrive and typically remain in that pen until they move on to the next stage of the process. The dispensing of feed, water, and the various antibiotics and pesticides used to prevent disease among the herd is handled by the machinery. Similarly, the cleaning mechanisms described previously are entirely automated. Operators tend to the machinery but typically do not interact with the hogs unless a problem is observed. In fact, a recruiter for one of North Carolina's larger corporate integrators routinely sought to persuade farmers to construct a 3,000-head hog operation by describing it as a "housewife operation." He would explain that the farmer's wife could operate the entire CAFO during the middle of the day while the kids were at school. As described in Lesson 4 and by the treadmill of production theory (see Lesson 2), replacing human labor or making it more productive with capital-intensive technologies creates increased demands for fossil fuel energy and typically involves the use of artificial chemicals. It is only the use of copious amounts of inanimate energy that makes it possible for a single person to operate a hog CAFO by himself or herself. Similarly, the hogs can exist in such crowded conditions only through the use of a large number of synthetic chemicals to suppress disease and insect pests. CAFO technology may produce more pigs with less human labor, but it also creates a much higher environmental footprint for each pig raised in such a fashion.

Externalities of Scale

The industrialization and restructuring of the North Carolina hog industry has had tremendous consequences on how hog waste is managed and disposed. It is being produced at an unprecedented volume in a very small geographical area. Its composition is even radically different than the waste produced on traditional hog farms 30 years ago. These changes in the volume, concentration, and makeup of hog waste illustrate a concept we describe as "externalities of scale." This concept refers to a constellation of adverse, but not yet fully understood, economic, social, and environmental impacts found in large-scale pork production but largely absent in small-scale, traditional methods typical at the beginning of the period described here.

In traditional operations, hog herds that number in the low hundreds can be rotated over different pasturelands. The waste from the hogs contains little besides organic matter, and the fields are large enough to fully absorb the nutrients from the waste, which go on to fertilize future crops. With a low enough hog-to-land ratio, there is no pollution and you have a zero-discharge system. In concept, large-scale CAFOs use a similar system with their lagoons and sprayfields. However, full **bioremediation** is impossible for a CAFO with herd sizes in the thousands as sufficient land is not available. Hogs excrete much more waste than humans. Claims of exactly how much more vary depending upon who is making the claims and their stake in the issue, but likely the amount is close to around four times as much. The reasons for this lie in a hog's growth rate. Consider that a market hog reaches a slaughter weight of 250 pounds at less than 6 months of age. A human who reaches 250 pounds at age 18 gains only 14 pounds a year. CAFO-raised pigs are gaining weight at a rate of 500 pounds per year. This tremendous growth rate requires a correspondingly tremendous rate of consumption and subsequent excretion. Consequently, a small hog CAFO with 2,500 pigs is going to be producing the wastes of approximately 10,000 people *each day*. This volume is far greater than that which can be absorbed and incorporated in the surrounding fields.

When more hog waste is applied to a field than the soil can absorb (oversaturation), the extra waste washes off and into the local watershed. Even if the soil can absorb the physical waste, when more nutrients are added to the soil than the crops can utilize, the surplus nutrients leach out into the ground water. At one point, three hog-producing counties in eastern North Carolina were generating more nitrogen than could be absorbed by all of the crops in the entire state! The wastes and nutrients that leave the CAFOs go on to have negative impacts on surrounding communities' health, prosperity, well-being, and natural environment. Since the costs of this waste are being passed onto the public while the owners of the pigs realize most of the benefits, an externality is being created. Because the formation of this externality is primarily due to the scale on which this process is being performed (excess waste is generated only by large-scale operations), we describe it as an "externality of scale."

Opponents of current CAFO and waste disposal practices often illustrate their concerns by suggesting that the 9 to 10 million hogs in eastern North Carolina represent the same excretory impact as 35 to 40 million people. Don Webb, a former hog farmer and founder of the Alliance for a Responsible Swine Industry, seldom misses the opportunity to portray the region as a giant cesspool, where the waste of 10 million hogs is simply laid on the land for nature to take its course. Others suggest that it is like four New York Cities moving to eastern North Carolina without the benefit of a single sewage treatment plant. Some critics emphasize that if 9 to 10 million humans lived in eastern North Carolina utilizing open-pit cesspools, it would be a public health crisis of epic proportions and a national embarrassment. Irreverent opponents joke about miracles of "immaculate excretion" when it comes to CAFO-raised swine. The bottom line is that waste is being produced on a scale far beyond that at which on-farm disposal is a feasible option.

In addition to discussing the amount of waste being produced, it is important to note that this tremendous volume is not being spread evenly over the eastern region. As hog farms have intensified and industrialized their production, they have concentrated more pigs on less area. An analysis of farm-registration data shows that hundreds of these farms lack sufficient acreage to absorb the volume of waste being produced. An even greater number do not cultivate a sufficient portion of their land to ensure that waste gets properly absorbed. So in addition to more waste being produced, it is being concentrated onto smaller areas, creating more of a runoff problem. In essence, the CAFO lagoon system stacks the waste into fewer and bigger piles.

Accompanying the differences in volume and concentration of hog wastes generated by CAFOs relative to traditional hog farms, the very composition of the wastes is radically altered by the CAFO system. In CAFOs many things beside excrement can fall through the slats in the floor and get flushed along with the waste into the lagoons, including afterbirths, trampled and stillborn piglets, old batteries, broken bottles of insecticide, and antibiotic syringes. A more important component of CAFO hog waste, however, is excess antibiotics, vaccines, and insecticides. The extremely high concentration of hogs at high temperatures (often higher than 90°F) in close proximity to their own wastes creates the most unsanitary conditions imaginable. Most CAFO operations depend on the subtherapeutic use of antibiotics as a substitute for disease control practices. Animals are routinely infused with antibiotics and vaccines and doused with insecticides (oxytetracycline, tulathromycin, ceftiofur, and tiamulin) in a preemptive attempt to combat the numerous pathogens that are festering in the relative filth of the hog barn. Whatever chemicals are not absorbed by the animals exit the barns as a component of the waste. Antibiotics can promote the growth of antibiotic-resistant bacterial strains in an already bacteria-rich medium. The toxic quality of hog waste is most clearly exhibited in the color of the waste lagoons, where the interaction between the bacteria, blood, waste, and chemicals turns the liquid not a decent healthy brown but various unnatural shades of pink.

"Externalities of scale" refers to all of the various ways that the social and environmental costs of large-scale, industrial forms of production may exceed those of more traditional methods. New production systems can be both technological, as with the shift to CAFOs, and structural, relating to how production is organized and how its costs and benefits are distributed. This second aspect of externalities of scale refers to how adverse social and environmental costs of production are often concentrated in socially and politically marginalized regions around the world, while most of the economic benefits of that production are channeled out of production zones to large corporations and their stockholders. In other words, the places and communities that most directly suffer the costs of production receive a much smaller share of its benefits (see Lesson 10). In the next two sections we discuss the social and environmental costs of industrialized pork production on North Carolina's coastal plain.

SOCIAL IMPACTS

The radical expansion and industrialization of the North Carolina swine industry has had a wide range of far-reaching consequences. The externalities of scale created by this transformation are costs that extend into the realms of health, economics, and quality of life. This section describes these social costs, starting with the health risks created by this new style of hog production. Next, we discuss the impacts of hog CAFOs upon the quality of life of members of surrounding communities. The third portion of this section deals with the economic impacts of this new model of agriculture. Finally, this section concludes with a discussion of the unequal distribution of these externalities among communities with high percentages of minorities and high levels of poverty.

The Health Risks of Hog Waste Exposure

A substantial body of research has accumulated on the adverse health impacts of occupational exposure to concentrated hog wastes for swine confinement house workers. In poorly ventilated buildings, workers can be exposed to a number of hazards, including harmful levels of gases (methane, ammonia, hydrogen sulfide, and carbon monoxide), dust, infectious agents, and airborne bacteria. These hazards contribute to a wide range of respiratory disorders, from headaches and shortness of breath to hydrogen sulfide poisoning, bronchitis, atopic asthma, and acute organic dust toxic syndrome. There have been cases reported of workers being killed by exposure to high concentrations of hydrogen sulfide gas or by falling into a waste lagoon. In one such instance, a worker performing repairs on a hog lagoon in Michigan was overcome by fumes from the lagoon and fell in. In an effort to rescue him, the worker's nephew, cousin, older brother, and father all separately jumped in. Like the initial victim, all four rescuers were overcome and killed by the toxic liquid and fumes.

More recent studies have examined health impacts among those living near swine CAFOs and have consistently found indications of adverse effects. Many studies have shown that the smell from swine CAFOs can be experienced by nearby residents as a sickening odor and a source of tension, depression, fatigue, and anger. Additionally, multiple studies have shown that residents living near hog CAFOs are experiencing higher rates of respiratory, sinus, and nausea problems caused by the dust and gases being released. Symptoms associated with proximity to a large-scale hog operation include, but are not limited to, burning eyes, runny nose, headache, cough, diarrhea, nausea and vomiting, dizziness, shortness of breath, and chest tightness. Moreover, the contamination of local drinking water, through lagoon leakage or sprayfield runoff, can allow pathogen transfer between pigs and people and lead to such human diseases as salmonellosis, giardiasis, chlamydia, meningitis, cryptosporidiosis, worms, and influenza. Additionally, waste lagoons have been linked to increased levels of nitrates in drinking water, which can cause methemoglobinemia, or "blue baby syndrome," a rare but potentially life-threatening condition for infants. Finally, a number of public health experts have expressed concerns over the linkage between hog CAFOs and H1N1, the swine flu. Some studies traced that outbreak's origins to a Smithfield Foods farrowing operation in Mexico. These numerous health risks associated with swine CAFOs and the wastes they produce clearly demonstrate the need to treat them as a dangerous hazard.

Quality of Life

In addition to the direct health risks associated with proximity to a large-scale hog operation, there have been numerous findings of negative impacts of hog CAFOs on nearby residents' quality of life. Individuals living near lagoons or hog barns can find themselves virtually trapped in their own houses, unable to open windows or go outside and sit on the porch in nice weather. Clothes hung out to dry are said to come back in smelling of hog waste. While difficult to quantify, the impact of hog waste on individuals' quality of life certainly constitutes an important externality. Some hog CAFO neighbors have found themselves trapped in their homes in a different way. Research clearly indicates that the value of homes close to hog CAFOs is less than that of comparable homes farther away. Similarly, the value of existing homes declines significantly if a nearby farmer decides to construct a CAFO. Thus, some neighbors who decide to just move away from the CAFO cannot do so because they are unable to sell their homes and cannot afford to continue to make payments on them while renting or buying another house elsewhere.

Economic Impacts

The North Carolina Pork Council has vigorously touted the industry as the economic backbone of eastern North Carolina. According to their claims, the North Carolina hog industry generates $6.7 billion in annual sales and supports 46,000 jobs. An economic input as large as this in an impoverished region is substantial and important. Yet, the "economic miracle" of the North Carolina pork industry comes with economic costs as well. First, no one disputes that the industry restructuring and conversion to CAFOs drove thousands of small farmers out of business and contributed to a wave of farm loss in North Carolina. Hog farmers who did not contract with corporate integrators were pushed out of the business entirely. The main mechanism for this came from slaughterhouse policies that would accept hogs only in lots of 1,000 or more. Independent producers, even those in co-ops of 40 or 50 farmers, could not amass 1,000 slaughter-ready hogs on the same day; only large corporate integrators could meet this demand. It is also worth challenging the claims of economic benefits with questions about how much of the money produced by the pork industry actually stays in the region. Due to the industry restructuring, the overwhelming majority of profits are realized by Smithfield Foods (a Virginia-based corporation) and its shareholders. The actual CAFOs are constructed by outside firms, not local businesses, and the feed for the pigs is imported from the Midwest. Meanwhile, most of the jobs associated with this industry are found at the Bladen County slaughterhouse (remember that CAFOs are capital-intensive and require little in the way of labor). The slaughterhouse largely employs immigrant laborers, not local workers.

Additionally, while industry proponents may claim that the pork industry is the economic backbone of the region, the state's single largest industry currently is tourism. This industry depends on the perception of an uncontaminated environment. North Carolina has about 300 miles of coast along the Atlantic Ocean and another 3,000 or so miles of inland coast along its sounds and tidal river systems. All of these areas are popular vacation and recreation destinations. They are also attracting a substantial inflow of retirees. Neither vacationers nor retirees want to smell a swine CAFO. Nor do they want to wonder what's in the water. Prominent national media coverage of hog operations in North Carolina between 1995 and 1997 and then again following the massive flooding from Hurricane Floyd that inundated the region in 1999 threatened to diminish the area's appeal as a vacation or retirement destination. Such fears motivated substantial segments of the state's business community to join with environmentalists in pushing for stricter regulation of the industry.

Environmental Injustice

Thus far we have discussed social, health, and economic impacts in general terms. However, the evidence is indisputable that these impacts have not been distributed evenly among the population of North Carolina, or even among residents of the eastern region. First, hog production, and thus any adverse impacts flowing from it, is concentrated in one region of the state. The region lies between Interstate 95 and the Atlantic coast and has been on the periphery, both economically and politically, throughout its history. Much of eastern North Carolina is socially isolated and has higher rates of poverty, a higher proportion of African American residents, and lower rates of homeownership and college graduation than other parts of the state. In many ways the region is a rural analog for what sociologist William Julius Wilson referred to as truly disadvantaged areas of concentrated poverty and social isolation (see Lesson 10).

Low-income, African American, and politically marginalized communities up and down the coastal plain complain that a disproportionate number of hog operations are locating in their communities, leaving them to suffer the consequences without sharing the benefits. At least five separate scientific studies have confirmed the accuracy of their claim of disproportionate exposure, finding that African Americans regardless of income and low-income residents regardless of race are significantly more likely to live close to a hog CAFO. As we discussed before, the presence of hog waste lagoons seriously diminishes both the health and the quality of life of those living nearby. Additionally, as they depress local property values, they further exacerbate the economic conditions of the low-income communities they are built in. Furthermore, a disproportionate amount of the farm loss associated with swine CAFOs is located within African American communities, as African American farmers are far less likely to receive contracts with corporate integrators. Overall, the trend in eastern North Carolina is that African American and low-income residents are more likely to suffer the adverse impacts of the swine CAFOs, while being systematically excluded from any of the associated benefits.

ENVIRONMENTAL IMPACTS

The Earth is a multifaceted ecosystem of systems within systems. Adverse impacts produced in one place diffuse globally, eventually affecting all places even if to a negligible degree. Nevertheless, the environmental damage caused by an industry's production will be most apparent in the specific places where that production is concentrated. Both the human and biotic communities living in zones of concentrated production will be more likely to pay the costs of environmental damage. This brings us again to our notion of "externalities of scale" and raises two interrelated questions about the environmental impacts of swine production: What kind of place is this zone of concentrated production ecologically? How well suited is it to tolerate the environmental stressors of hog CAFOs? This section explores and describes those costs, starting with a discussion on the unsuitability of eastern North Carolina for this particular mode of waste disposal. Following that is a description of the ways the lagoon system allows hog wastes to end up in the environment. Finally, this section concludes by discussing the impacts untreated hog waste can have on the ecosystems of eastern North Carolina.

Regional Vulnerability

Newcomers to the region are often overwhelmed by just how flat it is. The upper deck of the East Carolina University football stadium in Greenville may well be the highest point in the entire region. The Tar River in Greenville, 90 miles from the Atlantic Ocean, is no more than 10 feet above sea level when not in flood stage. This flat region, like other low-lying coastal zones, was once primarily swamps, or more accurately wetlands. Colonial settlers in eastern North Carolina used slave labor to dig a vast network of ditches throughout the region to drain the swamps so that they could be planted for agriculture. Without the network of drainage ditches, much of the region would still be underwater, or at least wetlands. Yet, this is the same region where the hog industry is concentrated. In this area the water table is close to the surface region-wide. By the time one digs 25 to 30 feet down to construct a waste lagoon, it is quite likely that the bottom of the lagoon will be very close to the water table, if not already in it.

Additionally, with the land so flat the waterways move very slowly. When swine waste is applied to land already saturated from rain, it runs off into the system of drainage ditches that serve as direct transport into creeks and rivers. Nutrients like nitrogen and phosphorus run off and enter the slow-moving estuarine waterways. In other types of river systems in less-flat land, the rivers would quickly carry these pollutants downstream and eventually out to sea, transferring the environmental problem into an ocean "sink." Yet, in eastern North Carolina the nutrients remain in the slow-moving creeks and rivers for days or weeks. Finally, the soils of eastern North Carolina are coarse and sandy, making them highly permeable to both liquid waste and small particulate matter. These geological features make the region extremely ill suited for the application of waste from 9 to 10 million hogs.

Nonpoint Source Pollution Still Pollutes

According to industry public relations statements, the lagoon/sprayfield system does not discharge hog wastes into waterways. Yet, as we describe in this section, substantial amounts of pollutants get into waterways from swine CAFOs. How can both statements be true? The answer lies in the important distinction between "point source" and "nonpoint source" pollution. **Point source polluters** are industrial facilities that are regulated under the federal Clean Water Act (CWA). These facilities must obtain a discharge permit from the U.S. Environmental Protection Agency, which regulates the type and amount of pollutants each facility is allowed to discharge. Municipal sewage treatment plants fall into this category. By contrast, **nonpoint source pollution** comes mainly from urban storm water and agricultural runoff. As the laws were understood prior to 2003, CAFOs qualified as point source polluters only if they had some distinct outlet (such as a ditch, drain, or culvert) through which wastes were entering waterways. Without such, by legal definition, they do not "discharge" pollutants and were not governed by the CWA. So when the industry claims that it does not discharge hog waste into waterways, all it is really saying is that hog CAFOs are nonpoint source polluters rather than point source dischargers. In truth, the waste lagoon and sprayfield system is consciously designed to transport pollutants off the farm through a variety of mechanisms.

Pollutants from swine waste most often leave the farm by runoff from sprayfields and waste lagoon leaks and occasionally by lagoon ruptures and discharges associated with flooding or very heavy rains. Any overapplication of hog waste to sprayfields results in waste running off into local waterways. Don Webb claims that millions of gallons of hog waste are reaching the state's eastern waterways every week in this fashion. Additionally, lagoon ruptures, while not common, pose a serious threat to surface water. When the contents of a lagoon are not pumped onto sprayfields in a timely fashion, the lagoon can fill to the point of bursting. This problem grows worse with heavy rainfall, a high risk in a region where hurricanes and tropical storms are frequent. There have been numerous cases of spectacular lagoon ruptures directly spilling millions of gallons of waste into the surrounding area. In 1995, heavy rains contributed to a series of lagoon failures, highlighted by a 22-million-gallon spill at Oceanview Farms, a 10,000-head operation in Onslow County. Spills of this type dump high volumes of pure hog waste directly into the region's waterways.

Hog waste lagoons are also vulnerable to flooding. As described, eastern North Carolina is quite flat, has a very high water table, receives high amounts of rainfall, and is prone to hurricanes. These factors combine to make the region very vulnerable to flooding. In 1999, Hurricane Floyd, on the heels of Hurricane Dennis, caused widespread flooding over a period of several weeks, with nearly every river basin in the eastern part of the state exceeding 500-year flood levels. The floodwaters inundated approximately 50 waste lagoons and filled many others beyond safe capacity. The amount of waste that entered waterways during this flooding is unknown but likely dwarfed isolated incidents like the Onslow County spill.

Additionally, swine waste can enter underground aquifers and contaminate groundwater reserves through leaking waste lagoons and the leaching of sprayfield waste. Again, eastern North Carolina soils drain quite quickly. A study by North Carolina State University showed that 38% of older, unlined swine waste lagoons leached nitrogen compounds into the groundwater at "strong" or "very strong" levels. A different study by the North Carolina Division of Environment and Natural Resources found that 25% of *newer*, lined lagoons may contaminate groundwater. A state program testing private wells near hog operations found that more than one third of the wells tested showed some contamination. These are all well-documented cases in which wastes from nearby hog lagoons and sprayfields leaked their way into the groundwater.

Finally, pollutants found in swine wastes leave the farms and lagoons through evaporation and subsequent condensation. Airborne emissions from hog confinement houses, waste-holding lagoons, and fields onto which wastes are sprayed have been found to contain such substances as methane, hydrogen sulfide, endotoxins, and ammonia. The very design of a lagoon and sprayfield system is built around disposing of nitrogen wastes by emitting them into the air, and as much as 70% to 80% of the nitrogen in a lagoon can be eliminated in such a fashion. The atmospheric nitrogen and phosphorus then enter surface water as they are carried downwind and dropped on nearby lands and waterways through atmospheric deposition. So waste from hog CAFOs will find its way into the environment even when a perfectly functioning lagoon and sprayfield system is employed.

The Ecological Consequences of Hog Waste

We have described the vulnerability of eastern North Carolina's geography to water pollution and the various ways through which hog waste can find its way into the region's waterways. We now turn to the impacts of those hog wastes on the local ecology. It is important to note that the region in which these hog CAFOs are concentrated contains both the Cape Fear and Neuse river basins, the latter of which drains into the Pamlico Sound. The Pamlico Sound serves as a breeding ground for a number of anadromous fish species (fish that migrate to fresh water to spawn) found from Maine to Florida. Therefore, damage to the sound threatens the ecology of the entire North Atlantic.

The primary effect of hog waste on waterways is the "nutrient loading" that occurs in the local watershed. Simple nutrients play a crucial role in aquatic ecosystems, providing the basic building blocks of freshwater plankton and basic aquatic plants. However, when nutrients build up into excessive levels in the shallow, slow-moving waters, they create a state of **eutrophication** that promotes excessive plant growth and decay. This state can completely disrupt an ecosystem through the creation of algal blooms and oxygen depletion in the water, both of which can prove fatal to fish and plants that normally live in the waterways. While algae produce oxygen through photosynthesis during the day, they use it up through respiration during the night. Therefore, an overabundance of algae in the water can lower oxygen levels below that of what other species require to survive. Additionally, as the algae die off they become food for bacteria, which multiply and use up available oxygen. So eutrophication can create an ecological breakdown by lowering oxygen levels below those required to support life. This damage is borne out by the numerous fish kills that occurred in eastern North Carolina during the 1990s, some of which totaled in the millions. Local residents tell stories of shorelines being completely covered with dead and rotting fish. At times, city employees in New Bern (a tourist town located along the Neuse River) had to remove dead fish from their boat ramp and picnic areas by the tons. These kills would be followed by periods in which the rivers seemed empty and lifeless.

In addition to the excess nutrients it contains, the pathogens found in hog waste can also severely disrupt aquatic ecosystems. Fecal bacteria and protozoans can disrupt a food system and, in sufficient quantities, can kill larger animals directly. In humans, these organisms can cause diseases involving flulike symptoms such as nausea, vomiting, fever, and diarrhea. Bacteria can thrive on river bottoms for weeks after initial exposure. In one instance in 1994, a recreational lake in Duplin County with seven nearby hog farms was found to have a fecal coliform count (an indicator of fecal contamination) 60 *times* the allowable level for swimming. At such levels, the bacteria and pathogens contained in hog waste are a threat to the balance of any aquatic ecosystem.

The presence of swine waste in eastern North Carolina's waterways has also been linked to blooms of a toxic unicellular organism, *Pfiesteria piscicida*. Under normal conditions *Pfiesteria* does not occur in sufficient numbers to upset the balance of an ecosystem. However, high nutrient concentrations, such as those caused by hog waste contamination, can stimulate its rapid growth. This aptly nicknamed "cell from hell" is capable of producing a neurotoxin that paralyzes fish and sloughs their skin in order to prey upon their blood cells. In concentrated form, the toxin has even been found to be harmful to humans. While some of the research surrounding *Pfiesteria* remains under debate, its association with hog waste and fish kills demonstrates yet one more way in which hog waste hurts the environment.

POLITICS AND PROTEST

Thus far we have focused on changes to the pork industry and the social and environmental impacts of those changes. However, the transformation of North Carolina's hog industry from a sustainable small-scale system into the corporate-owned "swine factory" system we now have did not occur in a historical or political vacuum. A combination of events and individuals guided this shift and shaped the nature of the 20-year overhaul. This section describes and details that history, highlighting the roles of various stakeholders in both promoting and resisting the transformation of this industry.

Early Growth

To understand why the hog industry could grow so quickly in North Carolina, we need to return to the influence of Wendell Murphy. In addition to being the leading hog producer in the state, Murphy had been the college roommate of four-term Democratic governor James Hunt and served in the North Carolina General Assembly from 1982 to 1992. While in office he passed legislative acts to promote pork production as an alternative to tobacco in economically distressed eastern North Carolina. These actions, widely referred to as "Murphy's Laws" by industry critics, included a bill that exempted large, CAFO-style hog operations from county-level zoning restrictions, an amendment that granted animal and poultry feeding operations immunity from North Carolina air and water standards, and a bill exempting the industry from selected state taxes and fees. Combined, this body of regulations was highly effective in promoting growth in the pork industry and shielding it from environmental regulation.

The Rise of Opposition

The transformation of pork production in North Carolina did not go unchallenged. A vigorous opposition to swine CAFOs in eastern North Carolina first surfaced in 1990–1991 with the formation of a number of grassroots organizations like the Alliance for a Responsible Swine Industry and Concerned Citizens of Tillery that "were tired of hogs stinking up their environment and decided to fight back." In 1993, Concerned Citizens of Tillery persuaded 42 North Carolina environmental and citizens' groups to form the Hog Roundtable. This unique coalition brought together grassroots, legal, and mainstream environmental organizations with the dual goals of protecting communities from the environmental health hazards associated with intensive hog operations as well as forging ties between environmental justice groups and mainstream environmental organizations (see Lessons 10 and 16). The Hog Roundtable further organized opposition to pork industry expansion and sought to put its social and environmental impacts on the public agenda.

Their efforts attracted serious press attention in 1995, when the *Raleigh News & Observer* published an investigative series entitled "Boss Hog: North Carolina's Pork Revolution." The series amplified the claims of industry critics who charged the pork industry with polluting the state's air and water, displacing traditional small farmers with integrated corporations, and using its political ties to state lawmakers to avoid economic and environmental regulations. The "Boss Hog" series touched off a firestorm of reaction from virtually every interest group in the state with a stake in the industry and went on to win a Pulitzer Prize for public service reporting. Further attracting attention to this industry, within months of the Boss Hog publication, heavy rains in eastern counties caused waste lagoons at seven hog facilities to burst. Over the next few weeks over 40 million gallons of untreated swine feces and urine spilled into the streams and rivers of the coastal region. An estimated 10 to 15 million fish died as a result, and 364,000 acres of waterways were closed to commercial and recreational fishing.

An End to Growth and Partial Resolution

Toward the end of 1995, North Carolina was at the center of growing national and regional debate and intensifying opposition to industrial hog operations. Then Governor Hunt responded with a blue ribbon commission to study agricultural waste. Public opposition, scientific study, and political debate over swine operations intensified, and by 1997 the politics of swine waste was the single largest and most contentious issue in North Carolina. Hog Roundtable groups mobilized public concerns over odor, water pollution, equity, and recreation into an effective lobby. Meanwhile, the North Carolina Pork Council responded with a statewide public relations media campaign, asserting that hog farms were the economic lifeblood of the state and claiming an unmatched record of environmental stewardship. After months of intense lobbying, the North Carolina General Assembly passed the Clean Water Responsibility Act (CWRA) in August 1997. The CWRA imposed increased regulatory controls over the industry to protect air and water quality as well as a 2-year moratorium on new and expanded hog operations. At the time, the passage of the CWRA was viewed as a tremendous victory for hog opponents.

While the CWRA halted industry growth, it did not eliminate public pressure for a long-term solution to the hog waste issue. With Smithfield Foods consolidating ownership of the North Carolina hog industry, it became the focal point of anti-industry sentiments and activities. It also created an opportunity for then Attorney General Mike Easley to negotiate an agreement with only one party that would defuse a potent issue. In the Smithfield–Easley agreement of July 2000, Smithfield Foods agreed to provide $15 million over 10 years to fund research into alternative waste disposal technologies and to pay $50 million toward cleaning up abandoned waste lagoons and compliance monitoring. Additionally, Smithfield pledged to adopt the new technology on all company-owned farms within 3 years, if the technology were to prove economically feasible. In exchange for this, the state of North Carolina implicitly agreed to maintain the status quo until the research team made its recommendations. The agreement was widely hailed as a successful resolution that demonstrated the potential of public–private partnerships to solve environmental problems. Nevertheless, critics pointed out several flaws. First, Smithfield's profits were so great at the time that the agreement essentially required them to exchange 4 months' worth of profits for 10 years of being left alone to continue polluting as usual. Second, the agreement applied only to the 276 hog operations directly owned by Smithfield, not the other 2,000-plus operations in the state that contracted with Smithfield. Efforts by environmentalists to point out these flaws in the agreement gained little attention.

Subsequent Developments

Following the passage of the CWRA and the Smithfield–Easley agreement, the hog issue largely dropped off the public radar. Hog industry opponents have exerted enough political pressure to maintain the moratorium on swine industry expansion, and it became a permanent law in 2007. However, the moratorium has proved to be a double-edged sword. Freezing the 1997 hog population in place did prevent the magnitude of environmental impacts from escalating, but the moratorium also undercut the political clout of future opposition by creating the perception among the general public that the problem had been solved. The waste from a stable population of 9 to 10 million hogs still produces substantial adverse impacts year in and year out, but the moratorium creates the perception of a problem solved. After 10 years of supporting the moratorium they worked so hard to get in place, North Carolina's environmental community reversed its stance and now opposes the moratorium in favor of a permanent ban on lagoon and sprayfield disposal technologies.

Regarding the issue of whether or not CAFOs qualify as point source pollution and therefore fall under the regulatory jurisdiction of the EPA through the CWA, there have been a number of developments. A series of lawsuits brought about by the Waterkeeper Alliance and the National Pork Producers Council led to adjustments and rewordings of the CWA in 2003, 2008, and 2012. The final ruling at the national level designated *all* CAFOs as point source pollution. However, CAFO owners and operators were not required to apply for a permit, only to have one if they discharged waste. While this ruling grants the EPA the right to prosecute CAFOs that can be shown to have released wastes into waterways, it does not give the EPA any authority to monitor whether or not CAFOs are doing so. At the state level, a settlement by Smithfield in North Carolina included an agreement that all Smithfield-owned and contracted CAFOs would obtain CWA permits. However, to date virtually none of them has done so. So the situation stands that any CAFO that is releasing wastes into eastern North Carolina's waterways is technically in violation of the law, but the burden of proof lies upon those affected.

During the 15 years of "business as usual," Smithfield Foods has used the profits made in eastern North Carolina to fund expansion into both national and global markets. Starting in 1998, Smithfield has expanded into the international market by acquiring 11 domestic and foreign competitors, including Animex in Poland (1999), Mitchell's in Canada (2000), NORSON in Mexico (2000), AFG in China (2002), and SFGP in France (1999). Smithfield currently boasts of being "the world's largest pork processor and hog producer" and records annual sales above $13 billion. The research that Smithfield funded through the Smithfield–Easley agreement produced a report in 2006 that detailed five alternative technologies. However, none of them was deemed to be cost-effective by Smithfield Foods, and to date none has been implemented. Instead, Smithfield has maintained its pollution-intensive industrial style of hog production and exported this model across the globe.

CONCLUSIONS

This lesson has described how the industrialization of hog production in North Carolina has created a host of "externalities of scale" that were absent in traditional hog farming. These externalities include health risks, farm loss, reduced quality of life, and environmental degradation. Currently, this situation remains unresolved, with the waste from the production and slaughter of 10 million hogs still concentrated in an ecologically fragile region that contains a disproportionate number of poor and minority residents. Massive fish kills on the lower Neuse River in the falls of 2009 and 2012 (both within the range of 15 to 50 million dead fish) provide excellent testimony as to the environmental damage that continues to this day. Smithfield Foods is still realizing incredible profits on the backs of eastern North Carolina's residents and ecosystems.

Furthermore, the lessons that can be drawn from CAFO-style pork production can easily be extended to apply to nearly all types of industrial protein production. Poultry, fish, shellfish, dairy, and beef are all currently being raised in a similar fashion. With this form of factory agriculture becoming the norm across the meat production industry, the issues and concerns raised about pork production in North Carolina have general implications up and down the global supply chain (see Lesson 12). Wherever animals are being raised in an industrial fashion, corporate profits are being accumulated at the expense of local communities and their physical environments.

SOURCES

Edwards, Bob, and Anthony E. Ladd. 2000. "Environmental Justice, Swine Production and Farm Loss in North Carolina." *Sociological Spectrum* 20:263–290.

Furuseth, Owen. 1997. "Restructuring of Hog Farming in NC: Explosion and Implosion." *Professional Geographer* 49:391–403.

Juska, Arunas, and Bob Edwards. 2004. "Refusing the Trojan Pig: The Trans-Atlantic Coalition Corporate Pork Production in Poland." In Joe Bandy and Jackie Smith, eds. *Coalitions Across Borders: Transnational Protest and the Neoliberal Order*, pp. 187–207. Lanham, MD: Rowman & Littlefield.

Ladd, Anthony, and Bob Edwards. 2002. "Corporate Swine, Capitalist Pigs: A Decade of Environmental Injustice in North Carolina." *Social Justice* 29(3):26–46.

North Carolina Department of Environment and Natural Resources. 1999. Framework for the Conversion of Anaerobic Swine Waste Lagoons and Sprayfields. Office of the Governor, Raleigh, NC.

Smithfield. 2007. "About Smithfield." Retrieved March 5, 2007 (http://www.smithfield.com/about/index.php).

Stith, Pat, Joby Warrick, and Melanie Sill. 1995. "Boss Hog: North Carolina's Pork Revolution." *News and Observer*, February 19–26, 1A–16A.

Tietz, Jeff. 2006. "Boss Hog." *Rolling Stone*, December 14. Retrieved March 5, 2007 (http://www.rollingstone.com/politics/story/12840743/).

Wilson, William Julius. 1990. *The Truly Disadvantaged: The Inner City, the Underclass, and Public Policy*. Chicago, IL: University of Chicago Press.

Wing, Steve, Dana Cole, and Gary Grant. 2000. "Environmental Injustice in North Carolina's Hog Industry." *Environmental Health Perspectives* 108:225–231.

14

Understanding Disaster Vulnerability
Floods and Hurricanes

Nicole Youngman

Remains of First Baptist Church following Hurricane Katrina, Biloxi, Mississippi.
Photo by Ken Gould.

We tend to think of "natural disasters" as sudden, extreme events that have their origins in the workings of the Earth's physical systems. Other kinds of disasters, like oil spills or failed dams, seem to have clearly anthropogenic (human) causes. But even though different kinds of disasters may have different *triggers*, which may or may not be the direct result of human activities, they are all caused by *interactions* among three overlapping systems: human social and cultural systems, the built environment, and the preexisting natural environments in which they are embedded. The impacts of all disasters, from tornado touchdowns to nuclear meltdowns, are directly related to how and where human societies organize themselves. And while disasters always create *community* (rather than simply individual) trauma, some residents of disaster-prone areas are much more **vulnerable** to extreme losses than others.

Two hurricanes that have recently struck heavily populated urban areas in the United States have clearly demonstrated how a myriad of human and nonhuman factors can come together to produce profoundly traumatic events. Hurricane Katrina, which struck the Mississippi and southeast Louisiana coasts on August 29, 2005, killed over 1,700 people. The flood that accompanied the storm engulfed 80% of New Orleans, inundated nearly all of St. Bernard and Plaquemines parishes (counties) to the city's south and east, and largely obliterated the Mississippi Gulf Coast. In this case, the disaster's trigger—a category 3 hurricane—was a natural and normal (though infrequent) event for the Gulf Coast. But while the unprecedented 30-foot storm surge that hit the Mississippi coast was directly generated by the storm, extensive development along the state's beaches, particularly the large number of casinos built in recent decades, had placed many more people and structures in harm's way than had existed there during previous hurricanes. In the New Orleans area, the effects of development were even more pronounced. The city's approximately 1,100 deaths and widespread destruction were caused by its failed flood-control system, which in turn was caused by a combination of poor engineering practices, the construction of a network of shipping and drainage canals that funneled the storm surge into the city, unwise urban development in areas below sea level, and the metropolitan area's long history of prioritizing economic growth over public safety. Not surprisingly, the city's most vulnerable residents—those who were poor, African American, and/or elderly—were hit especially hard (see Lesson 10). Rather than declaring the hurricane an "act of God" for which no one was responsible, the residents of New Orleans and its eastern suburbs responded to the disaster with feelings of anger and betrayal, insisting that the Katrina flood was a human-made, not a "natural," disaster.

Hurricane Sandy (also termed "Superstorm Sandy") devastated the New Jersey and New York City coastal areas when it struck on October 29, 2012. Sandy's winds were much weaker than Katrina's—it was technically no longer a hurricane as it came ashore—and it caused a much lower death toll, with over 140 lives lost in the United States and Canada (plus about 70 people in the Caribbean). Factors beyond wind speed turned Sandy into a monster, however: its enormous diameter of over 800 miles, its unusual late-season track up the Eastern Seaboard, and its merger with northern winter weather systems (a phenomenon that led recently appointed Federal Emergency Management Agency [FEMA] director Craig Fugate to quip that he hadn't "been around long enough to see a hurricane forecast with a snow advisory in it").

The unusual nature of the storm produced unprecedented flood impacts along the New York/New Jersey coastline, with storm surges of over nine feet on top of normal high tides in some locations. The storm washed away homes and rental properties throughout the area's low-lying coastal communities and knocked out much of New York City's transportation and electrical infrastructure, flooding subways and tunnels and creating massive blackouts across Manhattan and the surrounding areas. Over half of the New York-area deaths took place in the working- to middle-class communities on Staten Island, where a development boom in prior decades had wiped out much of the island's natural wetlands and greatly increased the area's storm surge vulnerability. Months after the storm, people in flooded communities throughout the area found themselves trying to survive the winter in mud-filled, mold-infested homes with no electricity, no heat, and nowhere to go.

THINKING ABOUT VULNERABILITY

Flood vulnerability is rising worldwide for a variety of reasons, including higher levels of urbanization and industrialization, rapid population growth and development along coastlines and river valleys, and sea-level rises induced by climate change. Disaster sociologists distinguish between **physical vulnerability** and **social vulnerability**, which have different but overlapping causes and consequences. Physical vulnerability generally refers to one's geographical location; different parts of the world, of course, are more prone to various kinds of natural disasters than others. More specific locations matter, too: living downstream or next to a dam or levee that might break, on a hillside prone to slide in heavy rains, or in a poorly constructed dwelling increases one's risk of experiencing a catastrophe. This type of physical vulnerability is sometimes referred to as "unsafe conditions." Social vulnerability refers to preexisting conditions, rooted in social inequalities, that affect potential disaster victims' ability to escape, survive, and/or "bounce back" from a disaster: race, class, gender, age, disability, health status, etc. Physical and social vulnerability are frequently intertwined in complex ways and can exist at the individual, household, or community level.

Both the New Orleans and the New York/New Jersey hurricanes provide clear examples of how physical and social vulnerability can overlap. In some ways, physical vulnerability in New Orleans cuts across racial and class lines. The city has both white/upper-class and minority/low-income neighborhoods that flooded catastrophically in Katrina due to their lack of elevation and/or proximity to drainage or shipping canals. Meanwhile, other well-to-do and poorer neighborhoods alike escaped flooding because they were built on higher ground in older sections of the city. This does not, however, mean that all of the city's flooded communities are equally vulnerable to disasters overall. Because residents in wealthier communities generally have considerably more financial resources and human capital at their disposal, they are much more likely to be able to eventually return and rebuild if they so desire or to "start over" elsewhere if they prefer. This is not to say that the recovery process is not difficult at best for all hurricane victims;

lengthy, exhausting struggles with insurance companies and government disaster assistance programs, for instance, abound throughout all affected areas. But even so, wealthier victims are more likely to have had sufficient insurance in the first place, to have well-paying jobs to return to and high-quality schools and daycare available, and to have the skills and social networks necessary to negotiate the piles of paperwork and extensive new regulations that flourish in a post-disaster environment. Race and social class also played important roles in Hurricane Sandy's impact. As the storm approached, New York's working-class, service-sector workers stayed at their jobs so that others with more means could stock up on supplies and prepare to keep their families safe. Hotel workers remained on site to look after wealthy evacuees who had checked in to take refuge away from the beaches. After the storm passed, much of the nation's media outlets focused their attention on the blow to New York City's infrastructure, particularly the widespread power outages and the flooded subway system. While experts from the Corps of Engineers worked to pump out the city's highway and subway tunnels—an effort sometimes compared to their work to de-water New Orleans in 2005—storm survivors away from the wealthy sections of Manhattan in the more modest communities of the Rockaways, Staten Island, etc. struggled to call attention to their desperate need for help after the storm wiped out their neighborhoods. Public housing residents were hit especially hard, with 402 buildings comprising 35,000 housing units damaged by the storm.

Gender issues, too, play an important role in determining disaster vulnerability. While our society is considerably less patriarchal (male-dominated) than it has been in the past, women of all races and social classes still tend to find themselves dealing with considerably heavier childcare, elder care, and housework responsibilities than men. For single mothers, this is obviously a huge burden, but even married women with jobs and incomes comparable to those of their spouses often find themselves in this position due to cultural norms that still consider such activities "women's work." In the aftermath of a disaster, these "traditional gender roles" tend to be exacerbated, even for couples that have tried to create more egalitarian relationships. With buildings and infrastructures heavily damaged and many residents unable to return, schools and daycare centers may be unable to reopen for months after the disaster or may close permanently. Traumatized children, who may have lost their homes and belongings and/or had family members die, often "act out" in ways that can be difficult for their caregivers to predict or cope with. Widespread damage to businesses and office buildings can create long commutes for those relatively lucky residents who are able to go back to work when their jobs are forced to relocate to more distant locations.

With no outside help caring for children or elderly family members, many women end up staying home to tackle these responsibilities full-time while their male partners (who usually earn more than they do, even if both had worked outside the home previously) put in extraordinarily long hours commuting to work. Both single- and two-parent families may find themselves unable to return home at all without childcare available since the situation makes it impossible for mothers to go back to work, and many families rely on women's incomes to survive economically. Women also tend to find themselves with the primary responsibilities of applying for disaster aid—which often involves standing in long lines for many hours, with young children in tow—and dealing with the contractors who arrive to repair their homes, some of whom turn out to be con artists who take victims' money and promptly disappear. The stresses of dealing with these kinds of situations on an everyday basis can lead to significant marital and other family problems, particularly when men and women are facing different kinds of stresses and may have different coping strategies (for example, talking about them vs. "being strong" and "bottling up" emotions), making communication difficult.

Hurricane evacuations also provide examples of different kinds of physical and social vulnerability. For low-income residents, the physical vulnerability of living in a disaster-prone location is frequently compounded by the physical inability to leave when disaster threatens. Pre-Katrina research in the New Orleans area had clearly demonstrated that at least 100,000 residents did not have cars and thus would be unable to leave in advance of a major hurricane. This problem became all too obvious when tens of thousands of New Orleans residents, almost all of them African American, fled to the Superdome and the Convention Center downtown before, during, and immediately after Katrina made landfall, remaining stranded in the blistering heat for days with little or no food, water, or sanitation. The preexisting social vulnerabilities these victims faced led directly to extreme physical vulnerability, making them exponentially more likely to become trapped (and perhaps die) in the storm or its chaotic aftermath. A similar dynamic unfolded in New York, complicated by the height and density of much of the city's housing. In more heavily urbanized areas, many thousands of low-income, disabled, and/or elderly people who were unable or unwilling to evacuate found themselves trapped in high-rise buildings with no power—and no elevators. National Guard troops and masses of volunteers working with the emerging "Occupy Sandy" movement combed the buildings for weeks trying to locate people in need of food, water, and medical supplies.

Not everyone who fails to evacuate in advance of a hurricane stays behind for simple lack of transportation. Figuring out when and whether to go, even when told by authorities that leaving would be the best option, can be very tricky. Gas, meals, and hotels while on the road can be very expensive, especially for those whose incomes are marginal. Employers and schools may be reluctant to close down until the very last minute, prolonging the decision-making process for those who are dependent on them. Traveling with children (and pets) is difficult and stressful under normal circumstances; spending hour after hour in traffic that barely moves is much worse. Not all cars are reliable, and even vehicles in good condition can break down in the stop-and-go circumstances of evacuating in 90-degree weather, leaving their occupants potentially stranded and in an even more dangerous situation while the storm approaches. And to make things worse, since it is impossible to predict exactly where the eye wall of a hurricane will hit more than several hours in advance, some evacuations turn out to have been unnecessary, resulting in wasted time, money, and stress for many thousands of people. It is hardly surprising, then, that many coastal residents are extremely reluctant to put themselves through such an ordeal and may choose to risk the storm instead.

Failure to truly understand one's physical vulnerability—or a stubborn refusal to accept it—can also lead to a failure to evacuate. Paradoxically, both a lack of experience with hurricanes and considerable experience "riding them out" can give coastal residents a false sense of security, leading them to underestimate the true danger of a major storm. In rapidly growing coastal areas, newer residents who have no experience with hurricanes and therefore no idea what to expect when a warning is issued may assume that the risk is manageable if they stay home. But even longtime residents, who often have been through many smaller storms (or only the edges of bigger ones) with little more than power outages and downed trees to deal with, can easily arrive at the faulty conclusion that they can get through any hurricane with only a few inconveniences. For New Yorkers, Hurricane Irene's near-miss the year before Sandy hit led many residents to believe that the media were over-hyping Sandy's potential impact just as they felt the media had falsely predicted doomsday with Hurricane Irene. This understandable frustration with the media's tendency to over-dramatize any large storm led many residents to brush off mandatory evacuation orders as nonsensical exaggerations, leaving an exasperated Governor Chris Christie of New Jersey to fume that waterfront and flood-zone residents who refused to go were being "stupid and selfish" by forcing emergency workers to risk their lives to rescue them when they became trapped by rising waters.

Those who have made it safely through truly horrendous storms are also likely to assume (not entirely irrationally) that since they and/or their homes survived the worst that nature could dish out, they can weather any subsequent storms. Some Mississippi residents who got through Hurricane Camille in 1969, for instance—a category 5 storm with 200 mph winds and a 28-foot surge—failed to evacuate for Katrina, mistakenly assuming that no storm could possibly be any worse than what they had already experienced. A long period of time between hurricane "hits" can play a role in development and evacuation decisions, too. Coastal communities tend to develop "**hurricane amnesia**" when memories of the last terrible storm fade, which encourages a push for more "economic growth" in their region, increasing the area's long-term physical vulnerability as more businesses, residents, and tourists move in. When Hurricane Sandy struck, the Northeast had not seen a severe hurricane in many decades, encouraging many residents to comfortably assume that the storm "wouldn't really be that bad" or that their neighborhoods—many of which were recently built and had never been hit by a major hurricane—weren't in any real danger of serious flooding.

Finally, it is important to note that more than 60% of the people who drowned in Hurricane Katrina were over 61 years of age. Hurricane Sandy's impact followed a similar pattern: though its death toll was a fraction of Katrina's, nearly half the people who perished were 65 and older. While many of these victims drowned, falls, hypothermia, fires, and carbon monoxide poisoning from generators also caused fatalities. These statistics demonstrate another way in which physical and social vulnerability can overlap. For older people, the evacuation process can be frightening and difficult enough that "riding it out" seems like a comparatively smaller risk. While the prospect of a long road trip—perhaps to an unknown destination for an undetermined amount of time—may seem manageable or even a bit exciting for those who are younger and healthy and have some financial resources to fall back on, the elderly frequently live on fixed incomes and often must deal with a variety of health and mobility problems: poor hearing or eyesight, difficulty walking, arthritis pain, etc. They are also likely to require medication for severe conditions such as heart problems, high blood pressure, or diabetes and thus depend heavily upon remaining close to their own familiar doctors and pharmacists. These difficulties can make traveling any distance unpleasant at best and dangerous at worst.

STRUCTURAL AND INFRASTRUCTURAL MITIGATION: DECREASING OR INCREASING VULNERABILITY?

Communities at risk for disasters have three basic options for trying to mitigate (lessen or prevent) their impacts: **structural mitigation, infrastructural mitigation, and nonstructural mitigation**. Structural mitigation generally refers to strategies in coastal areas and river floodplains that emphasize large engineering "megaprojects" to stop flooding and erosion, such as levees, floodwalls, groins, bank stabilization, and beach renourishment. Infrastructures are those things that physically tie a community together, including the drinking water, sewerage and drainage systems, roads and bridges, phone and Internet lines and towers, and power and gas lines. Infrastructural mitigation strategies, then, are efforts to make these systems more resilient to high winds, floodwaters, or seismic activity. Stronger building codes, too, are sometimes considered infrastructural mitigation. Nonstructural mitigation generally focuses more on keeping people (and property) out of harm's way in the first place: stricter zoning laws that prohibit or severely restrict building in some parts of a floodplain or coastal area, for instance, or restoring wetlands that absorb floodwaters and storm surges. In extreme cases this can mean moving entire communities to higher ground, which some small Midwestern towns chose to do after the enormous Mississippi River flood of 1993. Flood and other disaster insurance, too, can be considered nonstructural mitigation.

Infrastructural mitigation tends to be one of the first things emergency management officials and government agencies try to improve after a disaster strikes (or nearly strikes), in an effort to quickly and effectively reduce their community's vulnerability. Communications systems, in particular, are obviously crucial during search and rescue operations and all too frequently fail completely or prove to be incompatible among different agencies under extreme conditions. Post-disaster **mitigation** planning, then, frequently focuses on finding new ways to ensure that police, firefighters, and other "first responders" can continue to communicate with one another despite widespread devastation.

New Orleans' experience with improved evacuation routes is an interesting case of infrastructural mitigation that was, eventually, highly effective. In a strange way, the city was actually very lucky to have gone through a couple of "near misses" before being inundated by Katrina. The city is surrounded by water, limiting the routes available to evacuees to just a few main highways. Places where these evacuation routes bottlenecked badly during evacuations for Hurricane Georges in 1998 and Hurricane Ivan in 2004 led to significant improvements in the "contraflow" system (which allows traffic to travel "the wrong way" on interstate highways, doubling the roadways' capacity), allowing a much more effective evacuation for Katrina than might otherwise have occurred. While the plan in effect during Katrina was not perfect and traffic was still very slow, it was an enormous improvement over previous efforts, and several hundred thousand New Orleans-area residents (as well as many others in even higher-risk areas to the south) were able to leave before the storm made landfall. It is, of course, important to note that this approach was only "successful" for those who had the means to leave on their own and did nothing to help those without reliable transportation.

New Orleans' experience with the contraflow plans highlights three concerns that disaster researchers have been expressing for decades regarding mitigation efforts. First, at-risk communities tend to rely almost entirely on structural and infrastructural mitigation techniques, at the expense of nonstructural strategies (such as restoring adjacent wetlands or moving people out of an area's most flood-prone locations) that have the potential to be far more effective over the long term. Second, these mitigation efforts tend to be "event-driven" rather than "threat-driven," designed and implemented *after* a disaster strikes rather than as a result of a careful risk analysis beforehand. Finally, structural and infrastructural techniques do not protect all members of a community equally. All these tendencies actually serve to increase rather than decrease communities' long-term disaster risks, but persuading governments, businesses, industries, and residents to place more emphasis on nonstructural mitigation methods is difficult for several reasons.

Residents and business interests that have been traumatized by a major flood or hurricane understandably want their community back the way it was as soon as possible. City **growth machines**—coalitions of municipal government officials, prominent business interests, and the local media organizations that support their efforts—must work to encourage (re)investment in their area by somehow overcoming the negative images and impressions of their community as destroyed and chaotic, in order to restore confidence in its ability to rebound from the disaster and "get back to normal." Disaster victims tend to pressure their elected officials at all levels of government to find a way to "fix" their disaster vulnerability problem, to "do something, now!!" to ensure that such an event never happens again—but without forcing the community to make any drastic land-use changes. If ideas for long-term mitigation conflict with the community's immediate goals of getting the surrounding natural systems back under control, allowing residents to rebuild their homes, and returning to the normal routine of encouraging growth and development, they will almost always be rejected out of hand.

Not surprisingly, then, the post-disaster mitigation solutions that communities decide upon usually involve more (or improved) flood control structures, along with better evacuation routes and stronger building codes. Rezoning hazardous areas and moving human development away from them altogether, which would allow floodwaters to come and go in mostly unoccupied areas and thus provide better long-term risk reduction, are rarely considered seriously. Instead, at-risk communities repeatedly try to remove the dynamic, shifting aspects of the natural hydrological systems in which they are embedded and somehow make the land and water hold still indefinitely so that the area can continue to be developed. This approach ensures that as much land as possible will remain open to profitable (re)development, rather than being turned into less immediately beneficial spillways, "natural" beaches, or "green space." Ironically, communities hit by floods or hurricanes often find themselves in the midst of a building boom as the real estate industry works not only to rebuild what was destroyed but also to purchase and redevelop land that had once been vacant or built with small single-family homes, turning it into high-rise hotels and condominiums.

In decades past, these efforts to "conquer nature" were considered a noble cause that served to benefit the entire community. Experience has shown, however, that constructing elaborate structural flood mitigation systems frequently backfires. Such systems tend to create a vicious cycle that encourages more and more development in disaster-prone areas, which then needs increasingly higher levels of "protection," which then encourages still more development. Levees and seawalls give communities a false sense of security, something tangible that can make residents feel safe (and does, in fact, provide safety in smaller flood events) until they create an even bigger disaster when a flood too large for them to contain eventually occurs. Exceptionally large floods are actually more dangerous with levees than they would have been without, creating huge surges of rising water that wipe out everything in their path when the levees finally break, giving victims little or no warning or time to escape.

FLOOD INSURANCE: ENCOURAGING RISKY BEHAVIOR

Disaster researchers have also heavily criticized the National Flood Insurance Program (NFIP) for increasing flood risks nationwide. Created in 1968, the program was intended to help people living in flood- and hurricane-prone areas recover from catastrophic floods, but unfortunately it has had a number of unintended consequences. When Hurricane Betsy hit New Orleans in 1965, one of the most salient political issues during the relief and recovery effort was the fact that the vast majority of victims' losses had been uninsured because homeowners' insurance did not (and still does not) cover flood losses. The NFIP was supposed to help ameliorate this problem by providing low-cost, subsidized flood insurance to those who were already living in coastal areas and flood plains, while discouraging further development in such risky areas. Municipalities had to choose whether or not to join the program, which would then make insurance available to residents with the requirement that local governments adopt land-use policies that would not increase the number of residents and businesses in high-risk areas.

This provision of the NFIP, however, has been poorly enforced since its inception. While the program has in fact provided much-needed relief to homeowners who lost everything in floods—particularly for lower-income families living in floodplains because they simply cannot afford to move to higher ground—it has also inadvertently encouraged growth and development in low-lying and coastal areas by making insurance available in places that had previously been uninsurable and allowing repeat claims for properties that flood frequently. Economists refer to this phenomenon as a "**moral hazard**"—a change in peoples' risk-taking behavior brought about by the availability of insurance. While insurance is technically a kind of nonstructural mitigation, the problems created by the NFIP are very similar to those created by levees: helping to diminish risk in the short term, while actually making things worse in the long term.

The existence of a federal flood insurance program has also exacerbated disaster victims' already difficult task of applying for settlements from their homeowners' insurance companies. After a major hurricane, when insurance companies face many thousands of claims for the same event, it is to their benefit to award each homeowner as little as possible in order to keep their total payout lower. Because homeowners' insurance will pay for only wind damage, while the NFIP covers only flood damage, property owners with both kinds of policies frequently find themselves facing the rather surreal process of dealing with appraisers whose job it is to determine what percentage of their home was damaged and what percentage of that damage was due strictly to wind or to the storm surge. Given that hurricanes bring both, this distinction can be somewhat nonsensical in ordinary terms, but homeowners' insurance companies have a vested interest in declaring that most of the damage they survey is from water rather than wind, while appraisers from the NFIP may be making the opposite assertion. The catastrophic damages of the 2005 hurricane season—which along with Hurricane Katrina included Hurricanes Rita, Wilma, and a score of others—left the NFIP deeply in debt to the tune of $19 billion. In the summer of 2012, months before Hurricane Sandy, Congress passed the Biggert-Waters Act, which was intended to make the NFIP more financially stable by ending most flood insurance subsidies to people living in risky areas. This bill raises flood insurance rates drastically on those properties that are built too low in a flood zone, with the intention of reaching "actuarial rates"—that is, rates that reflect the actual risk these locations face—in five years. Properties that have been owned by the same people since before the NFIP was first passed and homeowners who raise their structures above the "base flood elevation" indicated on updated FEMA flood zone maps (which have greatly enlarged the New York metro areas that are officially in flood zones) will still qualify for extensive discounts on their policies. For property owners in the New York area who cannot afford the additional tens of thousands of dollars needed to raise a structure, however, these massive rate increases—which could easily mean policies costing $10,000 per year or more—may prove prohibitively expensive. While there are some government "increased cost of compliance" grants available to help property owners raise their structures, these grants generally take the form of reimbursements after the elevation work is already completed, which means only those property owners able to pay for such work up front can benefit from the program.

Other forms of government disaster relief, too, can be rendered considerably less effective thanks to insurance-related dilemmas. The "Road Home" program created in Louisiana after Hurricane Katrina, which was designed to provide flooded-out homeowners with rebuilding grants of up to $150,000, is a good example. The program was funded with federal appropriations but administered by a private company hired by the state; it was plagued with massive administration problems from its inception. This was complicated by the fact that the program was designed to augment, rather than replace, whatever settlements homeowners received from their preexisting policies. Road Home grants were decreased according to the payments applicants were supposed to receive from their insurance companies, even while insurance companies were reducing their awards so that the government program would make up the difference. Homeowners remained stuck in the middle for months or even years, with heavily damaged homes, two or three programs that were supposed to provide funding for rebuilding, and no actual checks in the mail, all while each program tried to pass off its costs onto the others. And buying new insurance or renewing existing policies post-Katrina turned out to be an even worse nightmare. With many insurance companies in the area dropping wind and hail coverage altogether, homeowners seeking to rebuild their homes or move into new ones found themselves forced to buy three separate insurance policies from three separate companies: homeowners' insurance for theft, fire, and liability; a second policy elsewhere for wind and hail; and an NFIP policy for floods. Needless to say, this reality sent insurance costs skyrocketing and, in some cases, kept storm victims from being able to repair or sell their homes or to buy new ones.

Insurance companies and city planners are also starting to take sea-level rise and the likelihood of more frequent severe storms into account when assessing flood risks. While no single storm can be directly attributed to

climate change, the increased number of catastrophic hurricanes in the early years of the 21st century is consistent with scientists' predictions that warming seas worldwide will lead to the formation of more and stronger tropical systems, which are basically meteorological "heat engines" that feed off warm ocean temperatures. A deadly combination of steady sea-level rises resulting from global ice melts, changes in Arctic wind patterns that can steer storms towards the Northeast more frequently, and thermal expansion of ocean waters is slowly eating away at coastlines in Louisiana, New England, and everywhere in between. Louisiana's coastal wetlands are disappearing at a particularly alarming rate, forcing entire communities to retreat to higher ground as their small towns disappear into the Gulf of Mexico.

DECREASING VULNERABILITY?

Finding viable solutions to the complicated, intertwined realities of flood and hurricane vulnerability is extremely difficult. Improved evacuation planning and more sensible and equitable insurance policies are certainly important but do very little to tackle the underlying issues of **disaster resiliency and sustainability**—enabling communities to "bounce back" quickly from an extreme natural event with a minimum of damage and losses over the long term. Instead, these approaches continue to rely on a philosophy that could perhaps be characterized as "run like hell, then come back and fix it if you can." The inequalities built into our social system, however, simply do not give all potential disaster victims an equal ability to run away, or to come back and fix the damage to their lives and property after the initial danger has passed. Stricter building codes, including elevation requirements, are certainly a step in the right direction, but they tend to be fought by real estate interests and become watered down or unenforced by state and local governments, to the point of being almost meaningless—and are frequently prohibitively expensive for residents to implement without considerable financial assistance.

Both the New Orleans and New York areas have considered taking structural mitigation efforts a giant step further by building giant storm surge gates across vulnerable bays and inlets, particularly those that are highly prone to funneling such a surge straight into highly developed areas. Such gates would provide another layer of protection for vulnerable communities and would ideally function in a manner similar to the Netherlands' Delta Works, which was constructed after a catastrophic storm coming out of the North Sea killed nearly 2,000 people in 1953. Such gates are extremely controversial, however: they would be extraordinarily expensive, have the potential to create unacceptable environmental impacts, and might merely serve to redirect storm surges to coastal areas adjacent to the area being targeted for protection.

Switching to a heavier reliance on nonstructural mitigation is problematic as well, both from a political and a social justice standpoint. Disaster relief in the United States has been increasingly federalized over the last several decades and focuses largely on upholding the institution of private property. While homeowners may be eligible for a variety of loans and grants after disasters, there are few programs aimed at helping renters or public housing residents move back home, find new permanent housing, and get back on their feet. Structural mitigation, too, is largely aimed at protecting (and sometimes even creating) private property, and communities are likely to choose those structures that take up the least amount of space (that is, levees over "green space" and floodwalls over levees) in order to allow as much development as possible. Property rights organizations are prone to fight any government attempts to restrict what owners can do with their property but still insist that owners' investments should be protected with massive projects built at taxpayers' expense, even if they are along a beach or in a floodplain.

Government buyouts of extremely vulnerable homes and businesses that have been destroyed by a catastrophic storm or have suffered repeated flood losses are often proposed after catastrophic storms or floods. Theoretically, such programs would be funded through disaster-recovery monies and would allow private property to be turned into "green space" such as public parks or restored wetlands, removing people from harm's way and creating flood-relief buffer zones that could help absorb high waters. These programs are extremely difficult to implement on a large scale, however, particularly since property owner participation is voluntary and most flood victims wish to stay in their own communities rather than moving elsewhere. The Louisiana "Road Home" program discussed above contained a buyout provision, but it was poorly designed and contained confusing time limits. After Hurricane Sandy, Governor Andrew Cuomo suggested a voluntary buyout program that would be available to some 10,000 homes in the most-at-risk areas. While some property owners expressed interest in the program, early estimates suggested that only 10% to 15% of those eligible would take advantage of the buyout offer, which would make the creation of large green spaces very difficult. New Jersey hopes to use federal money to buy out as many as a thousand homes in hopes of restoring floodplains, but as the buyouts are optional, this may not be possible. Successful buyout programs are not unheard of, though: one such effort in North Dakota purchased private property from several hundred homeowners after the Red River flooded in 1997, resulting in a drastic drop in property losses when the river flooded again in 2006.

It is important to understand that not all resistance to this sort of nonstructural mitigation planning comes from wealthy property owners who wish to maintain their vacation homes. Low- or modest-income residents often fear—not illogically—that attempts to rebuild their towns or cities with radically different "footprints" after a severe flood are merely thinly disguised "land grabs" aimed at taking over and destroying their public housing projects or long-established neighborhoods, turning them into city-owned parks or privately developed, highly profitable condominium complexes. Increasing emphasis on nonstructural mitigation after a catastrophe involves determining who will and will not be allowed to have their neighborhoods back, which raises difficult questions of equity, justice, and fair compensation.

While large natural disasters do provide opportunities for communities and disaster relief agencies to learn from their mistakes and improve their planning, response, and long-term mitigation techniques, they also serve to exacerbate rather than "even out" the preexisting social inequalities in devastated regions. While severe floods and hurricanes do in fact have a heavy impact on all kinds of people across the socioeconomic spectrum, they are far from being "great equalizers" that place everyone (perhaps literally) in the same boat. Finding ways to tackle centuries of discrimination and risky land-use decisions is considerably more difficult than improving communications technologies or contraflow plans, but it is essential for truly diminishing overall disaster vulnerability.

SOURCES

Colten, Craig E. 2005. *An Unnatural Metropolis: Wrestling New Orleans from Nature.* Baton Rouge, LA: Louisiana State University Press.

Cutter, Susan L., and Christopher T. Emrich. 2006. "Moral Hazard, Social Catastrophe: The Changing Face of Vulnerability Along the Hurricane Coasts." *Annals of the American Academy of Political and Social Science* 604:102–112.

Extension Disaster Education Network. "Flood Premiums Rising Dramatically." http://eden.lsu.edu/Topics/Hazards/Floods/NFIP/Pages/FloodPremiumsRisingDramatically.aspx

Godschalk, David R., David J. Brower, and Timothy Beatley. 1989. *Catastrophic Coastal Storms: Hazard Mitigation and Development Management.* Durham, NC: Duke University Press.

Haas, Edward F. 1990. "Victor H. Schiro, Hurricane Betsy, and the 'Forgiveness Bill.'" *Gulf Coast Historical Review* 6(1):66–90.

Kirby, Andrew, ed. 1990. *Nothing to Fear: Risks and Hazards in American Society.* Tucson, AZ: University of Arizona Press.

Knafo, Saki, and Lisa Shapiro. 2012. "Staten Island's Hurricane Sandy Damage Sheds Light on Complicated Political Battle." *Huffington Post.* Dec. 6. http://www.huffingtonpost.com/2012/12/06/staten-island-hurricane-sandy_n_2245523.html

Logan, John R., and Harvey L. Molotch. 1987. *Urban Fortunes: The Political Economy of Place.* Berkeley, CA: University of California Press.

Logan, John R., Rachel Bridges Whaley, and Kyle Crower. 1999. "The Character and Consequences of Growth Regimes: An Assessment of Twenty Years of Research." In Andrew E. G. Jonas and David Wilson, eds. *The Urban Growth Machine: Critical Perspectives Two Decades Later,* pp. 73–94. Albany, NY: State University of New York Press.

McQuaid, John, and Mark Schleifstein. 2006. *Path of Destruction: The Devastation of New Orleans and the Coming Age of Superstorms*. New York: Little, Brown, and Company.

Mileti, Dennis S., et al. 1999. *Disasters by Design: A Reassessment of Natural Hazards in the United States*. Washington, D.C.: Joseph Henry Press.

Murphy, Raymond. 2004. "Disaster or Sustainability: The Dance of Human Agents with Nature's Actants." *Canadian Review of Sociology and Anthropology* 41(3):249–266.

New York Times. Hurricane Sandy: Covering the Storm. http://www.nytimes.com/interactive/2012/10/28/nyregion/hurricane-sandy.html

———. Hurricane Sandy's Death Toll. http://www.nytimes.com/interactive/2012/11/17/nyregion/hurricane-sandy-map.html

———. Rebuilding the Coastline, but at What Cost? http://mwr.nytimes.com/2013/05/19/nyregion/rebuilding-the-coastline-but-at-what-cost.html?from=nyregion

Peacock, Walter Gillis, Betty Hearn Morrow, and Hugh Gladwin. 1997. *Hurricane Andrew: Ethnicity, Gender, and the Sociology of Disasters*. London: Routledge.

Platt, Rutherford H. 1999. *Disasters and Democracy: The Politics of Extreme Natural Events*. Washington, D.C.: Island Press.

Scientific American. Hurricane Sandy coverage. http://www.scientificamerican.com/search/?q=hurricane+sandy&x-0&y=0

Steinberg, Ted. 2000. *Acts of God: The Unnatural History of Natural Disaster in America*. Oxford, UK: Oxford University Press.

Van Heerden, Ivor. 2006. *The Storm: What Went Wrong and Why During Hurricane Katrina—The Inside Story from One Louisiana Scientist*. New York: Viking.

The Wave. "Read This! Special Editorial." http://www.rockawave.com/news/2013-03-29/Front_Page/Read_This.html

Wisner, Ben, et al. 2005. *At Risk: Natural Hazards, People's Vulnerability, and Disasters*. London: Routledge.

15

Normalizing the Unthinkable
Climate Denial and Everyday Life

Kari Marie Norgaard

Beachgoers at Jacob Riis Park in the Rockaways, Queens, New York, before being inundated by Hurricane Sandy.

Photo by Ken Gould.

In early January 2013 the National Oceanic and Atmospheric Administration (NOAA) announced that 2012 was the warmest year ever recorded in the United States. In fact, in 2012 every single state in the continental United States had recorded above-average annual temperatures. The average temperature for the contiguous United States was a full 3.2°F above the 20th-century average, and 1.0°F above the previous national record, which had been set in 1998. This should come as no surprise: For nearly three decades natural and physical scientists have provided increasingly clear and dire assessments of how climate change will alter the biophysical world around which human social systems are organized. I took an entire course on climate change as an undergraduate student in 1990, just two years after James Hansen's congressional testimony on the seriousness of climate change made the front page of the *New York Times*. Recently, new temperature records have been coupled with extreme weather events such as Hurricane Katrina, Superstorm Sandy, and the widest tornado on record that hit Oklahoma in May 2013.

Yet despite these heat records, extreme weather events, and urgent warnings from the scientific community, climate change has remained like a proverbial "elephant in the room." Climate scientists may have identified global warming as the most important issue of our time, but for urban dwellers in the rich and powerful Northern countries climate change is still mostly seen as "no more than background noise." For evidence of this disjuncture in the United States one need look no further than the titles of stories released by Gallup on their website reporting the results of their annual Environment Poll: "World's Top-Emitters No More Aware of Climate Change in 2010," "Fewer Americans, Europeans View Global Warming as a Threat" (2011) and "In U.S., Global Warming Views Steady Despite Warm Winter" (2012). Even after Hurricane Katrina hit, the March 2006 Gallup headline read, "Americans Still Not Highly Concerned About Global Warming." The category of climate change did not even make it onto the list of the Pew Research Center's annual January survey of national domestic priorities for the Government and Congress until 2007, some 24 years after the first front-page story in the *New York Times*!

While "apathy" in the United States is particularly notable, this gap between the severity of the problem and its lack of public salience is visible in most Western nations. Indeed, no nation has a base of public citizens that are sufficiently socially and politically engaged to effect the level of change that predictions of climate science would seem to warrant. Instead we are confronted with a series of paradoxes: As scientific evidence for climate change pours in, public urgency and even interest in the issue fails to correspond. As events from Hurricane Katrina and Superstorm Sandy to pine bark beetle infestations in Colorado and melting permafrost in Alaska reveal, changing climatic conditions will increasingly jeopardize state economic resources, exacerbate social inequality, alter community structures, and generate new patterns of economic and social conflict (see Lesson 14). How is it possible that predictions of major threats to social infrastructure such as sea-level rise, increased wildfires, and flooding fail to mobilize public response? What can explain the misfit between scientific information and public concern? Are people just uniformed of the facts? Are they inherently greedy and self-interested? These are the questions that chart the course of my work, which concerns not the outright rejection of climate science by so-called climate skeptics but the more pervasive and everyday problem of how and why people who say they are concerned about climate change manage to ignore it.

For nearly 20 years the main explanation for public silence from the scientific community has been that the public just doesn't understand the seriousness of what is unfolding—in other words, that lack of information is the limiting factor in public nonresponse. The thinking has been that "if people only knew the facts," they would act differently. Psychological and "science communication" studies emphasized the complexity of climate science, while sociologists described political economic corruption as reasons people do not adequately understand what is at stake. Researchers have described the problem of "faulty mental models," lamented the confusion between global warming and ozone depletion, investigated the role of media framing, and described how understanding global warming requires a complex grasp of scientific knowledge in many fields.

For example, psychologists Grame Halford and Peter Sheehan wrote, "With better mental models and more appropriate analogies for global change issues, it is likely that more people, including more opinion leaders, will make the decision to implement some positive coping action of a precautionary nature" (1991, p. 606).

On the sociological side, scholars have identified the fossil fuel industry influence on government policy, the tactics of climate skeptic campaigns, how corporate control of media limits and molds available information about global warming, and even the "normal" distortion of climate science through the "balance as bias phenomenon" in journalism (Boykoff 2011). Many scholars have now traced the process of how the fossil fuel industry and conservative think tanks have challenged the scientific consensus on climate change by "manufacturing uncertainty," altering government documents, and launching political attacks on key climate scientists. The climate skeptic movement has been mostly organized from the United States. Corporate associations including the U.S. Chamber of Commerce and the American Petroleum Institute together with conservative think tanks including the Heartland Institute, the CATO Institute, and the Marshall Institute have played key roles in this process (see Lesson 5). Interestingly, according to research by McCright and Dunlap (2011b), acceptance of climate change also varies by gender and race, with conservative white men being more likely than other Americans to subscribe to "denialist views."

The climate skeptic movement in particular has played a powerful role in the distortion of public understanding of climate change just in the past 10 years. Note that explanations for public nonresponse that highlight corporate media and climate skeptic campaigns also implicitly direct our attention to a lack of information as the biggest barrier to engagement, though for different reasons. Certainly there are cases when the public may either lack information or be outright misinformed, but are these issues the limiting factor behind greater public interest, concern, or political participation? Clearly knowledge is necessary to generate public response, but is knowledge sufficient? As Read and colleagues pointed out two decades ago, only two simple facts are essential to understanding climate change: Global warming is the result of an increase in the concentration of carbon dioxide in the earth's atmosphere, and the single most important source of carbon dioxide is the combustion of fossil fuels, most notably coal and oil. So how can it be that people around the world fail to understand these basic facts? And while such "information deficit" explanations are indispensable, they do not account for the behavior of the significant number of people who know about global warming and express concern, yet still fail to take any action.

While there have been many surveys and public opinion polls on climate change, there have been almost no in-depth, qualitative or ethnographic studies of how people actually experience climate change. I arrived in Norway with a concern about global warming and an intention to conduct research on how the environmentally progressive Norwegians made sense of it. Norway was not only a place I had spent significant time growing up in, but also a nation I admired for its strong environmental and humanitarian values. Plus, the Norwegians have substantial wealth, which can be an asset, at least in making technological changes. Since the time I first lived in Norway as a teenager, I had been fascinated by the extent of progressive environmental policy and awareness there. Now I returned with my comparative sociological lens to ask questions that at the time could not be addressed in my own country, the United States. Indeed, at the time the United States was the only country in the world where, thanks to extensive counter-campaigns by the oil industry and the George W. Bush administration, one quarter of the population still questioned whether global warming was actually occurring.

If any nation can find the ability to respond, it must be in a place such as this, where the population is educated and environmentally engaged. That winter and spring I spent a lot of time attending public meetings, reading the newspapers, talking with people on the street, and generally watching and listening to what was going on. I conducted 46 interviews with a range of community members. As it happened, there was unusually warm weather during the 10 months I spent in the community. November brought severe flooding. The first snowfall did not come until late January, some two months later than usual. By then, the winter was recorded as Norway's second warmest in the past 130 years. The local ski area opened in late December only with the aid of 100% artificial snow, a completely unprecedented event with measurable economic impacts on hotels, shops, taxi drivers, and others in the area. The local lake failed to freeze sufficiently to allow for ice fishing. Small talk commonly included references to "unusual weather" and to "climate change," accompanied by a shaking of heads.

It was not just the weather that was unusual that winter. As a sociologist, I was perplexed by the behavior of the people as well. Despite the clear social and economic impacts on the community, there was no social action in response to the warm weather. Nobody wrote letters to the local paper, brought the issue up in one of the many public forums that took place that winter, made attempts to plan for the local effects of climate change, put pressure on local and national leaders to develop long-term climate plans or short-term economic relief, decreased their automobile use, or even engaged their neighbors and political leaders in discussions about what climate change might mean for their region.

People could have reacted differently to that strange winter. The shortened ski season affected everyone in the community. In the words of one taxi driver, "It makes a difference if we move from five months of winter tourism to only three. It affects all of us, you know, not just those up on the mountain. It affects the hotels, the shops in town, us taxi drivers, we notice it too." Why didn't this awareness translate into social action? Throughout modern history, people have used a variety of strategies to draw attention to problems in their communities, such as staging marches and boycotts and writing letters to newspaper editors and political leaders. What might people have done differently? Community members could have done any number of things to express a sense of concern, from raising the issue in one of the many local political meetings to writing letters in the newspaper, developing plans for how their community might respond, or, at the very least, talking with one another about what climate change might mean for their community in the next 10 to 20 years.

Indeed, in other parts of the world that year reactions to climate change *were* different. Severe flooding in England that November was linked to climate change by at least some of the affected residents. People from affected communities in England traveled to the climate talks at The Hague to protest government policies. Since that time, several cities in the United States have taken action against the federal government over global warming. And although one cannot tie weather events *per se* to climate change, the fact that increased hurricane intensity is one clear outcome of climate change has led residents in Mississippi who are now homeless as a result of Hurricane Katrina to file a lawsuit against oil companies for their role in climate change. The residents of this town could have taken similar actions, rallying around the problem of the lack of snow and its economic and cultural impacts. But they did not.

"WE DON'T REALLY WANT TO KNOW"

That season global warming was frequently mentioned and people in the community seemed to be both informed and concerned about it. Yet at the same time I noticed that it was an uncomfortable issue. People were aware that climate change could radically alter life within the next decades, yet they did not go about their days wondering what life would be like for their children, whether farming practices would change, or whether their grandchildren would be able to ski on real snow. They spent their days thinking about more local, manageable topics. Vigdis, a college-age student, told me that she was afraid of global warming but that it didn't enter her everyday life:

> I often get afraid, like—it goes very much up and down, then, with how much I think about it. But if I sit myself down and think about it, it could actually happen, I thought about how if this here continues we could come to have no difference between winter and spring and summer, like—and lots of stuff about the ice that is melting and that there will be flooding, like, and that is depressing, the way I see it.

In the words of one person who held his hands in front of his eyes as he spoke, "people want to protect themselves a bit." Other community members in Norway described this sense of knowing and not knowing, of having information but not thinking about it in their everyday lives. As one young woman told me, "In the everyday I don't think so much about it, but I know that environmental protection is very important." As a topic that was troubling, it was an issue that many people preferred to avoid. Thus community members describe climate change as an issue that they have to "sit themselves down and think about," "don't think about in the everyday," "but which in between is discouraging and an emotional weight." Since members of the community did know about global warming but did not integrate this knowledge into everyday life, they experienced what Robert Lifton calls the *absurdity of the double life*, a phrase I adapt in coining the term *double reality*. In one reality was the collectively constructed sense of normal everyday life. In the other reality existed the troubling knowledge of increasing automobile use, polar ice caps melting, and the predictions for future weather scenarios. In the words of Kjersti, a teacher at the local agricultural school in her early thirties: "We live in one way and we think in another. We learn to think in parallel. It's a skill, an art of living."

What was happening in that community, and indeed what we can all observe in the public silence on climate change in United States and elsewhere, was not a rejection of information *per se* but the failure to integrate this knowledge into everyday life or transform it into social action. British sociologist Stanley Cohen calls this **implicatory denial**: "the facts of children starving to death in Somalia, mass rape of women in Bosnia, a massacre in East Timor, homeless people in our streets are recognized, but are not seen as psychologically disturbing or as carrying a moral imperative to act . . . Unlike literal or interpretive denial, knowledge itself is not at issue, but doing the 'right' thing with the knowledge" (2011, p. 9).

THREE DISTURBING EMOTIONS

Both my research in Norway and follow-up work in the United States describes how for many people thinking seriously about climate change evokes a series of troubling emotions. There is *fear about a future* with more heat waves, droughts, and increased storm intensity. There is *fear that our present political and economic structures* are unable to effectively respond. And for many there is *guilt* since Americans are among the main contributors to global climate emissions and Norwegians' high standard of living comes directly from their oil income. Finally, many people described a sense of not knowing what to do. Ultimately, sufficiently reducing global climate emissions is beyond the level of individual action. But neither national nor international efforts have been successful either. Awareness of this generates for many a feeling of *helplessness*. Younger people, especially in the United States, have suggested that anger is a fourth emotion that should be considered.

How we respond to disturbing information is a complex process. Individuals may block out certain information in order to maintain coherent meaning systems (e.g., cognitive dissonance), desirable emotional states, a sense of self-efficacy and to follow **norms of attention, norms of emotion**, and **norms of conversation**. The denial metaphor of the elephant in the room is useful because it reminds us that ignoring a serious problem is not easy to do. Ignoring the obvious can be a lot of work. In her work on apathy in the United States, sociologist Nina Eliasoph observes, "We often assume that political activism requires an explanation, while inactivity is the normal state of affairs. But it can be as difficult to ignore a problem as to try to solve it, to curtail feelings of empathy as to extend them . . . If there is no exit from the political world then political silence must be as active and colorful as a bright summer shadow" (1998, p. 6). How did people manage to outwardly ignore what was happening in the community? Did they manage to ignore it inwardly as well?

Eviatar Zerubavel argues that society organizes patterns of perception, memory, and organizational aspects of thinking. In other words, what people pay attention to, think about, remember, and more are in large part a matter of what we have been socialized to notice, think about, and remember. These things are also a function of what people around us are paying attention to, thinking about, and remembering. These cultural norms are in turn attuned to specific political economic relations. Governments and media outlets shape the collective thought process through direct censorship, of course, but much more often this happens through the process of framing stories, distraction, public rituals, and other seemingly more benign techniques. My own work has examined this. Thus, alongside the serious threat to democracy posed by capital's control of the production and dissemination of knowledge (e.g., the fact that increased corporate control of media limits and molds available information about global warming, and corporate-funded research centers generate conflicting knowledge) is another phenomenon that reinforces public nonresponse: how people cope with the information that *does* become available. Overt and more readily identifiable processes such as manipulation and control of information set the stage for the less visible (and to date less studied) process of socially organized denial that I describe here.

The concept of denial is generally considered the domain of psychology. But the information individuals find disturbing, and the mechanisms they employ to protect themselves from such information, may also be analyzed within the context of both social interaction and the broader political economy. Social context itself can be a significant part of what makes it difficult to respond to climate change. Sociologists remind us that notions of what is normal to think and talk about are not given, but are socially structured. Although individual people experience the disturbing emotions of fear, guilt, and helplessness, the act of denial is not individual; rather, it is something that people do together as a community. Again, I draw upon the work of sociologist Eviatar Zerubavel, who coined the term "**socially organized denial**." It is by paying simultaneous attention to individual responses and social context that we can begin to analyze people's reactions to global warming in reference to the larger political economy. Drawing next from my ethnographic data from Norway, I will describe how people use a variety of methods for normalizing or minimizing disturbing information, what can be called "strategies of denial."

Community members *collectively* held information about global warming at arm's length by participating in cultural norms of attention, emotion, and conversation, and by using a series of cultural narratives to deflect disturbing information and normalize a particular version of reality in which "everything was fine." For example, they tried not to think too far into the future, tried to avoid scaring one another or "being too negative," and often emphasized how "Norway is such a small country anyway" and "at least we're not as bad as the Americans." I have since done comparative work in the United States, where many of the feelings about climate change, as well as tactics of normalizing it, are similar to what I found in Norway—except that the "bad guys" are the climate skeptics and the Chinese.

CULTURAL DENIAL

People in the community managed to keep climate change at a distance from their safe everyday lives by following established cultural norms about what to pay attention to, feel, and talk and think about in different contexts. I categorized these as "cultural denial." From the perspective of sociology of cognition, people learn to think through socialization into different "thought communities." At the same time as they feel "just like everyday life," these culturally prescribed norms of attention reflect a particularly insidious form of social control. While outright coercion is a serious matter, it is also more easily recognized, identified, and, in (so-called) democratic societies, condemned. As Cohen notes, "Without being told what to think about (or what not to think about), and without being punished for 'knowing' the wrong things, societies arrive at unwritten agreements about what can be publically remembered and acknowledged" (2001, pp. 10–11). For example, to avoid emotions of guilt, fear, and helplessness, people in the Norwegian community I studied changed the topic of conversations, told jokes, tried not to think about climate change, and kept the concept off the agenda of political meetings. When disturbing ideas about climate change entered the conversation, people used a series of cultural narratives to deflect those ideas and to normalize a particular version of reality in which the scary problem of climate change was not occuring.

Thus information about climate change disappeared into daily life for reasons that were more culturally diffuse. For example, simply upholding norms of attention with respect to space made the lack of snow and warm temperatures seem less significant (depoliticized in part because connections to unusual weather events elsewhere were not made), while following norms of attention with respect to time encouraged community members to not think too far ahead into the future, hence minimizing the extent to which the implications of immediate events are forecasted. Cultural norms of emotion limited the extent to which community members could bring strong feelings they privately held regarding climate change into the public political process, which in turn served to reinforce the sense that everything was fine.

INTERPRETIVE DENIAL: COMBATING GLOBAL WARMING BY INCREASING CARBON DIOXIDE

A second, more explicit example of socially organized denial happened through narrative interpretation. Community members used a variety of social narratives, some produced by the national government, to deflect responsibility for and legitimate Norwegian climate and petroleum policy. I observed three types of narratives: **selective interpretation, perspectival selectivity**, and **claims to virtue.** According to Rosenberg (1991, p. 135), in the case of selective interpretation, to the extent that they are able, "people tend to assign those meanings to events that will produce the desired emotions." In this case, community members had a set of "stock stories" about who they were. By portraying Norwegians as close to nature, egalitarian, simple, and humble, these narratives of national identity served to counter the criticism and doubt Norwegians face with regard to climate and petroleum policies. Notions of "Mythic Norway" were portrayed in official government images and drawn upon by advertisers and everyday people in the town. References to Norwegians as humanitarian and egalitarian were common in the national press, and we bought "Norwegian Mountain Bread" complete with an image of a person skiing in the mountains on 400-year-old ski equipment at our local store.

People also normalized information about global warming using what Rosenberg calls perspectival selectivity: "the angle of vision that one brings to bear on certain events" (1991, p. 134). For example, people may manage unpleasant emotions by searching for and repeatedly telling stories of others who are worse off than they are. Three narratives in this category— "Amerika as a Tension Point," "We Have Suffered," and "Norway Is a Little Land"—served to minimize Norwegian responsibility for the problem of global warming by pointing to the larger impact of the United States on carbon dioxide emissions, stressing that Norway has been a relatively poor nation until quite recently, and emphasizing the nation's small population size. For example, multiple newspaper articles in the national papers in the winter and spring of 2001 mentioned that the United States emits 25% of total greenhouse gas emissions while accounting for only 4% of the global population. While obviously the United States must be held accountable for its emissions, framing the figure in terms of total emissions and population makes the difference between the United States and "little Norway" appear greatest. When looking at per capita emissions in each country, the contrasts are not so large. Perspectival selectivity was used to create what social psychologists Susan Opotow and Leah Weiss (2000) call "denial of self-involvement." These narratives are discussed in more detail in the book that I published based on this research called *Living in Denial: Climate Change, Emotions and Everyday Life*.

A third interpretive strategy is in the vein of what historical psychologist Robert J. Lifton calls "claim to virtue" (1982). He coined the phrase to describe how the Nazi doctors in concentration camps who gave Jews lethal injections interpreted their genocidal actions in terms of compassion. From the doctor's perspective, their acts were compassionate because, by killing people who were ill (or who might become ill), they were able to prevent the spread of disease in the camps. Through the claim that unjust acts are actually working toward the opposite end as they appear (in the case of the doctors, saving the Jews rather than killing them), these actions are made acceptable. Two such claims to virtue were in use that winter with respect to climate change. Although the Norwegian government speaks urgently of the need to reduce emissions of climate gases, they were at the time involved in two projects that do exactly the opposite: building two new natural gas facilities and expanding the petroleum sector by increasing oil development. Both actions have been justified by switching the focus from national targets and measures (as specified under the Kyoto Protocol) to emphasizing climate change as an *international* problem and attempting to meet Norwegian climate commitments by *trading* climate gas emissions rather than reducing actual output.

"GAS PLANTS ARE BETTER THAN COAL"

Beginning in the early 1990s, the Norwegian government in combination with oil and gas companies began presenting a series of justifications for the development of new natural gas facilities: As natural gas produced less carbon dioxide than coal, Norway could sell this excess energy to other nations and actually be helping overall global emissions (see Lesson 9). Thus, although the government acknowledges that Norway's emissions of climate gases must decrease, it has used a claim to virtue to argue that the building two new natural gas plants, thereby *increasing* Norway's contribution to climate gases, was actually helping to solve the problem of global warming. However, as Norwegian researchers Hovden and Lindseth pointed out: "While it is claimed that these would be offset by reductions elsewhere, this does not change the fact that emissions from Norwegian gas-based power would increase the CO_2 emission reductions that Norway would have to complete in order to fulfill its international obligations" (2004, p. 158).

"INCREASING PRODUCTION OF NORWEGIAN OIL WILL HELP THE CLIMATE"

A second example, the justification for increasing national oil production, follows a similar pattern. Norway had increased production of oil and gas threefold in the preceding 10 years, dropped its plan of a national carbon dioxide emissions stabilization target, and shifted from a focus on national strategies (mandated under the Kyoto Protocol) to a focus on international efforts. Within the new international perspective, the government has argued that "since Norwegian petroleum products are not the dirtiest in the international market, Norwegian oil and gas production is good climate policy internationally" (Hovden and Lindseth, 2004, p. 153). Hovden and Lindseth (p. 152) describe how

> Miljkosok, an environmental cooperative forum consisting of the petroleum industry, the government and various interest groups and organizations, produced a report in 1996 that in effect, concluded that Norwegian oil production was environmentally benign. The arguments were a) that a cut in Norwegian production would increase the price of oil on the world market, which would make coal more competitive, and, most importantly, b) that as Norwegian petroleum production has fewer emissions per unit of oil produced, it was environmentally preferable to the oil produced by other countries. The unavoidable conclusion was that Norway should increase its Continental Shelf activity, as this would, in sum, be beneficial with respect to the global emissions of CO_2 and No_x.

Thus, by shifting attention from the national level (on which Norway is retreating from the Kyoto Protocol and other earlier reduction goals) to the international (in which Norway produces "cleaner" oil than other nations), the Norwegian government claims that increasing oil production is the best thing it can do for the global climate, even though these activities increase carbon dioxide emissions and are in direct opposition to their agreement under the Kyoto Protocol!

The interpretive strategies of selective interpretation, perspectival selectivity, and claims to virtue worked together to reinforce one another. For example, selective interpretation and perspectival selectivity gave a background picture of Norwegian environmentalism and innocence, whereas claims to virtue were linked to particular contested climate and petroleum activities such as the expansion of oil and gas production or plans of carbon trading.

CONCLUSION

The view from this one town in Norway portrays global warming as an issue about which people cared and had considerable information, but one about which they didn't really want to know and in some sense didn't know *how* to know. I have traced the three disturbing emotions of guilt, fear of the future and helplessness, as well as how people normalized the idea of climate change in order to avoid these emotions. I describe how people changed the topic of conversations, told jokes, tried not to think about it, and kept the concept off the agenda of political meetings all by following the "rules" of normal behavior. Weaving these pieces together, I follow an arc of power that moves from the microlevel of emotions to the mesolevel of culture to the macrolevel of political economy and back again. According to my data both from Norway and from the United States, thinking about global warming is difficult for community members because it raises troubling feelings, feelings that go against a series of cultural norms. And these norms are in turn embedded in the particular social context and economic circumstances in which people live. Thus, in contrast to psychological and survey research that studies human perceptions of climate change on an individual level, I locate these emotional and psychological experiences in both *cultural* and *political-economic* contexts. As a result of this emphasis on cultural, economic, and social contexts, my approach shifts from an "information deficit" model, in which the public fails to respond because of a lack of information, to a "social organization of denial" model, in which the public on a collective level actively resists available information. As a result, what happened in this one town, and indeed what we can all observe in the public silence on climate change in the United States and elsewhere, was not a rejection of information *per se* but the failure to integrate this knowledge into everyday life or transform it into social action.

One implication of socially organized denial of climate change is that as individuals we must struggle to imagine the reality of our current situation. In writing on the threat of global nuclear war, a problem that now seems infinitely more manageable than climate change, Lifton described many of the same difficulties we face in coming to terms with climate change. He wrote of our "fragmented awareness," how "we have no experience with a narrative of potential extinction," and how therefore we "cling to a desperate conventionality." He pointed out that the emotion of fear inhibits our ability to break through "illusions" to "awareness." And at stake in our "struggle for awareness" is the fact that "the degree of numbing of everyday life necessary for individual comfort is at odds with the degree of tension, or even anxiety that must accompany the nuclear awareness necessary for collective survival." He noted that with the appearance of nuclear weapons, imagining the reality of our situation became "uniquely difficult, and at the same time, a prerequisite for survival" (1982, pp. 117, 108, 5).

Can such socially organized denial be overcome? And if so, how? With socially organized denial, the question becomes not how better to educate and inform the public, but the circumstances under which people are able to move beyond a sense of helplessness, guilt, or fear of the future and take actions that are in their collective, long-term survival interest. Climate change requires large-scale reduction of emissions, but our current political economic structure is intimately embedded in our petroleum- based economy (see Lessons 7 and 9). We need democratic engagement and response, yet individuals retreat out of a sense of helplessness. Part of what makes people feel helpless at present is an assessment of this very serious problem in a context where nobody else is acting, an assessment that political actions are socially unacceptable or politically unfeasible, and a sense that larger international efforts are even more unlikely. How can we escape this circular pattern? Must we go into the streets? Probably a lot more people do need to march with signs down the main streets of every town in the United States, Norway, and around the world in order to break the cycle of invisibility regarding climate change (see Lessons 16 and 18). But for those with different instincts, there are many other things that can and must be done to make climate change visible and to show each other and our political leaders that we demand action.

If socially organized climate denial is a cycle held in place by individual fear and silence, complicit cultural norms, and a state logic based on fossil fuel extraction and economic profit at any politically acceptable cost, then this cycle can be interrupted at multiple points. In any political struggle there are key strategic possibilities. In our present times of rapid social change such strategic moments will continue to emerge, and we can be ready for them. More generally, individuals can get involved in the many ongoing local, regional, and national political efforts. Social theorists like Hannah Arendt remind us of the importance of power from below: Even talking about climate change with family and friends is an important way to break the present cultural silence. Although they are not enough in isolation, local efforts to make climate change visible in one's community, to plan for coming changes in water supplies and energy use, and to reduce emissions at the county and regional levels that are based on existing community ties and sense of place and identity may provide a key for breaking through climate denial from the ground up. There is already a global movement building for communities to uncover how climate change is manifesting in their local contexts. Local political renewal cannot be enough on its own, but it may be the important next step for individuals in breaking through the absurdity of the double life and for renewing democratic process. As people participate in thinking about what is happening in their own place and how they will respond, they will begin to see why the facts of climate change matter to them and to develop a sociological imagination at the same time as they reconnect the rifts in time and space that have constructed climate change as a distant issue. Working together may over time create the supportive community that is a necessary (though not sufficient) condition for people to face large fears about the future and engage in large-scale social change. Facing climate change will not be easy, but it is worth trying.

SOURCES

Arendt, Hannah. 1958. *The Human Condition*. University of Chicago Press.
Boykoff, Maxwell. 2011. *Who Speaks for the Climate? Making Sense of Media Reporting on Climate Change*. Cambridge, UK: Cambridge University Press.

Cohen, Stanley. 2011. *States of Denial: Knowing About Atrocities and Suffering.* Cambridge, MA: Polity Press.

Eliasoph, Nina. 1998. *Avoiding Politics: How Americans Produce Apathy in Everyday Life.* Cambridge, UK: Cambridge University Press.

Halford, G., and Sheehan, P. 1991. Human responses to environmental changes. *International Journal of Psychology* 269(5):599–611.

Hochschild, Arlie Russel. 1983. *The Managed Heart: Commercialization of Human Feeling.* Berkeley: University of California Press.

Hovden, Eivind, and Gard Lindseth. 2004. Discourses in Norwegian Climate Policy: National Action or Thinking Globally? *Political Studies* 52(1):63–81.

Jacques, Peter. 2009. *Environmental Skepticism Ecology, Power and Public Life.* Burlington, VT: Ashgate.

Jacques, Peter, Riley Dunlap, and Mark Freeman. 2008. "The Organization of Denial: Conservative Think Tanks and Environmental Skepticism." *Environmental Politics* 17(3):349–385.

Lifton, Robert. 1982. *Indefensible Weapons: The Political and Psychological Case Against Nuclearism.* New York: Basic Books.

Mann, Michael. 2012. *The Hockey Stick and the Climate Wars: Dispatches from the Front Lines.* New York: Columbia University Press.

McCright, Aaron M., and Riley E. Dunlap. 2010. "Anti-reflexivity: The American Conservative Movement's Success in Undermining Climate Science and Policy." *Theory, Culture & Society* 27(2–3):100–133.

McCright, Aaron M., and Riley E. Dunlap. 2011a. "The Politicization of Climate Change: Political Polarization In the American Public's Views of Global Warming." *Sociological Quarterly* 52:155–194.

McCright, Aaron M., and Riley E. Dunlap. 2011b. "Cool Dudes: The Denial of Climate Change Among Conservative White Males in the United States." *Global Environmental Change* 21(4):1163–1172.

NOAA. "National Overview—Annual 2012" http://www.ncdc.noaa.gov/sotc/national/2012/13#over

Norgaard, Kari Marie. 2011. Living in Denial: *Climate Change, Emotions and Everyday Life.* Cambridge, MA: MIT Press.

Opotow, Susan, and Leah Weiss. 2000. "New Ways of Thinking about Environmentalism: Denial and the Process of Moral Exclusion in Environmental Conflict." *Journal of Social Issues* 56(3):475–490.

Oreskes, Naomi, and Erik Conway. 2010. *Merchants of Doubt: How a handful of scientists obscured the truth on issues from tobacco smoke to global warming.* New York: Bloomsbury Press.

Rosenberg, Morris. 1991. "Self-Processes and Emotional Experiences." In Judith Howard and Peter Callero, eds. *The Self-Society Dynamic: Cognition, Emotion and Action*, pp. 123–142. Cambridge, UK: Cambridge University Press.

Sutton, Barbara, and Kari Marie Norgaard. 2013. "Cultures of Denial: Avoiding Knowledge of State Violations of Human Rights Violations in Argentina and the United States." *Sociological Forum* 28(3):495–524.

Weber, Elke, and Paul Stern. 2011. "Public Understanding of Climate Change in the United States." *American Psychologist* 66(4):315–328.

Zerubavel, Eviatar. 2006. *The Elephant in the Room: Silence and Denial in Everyday Life.* New York: Oxford University Press.

Part 4

SOME SOCIAL RESPONSES TO ENVIRONMENTAL DISRUPTION

16

U.S. Environmental Movements

Robert J. Brulle

Brooklyn Green Party marching in Occupy Wall Street protest, Manhattan, New York.
Photo by Ken Gould.

The U.S. environmental movement is perhaps the single largest social movement in the United States. With over 6,500 national and 20,000 local environmental organizations, along with an estimated 20 million to 30 million members, this movement dwarfs other modern social movements such as the civil rights or peace movements. It is also the longest-running social movement. The first local environmental organizations were founded before the Civil War, and several still existing national environmental organizations, such as the Sierra Club, the National Audubon Society, and American Forests, were founded in the late 19th century.

The question facing social scientists is: How can we understand and examine this enormously complex social movement? There are three commonly used approaches. First, sociologists examine the belief systems that define the various components of this social movement, a process that is termed *discourse analysis*. Second, the development of the social movement over time is examined using *historical analysis*. Third, the techniques used to garner financial resources for the organization are examined through the perspective of *resource mobilization* analysis. By combining all three of these perspectives, one can gain a more complete picture of the environmental movement. The chapter ends with an analysis of the ongoing climate change movement.

DISCOURSE ANALYSIS OF THE U.S. ENVIRONMENTAL MOVEMENT

The first approach is to view this movement as a group of distinct communities, each based on a particular worldview. For example, if you were asked to describe organized religion in the United States, you could list all of the various denominations, such as Catholics, Jews, Episcopalians, and Muslims. When you describe religion using these terms, what you are saying is that there are a number of different religious communities, each based on a particular set of beliefs.

This approach can be applied to describing the U.S. environmental movement. Just like organized religion, the environmental movement is made up of a number of different communities, each based on a particular worldview. Sociologists label these different worldviews as "discursive frames." A **discursive frame** is the set of cultural viewpoints that inform the practices of a community of social movement organizations. Each discursive frame provides a cultural viewpoint from which the environmental organization acts. This discursive frame defines the goals and purposes of the organization and provides guidance for the actions of the organization.

For example, the Wilderness Society belongs to the discursive community defined by the discourse of **preservation**. This discursive frame focuses on the preservation of intact ecological systems and protection of biodiversity. Oriented by this viewpoint, the Wilderness Society seeks to create and maintain wilderness areas and to ensure long-term ecological diversity in these areas. Conversely, the Center for Health, Environment and Justice is informed by the discursive frame of **environmental health** (see Lesson 11). It seeks to protect the health of urban-area residents by eliminating toxic chemicals from their environment. So while both of these organizations have an environmental focus, their discursive frames are distinct.

When you look at the U.S. environmental movement from this perspective, it is clear that it comprises several distinct communities, each based on a unique discursive frame. It is important to recognize this movment's multiple foci based on unique discursive frames. There are 11 major discursive frames that define the environmental movement in the United States. Thus, to understand the environmental movement, you must be familiar with each one.

Wildlife Management

The oldest and first manifestation of concern over the natural environment appeared in the United States over the issue of hunting. Around the middle of the 19th century, wealthy Americans became concerned about the depletion of wildlife for hunting. These sportsmen organized the first environmental organizations. These organizations lobbied for the creation of bag limits on both game animals and fish. This expanded into a national movement toward the end of the 19th century with the appearance of organizations such as the Boone and Crockett Club and the National Audubon Society.

In the early 1930s, this movement underwent a profound shift. Up until this time, the only strategy was to control the demand on fish and game animals by limiting the number of animals that could be taken or limiting the hunting season to a specific time period. However, due to the loss of habitat, this strategy was unable to ensure that a sufficient number of game animals was available. Thus, a new strategy of **wildlife management** was created. This strategy focused on both reducing demand and increasing supply. To increase the supply of game animals, wildlife refuges were established. This strategy of managing both the supply and demand of game animals has worked successfully since its development. This approach defines a major environmental discourse in the United States, with the following key components:

- The scientific management of ecosystems can ensure stable populations of wildlife.
- The wildlife population can be seen as a crop from which excess populations can be sustainably harvested in accordance with the ecological limitations of a given area. This excess wildlife population thus can be utilized for human recreation in sport hunting.

The discourse of wildlife management defines both a unique viewpoint and the practices of a distinct community of organizations. This community is centered on wildlife conservation issues, and it defines its objective as conserving or rationally developing wildlife resources to provide for human recreational needs. It uses phrases such as "maximizing the supply of game" and "conserve our wildlife resources." Some major organizations in this discursive community are Trout Unlimited, Ducks Unlimited, and the National Wildlife Federation.

Conservation

Perhaps the most influential early discursive frames in the U.S. environmental movement were developed by the **conservation** movement. Around the turn of the 20th century, there was a great deal of concern regarding the overexploitation of natural resources by market forces. This concern led to the creation of the conservation movement. These organizations, such as the American Forestry Association (founded in 1875), advocated government control to ensure that these resources would continue to provide an adequate supply for the economy. This philosophy was put into practice during the administration of Theodore Roosevelt in the creation of the national forests. From 1900 to around 1960, this perspective dominated American environmental policy.

From the viewpoint of the discourse of conservation, nature is a resource to be used by society to meet human needs. This forms the basis for collective action to ensure that natural resources are used by applying the criteria of rationality and efficiency to achieve the maximum utility to society. Key components of this perspective are as follows:

- Physical and biological nature is nothing more than a collection of parts that function like a machine.
- Humans need to use the natural resources provided by nature to maintain society.
- Nature can be managed by humans through the application of technical knowledge by competent professionals.
- The proper management philosophy for natural resources is to realize the greatest good for the greatest number of people over the longest period of time.

Organizations based on this discourse define their objective as conserving or rationally developing our natural resources to meet long-term human needs. They use phrases such as "ensure wise use of natural resources" and "bring about efficient conservation and development." Some organizations in this discursive community are the Society of American Foresters, American Forests, and Scenic America.

Preservation

The third environmental discourse to emerge in the United States during the 19th century was preservation. As economic development expanded across the United States, there was growing concern regarding the disappearance of "wild" lands. In 1890,the Census Bureau made a dramatic proclamation; it could no longer define a frontier line. For a country that had previously thought of the West as an inexhaustible source of natural resources and land, this was a profound psychological shock. This meant that the United States was running out of natural resources and wild areas.

This led to concern over the loss of wilderness and the animals that occupied those areas. Based on this concern, a number of organizations arose, such as the Sierra Club (founded in 1892). These organizations advocated for the preservation of wilderness as both a natural and a spiritual resource. This discourse took the form of preservation. It defined a spiritual and psychological relationship between humans and the natural environment. In this discourse, nature in the form of wilderness, untouched by human activity, has intrinsic value. Nature also serves as a site for self-renewal through the experience of its aesthetic beauty. This translates into a concern over the preservation of scenic areas, wilderness, and wildlife. Key components of this perspective are as follows:

- Natural systems are self-creating evolutionary wholes that cannot be reduced to the sum of their parts. Hence, nature is not a machine but an intact organism.
- Human actions can impair the ability of natural systems to maintain themselves or to evolve further.
- Wilderness and wildlife are important components in supporting both the physical and spiritual life of humans.
- Human values go beyond those measured by the national income accounts to include the preservation of wild lands and life.
- Continued existence of wilderness and wildlife is critical to the spiritual well-being of humanity.
- Protection of wilderness areas and wildlife for the current and future generations is an essential environmental task.

Several key features identify organizations based on this discourse. First, the organizations define their objective as preserving wilderness in a pristine state, untouched by humans. This includes leaving all of the plants and wildlife that inhabit that area to develop in a "natural" manner—that is, unaffected by human influences. They use phrases such as "preserve and protect" and "ensure the continued existence of wilderness areas." Some preservation organizations focus only on a specific species or geographical region. This is reflected in the name of the organization. Some examples of these types of organizations are the Sierra Club, the Wilderness Society, and the Nature Conservancy.

Reform Environmentalism

The most dominant discourse of the present day is **reform environmentalism**. This discourse is, in fact, so dominant that it is generally used to refer to the multiple discourses that make up the current environmental movement. However, this was not always the case. Up until around 1966, environmentalists were commonly referred to as "conservationists." This changed in the mid-1960s. In an enormous expansion of the environmental movement, reform environmentalism rose to its current position of dominance in under a decade.

Concern about pollution has been around since the mid-1800s. The development of industrialization brought the burning of coal, the concentration of factories, and human crowding in urban areas. This created environmental problems in the industrial cities in the United States, including crowded tenement districts, air and water pollution, garbage disposal problems, and occupational hazards in the rapidly expanding factories. The brunt of these environmental problems was borne by the working class and the poor. As shown in Lesson 17, this environmental pollution had adverse impacts on workers' health and economic opportunities.

Concerns over urban environmental pollution first manifested themselves in the sanitary movement, which arose after the Civil War to address community health problems. Its aim was to improve urban living conditions, and it dealt with problems such as sanitary water supplies, sewage systems, garbage, and air pollution. This was followed by concern over the excess of refuse and garbage in urban areas. Several protests occurred and a number of civic organizations were founded in the 1890s to demand urban cleanliness. This movement became known as the "municipal housekeeping movement." It primarily took the form of antilittering campaigns, education about sanitary procedures, city cleanup days, and advocating for effective sanitation ordinances. Finally, around 1900, labor unions began pressing demands to address the exceptional levels of exposure to environmental pollution in urban factories.

However, these issues were not a major focus of the leading discursive frames of the early environmental movement in the form of wildlife management, preservation, or conservation. Following a number of highly publicized environmental pollution incidents and spurred on by the publication of Rachel Carson's book *Silent Spring*, pollution concerns rose dramatically among the American public. This gave rise to a new discursive community oriented around a concern that links human health and survival to environmental conditions. In this discourse, nature has a delicate balance and humans are part of it. This perspective emphasizes that nature is an ecological system—that is, a web of interdependent relationships. Humanity is part of this ecological system. Hence, human health is vulnerable to disturbances in the ecosystem. This animates action to identify and eliminate the physical causes of environmental degradation. Key components of this perspective are as follows:

- Natural systems are the basis of all organic existence, including that of humans.
- Humankind is an element within natural ecosystems, and hence human survival is linked to ecosystem survival.
- Ethical human actions (actions that promote the good life for humankind) necessarily promote action toward all life on Earth in an ecologically responsible manner.
- Proper use of natural sciences can guide the relationship between humanity and its natural environment.

Organizations based in this discourse identify their purpose as protecting the Earth's ecosystem and human health. These organizations tend to use phrases such as "to protect and enhance human welfare and combat environmental deterioration" and "this organization is dedicated to improving environmental quality and public health." Some of the well-known organizations in this discursive community include Greenpeace, Environmental Defense, and the Natural Resources Defense Council.

Deep Ecology

Following the rise of reform environmentalism in the 1960s and 1970s, there was increasing disillusion with the results that the existing environmental movement was able to realize. One area of concern was the increasing exploitation of the few remaining natural areas in the United States. These concerns gave rise to the formation of the **deep ecology** movement in the early 1980s. Although part of the environmental movement, it is much more radical in its belief that the requirements to maintain intact natural systems should take precedence over human needs. At the core of this discursive frame is a belief in the intrinsic value of all nature that will ground a respectful way of living in and with the natural, nonhuman world. In this discursive frame, nature is seen as a value in its own right, independent of human existence. Humanity is only one species among many and has no right to dominate the Earth and all of the other living organisms. This creates an ethic of radical wilderness advocacy. Unlike preservation, which seeks to keep what remains, deep ecology seeks the restoration of fully functioning ecosystems, in which the evolution of life, unaffected by human actions, can continue. It also advocates the inherent rights of all nonhuman beings to exist in their natural state. In this sense, deep ecology makes a moral argument for the preservation of the natural environment. Key components of this discourse are as follows:

- All life on Earth, in its richness and diversity, has intrinsic value.
- Humankind's relations to the natural world at present endanger the richness and diversity of life.
- Human life is privileged only to the extent of satisfying vital needs.
- Maintenance of the diversity of life on Earth mandates a decrease in the human impacts on the natural environment and substantial increases in the wilderness areas of the globe.
- Changes (consistent with cultural diversity) affecting basic economic, technological, and cultural aspects of society are therefore necessary.

The organizations based in deep ecology generally define their objectives as acting to preserve the rights of all nonhuman beings to a natural existence, unaffected by human intervention. These organizations define their aims using phrases such as "defending the intrinsic rights of species to life" and "placing ecological considerations first in any decision-making process." Some of the well-known organizations in this discursive community include Earth First! and the Sea Shepherd Conservation Society.

Environmental Justice

A second component of the U.S. environmental movement that arose in the early 1980s was the **environmental justice** movement (see Lesson 10). Like deep ecologists, environmental justice advocates had a profound sense of disappointment over the results of the 1960s and 1970s environmental movement. However, the concern of this community was not wilderness; rather, it was the unequal burden of pollution that was placed on poor and minority communities. Thus, they were concerned with exposures to persistent toxic pollution in the form of local toxic waste dumps, high levels of air pollution, or unhealthy and polluted living conditions. From these concerns, a unique community arose that focused on urban environmental issues in systematically disadvantaged areas.

The discursive frame of environmental justice accepted the link between human survival and ecosystem survival as defined by reform environmentalism. However, instead of focusing on the physical causes of environmental degradation, this frame sees environmental problems as creations of human social order. Hence, the solution of environmental problems lies in social change. Key components of this viewpoint are as follows:

- Domination of humans by other humans leads to domination of nature.
- The economic system and nation-state are the core structures of society that create ecological problems.
- Commodification and market imperatives force consumption to continually increase in the developed economy.
- Environmental destruction in low-income/racially distinct communities or Third World countries originates in the exploitation of the people who live in these areas by the dominant social institutions.
- Resolution of environmental problems requires fundamental social change based on empowerment of local communities.

Thus, environmental justice organizations focus on the social creation and resolution of environmental problems. While these groups focus on a large number of issues, they all seek to protect local communities from the adverse effects of environmental degradation. Additionally, regardless of their specific focus, groups based in the discourse of environmental justice define their objective as changing the social order in some manner to solve environmental problems. The means to carry out this goal include holding government and corporations accountable through democratic processes or by bringing legal suits to end toxic waste dumping. Some organizations with this orientation describe their purpose in phrases such as "create economic democracy through localized decision-making," "develop grassroots capabilities to involve local citizens in the resolution of their communities' environmental problems," and "abolish environmental racism." Some of the leading environmental justice organizations include the West Harlem Environmental Action Coalition, the Southwest Network for Environmental and Economic Justice, and the Indigenous Environmental Network.

Environmental Health

A discursive community closely associated with the environmental justice community is the environmental health movement (see Lesson 11). While the environment has always played a key role in community health, the relationship between environmental pollution and specific illnesses is still not widely acknowledged. However, in a number of diverse locations, individuals noticed a strong relationship between environmental pollution and their health. Some of the key examples are the extremely high rate of breast cancer among women on Long Island and the increasing rates of asthma among children exposed to automobile exhaust.

From this concern, a movement took shape in the late 1980s that focused on the relationship between environmental pollution and human health. This movement defined a unique discourse that encompassed the perspective of environmental health. Key components of this viewpoint are as follows:

- Human health is the outcome of interactions with physical, chemical, biological, and social factors in the natural environment, especially toxic substances and pollution.
- Ensuring community health requires a livable and healthy community, with adequate social services and elimination of exposures to toxic or polluting substances.
- The precautionary principle (no technology or material can be used unless it is proven environmentally harmless) should guide industrial development.

The organizations in this discursive community seek to reduce the use of toxic materials and to ensure a safe and clean environment for all people. Organizations in this movement describe their purpose in phrases such as "preventing exposure to toxic materials that cause breast cancer," "creating safe schools to protect our children's health," and "ensuring that medical waste from hospitals is disposed of in an environmentally responsible way." Some examples of actions taken by these types of organizations include demanding that all toxic materials are removed from schools to ensure that children are not exposed to them and calling for the safe disposal of industrial wastes. Some of the leading environmental organizations in this discursive community include the Center for Health, Justice and the Environment and 1 in 9: The Long Island Breast Cancer Action Coalition.

Ecofeminism

The fourth environmental discourse to develop in the 1980s was **ecofeminism**. This discursive community grew out of the feminist movement. Ecofeminism defines the problem of ecological degradation as originating in the treatment of nature as an object to be possessed and dominated, instead of a partner to be cooperated with. This cultural treatment of nature is tied to the development of a patriarchal society and the domination of women by men: Just as men dominate women, humanity dominates nature. Thus, the resolution of our ecological problems entails a shift from a manipulative and controlling culture toward both women and nature to a culture of cooperation. Key components of this discourse are as follows:

- Earth is home for all life and should be revered and nurtured.
- Ecosystem abuse is rooted in androcentric concepts, values, and institutions.
- Relations of complementarity rather than superiority between culture/ nature, human/nonhuman, and male/female are desirable.
- The many problems of human relations and relations between the human and nonhuman worlds will not be resolved until androcentric institutions, values, and ideology are eradicated.

The few ecofeminist organizations that exist focus on empowering women to function as decision makers. Some examples of phrases used by ecofeminist organizations include "representing the viewpoints of all women in international affairs" and "facilitating the development of women in leadership roles in the environmental movement." In addition, they seek to correct the perspective in economic development programs that fail to recognize the role of women and the household economy in the overall system of economic production. The largest and best-known ecofeminist organization in the United States is the Women's Environment and Development Organization.

Ecospiritualism

In 1967, a landmark essay by Lynn White titled "The Historical Roots of Our Ecologic Crisis" appeared in *Science* magazine. In this essay, White argued that the Western biblical tradition, on which both the Jewish and Christian faiths are based, was the root of the environmental crisis. Since the Bible created a separation of humans from nature, humans were seen as masters of and apart from the rest of creation. This image, White argued, created a wholly anthropocentric view of nature, in which humanity was commanded to subdue the Earth, so the exploitation of nature for human needs was natural and appropriate. The remedy for our ecological crisis was clear. He argued that if the biblical belief system created a disregard for the natural environment and led to our ecological crisis, we needed to develop a new religious viewpoint that would accommodate humans living in harmony with nature.

This viewpoint posed a major problem for Western theologians. The ecological crisis created doubt about the Christian idea that a providential god was providing for humanity. Following this essay, a number of different religious thinkers developed unique perspectives that integrated concern over the natural environment into religious belief systems. Out of these writings, a unique discourse of **ecospiritualism** emerged. Key components of this discourse are as follows:

- Nature is endowed with spiritual value.
- Humanity, as part of nature, has a moral obligation to preserve it intact.
- Religious beliefs need to be developed that embody this ethic.
- These beliefs can then inform actions to create an ecologically sustainable society.

This new viewpoint spread through the U.S. religious community, and by 1995, virtually all of the major churches in the United States issued proclamations on environmental degradation. Additionally, in 1993, the National Religious Partnership was formed. This organization is composed of the United National Council of Churches, the U.S. Catholic Conference, Consultation on the Environment and Jewish Life, and the Evangelical Environmental Network. This action united the major Protestant, Catholic, Jewish, and Evangelical communities into one organization focused on developing and implementing religious approaches to combat environmental degradation. This movement has a unique structure. Its organizations are not single-focus social movement organizations; rather, they involve religious organizations that are expanding their role into environmental affairs.

It is important to realize that there is no absolute line that defines the environmental movement. Rather, it is a gradient, moving from organizations that have an exclusive focus on environmental issues to those that deal with environmental issues as part of a group of associated issues. The final two discursive frames examined in this lesson fall into this category.

Animal Rights

The first related discursive frame is **animal rights**. Concern about the treatment of animals dates from 1866 in the United States, when the American Society for the Prevention of Cruelty to Animals (ASPCA) was founded. Although the primary focus of this movement has always been on domestic animals and pets, it has also been a significant actor regarding the treatment and preservation of wildlife. For example, Henry Bergh, who founded the ASPCA, was a key force in trying to stop the indiscriminant slaughter of bison in the 1870s.

This concern over animals has developed into a well-defined discursive community. In this discursive frame, all species are seen to have intrinsic rights to realize their own evolved characteristics and to live an independent life free from human direction or intervention. Key components of this discourse are as follows:

- All of creation is endowed with an ability to define itself and evolve.
- Life thus has a right to be left to develop according to its own character.
- Humanity has no right to infringe on the rights of other animals.

The organizations in this discursive community usually focus on the protection of both domestic and wild animals. One recent focus has been on the treatment of animals in agricultural production (see Lessons 12 and 13). A large number of organizations focus on the rehabilitation and release of injured or sick wildlife. Some of the better-known animal rights organizations in addition to the ASPCA include the Free Willy Keiko Foundation and People for the Ethical Treatment of Animals (PETA).

Anti-globalization/Greens

The second discursive frame related to the U.S. environmental movement is the anti-globalization/**greens** frame. This frame, which arose in the 1990s, focuses on the rise of a global economy and the impacts of this process on both the quality of life and the environment. Specifically, it sees the process of economic globalization and the weakening of national labor and environmental standards as encouraging a "race to the bottom" as nations lower these standards to attract business investments. Key components of this discursive frame are as follows:

- All humans and their communities deserve to live in an equitable, just, and environmentally sustainable world.
- Global abuses—such as ecological destruction, poverty, war, and oppression—are linked to global capitalism and the political and economic forces that have allowed the development of social inequality and injustices.
- The coercive powers of international financial institutions need to be eliminated so that national governments are accountable to the democratic will of their population.

The first large-scale collective action of this community in the United States was the series of demonstrations in conjunction with the meeting of the World Trade Organization in Seattle in 1999. This community is loosely organized in the U.S. Network for Global Economic Justice, a coalition of over 200 social movement organizations. Some of the better-known organizations in this community include the Ruckus Society and the Pesticide Action Network of North America.

Distribution of Organizations by Discursive Frame

The number of organizations in each discursive frame is shown in Figure 16–1. As this graph shows, the largest number of organizations are found in the long-established discursive frames of reform environmentalism, preservation, and conservation. Together, these three discursive frames represent 78% of the environmental movement. All of the other discursive frames represent 5% or less of the total organizations. Thus, although a great deal of

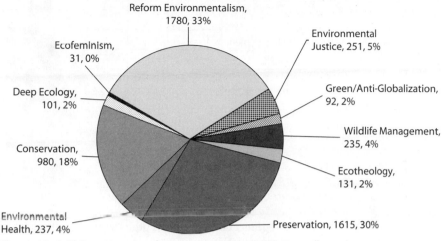

U.S. National and Regional Environmental Organizations Distribution by Discursive Frame

Reform Environmentalism, 1780, 33%

Ecofeminism, 31, 0%

Environmental Justice, 251, 5%

Deep Ecology, 101, 2%

Green/Anti-Globalization, 92, 2%

Conservation, 980, 18%

Wildlife Management, 235, 4%

Ecotheology, 131, 2%

Environmental Health, 237, 4%

Preservation, 1615, 30%

Figure 16–1 U.S. national and regional environmental organization distribution by discursive frame.

attention is given to the newer discursive frames in the academic literature, the environmental movement continues to be concentrated in these more conventional and long-lived discursive frames.

HISTORICAL DEVELOPMENT OF THE U.S. ENVIRONMENTAL MOVEMENT

The second approach to understanding the U.S. environmental movement is to examine its historical development over time. The current environmental movement is the result of the cumulative historical development of the different discursive communities over the past 150 years. This growth in organizations is shown in Figure 16–2. To simplify this presentation, the number of discourses illustrated has been reduced. First, due to the relatively small number of organizations with the discourse of wildlife management and its close ideological similarity with conservation, these two discursive frames have been combined. Second, due to their small numbers, organizations with the discursive frames of animal rights, deep ecology, ecofeminism, ecospiritualism, environmental health, environmental justice, and anti-globalization/green have been combined into one category, labeled "Alternative Discourses." As this graph illustrates, there was a substantial increase in the number of new organizations starting in the mid-1950s until around 1967. This was followed by explosive growth in 1968–1970 and again in 1988–1990.

To further examine this growth by different discursive frames, the relative growth rates of the different communities are shown in Figure 16–3.

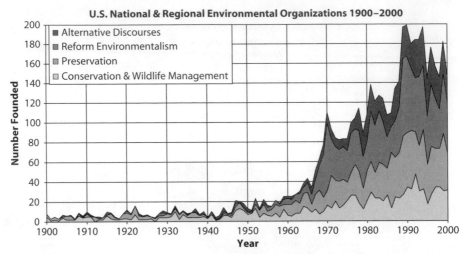

Figure 16–2 U.S. national and regional environmental organizations, 1900–2000.

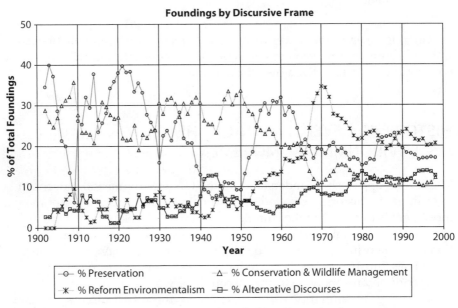

Figure 16–3 Number of organizations founded by discursive frame.

Note: Trends based on 5-year moving average.

This graph clearly shows that the discursive frames of preservation and conservation/wildlife management were dominant until the end of the 1930s. In the 1940s, there was a significant rise in the number of alternative discursive organizations. This was due primarily to the increase of environmental health organizations founded during World War II. Additionally, the founding of preservation organizations dramatically declined in the 1940s. However, in the 1950s, the number of new preservation groups increased rapidly, and the number of new conservation/wildlife management groups started a long, slow decline. Additionally, the number of new reform environmental organizations started a long and steady increase, which culminated in an explosive rate of growth around 1970. Additionally, as more alternative discursive frames were developed in the 1970s and 1980s, there was a slow but steady growth in these organizations in the period from 1960 on.

What Figure 16–3 shows is that there are unique developmental dynamics for each discursive community. The cumulative impact of these different developmental dynamics has led to today's highly differentiated environmental movement.

Economic Resource Mobilization

The third approach to understanding the U.S. environmental movement focuses on the economic resources that each discursive community has available to promote its particular environmental agenda. The mobilization of economic resources is an extremely important determinant of the effectiveness of a discursive community in realizing its goals. Every year, all nonprofit organizations are required to inform the U.S. Internal Revenue Service (IRS) of their income and expenses. Based on this information filed with the IRS in 2003, Table 16–1 shows the total income of these different discursive communities.

As Table 16–1 shows, fully 50% of the funding of the environmental movement is under the control of the organizations with a preservationist frame. This is followed by the other three mainstream discursive frames of reform environmentalism, wildlife management, and conservation, which range between 20.4% to 12.2% of the total income. The alternative discourses have

Table 16–1 Income Distribution by Discursive Frame, 2003 (in US Dollars)

Frame	N	% of N	Total Income ($)	% of Total	Mean ($)	Median ($)
Animal Rights	35	2.5%	95,542,298	1.9%	2,729,780	420,819
Conservation	223	16.0%	627,813,084	12.2%	2,815,305	345,421
Deep Ecology	34	2.4%	17,763,087	0.3%	522,444	270,092
Ecofeminism	4	0.3%	2,027,480	>0.1%	506,870	115,100
Ecospiritualism	12	0.9%	8,776,361	0.2%	731,363	149,452
Environmental Health	33	2.4%	36,683,659	0.7%	1,111,626	503,346
Environmental Justice	38	2.7%	57,301,562	1.1%	1,507,936	385,728
Green/Anti-Globalization	9	0.6%	8,844,870	0.2%	982,763	571,318
Preservation	536	38.6%	2,590,627,143	50.3%	4,833,260	296,873
Reform Environmentalism	404	29.1%	1,048,293,688	20.4%	2,594,786	395,409
Wildlife Management	62	4.5%	656,084,214	12.7%	10,582,003	310,477
Total	1,390	100.0%	5,149,757,446	100.0%	3,704,861	348,058

Table 16–2 Income Distribution, Top 50 U.S. Environmental Organizations, 2003 (in US Dollars)

Organization	Income ($)	% of Income
Nature Conservancy	972,368,622	18.85
Wildlife Conservation Society	347,533,674	6.74
Sierra Club Foundation	241,236,005	4.68
Conservation International Foundation	229,267,098	4.44
Population Council	197,888,299	3.84
World Wildlife Fund	175,582,103	3.40
National Audubon Society	172,642,826	3.35
Trust for Public Land	153,915,522	2.98
National Wildlife Federation	132,004,722	2.56
Sierra Club	88,203,029	1.71
Tides Center	69,567,396	1.35
American Land Conservancy	68,110,320	1.32
Fresh Air Fund	65,459,125	1.27
Chesapeake Bay Foundation	61,007,116	1.18
Conservation Fund	60,133,583	1.17
Rocky Mountain Elk Foundation	55,418,970	1.07
Environmental Defense	51,657,887	1.00
Natural Resources Defense Council	50,063,972	0.97
World Resources Institute	48,241,872	0.93
Brandywine Conservancy	39,007,586	0.76
Earthjustice	34,266,715	0.66
Ocean Conservancy	31,981,555	0.62
Ducks Unlimited	31,475,354	0.61
Institute of Ecosystem Studies	30,206,097	0.59
Association of Village Council Presidents	29,865,852	0.58
Pheasants Forever	27,824,126	0.54
Yosemite Foundation	25,967,512	0.50
Wilderness Society	23,180,201	0.45
National Parks Conservation Association	22,147,238	0.43
Defenders of Wildlife	21,779,921	0.42
National Arbor Day Foundation	21,337,542	0.41
African Wildlife Foundation	18,861,831	0.37
Student Conservation Association	18,714,956	0.36
Water Environment Federation	18,687,081	0.36
People for the Ethical Treatment of Animals	18,652,096	0.36
Wetlands America Trust	17,171,656	0.33
Anti-cruelty Society	16,932,539	0.33
International Fund for Animal Welfare	16,634,365	0.32
Energy Federation Inc.	15,537,392	0.30
Environmental Careers Organization	15,468,856	0.30
Save the Redwoods League	14,546,107	0.28
American Forest Foundation	14,351,443	0.28
Coastal Conservation Association	14,265,263	0.28
Center for International Forestry Research	12,466,225	0.24
Aspen Center for Environmental Studies	12,402,810	0.24
Water Environment Research Foundation	12,042,492	0.23
National Save the Sea Turtle Foundation	11,349,324	0.22
Manomet Center for Conservation Sciences	11,212,735	0.22
Greenpeace Foundation	10,986,369	0.21
National Environmental Trust	10,715,102	0.21

very low levels of economic resources: Even if they are combined, they total less than 5% of the total income distribution.

This economic distribution is mirrored in the income ranking of individual organizations. Table 16–2 shows the total and percent income distribution for the wealthiest 50 U.S. environmental organizations. Income among environmental organizations is highly skewed to a few extremely wealthy organizations. The Nature Conservancy, a large land trust organization, receives nearly 19% of the total environmental movement's income.

It is important to note that this list shows only the top 50 organizations; another 1,339 organizations are not shown in this table, and between them they divide the remaining 25.2% of total income. Thus, the vast majority of environmental organizations have very limited economic resources available to them. It is no surprise, then, that the organizations that mostly appear in the press and before Congress are those with sufficient funding to build and maintain a strong staff and organizational structure. Accordingly, one of the key areas of focus in current research into the environmental movement is why these funding differentials exist.

THE U.S. CLIMATE CHANGE MOVEMENT

As climate change has risen in importance (see Lesson 15), a number of organizations and coalitions have arisen to address this issue. There are three dominant discursive frames within this movement:

1. *Weak Ecological Modernization.* In this perspective, the appropriate approach to deal with climate change is through technological development. By shifting to renewable energy, this approach argues that this technological shift can result in a decrease in carbon emissions and a decoupling of economic growth and energy production with carbon emissions. At the core of ecological modernization theory is the idea that the existing social, economic, and governmental institutions can deal effectively with environmental issues, and there is no need for radical structural changes in industrial society.

2. *Strong Ecological Modernization.* This approach focuses on embedding environmental and ecological concerns in society by reconfiguring existing political and economic institutions. This includes adjusting economic systems to include the value of natural capital in production decisions, modifying the existing political system toward more democratic participation, and including developing countries' social justice and equity concerns in global environmental governance. However, the basic structure of a capitalist global economy is seen as sufficient after adoption of these reforms.

3. *Civic Environmentalism.* This perspective argues that neither weak nor strong ecological modernization is adequate to address climate change.

From this discursive perspective, both ecological modernization and global governance are seen as favoring the interests of the existing power elites and the dominant industrialized countries and thus will result in the marginalization of poor people and less developed countries. Instead, this discursive frame aims for a fundamental transformation of consumption patterns and existing institutions to realize a more sustainable and ecologically conscious world order. Thus, addressing climate change will require a fundamental transformation of the existing global institutions.

Within the U.S. climate change movement, the dominant discursive frame on climate change in the U.S. at the national level is a form of the first of these three, weak ecological modernization. A few peripheral organizations operate within the discursive frames of strong ecological modernization and civic environmentalism.

In my analysis (Brulle, 2013), I examined the network structure of 21 climate change coalitions that existed in 2010. A sociogram of this network structure is shown in Figure 16–4. As this figure illustrates, there is a great deal of diversity in the types of organizations that make up the different coalitions. The largest coalition is 350.org, which is primarily composed of nongovernmental organizations (NGOs) and also has links to nine other coalitions. The structures of the next two largest generalist coalitions, TckTckTck and the U.S. Climate Action Network, are quite similar. There are three coalitions that are primarily composed of for-profit corporations: Inter-west Energy Alliance, Sustainable Energy Coalition, and U.S. Climate Action Partnership. In addition, both Apollo Alliance and Blue Green Alliance are composed primarily of labor unions and NGOs.

There is a relationship between the discursive orientation of a coalition and the organization's composition. Coalitions with a discursive orientation of weak ecological modernization have the highest participation of for-profit corporations and the lowest percentage participation of NGOs. Conversely, coalitions with a civic environmentalism discursive frame have the lowest level of corporate participation and the highest involvement of NGOs and other coalitions. Coalitions with a strong ecological modernization discourse are more similar to civic environmental organizations in that they have low corporate involvement and high NGO involvement. In addition, an examination of the absolute size of the different coalitions based on discursive frame shows an overwhelming preponderance of organizations in the larger frame of weak ecological modernization.

CONCLUSION

The U.S. environmental movement is not a monolithic structure; rather, it is composed of a number of different discursive communities, each with its own specific issue focus. The organizations developed under different historical

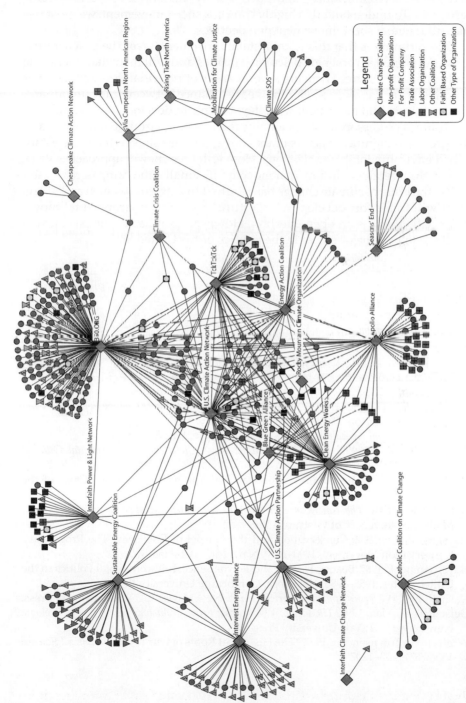

Figure 16-4 Sociogram of U.S. national climate change movement, 2010.

Legend

- Climate Change Coalition
- Non-profit Organization
- For Profit Company
- Trade Association
- Labor Organization
- Other Coalition
- Faith Based Organization
- Other Type of Organization

Chesapeake Climate Action Network
Via Campesina North American Region
Rising Tide North America
Mobilization for Climate Justice
Climate SOS
Climate Crisis Coalition
Tck Tck Tck
Energy Action Coalition
Seasons' End
350.ORG
Rocky Mountain Climate Organization
Apollo Alliance
U.S. Climate Action Network
Blue Green Alliance
Clean Energy Works
Interfaith Power & Light Network
Sustainable Energy Coalition
U.S. Climate Action Partnership
Interwest Energy Alliance
Catholic Coalition on Climate Change
Interfaith Climate Change Network

and political circumstances and have widely varying levels of economic resources. To understand this highly complex social movement, we must use the full range of social movement perspectives.

One certainty is that this is not a static movement. Over the past century, it has developed several new discursive frames and will most likely continue to do so in the future. There are several areas of potential development. For example, there has always been an uneasy alliance between trade unions and the environmental movement. Will they be able to develop a united political program? (See Lesson 17.) Additionally, the rise of environmental justice and the greens as significant actors in the movement has shaken the more established environmental organizations. How will these newer approaches work within the overall environmental movement? Finally, the campaign focused on the the issue of climate change has resulted in new groups such as 350.org. How will this effort develop in the future? How the environmental movement will evolve is an open question. However, as it has in the past, it will continue to be a major player in the politics of the United States.

SOURCES

Bernstein, S. 2001. *The Compromise of Liberal Environmentalism*. New York: Columbia University Press.

Brulle, Robert J. 2000. *Agency, Democracy, and Nature: The U.S. Environmental Movement from a Critical Theory Perspective*. Cambridge, MA: MIT Press.

Brulle, Robert J. 2013. "The Development, Structure, and Influence of the U.S. National Climate Change Movement." In Yael Wolinsky, ed. *Climate Change Policy and Civil Society*. Washington, D.C.: Congressional Quarterly Press.

Buell, F. 2004. *From Apocalypse to Way of Life*. London, UK: Routledge.

Bullard, Robert D. 1990. *Dumping in Dixie: Race, Class and Environmental Quality*. Boulder, CO: Westview Press.

Dowie, M. 1996. *Losing Ground: American Environmentalism at the Close of the Twentieth Century*. Cambridge, MA: MIT Press.

Fox, Stephen. 1981. *The American Conservation Movement: John Muir and His Legacy*. Madison: University of Wisconsin Press.

Hays, Samuel P. 1972. *Conservation and the Gospel of Efficiency: The Progressive Conservation Movement, 1890–1920*. New York: Athenaeum.

Hays, Samuel P. 1987. *Beauty, Health, and Permanence: Environmental Politics in the United States, 1955–1988*. New York: Cambridge University Press.

Nash, R. 1967. *Wilderness and the American Mind*. New Haven, CT: Yale University Press.

Oelschlaeger, Max. 1991. *The Idea of Wilderness: From Prehistory to the Age of Ecology*. New Haven, CT: Yale University Press.

White, Lynn Townsend, Jr. 1967. "The Historical Roots of Our Ecologic Crisis." *Science* 155(3767):1203–1207.

17

Labor and the Environment

Brian K. Obach

Abandoned Bethlehem Steel mill, Bethlehem, Pennsylvania.
Photo by Ken Gould.

Imagine that you have worked in a lumber mill in a rural area in the Pacific Northwest for the last 15 years. Your father worked in the timber industry, as did his father before him. The timber industry is the primary economic engine in your area. Tourism has been growing, and the wilderness enthusiasts who come to town have also helped to bolster the economy through their spending on lodging, supplies, and services. But the jobs associated with serving these visitors do not pay very well, and the mill remains the main employer. However, timber sector jobs have been disappearing in recent years. Several mills elsewhere in the region have shut down, and your mill has laid off several workers. So far, you've been able to keep your job, but unemployment is high, and there is much fear and concern among the mill workers about their job situation.

The company says that the industry is being harmed by environmental groups that charge that logging is destroying the habitat of an endangered owl. The mill owners say that measures being promoted by "big-city environmentalists" would "lock up" a good deal of forest land that the industry depends upon. Lawsuits filed by some environmental groups have already delayed logging on some parcels, and the company claims that this is what led to the recent layoffs. Along with your last paycheck the company included a request that everyone write to their congressional representatives to oppose any new logging restrictions. Many of your fellow workers have already done so, and talk about these "damn environmentalists who want to destroy our jobs" is common throughout the community.

What do you think you would do in this situation? How do you think you would feel about environmentalists and the need for forest protection?

People form opinions and take political action on the basis of many different factors. As sociologists we recognize that people have different interests and are exposed to different ideas and influences depending on their social position—that is, their economic class, the region they live in, their age, their race, their gender, their education, and other important facets of their lives. Unless you are returning to school, as a college student you are probably fairly young, you are already relatively well educated, you might have a part-time job or work over the summer in the service sector, and, while you may not necessarily be well off now, your education level will likely place you in a job that does not involve manual labor and that will provide you with a relatively decent income in the future. On the basis of your social position and the influences to which you are exposed within that location, your views on many issues are likely to be different from those of a middle-aged career mill worker.

Research demonstrates that, as with most issues, views on environmental protection vary depending on one's social position. Thus, to understand (and to shape) our environmental future, it is important that we examine what influences people's attitudes regarding the need for environmental protection. If people are in a position that leads them to deny the existence of real environmental problems, we need to understand why and to consider ways that would help to unite people to confront environmental changes that threaten human well-being. One's employment situation can be an important aspect of shaping one's views on environmental issues.

If you were the mill worker described above, you might view the need for forest protection with some skepticism. Logging restrictions would pose a potential threat not only to the basic economic interests of you and your family, but to your whole way of life and the community in which you live. If the mill were to shut down, you would find yourself out of work, your community would likely deteriorate without its primary economic engine, and you would be cut off from some of the cultural traditions that extend back in your family for generations. In addition, your employer, who not only signs your paychecks but whom you probably consider to be knowledgeable about the industry, is telling you that environmentalists are responsible for this threat. Many of your friends and coworkers share the view that environmentalists are a problem. And what's more, these environmentalists are outsiders whom you do not know and do not necessarily trust. You know that logging has been carried out in your area for decades, even by members of your own family, and there have not been environmental problems before. What would these environmental activists, lawyers, and lobbyists based in Washington, D.C., or other big cities know about the forest that they probably never even visited in the first place? It is likely that if you were in that mill worker's social location, you would be suspicious about these environmental claims and possibly even hostile to environmental advocates and the cause that appears to threaten your livelihood.

This is not to suggest that every person in such a position is going to react to this situation in exactly the same way. Human beings are extremely complex, and while we know that social position *influences* the beliefs and behaviors that people develop, that position does not *determine* the opinions and attitudes of every individual. Nonetheless, as sociologists, we are able to detect patterns that help us to understand how one's social position influences behavior and attitudes.

It is clear that one's employment situation and the associated influences can affect the way one views issues, including that of environmental protection. Examining the relationship between labor and the environment will help us to answer important questions: Will environmental measures harm the economic condition of workers? Or might a failure to act to protect the environment harm some industries and destroy jobs? Who will be most affected by environmental measures and in what way? How will employment concerns shape workers' perspectives on environmental protection? How will such concerns shape their political behavior? Are there ways to effectively address both environmental concerns and the economic interests of working people? What is the role of government, of labor unions, of employers, and of environmental organizations in this process? Our future as a society will depend on what policies we develop to address environmental issues. Those policies will be shaped, in part, by mobilized segments of the public, people whose views about the need for environmental protection are in turn shaped by their employment situation. Thus, it is crucial that we seek to understand the relationship between work and the environment.

ENVIRONMENTAL PROTECTION AND JOBS

Workers have obvious reasons to be concerned about environmental measures if they pose a direct threat to their jobs. But in reality, environmental regulations threaten very few jobs and, in many cases, actually *add* to employment. Overall, environmental protection measures have generated millions of jobs. The U.S. Labor Department reports that almost 4 million workers are employed in **green jobs**—that's 3.1% of the total U.S. labor force. These workers are employed doing things such as manufacturing hybrid vehicles or wind turbines, growing organic foods, recycling waste, or designing energy-efficient homes. Environmental protection also creates and sustains jobs in other sectors. Ecotourism has grown dramatically in recent decades, and in many regions, where attractive environmental features have been preserved, communities have prospered by selling services to tourists (see Lesson 20). Thousands more are employed as researchers, lawyers, lobbyists, and policy-makers in positions related to environmental protection. Given environmental imperatives and international measures being taken to address them, nations that have taken the lead in promoting environmentally sound, energy-efficient practices are likely to thrive economically relative to those that fail to act (see Lesson 9). Thus, pursuing these goals will have a dramatic, positive impact on employment.

It is also important to keep in mind that in some cases a failure to act to protect the environment may harm certain employment sectors. For example, manufacturing industries grew dramatically along the Hudson River in New York State during the early to mid-20th century. However, the pollution that these factories released into the river, including many toxic substances, ultimately decimated the fishing industry, which was an important part of the regional economy. Thousands of workers lost their jobs as a result, and the fishing industry never fully recovered.

Although environmental protection measures result in net job gains and protect workers in industries dependent on a healthy environment, in some rare instances particular jobs may be threatened by environmental policies. These factors are never as significant as other major influences on employment, such as trade policy, corporate restructuring, technological change, and the general ups and downs of the business cycle characteristic of capitalist economies (see Lessons 4 and 7). The relatively small impact of environmental regulation is not surprising given that environmental protection costs typically make up less than 2% of a firm's expenditures. Yet environmental compliance can still cost jobs in some instances. One economic analysis indicates that roughly 3,000 jobs are lost annually in the United States due to environmental regulation. This represents a tiny fraction of jobs lost nationally. The economic recession that began in 2007 alone resulted in over 8 million lost jobs. In fact, more workers lose their jobs as a result of natural disasters than they do from measures taken to protect the environment.

Despite the fact that job loss due to environmental protection is very small and that many more jobs are created by environmental measures, any job loss represents serious hardship for the affected workers. Perhaps more significantly, the very idea that there is a tradeoff between jobs and environmental protection is a powerful rhetorical tool that some have used to argue against important environmental measures (see Lesson 4). Thus, it is important to understand the relationship between jobs and the environment, not just to safeguard workers, but also to understand how the issue is used politically to shape environmental policy.

Who actually stands to lose their job as a result of environmental protection? Some early studies found that environmental measures have contributed to job loss in the metal, chemical, and paper industries, but environmental economist Eban Goodstein found that workers in the extractive industries have borne the brunt of the job loss. For example, his research indicates that the

Clean Air Act resulted in the loss of about 10,000 coal-mining jobs in the 10 years following its passage. He found that a similar number of timber industry workers lost their jobs following the implementation of measures designed to protect the endangered northern spotted owl in the Pacific Northwest, the basis for the scenario introduced above.

It is worth noting that these job losses have primarily affected male blue-collar workers, a population that has already been hit hard by automation and economic globalization. Employers have introduced labor-saving technologies that have displaced millions of workers in manufacturing industries (see Lesson 7). And the outsourcing of manufacturing jobs to low-wage regions overseas has also resulted in significant job loss for blue-collar workers. In fact, many timber industry jobs were lost when business owners started exporting raw logs for processing in low-wage countries in Asia before reimporting the wood back to the United States. These factors have resulted in significant job loss and wage depression for blue-collar, primarily male workers. This economic vulnerability makes this group particularly susceptible to claims that environmental regulation poses a threat to their livelihood.

"JOBS VERSUS THE ENVIRONMENT" CONFLICTS

Even though the number of workers negatively affected is very small, the "jobs versus the environment" issue commands a great deal of public attention, and it can have a significant impact on environmental policy. The "timber wars" of the 1980s and 1990s took on special significance for political candidates seeking to capitalize on voters' general economic insecurity. While running for president in 1992, Republican candidate George Bush, Sr., claimed that if his more environmentally sympathetic opponents were elected, "we'll be up to our neck in owls and outta work for every American."

Environmental measures and their relationship to jobs have also taken center stage in more recent political conflicts. As a presidential candidate, Barack Obama promised to create jobs through environmental policy. He sought to institute a measure that would raise funds through a mechanism designed to limit greenhouse gas emissions, then use that money to build green industries such as renewable energy, electric cars, and public transportation. Once in office, this effort was thwarted when Congress failed to pass the climate change measure. Nonetheless, following the economic recession of 2007, President Obama sought to stimulate the economy through government spending on job creation, much of which was targeted for green industries.

The contrast between the policies advocated by Democratic and Republican leaders reflects a larger ideological disagreement about the role of government in the economy and in job creation. While both parties adamantly embrace capitalism and both support massive military expenditures, Democrats tend to see a broader constructive role for government in addressing social problems like the lack of affordable healthcare, poverty, and access to education. They also see a more active role for government in environmental protection and through the regulation of business generally. Thus President Obama and other liberal-leaning thinkers tend to focus on the positive relationship between environmental protection and jobs. They believe that polluting industries can be reformed and that "clean industries" can be nurtured through proper governmental policy intervention, yielding environmentally sound, sustainable employment. Without this intervention, liberals tend to believe that businesses will focus exclusively on short-term profit for their shareholders, sacrificing the environment and undermining the well-being of working people.

In contrast, most Republican officials and other conservative thinkers tend to believe that any government intervention in the economy, be it restrictions on international trade, taxes, minimum wage laws, public healthcare, or regulations, including environmental regulation, harms free market functioning and causes a loss of jobs and prosperity. These leaders often refer to "job-killing environmental regulations." The conservative Congressional representative from Minnesota, Michele Bachmann, who briefly ran for the Republican presidential nomination in 2012, gave voice to this belief when she stated that the Environmental Protection Agency should be renamed the "Job-Killing Organization of America."

While elected officials are the most visible figures voicing these contrasting perspectives and it is they who actually make policy, it is important to bear in mind that political candidates take positions that reflect their base of support. Environmental organizations more commonly support Democratic candidates who, in turn, tend to take somewhat stronger positions in favor of environmental protection. But perhaps more influential are the business interests that back candidates running for office. Some businesses, such as the renewable energy industry, stand to gain financially from environmental protection measures, so they often back candidates who support such efforts. Many others, such as the very powerful fossil fuel and energy industries, seek to protect profits by blocking environmental measures, thus avoiding the costs of complying with such regulations.

Business interests who see costs associated with environmental compliance will often carry out publicity campaigns and fund research purporting to show that regulations will harm their industry and cost jobs (see Lesson 5). When the Obama administration instituted rules that would limit toxic mercury emissions from power plants, a coal industry organization issued a report claiming that the measure would result in the loss of 1.44 million jobs. Similar claims have been made in regard to other recent environmental policy issues, such as the regulation of hydraulic fracturing, or "fracking," a technology now being used to extract natural gas from rock deposits deep underground. While environmentalists fear this practice may contaminate groundwater and cause other health and environmental problems, the gas industry has touted the economic benefits of developing this domestic industry.

The job loss claims made by employers in relation to environmental measures are often wildly exaggerated. As discussed earlier, negative job impacts from environmental measures are very rare and very small. Business owners oppose regulation primarily because they want to protect their profits and avoid the cost of complying with such rules. It would be difficult for them to rally public opposition to environmental measures in order to protect industry profits, so instead they frame the issue in terms of job loss. Some refer to this strategy of enlisting workers in the fight against regulation as **job blackmail**. Just as the timber business operator encouraged his workers to contact their elected officials in the opening scenario, employers often seek to mobilize workers by shifting the focus from environmental protection to the alleged economic impacts. Employers will claim that burdensome regulations will drive them out of business or force them to relocate to countries that do not have strict environmental protections, thus stoking fears among insecure workers.

In addition to fostering job loss concerns, employers may also take advantage of the cultural differences that exist between blue-collar workers and the middle-class professionals who often fund or make up the active membership base of many large environmental organizations. In *Coalitions Across the Class Divide*, Fred Rose argues that due to their different education and work experiences, middle class professionals have different understandings about the natural environment, about work, and about the value of scientific expertise relative to direct experience. These differences in **class culture** can be used to heighten fears about unfamiliar outsiders who threaten the workers' way of life. The situation is made worse when environmental advocates are insensitive to workers' concerns or when they harbor stereotypes about ignorant blue-collar workers who don't understand what is really good for them. These cultural differences by themselves can result in suspicion that inhibits compromise and the pursuit of mutually beneficial approaches to environmental problems. But this cultural gap is particularly difficult to overcome when employers or politicians exploit these differences to foster divisions involving environmental issues and their job implications.

THE ROLE OF LABOR UNIONS
IN ENVIRONMENTAL CONFLICT

As sociologists, we know that we can learn a great deal about people by examining the conditions under which they live, and clearly one's employment situation is a very significant aspect of one's life. After all, for most people, it is through their labor that they earn their livelihood. It is also what many of us spend much of our lives doing. As a college student you may already be working at a part-time or full-time job. But even if you are not currently employed, enrollment in college is probably tied to your aspirations for future employment. Because it is so central to our lives, sociologists, from the founding of the discipline, have placed a great deal of attention on economic institutions. The classical theorists each focused on aspects of the economy, from Emile Durkheim's analysis of the division of labor to Max Weber's research on the origins of capitalism to Karl Marx's detailed examination of class. Marx in particular was attuned to the conflicts that emerge around economic issues and the power that some groups have relative to others; thus, the general branch of theory emerging from his work is sometimes referred to as "conflict theory."

We could apply conflict theory to understand how business owners exercise power to advance their interests within the economy, interests that, in at least some instances, facilitate ecological degradation. This power can be seen on the macro level, in terms of influence over the political and economic systems and control of the mass media, down to the micro level control that an individual supervisor can exercise over an employee. Business owners have power in that they can choose to disinvest and close down their business or move it elsewhere, thus dramatically affecting the lives of hundreds or even thousands of workers. They can also influence government policy through lobbying and campaign support, thus shaping the laws that govern every member of society. At the micro level, they can use their power and influence at the workplace to pressure individual workers into opposing environmental measures that may threaten profitability. Although those who own the means of production have a great advantage when seeking to influence government action, such as environmental policy, in some cases other workplace actors can play an important role in influencing individual workers and even, at times, in influencing larger policies and the general distribution of power within society. The organizations that play this role are **labor unions**.

Capitalist economies tend to foster organization among workers to counter the imbalance of power within a system based on the private ownership of the means of production. Most individual workers, because they lack assets of their own off which they can live, are forced to sell their labor to those who own the means of production. These capitalists employ workers to produce goods so that they can obtain profit by selling those goods on the market at a rate higher than that which it cost them to have the goods produced. One way in which capitalists can increase profits is by minimizing labor costs—that is, by paying workers as little as is necessary.

Workers usually understand their lack of power as individuals within this situation. After all, a single worker is rarely of great value to any large enterprise, and in any case, within market economies there is always a pool of additional unemployed workers for the owner to draw from if any single worker needs to be replaced. But at times workers recognize that if they were to join together and act collectively, they would be better positioned to challenge their employer and to demand better treatment. Workers, and disadvantaged people generally, have done this in one way or another throughout history. In the context of the workplace in capitalist economies, this takes the form of labor unions.

By forming unions, workers pledge to act together as a unit to counterbalance the advantage of the employer. While the employer can carry on unharmed without any single employee, if all the workers were to walk off the job simultaneously—that is, if they were to strike—this would impose significant costs on the business owner. Of course, employers still have a great advantage because, unlike the workers, they have the wealth necessary to secure their own survival (not to mention their very significant influence over other institutions such as the political system, the police, and the military). However, at least under some circumstances, employers may find it to be in their interest to make concessions to workers in the face of a strike or other workplace disruption rather than escalate the conflict or risk further delays in production.

Because conflicts between workers and owners are so common, most countries have developed **labor relations systems** to manage these relationships. Governments create a set of rules to moderate how the conflict between employers and workers will occur. The system of labor relations varies a great deal from nation to nation: Some create rules that reinforce the advantage that owners have, and others go to great lengths to level the playing field between owners and workers. In some countries, such as Vietnam, independent unions are illegal and workers are allowed to organize only through unions closely tied to the ruling political party, which controls the government. In others, such as Colombia, unions are not prohibited but they have few enforceable rights, which leaves them vulnerable to violent repression by employers or their agents. Other nations, such as Sweden and Germany, have labor relations systems in which unions are afforded a number of legal protections that enable them to operate almost as equals with employers in making important decisions about issues such as workplace organization and compensation levels.

In the United States, unions have few protections relative to other industrialized democracies like those found in Europe. Laws are designed and enforced in ways that make it fairly easy for employers to impose their terms on unions or to prevent workers from forming unions altogether. During the late 19th and early 20th centuries, prior to the creation of a formal industrial relations system, only skilled craft workers were successful at establishing lasting unions. Because their skills were needed by employers, they were advantaged compared to unskilled workers who were more easily replaced. But by the mid-20th century, through the use of militant tactics and newly developed legal protections, unskilled manufacturing workers were able to form unions of their own. Although the labor relations system that developed placed workers at a grave disadvantage, the period of great economic growth and prosperity that followed World War II allowed employers to accommodate U.S. unions while still profiting immensely. Unionized workers were able to command decent wages, and this spilled over, benefitting even workers who were not in unions. If your grandparents were working in the United States during the 1950s, chances are they were in a union. More than one in three workers were union members at that time. It was a result of this effort to distribute the wealth generated during this period that the middle class was built in the United States. It is not surprising that today, with unions in decline, we see growing economic inequality and the shrinking of the middle class.

The most significant decline in unions can be traced back to the 1970s, when the U.S. was hit by a major recession. At that time of declining prosperity employers sought to protect profits by taking advantage of weak labor protections to challenge unions and drive down wages. Since then, a number of political and economic developments have furthered organized labor's decline in the United States. New technologies allowed employers to automate many of the tasks previously performed by workers, thus eliminating manufacturing jobs and reducing union numbers (see Lesson 4).

Economic globalization has also weakened unions and provided employers with greater leverage in the labor relations system. Starting in the 1980s many large corporations pressed political leaders to enter into **free trade agreements** with other nations. This enabled businesses to shift production around the world in search of low wages, weak regulations, or other conditions that would allow for increased profitability. Many businesses, especially those in manufacturing industries, have moved operations overseas. If you look at your clothes or your computer or television or even your car, there's a good chance that none of it was manufactured in the United States. But even those companies that have not actually moved operations can use the threat of relocation to extract concessions from their workers. This further diminished labor's bargaining power within a labor relations system that afforded them few real protections to begin with.

As a result of these factors and an aggressive anti-union assault by employers, the United States has seen its rate of unionization decline precipitously from roughly 35% of the workforce in 1955 to about 11% today. The decline has been most severe in the manufacturing sector, labor's traditional stronghold, but workers in other sectors are also under attack. Conservative elected officials have undertaken efforts to weaken unions representing public sector workers such as teachers, bus drivers, and firefighters. Private service sector employment is the largest employment sector of the U.S. economy today. The service sector includes most jobs where workers are employed providing a service as opposed to manufacturing a product. Workers in retail stores, healthcare facilities, hotels, and restaurants are all service sector workers. This employment sector was never extensively unionized, although some of these workers are seeking to organize unions today. With low unionization in the service sector together with the decline of unionized manufacturing employment and attacks on public sector unions, the U.S. labor movement is among the weakest compared to those in other economically developed democracies.

Despite their current weakness, unions have a potentially very significant role to play in relation to environmental policy. Unions help to synthesize workers' concerns and enable individuals to act collectively to advance their interests, and clearly workers, like all people, have an interest in a safe and healthy environment. In fact, survey research indicates that union members report stronger support for environmental measures than the average worker. Unions could serve as vehicles for advancing these sentiments, and sometimes they have. Yet their position on environmental issues is complicated and inconsistent. In some instances unions have mobilized workers to promote environmental protection, yet in other cases they have sided with employers to oppose environmental measures.

Some of this positioning has to do with the particular industry in which the union members are based. For those workers who face real potential threats to jobs, it is easy to see why their union might oppose certain environmental regulation. For example, the United Mine Workers have opposed a number of air pollution measures that they perceived would harm their industry and contribute to job loss. A recent environmental issue that has divided the labor movement along sectoral lines is the construction of the Keystone XL Pipeline, a major pipeline project that would bring tar sands from Canada down to Texas for refining into fuel. With unemployment among construction workers very high due to the recession, union leaders in the building trades saw the project as a promising job creator. Environmentalists, on the other hand, have opposed the project both because of the risks of ecologically damaging spills and, more generally, because the use of this dirty fossil fuel will draw us further away from developing renewable energy sources. When the project was halted on environmental grounds, one construction union leader denounced environmental opponents as "job killers" out to "destroy the lives of working men and women." However, other unions, such as the Communication Workers of America and the United Auto Workers, sided with environmentalists in opposition to fast-tracking the project.

The different positions taken by these unions can in part be attributed to the different interests that workers have in the issue. Auto workers and those in the communication industry did not stand to gain jobs from the project; they chose instead to fight for the environmental interests of their members. But there are other factors that shape union behavior more broadly.

In general, the U.S. labor relations system channels unions into focusing on specific job-related issues, most significantly compensation. As a result union members come to view their union primarily as an organization that will protect their interests at work, especially in terms of the pay they receive. Some union leaders also come to see their role in that light. Union members don't often think of their union as a means to protect their broader interests in the political sphere. But the fact is that unions are one of the primary vehicles for protecting the interests of working people, even on issues that extend well beyond the workplace. Unions have championed causes like public education, Social Security, and access to healthcare through their political efforts.

As the primary political voice for working people, unions could also play a significant role in efforts to advance environmental legislation. But because the labor relations system encourages unions to focus on specific job-related matters, many union leaders have been reluctant to promote an environmental agenda. What's more, when an issue arises that allegedly creates a trade-off between jobs and environmental protection, unions may focus on the jobs issue instead of the more general interests of their members, including a safe and healthy environment.

So despite the fact that environmental sentiments may be strong among union members, their unions rarely involve themselves with such issues, especially when environmental measures may threaten their own economic interests or those of other union workers. Thus, for the most part, labor's political priorities have focused on job protection and economic expansion, policies that tend to threaten the environment through unchecked material consumption (see Lesson 4).

There are also historical reasons why unions, like those representing construction workers, take different positions on environmental issues than industrial unions, like the United Auto Workers or the Steelworkers union. As mentioned earlier, skilled workers, like those in the construction trade, were among the first to form successful unions. They were able to use their control over needed skills to advance their economic interests through their unions. The industrial unions, which represented unskilled workers, formed later. Because their members didn't have rare skills that they could withhold from employers to gain monetary concessions, the industrial unions tended to adopt a more encompassing vision of their role. They more often tended to view conflict in broad class terms. Disputes with employers at the workplace over wages or time off were just one part of the larger conflict between the classes. And these industrial unions more often engaged with the political system to try to advance workers' interests more generally—not just in terms of core economic interests, but also in their overall quality of life, including access to healthcare, aid for retired workers, and education for their children.

These broader concerns for the well-being of workers as a class at times led some unions to fight for environmental protection. Despite the channeling effect of the American labor relations system and the historical forces that led some unions to focus narrowly on economic interests, unions have nonetheless played a significant role in some important environmental legislation. While at times there were clear job gains to be had through environmental measures, as with labor's strong support for the creation of public sanitation systems, in other instances unions backed environmental policies even when they did not have direct implications for economic concerns. For example, unions were early supporters of clean water and clean air legislation. The American Federation of Labor-Congress of Industrial Organizations (AFL-CIO), the main labor federation representing almost all unions at the time, endorsed the creation of a wilderness preservation system as early as 1960, years before the rise of the modern environmental movement. They argued that working people should have access to nature for recreational purposes and for spiritual renewal, not just elites who could afford to buy land for their own use.

One area where labor has been particularly active historically is that of environmental health and safety (see Lesson 11). Health and safety issues have always been on labor's agenda, although this has never been given the same attention as wages and benefits. But because unions seek to protect workers' health, this creates fertile ground for cooperation with some in the environmental community (see Lessons 10 and 16). Historically, unions were supportive of environmental groups that took industrial pollution as their focus. This environmental health movement emerged from a different social context than that of the wilderness advocates who also began to mobilize in the late 19th and early 20th centuries. While early conservationists and pres-ervationists tended to be elites seeking to protect resources for industrial or recreational uses, environmental health advocates were rooted in working-class urban areas where working people and their families were being sub-jected to the toxic effluents from industrial production.

This link between environmentalism and worker health has, to this day, provided an opportunity for unions and environmental advocates to come together. After all, the toxic materials that can threaten workers' health inside the plant are the very ones that threaten the outside community and the natural environment when they leave the plant. The 1980s saw heightened cooperation between unions and environmentalists in terms of these issues. Spurred on by their common political adversary, President Ronald Reagan, who sought to roll back all manner of government regulation and services, unions and environmental organizations worked closely together to advance the regulation of hazardous materials.

LABOR AND THE ENVIRONMENT TODAY

Given the basic structure of our economic and political institutions, there are always likely to be some tensions, real or perceived, between labor and the environment. When workers are unorganized, they are particularly vulnerable to job loss claims from employers who seek to mobilize them against environmental measures. Non-unionized workers do not have an organization that can conduct research and challenge false claims being made by employers about the threat of environmental regulation. And even when workers are organized, when unions cling to a narrow agenda of economic self-interest and job protection, they can compound the prob-lem by siding with employers against environmental advocates. But unions are increasingly expanding their agendas to include issues of broader con-cern to workers, including environmental protection, and they are more open to cooperation with other progressive groups like environmental organizations.

In part this newfound willingness among union leaders to join with other movements can be interpreted as an act of necessity. Unions have lost so much of their power that they recognize the need for support from others to advance their goals, and, by necessity, that entails offering reciprocal sup-port for other causes.

From labor's perspective, these alliances must still be strategically assessed in terms of whether they stand to advance core economic goals. After all, the basic structure of the labor relations system remains in place, and workers still expect that their union will primarily act to advance their work-related interests. Thus, unions, and for that matter environmental organizations, are still constrained in the extent to which they can fully support one another's goals when there is not a direct link to the primary mission of their own organizations. But there is a growing willingness on the part of both labor and environmental advocates to seek those opportunities for cooperation. This shift can be tied to the larger economic trends that have affected both movements.

One major economic trend that threatens the interests of both workers and environmentalists is **trade liberalization** (a trade policy that is part of a broader "neoliberal" political perspective). As mentioned earlier, businesses have pressed for the elimination of government restrictions on international trade. Historically, governments have regulated trade and taxed the importation of goods to protect domestic industries, to raise funds, or to prevent the sale of goods considered unsafe or otherwise harmful to consumers. Proponents of trade liberalization, including many large corporations with operations spread across several countries, argue that restrictions on trade or overseas investment inhibit the efficiency of the free market, thus driving down profits and increasing the costs of goods. Yet, as noted earlier, employers have used loosened trade rules as a means to weaken unions and drive down wages. The prospect of moving operations overseas and throwing everyone out of work is a potent threat that has placed workers at a severe disadvantage. But the ability to move operations not only allows employers to seek lower-wage workers, it also allows them to escape from environmental regulations. Free trade allows polluting businesses to seek locations where there is little or no environmental regulation, thus decreasing production costs and increasing profits. For this reason, trade liberalization is viewed skeptically by both workers and environmentalists.

Opposition to trade liberalization is an important force in bringing workers and environmentalists together. Unrestricted trade greatly diminishes the ability of workers and environmentalists to improve conditions domestically as all nations become caught up in a "race to the bottom" as they seek to entice private investment through lower wages and weaker regulation. Some of the most significant examples of labor–environmental alliance building have occurred as a result of mutual opposition to trade liberalization. In the early 1990s some environmental organizations joined with organized labor in opposing the North American Free Trade Agreement (NAFTA), a trade treaty between the United States, Canada, and Mexico. But the most dramatic instance of mutual effort in this area came during the 1999 protests against the **World Trade Organization** (WTO) in Seattle, Washington. There, tens of thousands of unionists and environmental advocates, among others, came together to speak out against the neoliberal policies being advanced through the WTO. Although headlines focused on the violence that erupted when police engaged protesters, the most notable aspect of the event was the coming together of such a diverse coalition. While each group had its own reasons to oppose the WTO agenda, the event nonetheless demonstrated the possibility of a united labor–environmental movement. But this kind of cooperation has come in starts and stops: Soon after the WTO protest, goodwill was undermined by divisions between some unions and environmentalists over energy policy.

Still, unions and environmentalists are becoming more creative about finding ways to cooperate and to identify common ground. Issues of health and safety have continued to serve as an area of intermovement cooperation. New organizations have sprung up in recent decades, following in the footsteps of the early public health organizations that addressed environmental concerns during the early industrial period. Organizations have formed to fight the environmental and health effects resulting from the use of poisonous chemicals in manufacturing and agriculture. Environmental justice organizations, composed primarily of working-class people of color, have formed to fight against environmental health threats that disproportionately plague their communities (see Lesson 10). These organizations typically develop out of local struggles against immediate environmental health threats. While still generally considered to be part of the broader environmental movement, their members tend to have more in common culturally and economically with blue-collar union workers than they do with traditional middle- and upper-class conservation and preservation organizations. But even the larger professional environmental groups have in many cases integrated health and social justice issues into their agendas, thus creating more opportunity for overlap with their union counterparts.

Labor–environmental alliance-building efforts, even when initially based upon calculated self-interest, open the door to further cooperation. Many cases provide evidence to show that instrumental cooperation of this sort can grow into a true merging of interests. As unionists get to know and work with environmental advocates, stereotypes about insensitive elitists or deluded "tree huggers" begin to fall away, and they come to recognize that environmentalists are sincere people concerned about real threats to the environment and to human well-being. Similarly, environmentalists who work with labor advocates come to understand that unionists are not selfish or ignorant "hardhats" but people who are trying desperately to protect the basic economic security that many workers feel is slipping away. As this mutual understanding grows, both unions and environmental organizations are more likely to integrate all of these concerns into their advocacy agendas.

LABOR AND THE ENVIRONMENT TOMORROW?

At this historical juncture advocates for both workers and the environment face tremendous challenges. Although the environmental movement has been successful at raising awareness about threats to the environment, efforts to actually stave off environmental crises have not made substantial progress. National environmental policies and global treaties designed to address important issues such as global warming, species loss, and forest preservation have failed to fundamentally alter the historical trajectory of ongoing ecological degradation. Workers are also losing ground. Economic inequality is growing globally and within most nations. Little progress has been made to alleviate the extreme poverty that plagues a significant percentage of the world's population. Economic globalization has undermined the ability of both unions and environmentalists to hold accountable increasingly mobile corporate actors. Thus, on both fronts, many conclude that the prospects for rapid, significant changes are poor. But these meager hopes are greatly diminished when workers and environmental advocates engage in conflict with one another. Both have an interest in challenging the private interests that seek to exploit workers and the environment. Although their positions within existing political and economic institutions can, on some occasions, place them at odds on the basis of certain narrowly defined interests, an alliance between these movements or a new movement that embodies their respective goals represents perhaps the greatest hope of achieving a world that is both sustainable and just.

Let's return now to the hypothetical scenario with which we began, only now you are the son or daughter of the mill worker, and workers and environmentalists have united to reform labor and environmental policy. Your mother, who by now has lost her job at the mill, is currently enrolled in an accounting program at a nearby college where her tuition is being paid by a federal program that has also extended her old mill salary for 2 years while she is retrained. She hopes to get a job with a computer software firm that recently moved to the area, attracted by the high quality of life in the region, which can be attributed, at least in part, to strong environmental protection measures. Other former mill workers have taken jobs at a new artificial wood manufacturing facility that uses recycled plastics and paper milk cartons to make a highly durable wood substitute. This facility was developed through a federal program that brought together environmental technology investors with the Paper, Allied-Industrial, Chemical and Energy International Union. These unionized workers now earn more than they had at the former mill. You are working at a camping supply store during the summer serving the growing tourist population, but you are going away to college in the fall to study history and business. You plan to return to your community after graduation to open a bed-and-breakfast with an adjoining historical education center that focuses on the history of the timber industry.

Consider how you might feel about environmental protection policies from this vantage point. As in the original scenario, your views are going to be shaped by your social position, and a significant aspect of that is your labor force status and associated economic prospects. But institutional and policy changes have greatly altered the constraints and opportunities presented to you, and this is likely to affect your attitudes about environmental protection, perhaps in ways that would lead to still more environmental policy improvements.

The need to drastically change the way that society interrelates with the rest of the natural environment is imperative. But existing institutional arrangements in many cases perpetuate ecologically destructive practices. The distribution of power in our society and the conditions under which people live and work create a confluence of forces that inhibit desperately needed changes. Our role as sociologists is to seek to understand how these institutional arrangements operate and, more importantly, to identify ways to reshape those institutions so that we can create a socially just and ecologically sustainable society. Examining how work life can be made compatible with such goals is a central part of that mission.

SOURCES

Bureau of Labor Statistics. Green Jobs. http://www.bls.gov/green/home.htm

Dewey, Scott. 1998. "Working for the Environment: Organized Labor and the Origins of Environmentalism in the United States: 1948–1970." *Environmental History* 1:45–63.

Dreiling, Michael. 1998. "From Margin to Center: Environmental Justice and Social Unionism as Sites for Intermovement Solidarity." *Race, Class and Gender* 6(1):51–69.

Foster, John Bellamy. 1993. "The Limits of Environmentalism Without Class: Lessons from the Ancient Forest Struggle of the Pacific Northwest." *Capitalism, Nature and Socialism* 4(1):1–18.

Goodstein, Eban. 1999. *The Trade-Off Myth: Fact and Fiction About Jobs and the Environment.* Washington, D.C.: Island Press.

Gottlieb, Robert. 1993. *Forcing the Spring.* Washington, D.C.: Island Press.

Gottlieb, Robert. 2001. *Environmentalism Unbound.* Cambridge, MA: MIT Press.

Gould, Kenneth, Tammy Lewis, and J. Timmons Roberts. 2004. "Blue–Green Coalitions: Constraints and Possibilities in the Post 9–11 Political Environment." *Journal of World-System Research* 10(1):90–116.

Kazis, Richard, and Richard Grossman. 1991. *Fear at Work.* Philadelphia, PA: New Society Publishers.

Mayer, Brian. 2009. *Blue-Green Coalitions: Fighting for Safe Workplaces and Healthy Communities.* Ithaca, NY: ILR Press.

Obach, Brian K. 2004a. "New Labor: Slowing the Treadmill of Production?" *Organization and Environment* 17(3):337–354.

Obach, Brian K. 2004b. *Labor and the Environmental Movement: The Quest for Common Ground.* Cambridge, MA: MIT Press.

Rose, Fred. 2000. *Coalitions Across the Class Divide.* Ithaca, NY: Cornell University Press.

18

Environmental Movements in the Global South

Tammy L. Lewis

Protesting against the introduction of genetically modified corn, Porto Alegre, Brazil.
Photo by Ken Gould.

The term "environmentalist" means different things to different people. In North America, someone who recycles and buys "green" products might call himself or herself an environmentalist, as might someone who is concerned with the environmental effects of overpopulation, while another environmentalist argues that capitalism destroys nature. In the North American tradition, environmentalism has been strongly associated with membership in environmental organizations, such as the Sierra Club and the Nature Conservancy. Environmentalists in the Global South (lower-income countries of Latin America, Africa, and parts of Asia) also cover a broad range of beliefs and practices and do not fit neatly into one single box. In the Global South, there is less emphasis on membership in environmental organizations as defining an "environmentalist." While there are overlapping concerns between environmentalists of the North and South, I begin by outlining some fundamental differences between environmentalists and environmental movements in the Global North and in the Global South.

DIFFERENCES BETWEEN ENVIRONMENTALISM IN THE GLOBAL NORTH AND IN THE GLOBAL SOUTH

In *Environmentalism: A Global History*, Ramachandra Guha (2000) asked readers to consider the differences between the "ecology of affluence" and "**environmentalism of the poor**." Guha, and others writing from the perspective of the Global South, argued that there is a strong environmentalism in the Third World (now called the "Global South") that looks different from the environmental movement in the United States and other nations in the Global North (including Canada, Japan, Australia, and countries in Western Europe).

The first and most visible difference is simply in organizational structure and tactics. The U.S. movement is considered "professionalized" in that it is made up of formal organizations, with paid leaders and staffs, large budgets, lobbying arms, and extensive fundraising mechanisms. These **professionalized environmental organizations** differ from **collective action groups**, which use volunteer labor, have small to no budgets, and organize people to engage in direct action to preserve their local means of subsistence (the "environment").

The organizational differences are actually a result of different origins. Many Southern struggles are struggles in defense of economic livelihood. They arise from threats to people's economic survival. For instance, local "environmental" opposition forms when local economic resources are threatened. One of the most popular examples of this is the rubber tappers' movement in Brazil from the 1980s. The rubber tappers extracted rubber from trees in a sustainable manner to earn a living. When the rubber trees were threatened by cattle ranchers who wanted to clear the forests for ranching, the rubber tappers' union resisted the ranchers and fought for control of the land they had long used to make a living. They resisted environmental change because it threatened their economic well-being. Whether we classify this as an "economic" movement or an "environmental" movement is an interesting question. Guha (2000) asked us to consider the relationship be-tween "environmental" issues and livelihood struggles in general:

> Commercial forestry, oil drilling, and large dams all damage the environment, but they also, and to their victims more painfully, constitute a threat to rural livelihoods: by depriving tribals of fuelwood and small game, by destroying the crops of farmers, or by submerging wholesale the lands and homes of villagers who have the misfortune to be placed in their path. The opposition to these interventions is thus as much a defense of livelihood as an "environmen-tal" movement in the narrow sense of the term. (p. 105)

These types of struggles contrast with popular campaigns of environmental groups in the Global North that call on members to "Save the Whales" (or elephants, or pandas, etc.). Many Northern campaigns solicit urban dwellers to contribute to causes that are disconnected from their immediate sur-roundings or their lived experiences.

This leads to the third big difference in environmentalism of the North and South: the understanding of how humans fit into nature. Guha argued that a major difference between environmentalism in the Global South and that in the Global North has been the South's view that the environmen-tal struggle is inseparable from the struggle for social justice. Humans and nature are part of an interconnected and interdependent web. The **nature–society dichotomy** that is prevalent in Western thought is not as widespread in other cultures (see also Lesson 19). Therefore, movements in some other societies see humans as part of the environment, and thus the struggle for human rights is integrated into a movement to preserve the en-vironment. When working to save the environment, these groups see that they are working to save themselves.

Environmentalism in North America was founded with the idea of pre-serving nature for nature's sake (what we might now call "biodiversity pres-ervation") and for the good of humanity (see Lesson 16). John Muir, the first president of the Sierra Club (1892), argued for protecting undeveloped and undisturbed habitats, like national parks, so that the public could visit these areas for spiritual uplift and to enjoy recreational activities. Later, U.S. con-servationists such as Gifford Pinchot (the chief of the U.S. Division of Forestry, 1898) would argue that we needed to conserve lands for future development and the "wise use" of resources (though still not viewing humans as "in" nature).

U.S. environmentalism is often stereotyped as an **"elitist" movement.** This stereotype has some validity if we look only to the history of land pres-ervation and conservation. Muir, Pinchot, and others advocating for land protection were elite, well-educated white men. However, if we expand our historical lens and take a broader view of environmentalism in the early part of the 1900s, we see that there were movements in U.S. cities, often led by women, who were fighting for adequate sanitation and appropriate trash disposal. While they are not commonly thought of as part of the United States' "environ-mental" history, today we might call them "urban environmentalists." In the

United States, stereotypes of elitism in the environmental movement have also changed with the growth of the environmental justice movement (see Lesson 10). The environmental justice movement draws its constituents from a range of groups, including the working class and racial and ethnic minorities. Today, we have environmentalism within both wealthy and poor nations challenging the conventional wisdom that environmentalism is simply an elite movement.

Just as the charges of "elite" environmentalism are largely false in the United States, they are also false across the globe. Though affluence creates opportunities to participate in the movement, concern about the environment is not limited to elites. In fact, there are high degrees of concern about the environment in both North and South; in some cases, there is more concern in the Global South. Not only "elite" (rich) nations are environmentalist. Steven R. Brechin and Willett Kempton (1994) analyzed responses to public opinion data from around the world that show that richer nations do not have a higher level of environmental concern than poorer nations. In fact, in many cases, the opposite is true. For example, 77% of Mexicans surveyed perceive air pollution to be a serious problem and 81% perceive species loss as "very serious." By contrast, in the United States, the figures are 60% and 50%. In their analysis, they showed that individuals in wealthier nations are more willing to pay more for environmental protection. However, people in poorer nations are more willing to pay in time (a resource more available than money for many in these nations) than were the respondents in richer nations. Riley Dunlap and Richard York (2008) followed up on these results with international survey data through to 2001 and confirmed that citizens' concern for environmentalism does not depend on affluence In sum, survey data from multiple surveys and multiple years suggest that environmental concern is not just a concern for the rich; the concern is global.

GRASSROOTS CASES FROM INDIA, NIGERIA, AND BOLIVIA

Three brief examples from three different continents will illustrate how environmental actions (variously called "movements," "campaigns," and "environmentalisms") in the Global South are intertwined with livelihood struggles and how they are closely tied to attempts to promote social justice. There are numerous examples to draw from; I have selected one case each from Asia (the Chipko movement in India), Africa (the Movement for the Survival of the Ogoni People in Nigeria), and Latin America (the "water war" in Bolivia). While reading about these cases, keep in mind the environmental justice struggles going on in the United States (see Lesson 10). Some of these struggles take place in indigenous communities and others take place in industrial workplaces (see Lesson 17). They also occur in places where people live, especially in working-class and minority communities (see Lesson 10). So, while we make a distinction between environmentalism of the rich and environmentalism of the poor, these are not just differences between rich and poor nations, for there is also diversity of movement types within nations. The three cases that I present are well-known, often-referenced, historically important cases.

Asia: The Chipko Movement in India

The Chipko Movement began in 1973 and is perhaps the first internationally recognized "ecology" movement from a developing country. It became well known because of its use of direct action and due to the participation of women in the struggle.

After years of coping with flooding and the need to travel long distances for fuel wood, problems caused by deforestation and soil erosion, peasants in the Himalayan village of Mandal decided to put a stop to logging in the state-owned forests around their village. The village activists, many of whom were women, literally placed their bodies between the loggers and the trees. The loggers stopped; they did not cut the trees. This practice spread to other areas—the Reni forests and other parts of the region. It was not a centralized movement; rather, disparate communities replicated the protest. Numerous slogans were repeated throughout the countryside, including the famous "What do the forests bear? Soil, water and pure air."

Though "chipko" literally means "to cling," the movement was popularized as the movement of "tree huggers." The action was within the Gandhian tradition of nonviolent direct action, and it was directed at the state. Because of women's participation, this movement has also been considered a feminist movement. However, in a thorough historical examination of the movement, Guha argued that in many ways the Chipko Movement was neither an environmental movement nor a feminist movement. Instead, he contended, it was simply a peasant movement against state attempts to control village life; in this case, to control their means of survival (the environment). Regardless of how we label Chipko, its interpretation as an "environmental," "feminist," and "peasant" movement serves to further demonstrate how Southern environmental movements represent a more integrated understanding of social justice and the relationship between social systems and ecosystems.

Chipko is just one of many cases from the vast continent of Asia; many others could have been highlighted. For instance, J. Peter Brosius (2001) has written extensively about the struggles of the Penan (an indigenous group), who reside on the island of Borneo in Malaysia. Their efforts to preserve the Sarawak rain forest were transformed into an international campaign for indigenous rights. In Asia, damming rivers for hydroelectric power has been a controversial issue, especially where it has caused the displacement of people. In India, the Sardar Sarovar Dam on the Narmada River has drawn international attention, as has the damming of the Yangtze River by the Three Gorges Dam in China. As China continues its rapid development, we can expect to see growing problems related to industrial development, such as air and water pollution in cities and their associated environmental health problems.

Africa: The Ogoni Resistance in Nigeria

The Chipko Movement was essentially a battle between the people and the state. The Movement for the Survival of the Ogoni People (MOSOP) focused its attention on a transnational corporation (TNC): the Royal Dutch Shell Corporation. However, this was not simply a people-versus-TNC battle; in this showdown, the state played a complicating role because the military government sided with Shell. Why was that? Simple: in Nigeria, 80% of the state's revenues come from oil exports.

Shell had been drilling in the oil-rich regions of Nigeria since 1958. When they started, the people were promised "development." However, years and years passed and the promises were not delivered. In Ogoniland, half a million indigenous Ogoni lived in poverty and ecological devastation. Their villages were crossed by pipelines and surrounded by open gas flares. Oil spills polluted land and water, hurting fishing and farming. According to the *Ecologist* magazine, "From 1982 to 1992, 1.6 million gallons of oil were spilled from Shell's Nigerian fields in 27 separate incidents." The Ogoni were promised clean water, schools, and healthcare, but after over 30 years of drilling, they were much worse off. Both Shell and the Nigerian government benefited from the extraction within the Ogoni territories; the local Ogoni paid the costs.

MOSOP was founded in 1990 by author and outspoken Ogoni Ken Saro Wiwa and others to oppose the environmental destruction created by Shell's oil production and because Shell did not compensate the Ogoni as it said it would. MOSOP attempted to bring international attention to the mess that Shell made on their lands. They demanded compensation and wanted Ogoni control of their environment. MOSOP was not just an environmental organization; it worked, and still works, for democracy, to protect the practices of the Ogoni, and for social and economic development. MOSOP called for an international boycott of Shell. Greenpeace and Amnesty International became involved in the case.

The military government did not like the problems that MOSOP was causing for Shell and for its revenues. The state used its power to quell resistance. There were violent conflicts in the region, with the police repressing demonstrations and torturing activists. In January 1993, the Year of Indigenous Peoples project brought 300,000 people to the region in protest. That same month Shell withdrew its staff from the area. The Nigerian government sent security forces to dispel dissent and make the area safe for Shell. They continued to torture, detain, and kill Ogoni activists.

In 1995, Ken Saro-Wiwa and eight other activists were arrested. The government claimed that they had murdered Ogoni leaders. International observers did not believe they committed these crimes and called the military tribunal that found them guilty "unjust." In the end, the Nigerian government hung Ken Saro-Wiwa and the eight activists. This brought more international attention to Nigeria and turned Ken Saro-Wiwa into a martyr.

Sadly, this case from Africa highlights the deadly course that fighting for environmental and human rights can take. The MOSOP case was exacerbated by the Nigerian government's entrenchment with Shell. The people wanted schools and hospitals; the TNC and state wanted profit. The state ruled by force to silence protest and ensure its revenues. Most believe that the Nigerian military and Shell worked hand in hand to ensure this. Though the state in Africa has a reputation for corruption, this rather blatant case of the state's reliance on growth for its own capital accumulation is simply the grossest manifestation of what happens when capital accumulation outweighs a state's need for political legitimacy. Also, lest we think that violent repression of environmental activists happens only somewhere else, I recommend the 1996 book by Andrew Rowell, *Green Backlash*, which highlights attacks against environmentalists fighting the growth coalition in many nations, including the United States. One example is Judy Bari, the Earth First! and labor activist whose car was bombed in 1990.

Latin America: The "Water War" in Cochabamba, Bolivia

The final case study is a more recent one. It came to a conclusion in 2000 and is heralded as a success for the people against the transnational giants of **neoliberalism**. I also discuss it because it illustrates an urban movement that intertwines environmentalism with radical democracy, and I expect that as more and more of the Global South moves to urban areas, these areas will be the sites of future environmentalisms.

Cochabamba, with a population of over 600,000, is the third largest city in Bolivia. Due to pressure from international financial institutions like the World Bank, the government of Bolivia began privatizing what had formerly been public resources. While the laws that started the trend dated back to the mid-1980s, the issue came to the fore in 1999/2000 when the state attempted to privatize water in Cochabamba. This was required by the International Development Bank as part of the conditions of a loan. At the time, half of Cochabambans were connected to a central water system and the rest used community water systems organized by neighborhood groups and nongovernmental organizations (NGOs). The government changed the laws so that the latter forms of water acquisition would be illegal. Instead, a company, Aguas del Tunari, a subsidiary of Bechtel, a TNC based in San Francisco, would run the water system.

The people protested. They saw access to water as a fundamental human right, and the common good was being sold so that a corporation would benefit. People refused to pay. Neighborhoods were organized. Demonstrations were held. Oscar Olivera, a union organizer in the shoe factory, and others formed the Coordinadora (the Coalition in Defense of Water and Life). The Cochabambans were not willing to give up the right to decide how their natural resources would be used, bought, and sold. In the end, through multiple mass demonstrations, the people won and retained the right to access their water. This also reinvigorated Bolivian conceptions of democracy. Olivera (2004, p. 20) explains:

> What is happening more and more today is that *democracy is becoming confused with elections.* At one time democracy—at least to us—meant participation in the distribution of wealth; collective decision-making on issues that affect us all; and pressure and mobilization in order to influence state policies. Now the only acceptable meaning of "democracy" seems to be *competition in the electoral market.* (italics in original)

In 2005, Bolivia elected its first ever indigenous president, Evo Morales, who was part of the "water war." Bolivians are considering how to deal with their natural gas—how they will choose to use this resource and distribute its benefits. This movement, like the others discussed, is not just an environmental movement; it is about social justice, the environment, and the nature of globalization.

Latin America is rich with such cases of resistance. For example, the indigenous people of Ecuador's Amazon region took Texaco to court in New York for environmental damage. The globalization of the economy makes it more and more likely that actors in the Global South will fight agents in the Global North. In this David-and-Goliath fight, Cochabamba shows us that David can sometimes win.

CONSEQUENCES OF GLOBALIZATION OF OTHER INSTITUTIONS FOR THE ENVIRONMENT

From these examples, it might make sense to conclude simply that globalization (particularly economic) is bad for the environment. In the Bolivian and Nigerian cases, local populations responded to threats from TNCs that were aided in their quest for natural resources by national governments (**growth coalitions**). However, other aspects of globalization have been positive for the environment. For example, most organizations have been "greened" to some degree: states, international NGOs, intergovernmental organizations, and international financial institutions. In general, we are living in a historical era in which "the environment," as a concern, is taken seriously. This environmental moment does not show signs of ending anytime soon.

Take the following examples as evidence that the environment is an enduring concern. Over the past century, states around the globe have increasingly become more "green." A few ways this has been measured has been in the number of national environmental ministries, national laws requiring environmental impact statements, and national parks worldwide. At the international level, the number of NGOs and international governmental organizations dedicated to the environment continues to grow, year after year. International financial institutions, such as the World Bank, have enacted environmental standards for their lending programs. United Nations (UN) conferences on the theme of the environment have created an international forum for environmentalism to be discussed globally. In 1972, the UN Conference on the Human Environment was held in Stockholm, Sweden. This was followed 20 years later by the UN Conference on Environment and Development (popularly termed the "Earth Summit") held in Rio de Janeiro, Brazil. In 2002, this was followed by the World Summit on Sustainable Development in Johannesburg, South Africa, and in 2012, the UN Conference on Sustainable Development (also known as Rio + 20), was again held in Rio.

There is a complicated relationship, then, between Southern environmentalism and globalization. For the environment, globalization is a double-edged sword. On the one hand, there is resistance to TNCs, the economic agents of globalization. On the other hand, people in the Global South are often aided by institutions that have been greened by globalization, such as international governmental organizations. In this sense, the idea of a "local" movement really does not make much sense. There are groups that are focused on specific geographical areas, but they are connected to the "global" world. Earlier, I mentioned the rubber tappers of Brazil and their struggle against local ranchers. This was a fight among Brazilians for the most part, but it drew on the "globalization of environmentalism."

The case of the rubber tappers is chronicled in at least two films, one a documentary and the second a dramatization (*The Killing of Chico Mendes* and *The Burning Season*). To make a long and very interesting story short, essentially what happened was that there was a conflict between rubber tappers and cattle ranchers in the Acre province of Brazil. Chico Mendes was a union organizer for the rubber tappers (*seringueros*). In the 1970s, he began organizing rubber tappers in Brazil against the cattle ranchers who were clearing lands for pasture. There were violent confrontations between the two groups. This local battle went international when the World Bank and the Inter-American Development Bank (IADB) approved loans to build a road that would essentially open up the land for more clearing. Locals were not consulted in the process. Mendes worked with NGOs in the United States, notably the Environmental Defense Fund, and eventually came to Washington, D.C., to convince the U.S. Senate that it should not support the IADB loan. The Senate withdrew its support, the IADB suspended its loan payments, and the road was stopped. Mendes and the rubber tappers short-circuited the Brazilian government to halt its road development plans. Eventually, the government, the *seringueros*, and the ranchers came to an agreement to create an "extractive reserve"—that is, an area like a national park that the rubber tappers could use to tap rubber yet maintain as a forest (this fits into a "sustainable development" scheme, as discussed in Lesson 20). This innovative idea joined the interests of local people's livelihoods with the larger "environmental" interests of the "global" environmental community. As with other Southern campaigns, we should ask whether the rubber tappers were really environmentalists or whether they were framing their interests creatively to best appeal to the shifts in international thinking regarding the environment.

If they had framed this battle as one of human rights or workers' rights, it may not have succeeded at this time in history. Unfortunately, this story does not have a happy ending. Mendes went on to help other communities facing similar battles. In 1988, he was shot and killed by cattle ranchers. In some areas of Brazil, he is considered a hero. In 1989, the Brazilian government agreed to protect 50 million more acres in extractive reserves. This case shows how "local" environmental groups were able to gain support from global environmental actors to win (or at least make some gains) locally.

In my own work, I have looked at the consequences of transnational cooperation involving conservation movements with a focus on Latin America. In Ecuador, international NGOs have had a positive effect on conservation. Ecuadorian conservationists tell me that the Ecuadorian government has protected additional areas because of actions taken by transnational environmentalists and that, without these actors' interventions, Ecuadorian forests would be worse off. In the 1980s, international NGOs created a funding mechanism for conservation called a "debt-for-nature swap." In short, what happens is that conservation groups negotiate with banks on behalf of Southern nations so that instead of states making their full loan payments, a fraction of their payment is channeled within their country to pay for conservation and to fund conservation organizations. A number of swaps took place in Ecuador, which kept funds in the country that were earmarked for environmental activities and were tremendously important for conservation. In Ecuador, international conservationists helped protect a large percentage of land. They also helped found and fund environmental organizations. These were the upsides; the downside was that it created competition among Ecuadorian environmental groups for resources that were distributed by agents from the Global North. The competition among organizations for resources persists in Ecuador today and hinders the cooperation of Ecuadorian conservationists. Again, the "globalization of environmentalism" has had some complicated outcomes. While there are more groups working for the environment in Ecuador, they are not working together.

Another twist is that the organizations that were created by the influx of funds are professionalized organizations and their practices are more similar to NGOs in the Global North than to the grassroots resistance organizations described in the case studies. Environmental groups have been founded by international interaction throughout the Global South. In general, early environmentalism in these regions fit the patterns of livelihood struggles described in the case studies. Over time, however, as organizations sought international support, their forms became more institutionalized. In an analysis of the origins of environmental groups around the world, Wesley Longhofer and Evan Shofer (2010) noted that in the "industrialized west" (Global North in the terms of this lesson), the average date of founding for environmental groups was 1958. In South and Central America, the average date was 1983. What this suggests is that while grassroots environmental campaigns, without official organizational status, or perhaps under the auspices of other groups like labor unions, existed prior to 1983, what happened in the 1980s and later is that organized, professional groups came into being.

RESISTANCE TO ECOLOGICAL IMPERIALISM

When international NGOs work in Ecuador to protect lands for the "good of humankind," what does this mean for locals? For sovereignty in Ecuador? Whose needs are being met? What if Japan wanted to buy a chunk of the Pacific Northwest to protect it? How would people in Oregon respond? Who controls the environment and decisions regarding its use?

Transnational environmentalism has been criticized by some from the South as a form of "**ecoimperialism**." This critique parallels criticisms of development. "Development" was intended to change "backward/traditional" societies into "modern" societies; however, much official development has led to greater inequality between the Global North and the Global South, and many nations that started out poor are now poorer and further in debt and have less control over their choices. The critique of transnational environmentalism is that organizations "helping" with environmental issues are creating the same problem. By becoming involved in the Global South, actors from the Global North are attempting to exert control over foreign environments. For example, Arturo Escobar (1998) looked at what he called the "dominant biodiversity discourse" that comes from the West and suggested that there are multiple ways that other actors understand biodiversity. He argued that international conservation projects based on the Western, "global" conception of biodiversity (which he called the "resource management dominant view") are just one way of understanding, and that locals have alternative conceptions of the nature–culture relationship. In the current formulation, the "globalization of the environment" has opened doors to funding flows between North and South. This makes more and more possibilities for the North to "manage" the South.

Along this same line, Akhil Gupta (1998, p. 306) argued that "In contrast to the humanistic pronouncement of 'sharing one world,' made mostly by leaders and activists from the North, is the view of representatives of poor countries that the environment is a crucial arena where conflict between the haves and have-nots manifests itself." There have been specific instances of local groups in the Global South resisting the North's environmentalism. Back again to Ecuador: In 1995 frustrated, angry fishermen from the Galápagos Islands took their machetes and rounded up researchers from the Charles Darwin Research Station and held them hostage for 4 days. Why? The government limited fishing in the area on the basis of the Northern environmental scientists' assessment. The fishermen's access to fish, and thus their economic survival, was limited by Northern recommendations to limit withdrawals. This conflict in the Galápagos, between the local economy and international environmental protection, has been ongoing. This conflict, like ones dealing with sustainable development, highlights conflicts between the Global North and the Global South in which the North focuses on the environment at the expense of development and vice versa (see also Lesson 20).

Some interesting changes have been taking place with regard to "alternative development" and the environment, especially in Latin America. In Ecuador, Rafael Correa was elected president in 2006 and took office in 2007. *Alianza PAIS*, the political party that Correa founded, promised to create a new 21st-century socialism. Under President Correa, there was a referendum to elect a constituent assembly that would rewrite the constitution. The new constitution included constitutional rights for nature. Nature has "the right to exist, persist, maintain and regenerate its vital cycles, structure, functions and its processes in evolution" and the government is required to protect such rights. This was the first time nature has ever had these rights, anywhere. Bolivia adopted a similar change to its constitution in 2011. The Ecuadorian constitution also included language, written in Spanish and Kichwa (one of the dominant indigenous languages spoken in the country), expressing the right to *"buen vivir,"* and *"sumak kawsay"*—a right to living well. Many suggest that these changes create openings for Ecuadorians (and others) to create an alternative development model that incorporates nature rather than simply extracting it for human use. The Pachamama Alliance, an organization that works with indigenous peoples in the Amazon and is based in San Francisco (with a sister foundation in Ecuador), summarizes aspects of the indigenous conception of *sumak kawsay*:

> Sumak kawsay values people over profit. It is also a new way of viewing "developing nations" because it expresses a relationship with nature and surroundings that epitomizes the opposite of profit and commodification. A key piece is how development is defined: it calls for a decreased emphasis on economic and product development, and an increased focus on human development—not in population, but an enrichment of core values, spirituality, ethics, and a deepening of our own connection with pachamama [mother earth]." (The Pachamama Alliance, 2012)

These views of development and nature are at odds with the dominant worldview of the Global North.

One of the concrete proposals that have come out of President Correa's administration, which seems to be influenced by *sumak kawsay*, is a proposal that attempts to address global warming and lead the world to a "post-fossil fuel society." President Correa presented his ITT-Yasuní Initiative at the UN in 2007. The basic plan is that the state will not grant oil concessions in the ITT oil corridor that runs through Yasuní National Park if the international community can compensate Ecuador for half of the revenue that it would have earned over a 10-year period (in other words, asking for $3.6 billion in environmental donations in lieu of $7.2 billion in oil export profits). The argument is that the plan would protect one of the most biodiverse places on earth AND reduce greenhouse gas emissions AND protect indigenous people living on those lands. Environmental organizations have formed to promote the project and solicit funding. By the end of 2013, Ecuador had not received the funds it requested. As I write, Ecuador's government is making plans to drill in part of the park amid protest. It is not clear what will unfold in the near future, but it is a story worth following. If Ecuador is able to "keep the oil in the soil," this would mark a stark contrast to the days when the Ecuadorian state allowed Texaco to drill and create environmental devastation and endanger indigenous peoples' livelihoods in the Amazon.

CONCLUSION

Grassroots environmentalism in the Global South is more akin to environmental justice struggles in North America than to the professionalized movement industry represented by mainstream groups like the Sierra Club and the Environmental Defense Fund. Over time, however, the Global South's environmental movement has become more professionalized along the lines of environmental organizations in the Global North, and it is creating two different forms of organizations in the Global South: (1) grassroots-based direct action activists and (2) professionalized environmental groups who work from their offices.

Environmental movements in the Global South must attend to the concerns of those who are poor and want economic development and those who are poor and suffering from the negative effects of economic development. In many cases in the South, there have been outright attacks against environmentalism, as in the case of attacks and killings of activists working for the U'wa and Ogoni as well as Chico Mendes, since environmentalism often comes into conflict with states' and TNCs' interests. Economic globalization is one of the biggest foes of the environment in the Global South and represents an issue that is bigger than what most single-campaign organizations can focus on. When I ask environmentalists in Latin America if they've been successful, they respond, "Yes, we've slowed environmental degradation, but as long as we continue on this economic development path, the environment is bound for destruction." Some alternative models, such as that presented by Ecuador, suggest that alternative forms of "development" and "good living" may be possible.

SOURCES

Brechin, Steven R., and Willett Kempton. 1994. "Global Environmentalism: A Challenge to the Postmaterialism Thesis?" *Social Science Quarterly* 75:245–269.
Brosius, J. Peter. 2001. "Local Knowledge, Global Claims: On the Significance of Indigenous Ecologies in Sarawak, East Malaysia." In J. Grim and L. Sullivan, eds.

Indigenous Traditions and Ecology, pp. 125–157. Cambridge, MA: Harvard University Press and Center for the Study of World Religions.

Collinson, Helen, ed. 1996. *Green Guerrillas: Environmental Conflicts and Initiatives in Latin America and the Caribbean.* London, UK: Latin American Bureau.

Dunlap, Riley E., and Richard York. 2008. "The Globalization of Environmental Concern and the Limits of the Postmaterialist Values Explanation: Evidence from Four Multinational Surveys." *The Sociological Quarterly* 49:529–563.

Escobar, Arturo. 1995. *Encountering Development: The Making and Unmaking of the Third World.* Princeton, NJ: Princeton University Press.

Escobar, Arturo. 1998. "Whose Knowledge, Whose Nature? Biodiversity, Conservation, and the Political Ecology of Social Movements." *Journal of Political Ecology* 5:53–82.

Escobar, Arturo. 2011. "Sustainability: Design for the Pluriverse." *Development* 54(2): 137–140.

Frank, David John, Ann Hironaka, and Evan Schofer. 2000. "The Nation-State and the Natural Environment over the Twentieth Century." *American Sociological Review* 65:96–116.

Gedicks, Al. 1993. *The New Resource Wars: Native and Environmental Struggles Against Multinational Corporations.* Boston, MA: South End Press.

Gedicks, Al. 2001. *Resource Rebels: Native Challenges to Mining and Oil Corporations.* Boston, MA: South End Press.

Guha, Ramachandra. 1989. *The Unquiet Woods: Ecological Change and Peasant Resistance in the Himalaya.* Berkeley, CA: University of California Press.

Guha, Ramachandra. 2000. *Environmentalism: A Global History.* New York: Longman.

Guha, Ramachandra, and Juan Martinez-Alier. 1997. *Varieties of Environmentalism: Essays North and South.* London: Earthscan.

Gupta, Akhil. 1998. *Postcolonial Development: Agriculture in the Making of Modern India.* Durham, NC: Duke University Press.

Humphrey, Craig R., Tammy L. Lewis, and Frederick H. Buttel. 2002. *Environment, Energy, and Society: A New Synthesis.* Belmont, CA: Wadsworth/Thompson.

Keck, Margaret E., and Kathryn Sikkink. 1998. *Activists Beyond Borders: Advocacy Networks in International Politics.* Ithaca, NY: Cornell University Press.

Lewis, Tammy L. 2000. "Transnational Conservation Movement Organizations: Shaping the Protected Area Systems of Less Developed Countries." *Mobilization* 5(1):105–123.

Lewis, Tammy L. 2011. "Global Civil Society and the Distribution of Environmental Goods: Funding for Environmental NGOs in Ecuador." In Julian Agyeman and JoAnn Carmin, eds. *Environmental Inequalities Beyond Borders: Local Perspectives on Global Inequities,* pp. 87–104. Cambridge, MA: MIT Press.

Longhofer, Wesley, and Evan Shofer. 2010. "National and Global Origins of Environmental Associations." *American Sociological Review* 75(4):505–533.

Olivera, Oscar, in collaboration with Tom Lewis. 2004. *¡Cochabamba! Water War in Bolivia.* Cambridge, MA: South End Press.

Pellow, David N. 2007. *Resisting Global Toxics: Transnational Movements for Environmental Justice.* Cambridge, MA: The MIT Press.

Rowell, Andrew. 1995. "Oil, Shell and Nigeria." *Ecologist* 25(6):210–213.

Rowell, Andrew. 1996. *Green Backlash: A Global Subversion of the Environmental Movement.* New York: Routledge.

Smith, Jackie. 2008. *Social Movements for Global Democracy.* Baltimore: The Johns Hopkins University Press.

Taylor, Bron Raymond, ed. 1995. *Ecological Resistance Movements: The Global Emergence of Radical and Popular Environmentalism*. Albany: State University of New York Press.

Taylor, Dorceta E. 2009. *The Environment and the People in American Cities, 1600s–1900s*. Durham, NC: Duke University Press.

The Pachamama Alliance. 2012. Sumak Kawsay: Ancient Teachings of Indigenous Peoples. http://www.pachamama.org/sumak-kawsay. Accessed 4 January 2014.

19

Indigenous Cultures
Environmental Knowledge, Practice, and Rights

Bahram Tavakolian

St. Regis Mohawk Tribe Environment Division vehicle, Akwesasne.
Photo by Ken Gould.

AN ANTHROPOLOGICAL PERSPECTIVE

What can a cultural anthropologist contribute to a volume on environmental sociology? As an anthropologist I take it as a given that the greater the variety of cultures we know about, the greater our understanding of the human condition and the potentialities of human relationships with the natural environment. A comparative or cross-cultural approach is the essential element of most anthropological research and analysis. In addition, it appears that cross-cultural similarities and differences are not merely random in their distribution, nor can they be reduced to explanations dependent upon only one or two factors. While the "variables" that are most responsible for similarities and differences in the ways of life of different populations are a major part of anthropological concern, these variables also must be understood in their immediate cultural contexts. In the anthropological view, cultural institutions, such as power, economics, gender, family, and systems of beliefs and values, need to be examined *holistically*, or as part of a set of interconnections within a "whole" or total pattern. Indeed, such a contextual understanding is essential before institutions and their practical purposes and symbolic meanings can be accurately compared with seemingly similar institutions in other societies if we lack a holistic understanding, we risk taking cultural practices and beliefs out of context and misinterpreting or mistranslating them across cultural lines, or as the late Clifford Geertz once observed, comparing apples and oranges.

To gain an awareness of the meanings that different populations attribute to the worlds around them, anthropologists attempt to learn about the subjective cultural knowledge that human beings develop within specific cultural settings. The diverse voices of multiple respondents both within and across cultural systems remind us of the considerable variation in what people think, know, believe, and practice. In addition, however, the anthropological researcher must somehow comprehend and communicate information about this diversity across cultural lines, in particular to students, readers, and other researchers in typically literate, urban, industrial, stratified, highly specialized, and "scientific" societies. An *intersubjective* approach, which seeks to integrate culturally specific knowledge with a more universal conceptual vocabulary and analytic framework, is therefore also a necessary component in the anthropological perspective.

In addition, neither are cultural similarities found only among peoples who inhabit similar environmental zones (e.g., desert, savanna, steppe, tropical forest, coastal maritime, tundra, and polar regions), nor are such zones conducive to the development of only a single form of cultural adaptation. Thus, the expansion of anthropological research throughout the past 150 years has demonstrated considerable reason to dispute a one-to-one relationship between environmental conditions and social or cultural characteristics. Instead, we must understand the processes through which unique cultures and the interconnected aspects of their ecologies, technologies, social institutions, and cultural beliefs and values have developed over time but not assume that only one or a few "causal factors" or "determinants" are the sole bases for explanation and interpretation. A *processual* approach has as its dual objectives the explanation of *diachronic* (over time) processes and changes as well as *synchronic* (same time) interpretations of how cultural institutions and behavioral practices are interconnected within the contemporary period.

It seems to me that a comparative, holistic, intersubjective, and processual perspective raises a number of issues and concerns that are of interest to both anthropologists and sociologists and across a broad range of societies in the contemporary world. The most provocative question of all may be the one raised by Philippe Descola and Gisli Palsson (1996) when they asked "Does nature really exist?" To students in the West, answers to this question may seem obvious and irrelevant, if not silly, but an anthropological approach brings to mind a long list of ethnographic examples from every continent except Antarctica of peoples who reject a dualistic separation between nature and society. Emilio Moran (2006) echoed this view by pointing out that many indigenous peoples consider the dividing line between the person and the environment to be a very permeable one, such that the environment is part of the makeup of the person and, of course, people are part of the environment.

Through use of multiple cross-cultural examples, a comparative perspective encourages us to learn that among many peoples of the world, "the environment" is not merely a setting or a complex of material circumstances and natural resources; it is also a set of ideas and practices that people have developed in relation to their natural, sociopolitical, and symbolic surroundings, including their connectedness to other life forms as well as to topographic features and climatic conditions.

Environmental Ideas and Knowledge

Such a cross-cultural examination reveals considerable diversity both in how "nature" is conceptualized by different societies and in how the flora, fauna, terrain, and energy of the physical environment are used in practice. Thus, the commonsense view that we typically assume in the West, of nature as an entity with primarily objective, physical, and often marketable characteristics, is both historically and culturally unusual rather than either universal or inevitable. Descola, Palsson, and their coauthors in Nature and Society (1996) used a comparative ecological approach to reveal substantial historical and cultural variation in how people in different societies imagine and adapt to the constraints and possibilities of their environments. A major aspect of this variation is the significance of symbols, beliefs, values, and meanings in shaping how nature is subjectively and morally known and treated. As mentioned, there is no one-to-one correlation between environmental characteristics and cultural patterns. Rather, culture is an autonomous factor in its relations with the natural environment and may be both constraining and enabling in its influences on patterns of environmental knowledge and adaptation. One attribute of most indigenous cultures is that they know and live within their environments in situations of considerable intimacy, as part of everyday life and routine activity rather than as a separable domain or condition of existence.

Does this mean that indigenous peoples and their cultures are uniformly "closer to nature" than other populations? Do they invariably demonstrate greater wisdom in their understanding of and response to the rest of nature? For that matter, is ideological oneness with nature the same as "kindly use" of the environment? Quite the contrary, according to Shepard Krech III (1999): The stereotype of the "ecological Indian" is more likely to be an example of subtle racism than it is an ethnographic reality. To assume that all Native Americans are homogeneous in their cultural conceptions, practices, and environmental histories reduces diverse and innovative human populations to essentialized and stereotypical caricatures.

Furthermore, what does "closer to nature" actually mean? We must be careful to avoid the racist notion that any population has "instinctual" feelings or senses that tie them to their surroundings. Philosophical monism, as in the ethical movement associated with "deep ecology," which seeks an understanding of the unity and interconnectedness of people and nature, has parallels to many indigenous conceptualizations of nature. However, such a similarity need not imply that indigenous peoples follow such Western practices as veganism, not to mention the newly coined concept of "freeganism" by which, ideally, all consumption is freed from its impact on the need for further production, through use of food rescued from dumpsters, among other practices. Human populations practice many different food taboos, but there is no consistency across cultures in following vegan precepts that respect for other species of life renders them inedible. Rather, some animal species may be especially celebrated and honored by being hunted and consumed. Similarly, for very practical and rational purposes—rather than purely ethical or moral ones—indigenous peoples are careful to avoid overconsumption of material resources in order to allow for environmental replenishment and long-term utilization. Therefore, rather than on a very spurious connection between biology, culture, and morality, my anthropological emphasis is on the carefully developed environmental knowledge that comes from everyday practices, and on the sustainable use patterns that emerge from recognizing the constraints imposed upon utilization of natural environments over extended periods of time.

If we carefully conduct holistic examinations and look for the many linkages between material, structural, and ideational elements within diverse cultures, we will be better able to understand technological strategies, sociopolitical adaptations, and symbolic representations in relation to their own natural and social environments. In the anthropological view, indigenous forms of environmental knowledge and practice are not "poor substitutes" for Western culture and environmental relations. Rather, they must be understood and appreciated within their own geographical, historical, and cultural contexts. In addition, by identifying multiple roots of environmental practices, a holistic investigation of interconnections among cultural institutions can help ask further questions about "how" and "why"; that is, what are the processes by which cultural–environmental relationships have emerged and changed over time? As I will turn to in the next section of this discussion, some anthropologists, such as Marvin Harris and other "**cultural materialists**," prefer an analysis of ecological patterns that emphasizes material aspects of culture and their "shaping" influence upon other cultural characteristics. Other researchers have given their primary attention to ideational and symbolic characteristics of culture, and I will refer to them as "**cultural idealists**." Both theoretical approaches are feasible and informative, and in my view a more complete and accurate understanding of the relationships between culture and environmental knowledge and practice requires a synthesis of aspects of both frameworks.

ECOLOGICAL PROCESSES: MATERIAL ADAPTATIONS

By "material aspects of culture" I am referring to such factors as population size, growth rates, and distribution (demography); the forms of technology and production patterns that characterize different societies and communities; and the variety of floral and faunal species that people use within their territories. Some analysts, following the line of thought presented by the late Marvin Harris's "cultural materialism" (1979), consider these cultural elements to be the primary factors that shape or constrain ways that people are socially and politically organized, as well as the degrees and kinds of differences that exist among a society's members in terms of access to resources, power, wealth, status, and control. Harris is well known for his analysis of such practices as food prohibitions, cannibalism, female infanticide, warfare, and male supremacy with respect to their ecological implications and the material advantages that accrue from them.

According to Eric Ross (1978), one of Harris's students and followers, material conditions and adaptations also influence the kinds of ideas, symbols, and values that people use to explain their relations to nature and to one another. Thus, a food taboo may be based, for example, on the belief that certain animal species represent reincarnated ancestral spirits and should not be hunted or consumed. Among the Achuara Jivaro of eastern Peru, such ideational restrictions are placed on the hunting of relatively large and more difficult-to-locate deer, tapir, and capybara. The alternative emphasis on the acquisition of more abundant, more easily found, and more efficiently hunted species of small game also contributes to better use of the time, territory, and organization devoted to hunting activities.

ECOLOGICAL PROCESSES: CULTURAL MEANINGS

A different kind of interpretation of ecological processes that is favored by cultural idealists emphasizes ideational (having to do with ideas) aspects of culture and proposes that people organize their relations to their environments through their subjective thoughts, symbols, images, ideas, beliefs, moral requirements, and rituals. Through his many years of research with the Achuar of the Upper Amazon in Ecuador, Philippe Descola (1994) has demonstrated that interspecies material, social, and ideational relations are not limited to a few materially valuable or costly species, as is suggested by Ross. Rather, almost all plants and animals are considered to be comparable to persons and social groups in their qualities and affiliations. There is even a gendered breakdown in nature comparable to human social and economic patterns, such that game animals are the *affines*, or "in-laws," of men, who are the primary hunters in the population, while women are associated with cultivated plants as well as the labor of horticultural production.

The Achuar extend their own kinship system to the male woolly monkey, who—like the Achuar themselves—is supposed to breed only with his bilateral cross-cousin. In contrast, the hummingbird is not faithful to his mate(s) but constantly pursues new conquests. As Descola (1994, p. 96) wrote, "just as there are a few shameless individuals among the Achuar, so too certain species of animals evidence their asocial character by behaving like beasts." People as geographically disparate as Yonggom gardeners in Papua New Guinea and Koyukon hunters, trappers, and fishers in Alaska share a commonality with one another with respect to their symbolic uni-fication of human and other species. They treat other animals as equivalent to human beings in their possession of agency, spiritual power, and the right to respectful and reciprocal treatment. Both populations seek to attract other species to lend themselves to being captured, killed, and con-sumed. They do not assume human domination or unrestricted rights of consumption. Rather, they maintain ties to other species that are depen-dent on both the continued survival of these species and on symbolic restrictions on the ways that these species become part of human utiliza-tion patterns.

A particularly interesting example of "indigenous analysis of social and environmental relations" is found in Stuart Kirsch's *Reverse Anthropology* (2006), based upon his research with the Yonggom people of New Guinea. The Yonggom believe that both people and other animals are *agentic* (have the ability to initiate action) and belong to a single speech community. Hence, animals are not merely hunted but must be verbally and ritually cajoled into allowing themselves to be hunted and captured. In return, human beings must practice reciprocal relations with other elements of their environments, including mines and rivers as well as plant and animal species, for unre-quited reciprocity is the source of resentment, anger, danger, and misfor-tune. As far away as the Alaskan boreal forest, Koyukon hunters practice a similarly humble, respectful, and interagentic relationship with the species of fish, birds, and mammals they depend upon for their subsistence. Without an intersubjective understanding of these beliefs and ideas, it would be very difficult to interpret a variety of ecological practices among the Achuar or Yonggom or Koyukon, who clearly "know" and "see" their settings and surroundings differently than inhabitants of urban, industrial, and "con-structed" environments.

But rather than suggesting that only one of these interpretive frameworks— cultural materialism or cultural idealism—is more correct or analytically valuable than the other, it is more fruitful for a holistic ecological analysis to think of both perspectives as telling us a significant and essential portion of the story and of each requiring the other to complete its own viewpoint. In this manner, the two perspectives and the cultural elements they focus upon may be seen to be involved in a dialectical, complementary, and syn-thetic relational process with one another, rather than a deterministic one in which ideas and practices, or meanings and adaptations, are artificially separated from one another.

INDIGENOUS ECOLOGICAL PRACTICE

In Lesson 1 of this volume Čapek discussed Gary Fine's concept of *naturework*, referring to the ways that human populations construct their environmental ideas and practices through the filters of other cultural symbols, meanings, and understandings of "reality." Given the variety of ways in which nature is made "real" across different cultures, rather than having a universal conceptual identity and material value, a major aspect of anthropological concern is what relationship there is between cultural conceptualizations of the environment and the ways that potential resources of the environment are defined and utilized (see Lesson 1). As I have already mentioned, many peoples may attribute qualities of agency and responsibility and reciprocity to other species and are also more respectful of the "rights" of nonhuman species. Does this necessarily mean, however, that indigenous cultures—especially foragers, gardeners, and pastoralists—leave smaller "ecological footprints" by consuming and wasting less of the environment's bounty? Conversely, are societies whose members seek to control and dominate nature more likely to experience greater social inequalities and cyclical shortages in access to material resources, as well as greater frequency of competition and conflict over material access both within their own societies and with other societies? A related question is this: What happens to environmental relations and cultural patterns as a consequence of economic development, the penetration of market economies, and both economic globalization and so-called cultural modernization?

These are among the questions that I examine in the following section as I lay out some ways in which such issues matter not only among indigenous peoples but for us all—other species included. To reiterate a point made in the beginning of this discussion, in no way do I mean to suggest that indigenous peoples represent a "type" of human being but only that, by and large, their smaller populations, more limited technologies, as well as self-imposed ideational restrictions on levels of consumption and waste contribute to more sustainable and resilient relations between human populations and other elements of nature.

In addition, it becomes obvious that the difficulties that indigenous peoples may have in adjusting to contemporary environments are not primarily ecological but often political. That is to say, indigenous peoples have typically been successful in adapting sustainably to their local environments for many generations, if not centuries and perhaps even millennia. That their lifestyles are under attack and increasingly jeopardized by contemporary conditions is typically not a consequence of their irrational or inefficient practices. Quite the contrary. They have been able to survive on relatively limited resources despite the political and economic pressures placed upon them by the expansions of other populations into their traditional territories. They are the "long-term success stories," according to John Bodley (1999), while Western institutions and practices are both relatively recent and environmentally suspect. The survival of indigenous peoples in marginal lands into the 21st century is a measure of their resiliency but also an indication of the much greater burden placed upon their former territories and resources by the presence of other populations and ways of life.

Finally, another aspect of anthropological concern I will address later is a reminder that the cultural and technological successes of human populations have not immunized them from having to live within the constraints on energy and other resources found in the Earth's environment. As phrased by William Catton and Riley Dunlap (1978), one of the obstacles to understanding ecological conditions and their impacts upon human populations is *human exemptionalism*, or the idea that modern human societies have somehow overcome the limits experienced by other species in needing to balance population with resource and energy restrictions and consumption with production. There are obvious limits to growth on our planet as a result of population growth, resource scarcity, and both pollution and environmental degradation. Indigenous peoples demonstrate an awareness of this aspect of the human condition in a way that we may hope will eventually become understood within all human populations.

THE CULTURAL ECOLOGY OF NOMADIC PASTORALISM

I first became attracted to ecological anthropology after reading a 1956 essay by Fredrik Barth, the well-known Norwegian anthropologist, entitled "Ecologic Relations of Ethnic Groups in Swat, North Pakistan." Barth conducted field research with Pashtuns (then still known by the British Indian designation of "Pathans"), Kohistanis, and Gujars in the Northwest Frontier Province of Pakistan, and in this essay he demonstrated the intricate ecological, economic, and political interrelationships between three ethnically, linguistically, and technologically distinct populations. Each group inhabited a different ecological microniche and carried out a different form of technoeconomic adaptation. In combination with one another, they optimized the relationships between human populations and the natural environment through unique and interdependent strategies of territorial location and land use.

In the district of Swat, Pashtuns represent the largest and most powerful group, owning most of the land and cultivating wheat, maize, and rice in irrigated fields. Through their greater numbers and complex, stratified, and specialized political structure, Pashtuns were able to take over most of the area from earlier populations of Kohistanis (or "mountain people"), who were forced into higher and agriculturally more marginal areas. To supplement their cultivation of maize and millet on narrow, terraced fields at higher altitudes, Kohistanis practice a mixed economy that depends equally upon the raising of sheep and goats through *transhumant patterns* (migration across different ecological zones, such as between seasonal pastures at different elevations and with different climatic conditions). Unlike the highly stratified Pashtuns, who depend upon a double-cropping agricultural schedule and surplus production to support their more specialized population, Kohistanis are more subsistence-oriented in their production system and relatively more egalitarian in status and wealth relationships. They also refrain from many of the symbolic meanings that Pashtuns associate with patriarchy, power, honor, and bravery, all of which depend upon Pashtun patterns of stratification and a specialized division of labor, not only between women and men but also between families and men of higher and lower status.

Meanwhile, Gujars, the third and smallest ethnic group in the region, migrated into the area from more southerly regions. Gujars depend upon herding sheep, goats, cattle, and water buffalo, and they serve as clients of powerful, landowning Pashtuns. Gujars provide agricultural labor in exchange for pasture use and for surplus grain produced by Pashtuns. In addition, their herds provide meat, milk, and wool for Pashtuns, and livestock also help to fertilize the agricultural fields and prepare them for planting by eating stubble and breaking up the soil.

From Barth's description, the cultural–environmental relations in Swat seem to represent an almost ideal, intricate, symbiotic ecological pattern, in which three groups with diverse technologies, social structures, values, and meanings are able to coexist in a limited territorial space and to make efficient and productive use of its potential environmental resources. In Barth's interpretation, each ethnic group is characterized by unique adaptations to its own ecological microzone while also benefiting from the complementary activities and surplus production of other groups. While Barth did examine the political contexts of access to environmental resources, which was itself an important development in cultural–ecological analysis, he might have gone much further in investigating the ways that human–environmental relationships are outcomes not merely of local political processes but also of relations between localized populations and the nation-state.

More than a decade later, through field research in the late 1960s with nomads and farmers in southeastern Turkey, Daniel Bates (2005) developed a more powerful explanation of ecological mutualism—or the interdependence between different cultural groups within a single environmental location. Bates examined the combination of natural and political constraints that affect the technoeconomic and structural characteristics of social groups. He presented particularly valuable insights about the role of the state in controlling the power and territorial distribution of specific ethnic groups and their modes of technoeconomic activity. Historically, the role of the Turkish state has been to allow ethnically and linguistically "Turkish" Yörük sheep and goat herders to practice transhumant nomadism, while restricting the ability of Kurdish and Turkmen populations from doing the same. However, the Yörük themselves are constrained in their use of pasture and migration routes and schedules by state-based regulation of pasture ownership and legal intervention in instances of crop damage done by their herds on the cultivated fields of villagers. Through use of a holistic and processual perspective, Bates was able to show that what would constitute optimal grazing and migration patterns in connection with Yörük social institutions and cultural values is mitigated by nonbioecological, state-based, and political aspects of environmental relationships. Despite many similarities with pastoralist ecology in northwest Pakistan, the unique characteristics of Turkish history, politics, ethnicity, and availability of pasture and migratory routes all play a crucial part in the ecology of Yörük pastoralism.

Between 1976 and 1977, I had the opportunity to conduct field research with Pashtu-speaking Sheikhanzai pastoral nomads in western Afghanistan. My focus was on the material adaptations to their natural environment made by the Sheikhanzai—that is, their population size and herd composition, migration routes and schedules, patterns of land and water ownership and use, and economic relations with sedentary populations and with markets and merchants. I also conducted a holistic investigation of how the latter techno-economic factors were interconnected with patterns of marriage, family, coresidence relationships within camp groups, gender roles, social status, political leadership, religiosity, and cultural values. During the field research I became interested in the effects of national and international development projects on local populations, especially with respect to their neglect of the cultural factors involved with directed programs of economic and social change.

Like Barth, I was interested in how diverse and unrelated ethnic groups interacted within an economic nexus; but like Bates, I observed considerably more friction, competition, and animosity—fortunately, mostly verbal rather than physical—among rival, often ethnically distinct populations. Similar to Bates's analysis, a major contrast I found with Barth's interpretation of ecological symbiosis was the interventionist role of the state and the apparent favoritism that government officials showed for sedentary populations (though, oddly, in this instance, across ethnic lines, with Pashtu-speaking government officials often favoring non-Pashtun sedentary villagers who were more amenable than nomads to government schools, taxes, and military conscription). But a more significant factor than state-based politics alone that helped to explain the conflictual relations between ethnic groups in western Afghanistan was the basic ecological context of the resident populations and their discrepant, contradictory, and competitive—rather than mutualistic or symbiotic—patterns of resource utilization and coexistence.

For those of you unfamiliar with pastoralism, imagine a group of interrelated families—as many as 10,000 Sheikhanzai and upward of 2 million Pashtun nomads in Afghanistan—who have no permanent abode and are on migration almost half the year to take their sheep, goats, and camels to grassy pastures, water sources, and markets. The people live in black goat-hair tents throughout the year, and they establish social clusters of four or five camp groups, with two to ten tents per camp, in their summer pasture areas in the highlands of central Afghanistan, while they live in much larger camps of 30 to 35 tent households throughout the winter months in the western desert plains near the Iranian border. You don't need to know all the details, but it is important to understand that people such as the Sheikhanzai must rely upon an intimate knowledge of climate, the availability of water, types of forage, adequacy of feeding and rest cycles for animals, risks from wolves, competition for pasture access with other populations, and market prospects for surplus animals and animal/dairy products.

The difficulty of maintaining such a form of social organization and ecological adaptation in the modern era is that lands that are used without legal title are increasingly vulnerable to pressures by state institutions and their concessionaires as well as by other social groups in the region. The Sheikhanzai found the migration routes and pastures they had used for multiple generations reduced in size each year as a result of the expansion in cultivation by villagers, almost always belonging to other ethnic and linguistic groups and therefore not subject to the forms of economic reciprocity and conflict resolution that tied the Sheikhanzai to one another and to other Pashtun nomads.

Another obstacle to their traditional ecological patterns that Sheikhanzai nomads began to experience (well before the communist revolution in Afghanistan in 1978 and the subsequent Soviet invasion and occupation from 1979 to 1989) was the increasing inroads made by capitalist market pressures on pasture land and herding activities. Beginning in 1974 the World Bank established a program for the "rationalization" of pastoralism that attempted to encourage the adoption of range management schemes comparable to those established in Kenya and Tanzania among Maasai and other pastoralist populations. Such programs involved coercive *sedentarization* (the requirement of permanent settlement) of nomadic pastoralists and an overall reduction of the pastoralist population, along with market-based controls on herd sizes and livestock prices. In addition, the World Bank venture focused upon the raising of sheep for slaughterhouses and export, not only excluding goat and camel raising from the program but also deemphasizing the dairy products and wool provided by both sheep herds and goat flocks. Most significantly, the program assumed private ownership of animals, and specifically ownership by males, whereas the traditional Sheikhanzai pattern emphasized household-based ownership and considerable *de facto* control in the hands of women over dairy and wool production and distribution of surplus goods.

What the World Bank failed to recognize was the considerable power and decision-making ability held by Sheikhanzai women, who owned household tents, belongings, and even livestock and pasture rights. The World Bank's assumption of universal patriarchy among pastoralists demonstrates the lack of the cross-cultural, contextual, and holistic perspective I emphasize throughout this lesson. In addition, the World Bank project did not attempt to understand how women's power is associated with their control of dairy production activities as well as their status and rights within kinship units that include their brothers, fathers, and frequently husbands (often patrilateral first cousins).

Ecologically the program would have been disastrous for pastoralism if it had been successful in defining the purposes of sheep and goat herding primarily in terms of market prices for sheep carcasses. For one thing, the basic character of seasonal migrations by Sheikhanzai and other nomads was misunderstood by the World Bank–funded development agents as a quaint holdover from earlier times and perhaps even a reflection of human "wanderlust." This simultaneously romantic and racist image of exotic nomads, supposedly free from the constraints of government, settlement, and civilization, ignores the climatic and floral patterns that affect water and pasture resources, not to mention the severe contrasts between the seasonal temperatures of deserts and mountain valleys. The spring and fall migrations of the Sheikhanzai and their herds allow them to escape the extremes of heat in the summer and cold in the winter and to use pastures throughout the year that can be replenished in subsequent seasons and years as grazing sites. A sedentary existence would have been harmful to the quality of pastureland and the health of livestock, not to mention disintegrating the social ties that exist between multiple camp groups and villages in sparsely populated and agriculturally marginal areas. And, of course, it would have eliminated the economic production roles of women and their corresponding power in aspects of decision making about migration, herd size, livestock distribution, and both marital and political relationships and replaced them with monopolies of power held by the highest-status and most profit-oriented male livestock owners.

Essentially, the World Bank program paid little heed to the natural constraints of the environment and the livestock raised there, and it gave even less consideration to the social and cultural meanings and purposes of pastoralism. For the Sheikhanzai, nomadic pastoralism is not merely a way of making a living but a way of life. As such, it contains values and meanings of autonomy and self-sufficiency that are not available to sedentary village populations regulated by state institutions and market conditions. The Sheikhanzai used livestock markets without being dependent upon them. They sold surplus animals and wool to urban merchants when they wanted to obtain cash but not as a necessity within their own economic system.

In contrast, the World Bank adopted a culturally specific view of range management from Australia, declared itself successful in previous implementation efforts in eastern and southern Africa, transported it to Afghanistan, and blamed Sheikhanzai cultural resistance and backwardness for the failure of the program. Furthermore, similar to Pellow's discussion in Lesson 3, the World Bank's goals were in line with central state efforts to bring recalcitrant populations such as the Sheikhanzai into line with state policies and controls. The World Bank failed in its own right by giving little or no attention to the cross-cultural, holistic, processual, and intersubjective goals I have emphasized in this lesson. Their project did not succeed in attracting Sheikhanzai participants, and had it done so it would have succeeded in destroying both pastoralism and the pastoral environment for generations to come.

ENVIRONMENTAL IMPERIALISM: WHY DOES IT MATTER, AND TO WHOM?

In a 1999 book whose title at first seemed only ironic and now appears tragically prescient, John Bodley's *Victims of Progress* offers "a critique of the ethnocidal national and international policies toward indigenous peoples." Today, we refer to *ethnocide*—or the forcible eradication of unique cultures—in terms of euphemisms such as "globalization," "market expansion," and "cultural homogenization." But the latter tendencies are part of the same long-term process as the empire building by colonial powers in the 19th century and the first half of the 20th century. Today, the agents of change are generally transnational corporations and the impersonal "market" rather than nation-states and world empires, but the negative outcomes for indigenous peoples and cultures not only resemble earlier colonial experiences but occur at a much more rapid pace (see Lesson 20).

Despite warnings from Bodley (1999), Arun Agrawal (2005), Arturo Escobar (1995), Anna Tsing (1993), and many others, state and commercial attempts to take over indigenously owned land and to eliminate indigenous environmental knowledge, social organization, and subsistence practices have continued to expand almost unabated, but not without indigenous objection and resistance. While some programs have failed because of their own mistaken assumptions and expectations and have disappeared over time, such as the World Bank project in Afghanistan, others have so modified and destroyed land and traditional technologies that entire villages and regional populations have had no other recourse but massive emigration and recruitment as agricultural and sweatshop labor. As Deborah Barndt (2002) carefully documented in her discussion of the North American trade in tomatoes, the "tangled routes" of globalized agriculture have provided considerable economic progress for agribusiness and often only destitution for emigrants as well as those left behind to serve as the labor for commercial agricultural enterprises.

In addition to the harm to indigenous peoples and their cultural practices, the cultural and political hegemony of Western capitalism has frequently succeeded in producing a sense of the environment, both in the West and abroad, as merely a source of marketable and consumable resources. Again, we are reminded by Čapek (see Lesson 1) that ideas and uses of the environment are symbolic constructions that may sharply contrast across cultural lines. The intrinsic value of the environment as a landscape full of historical memories, a region of scenic beauty, a zone of spiritual consequence, or a site of personal and social identity is of little consequence in the effort by commercial, political, and military interests to define the world's environments simply in terms of Western interests and objectives. *Environmental imperialism,* in my usage, is the appropriation of the homes, forests, agricultural lands and pastures, and riverine or coastal lands of indigenous peoples for foreign economic and political goals. Whether with respect to the pastures and livestock of the Sheikhanzai, the forests and rivers of the Yonggom, or the agricultural lands and activities of Mexican peasant farmers in Chiapas, environmental imperialism, often as a byproduct of globalization within the contemporary world capitalist system, is as devastating to cultural autonomy, identity, and continuity as more direct forms of colonial annexation and political domination. In addition, the coercive cultural changes that accompany the cultural transformations experienced by indigenous peoples jeopardize the adaptive and renewable patterns of environmental knowledge and practice that have sustained these populations over extensive periods of time.

But does it have to end in this way for indigenous peoples? Is globalization not only politically and culturally "good" but also economically "necessary" and "inevitable"? Unfortunately, most people in the West, including ordinary citizens and not just politicians and corporate leaders, would agree with the latter sentiments. To most of us in the advanced, industrial capitalist societies, it seems only logical that the path that we have traveled for the past two centuries is desirable because of the "standard of living" that it has provided for us—at least some of us—and it would seem almost immoral not to share the benefits of our wisdom and success with other peoples. But, aside from the question of who should be empowered to make such decisions, are we even sure of their long-term impacts on ourselves, let alone on people who have never been offered the opportunity to engage in the process of debating the alternatives?

Not only does continued environmental imperialism demonstrate the arrogance of power—of human domination over other species of life, of the West over the rest, and of the haves over the have-nots even in Western industrial societies—but it also risks destroying the very "goose that laid the golden egg." In the posture that many in the West have adopted for themselves and that Catton and Dunlap (1978) have labeled the "human exemptionalism paradigm," there is the assumption of unlimited innovation, growth, progress, and technological fixes. Unfortunately, for both the paradigm and life on Planet Earth, global environmental problems have proven resistant to easy technological solutions, including the "green revolution," and have been exacerbated by the destruction of physical and biotic environments and cultures that had previously demonstrated long-term stability and resilience in deserts, steppes, and rainforests throughout the world.

Many indigenous peoples have already been the "victims of progress," and it seems now that some of the perpetrators of so-called progressive efforts to bring about growth at any price, with concomitant expectations of consumption and heavier demands upon energy and natural resources, have begun to realize that existing processes of energy consumption, pollution, and land degradation cannot continue. While our standard of living has supposedly improved, at least on average, the quality of life with respect to social relations and both personal and spiritual satisfaction has declined. Also, for very practical and economically oriented reasons, even major energy corporations and manufacturers have begun to see the necessity for "green business." Increasing numbers of politicians, labor organizers, and citizens argue for supporting local businesses and becoming more concerned about local environments. With enough communities decrying "Not in my backyard," both in the West and in the world as a whole, there is hope— contrary to the suggestion made by Lawrence Summers, former U.S. Secretary of the Treasury and former President of Harvard University, that less developed societies are "underpolluted"—that there will be no place for the exploiters and polluters to go. "Things fall apart. The center cannot hold," wrote

W. B. Yeats. But perhaps that is a good thing, after all, if it contributes to a reinvigoration and spread of localized, agentic, and responsible environmental knowledge and practice as has been documented among the many remaining and remarkably resilient indigenous peoples of the contemporary world. Furthermore, the adoption of parallel forms of knowledge, practice, and a sense of reciprocal environmental rights and responsibility would be a valuable antidote to the patterns of consumption, environmental destruction, and waste that so often characterize environmental relations in the Western industrial world.

SOURCES

Agrawal, Arun. 2005. *Environmentality: Technologies of Government and the Making of Environmental Subjects.* Durham, NC: Duke University Press.

Barndt, Deborah. 2002. *Tangled Routes: Women, Work and Globalization on the Tomato Trail.* Lanham, MD: Rowman & Littlefield.

Barth, Fredrik. 1956. "Ecologic Relations of Ethnic Groups in Swat, North Pakistan." *American Anthropologist* 58(6):1079–1089.

Bates, Daniel G. 2005. *Human Adaptive Strategies: Ecology, Culture, and Politics,* 3rd ed. Boston, MA: Pearson.

Bodley, John H. 1999. *Victims of Progress,* 4th ed. Mountain View, CA: Mayfield.

Catton, William R., and Riley E. Dunlap. 1978. "Environmental Sociology: A New Paradigm." *American Sociologist* 13:41–49.

Descola, Philippe. 1994. *In the Society of Nature: A Native Ecology in Amazonia.* Cambridge, UK: Cambridge University Press.

Descola, Philippe, and Gisli Palsson, eds. 1996. *Nature and Society: Anthropological Perspectives.* London, UK: Routledge.

Dove, Michael. 2006. "Indigenous People and Environmental Politics." *Annual Review of Anthropology* 35:191–208.

Ellen, Roy, Peter Parkes, and Alan Bicker, eds. 2000. *Indigenous Environmental Knowledge and Its Transformations.* London, UK: Routledge.

Escobar, Arturo. 1995. *Encountering Development: The Making and Unmaking of the Third World.* Princeton: Princeton University Press.

Grim, John A., ed. 2001. *Indigenous Traditions and Ecology.* Cambridge, MA: Harvard University Press.

Harris, Marvin. 1979. *Cultural Materialism: The Struggle for a Science of Culture.* New York: Random House.

Kirsch, Stuart. 2006. *Reverse Anthropology: Indigenous Analysis of Social and Environmental Relations in New Guinea.* Stanford, CA: Stanford University Press.

Krech, Shepard III. 1999. *The Ecological Indian: Myth and History.* New York: W.W. Norton.

Moran, Emilio. 2006. *People and Nature: An Introduction to Human Ecological Relations.* Malden, MA: Blackwell Publishing.

Ross, Eric B. 1978. "Food Taboos, Diet and Hunting Strategy: The Adaptation to Animals in Amazon Cultural Ecology." *Current Anthropology* 19(1):1–36.

Tsing, Anna Lowenhaupt. 1993. *In the Realm of the Diamond Queen: Marginality in an Out-of-the-Way Place.* Princeton, NJ: Princeton University Press.

20

The Paradoxes of Sustainable Development
Focus on Ecotourism

Kenneth A. Gould and Tammy L. Lewis

Ecotourism business, Punta Gorda, Belize.
Photo by Ken Gould.

WHAT IS SUSTAINABLE DEVELOPMENT?

When we ask our classes "What is **sustainable development**?" they usually respond, confidently, along the following lines: "It's development that doesn't deplete natural resources." Ok. We push this a bit. We follow with, "What is development?" They respond this time, pausing: "Making things better?" Ok. We press on. What should be sustained? The environment? The economy? Human welfare? What should be developed? Who should be developed? Is development growth? And so on. The answers become murkier, and what sounded so nice and neat at first begins to unravel upon deeper scrutiny.

The most commonly used definition of sustainable development is from a 1987 report by the World Commission on Environment and Development titled *Our Common Future*. In the report, the term is defined as "development that meets the needs of the present without compromising the ability of future generations to meet their own needs." The term gained popularity at the 1992 Earth Summit (officially titled the United Nations Conference on Environment and Development). At the Earth Summit, heads of state of 178 nations met to address both the "environment problem" and the "development problem." Tensions between the relative priorities of countries in the Global North and those in the Global South were a key feature of the discussions. Many Southern nations viewed alleviation of the crushing poverty in the Global South and the growing economic inequalities between the Global North and Global South as central issues. In contrast, many Northern nations viewed habitat protection (particularly rainforests) as central, with Southern poverty secondary and North–South inequality largely peripheral. In that context, the concept of sustainable development was appealing since it presumed that **economic growth** and environmental protection could be reconciled. Northern and Southern economies could grow, and **biodiverse** habitats could be saved. The priorities of both the Global North and the Global South could be addressed in a "win–win" scenario of improving material standards of living and increasing environmental protection. Up until that point, many viewed "environment" and "development" as adversaries. Sustainable development opened up new avenues to discuss alternative ways to protect the environment and "develop" societies.

While the definition from *Our Common Future* has the greatest recognition, a range of definitions have emerged since that time. The common thread among these definitions is what *Our Common Future* identifies as the three main, but not equal, goals of sustainable development: (1) economic growth, (2) environmental protection, and (3) social equity. Different interest groups highlight different goals. For example, industrialists focus on economic concerns, environmentalists on environmental protection, and some governments and nongovernmental organizations, especially those concerned with poverty alleviation, on **social equity**.

The ideas embodied in the term "sustainable development" were not entirely new in 1987. The concept of sustainable development draws upon environmental discourses from the 1970s and 1980s, such as limits to growth, appropriate and intermediate technology, soft energy paths, and ecodevelopment. For instance, the limits-to-growth debate was centered on a study produced by the Club of Rome in 1972 titled *The Limits to Growth*. In short, the study presented evidence that severe biophysical constraints would impinge upon the economic growth and development of societies. It predicted ecological collapse if current growth trends continued in population, industry, and resource use. The study generated tremendous debate and critique about the quantity of remaining, exploitable resources and what could be accomplished with technology. In addition, the limits-to-growth idea became politically unpopular in the Global South: Governments from poorer nations did not believe it was fair that they limit their economic growth in order to protect the global environment for the benefit of wealthier countries in the Global North, which had already depleted substantial resources for the benefit of their own economic growth. This was a precursor to debates over issues such as the Kyoto Protocol and global warming, in which rich and poor nations have divergent views regarding which countries should take the biggest steps toward lowering their emissions of greenhouse gasses. Sustainable development tried to bypass the idea of limits by postulating the possibility of growth within existing environmental constraints.

From the 1970s to the present, a remarkable change has occurred in a common understanding of the relationship between "environment" and "economic development." While the limits-to-growth debate asked whether environmental protection and continued economic growth are compatible, the mainstream sustainable development language assumes that the two are complementary and instead focuses on how sustainable development can be achieved. The sustainable development discourse does not assume that there are fixed limits; it is pro-growth and pro-technology. *Our Common Future* clearly states

> The concept of sustainable development does imply limits—not absolute limits but limitations imposed by the present state of technology and social organizations on environmental resources and by the ability of the biosphere to absorb the effects of human activities. But technology and social organization can both be managed and improved to make way for a new era of economic growth.

International aid agencies, such as the United States Agency for International Development (USAID), and international financial institutions (IFIs), such as the World Bank, adopted the sustainable development framework for the design of their programs. The emergence of the concept also coincided with the reframing of problems as "global problems." No longer was it enough to "think globally, act locally." In an era of sustainable development and globalization, the new interpretation of environmental problems suggested that we must "think globally, act globally."

A range of critics have attacked sustainable development. A leading criticism points to the lack of clarity in the meaning of the term. What should be "sustained"? The economy? The environment? Human welfare? What should be "developed"? Does development mean productive growth, which is typically measured by growth of **gross national product** (GNP)? Does it refer to environmental growth, such as an increase in environmental resources? Does it refer to growth in human welfare, including better health and working conditions? Similarly, when the "sustainable development" definition refers to "needs," whose needs are these? The definition of "needs" in the Global South contrasts sharply with the concept of "needs" in the Global North, which tends to expand into consumer "wants." How much socioeconomic inequality is sustainable? What type of objective criteria could be constructed to determine if we are moving toward or away from sustainable development?

In part due to the lack of consensus of meaning, critics argue that being in favor of sustainable development comes commitment-free. Bruce Rich (former World Bank employee and Environmental Defense Fund senior attorney) notes, "Sustainable development is a mother-and-apple-pie formulation that everyone can agree on; there are no reports of any politician or international bureaucrat proclaiming his or her support for unsustainable development." The "sustainability" tag is used to describe so many desirable institutions that it has lost meaning. Who could argue against sustainable cities? Sustainable agriculture? Sustainable tourism?

THREE PERSPECTIVES ON SUSTAINABLE DEVELOPMENT

Free-Market Environmentalism

Sustainable development ideology works in a culture in which there is an almost unquestioned belief that the operation of the free market is the best way to address social problems. It does not question the existing economic or political arrangements. Instead, it calls for individuals and corporations to take voluntary actions to improve the environment. William Sunderlin (1995) calls this approach to environmental problems "**free-market environmentalism**." From this perspective, one can be hopeful that individuals, through green consumerism and boycotting harmful products (voting with their dollars), can pressure producers to change environmentally harmful processes, thus changing corporate behavior (see Lesson 12). Proponents of this perspective believe that everyday citizens transform culture by putting their beliefs into actions through commitments to ideals such as "sustainable consumerism."

Many corporations also embrace the voluntary aspect of sustainable development. Business leaders making up the World Business Council for Sustainable Development (WBCSD), including Germany's Volkswagen, Japan's Mitsubishi, Brazil's Aracruz Cellulose, and the United States' 3M, see themselves as part of the solution to the global environmental crisis. BASF, Bayer, Dow Chemical, and General Electric are also members of the WBCSD. Those companies are also among the 10 worst air polluters on earth, as indicated in the 2012 "Toxic 100" list. Corporations have created a number of voluntary agreements, such as the CERES (Coalition for Environmentally Responsible Economies) principles. Corporate signers pledge to participate in voluntary environmental reporting and ongoing environmental improvements. Businesses such as American Airlines, Coca-Cola, General Motors, and Nike have signed the CERES principles. Associating with such voluntary principles provides positive public relations benefits without requiring dramatic shifts in actual corporate behavior, and signals that there is little need for government intervention. Another example is the International Organization for Standardization's ISO 14000 framework. It is a way for industries to measure and evaluate their corporate environmental programs' movement toward sustainable business development.

An example of a corporation ostensibly attempting to follow sustainable development principles is 3M (Minnesota Mining and Manufacturing).

3M produces a number of consumer products, including tape. 3M was an early initiator of voluntary environmental actions through its Pollution Prevention Policy (3P). According to 3M's literature, "3P was established because it is more environmentally effective, technically sound and economical than conventional pollution standards." The company tries to prevent pollution at the source rather than by managing its wastes. They view this as a way to save treatment and disposal costs and reduce environmental impacts. 3M has four strategies to do this: product reformulation, process modification, equipment redesign, and recycling/reuse of waste. An example of 3P was the redesign of a resin spray booth that cost $45,000 to implement and saves $125,000 a year in resin incineration disposal. 3M has saved money, reduced pollutants, and won awards since implementing its strategies. In 2012 3M established its "2015 sustainability goals," which include reducing volatile air emissions by 15%, improving energy efficiency by 25%, and reducing greenhouse gas emissions by 5%. Its stated ideal is to move toward zero emissions. This is also the goal of "industrial ecology" and "ecological modernization."

Ecological modernization approaches (see Lesson 2) also fit into this line of reasoning. Theorists in this tradition argue that there is a material environmental problem that can be improved through industrial production that is cleaner, more efficient, and more profitable. Leading proponents of this theory Arthur Mol and Gert Spaargaren (2000, p. 36) stated, "More production and consumption in economic terms (GNP, purchase power, employment) does not have to imply more environmental devastation (pollution, energy use, loss of biodiversity)." Simply put, they believe green capitalism-based sustainable development is possible.

Policy/Reformist Sustainable Development

A policy-oriented approach to sustainable development similarly does not question existing political or economic structures; instead, it looks to how policies can be reformed to integrate sustainable development. Like "free-market environmentalists," the **policy-oriented environmentalists**/developmentalists embrace the ideology of economic growth. For instance, even Al Gore, the most environmentally focused presidential candidate of a major American political party, still advocates for "greening" within the bounds of economic growth. Political actors at all levels (local, state, national, and international) take a reformist approach to sustainable development. In other words, don't change the system; adapt it to meet the goals of environment, economy, and social equity. Often, an assumption of this approach is that poverty is linked to environmental degradation; thus, ending poverty through economic growth will also curb environmental damage. Environmental degradation linked to affluence is not addressed. Policy actors are concerned with how sustainable development can be put into action, especially through existing "development" programs. Rather than reconstruct their entire way of doing things, these actors try to adapt sustainable development into themes of current programs.

For countries in the Global North, such as the United States, incorporating sustainable development into policies has led to refocusing the activities of their **aid agencies** (such as the USAID). USAID supports many environment and development projects in the Global South, such as pollution prevention programs in India and Chile, biodiversity protection in Madagascar and Peru, and the training of energy professionals in Ecuador and Nigeria. USAID believes that poverty can be eliminated by economic growth (rather than redistribution) and that environmental quality will then improve. Other nations in the Global North, such as Canada, have also incorporated sustainable development into their aid agencies. **International financial institutions**, such as the World Bank, have also "greened" their image, and their activities now have emphases on the environment. For example, the World Bank is partnered with the United Nations' Environment Program and the United Nations' Development Program to administer the Global Environment Facility, which transfers funds to the Global South for environmental programs.

If sustainable development is a goal, there is also the question of how we know if we're getting closer. While GNP per capita tells us about economic growth, it doesn't really explain anything about the environment or equity or quality of life. A number of measures have been proposed to examine sustainable development. These include the Happy Planet Index (HPI), which takes into account ecological footprints and "happy life years," and the Genuine Progress Indicator (GPI). The GPI is used to compare actual levels of economic activity with sustainable levels of activity. It takes into account additional costs, such as costs of environmental restoration, to traditional income statistics. While higher consumption levels lead to traditionally "better" economic statistics, the GPI accounts for the environment-degrading effects of consumption, such as the negative effects of vehicle use and eating vegetables out of season. Using this measure, many development schemes are accounted for as net losses rather than gains because the environmental costs are calculated as outweighing the economic benefits.

Critical Structural Approach to Sustainable Development

A structural approach to sustainable development offers a radical critique, examining the degree to which the mechanisms of sustainable development serve to reproduce global inequality. In particular, the critique focuses on three linkages between the Global North and the Global South: trade, aid, and debt. Critics of sustainable development argue that the unequal relationship between the Global North and the Global South during the post-World War II "developmentalist" period is reproduced in the sustainable development paradigm; thus, it is simply old wine in new bottles. In this view, the sustainable development concept emerged to avoid addressing difficult conflicts between the environment and economic growth, the Global North and Global South, the rich and poor; and unless those conflicts are addressed, neither long-term environmental protection nor poverty alleviation will be achieved. Such critics do not believe that sustainable development offers a real alternative to old practices that serve those in power at the expense of the "have-nots" and the environment. Instead, they see sustainable development as currently practiced as a ploy to co-opt demands for more effective efforts to protect the environment and address poverty and inequality.

Theorists writing in the critical structural tradition, such as Allan Schnaiberg and Kenneth Gould on the "treadmill of production," James O'Connor on the "second contradiction of capitalism," and John Bellamy Foster on "ecological Marxism," would disagree with the basic premise of sustainable development by arguing that it is within capitalist logic to maximize profit at the expense of the environment (see Lesson 2). Thus, any action, voluntary or not, that would limit profit making would be ultimately impossible for corporations to pursue as the need to remain competitive outstrips any desire to be better environmental citizens. Economic logic will always win over ecological and social logics as long as free markets dominate. They argue that limiting pro-environmental and pro-equity actions to those efforts that can also be profitable will not be sufficient to reverse the trends toward greater environmental degradation and social inequality. From that perspective, the very logic of the global economy demands ever-increasing levels of ecological withdrawals and additions in order to sustain itself. The conclusion is that only dramatic changes to the structure of the global economy, the goals that drive it, and the distribution of what it produces (both goods and bads) could bring us to a socially and ecologically sustainable relationship between social systems and ecosystems.

Frederick Buttel (1998) argued a middle ground, taking us back to a policy perspective. He suggested that efficiency in the use of resources and in the minimization of waste could be a means for capitalists to reduce costs and increase profits and that this could be especially true if policies penalize resource destruction and pollution and reward more environmentally benign behaviors. However, he also questioned whether capitalism can be sustainable, in the line of argumentation taken by theorists in the "treadmill of production" tradition.

While these competing theoretical frameworks provide us with lenses through which to view, analyze, and evaluate sustainable development as a concept, ultimately sustainable development can only protect environments (or fail to) as an actual enterprise. It is the real-world application of the concept that we must turn to in order to understand the difficulties, contradictions, and trade-offs that sustainable development paths present. To provide a look at real-world efforts to achieve sustainable development, we turn to the example of ecotourism. Ecotourism has been promoted as a means of simultaneously achieving economic growth and environmental protection, while alleviating rural poverty in the Global South. Ecotourism therefore offers us a good opportunity to explore the application of the sustainable development concept in action.

ECOTOURISM: A POTENTIAL MODEL FOR SUSTAINABLE DEVELOPMENT?

Ecotourism has been heralded as a model for sustainable development. International aid agencies, national governments, nongovernmental organizations, and indigenous groups have promoted ecotourism as a means to protect land and important biological diversity while at the same time providing long-term social and economic benefits through sustained resource use. Ecotourism and "wildlife tourism" have the potential to be big moneymakers: Tourism is one of the fastest-growing industries in the world, according to the World Tourism Organization.

Like "sustainable development," the concept of "ecotourism" is full of hidden conflicts and contradictions. Where ecotourism is promoted as a vehicle of sustainable development we find paradox. Just as sustainability has been employed in many different ways and to many different ends, ecotourism been used to label a wide variety of seemingly contradictory rural development forms. In some cases, ecotourism has been used to indicate a type of ecologically low-impact tourism development. But ecologically low-impact tourism could include touring San Francisco on $30 per day, which is an activity not commonly understood as ecotourism. In other cases, ecotourism has been used to refer to the touring of relatively intact natural ecosystems. However, this could include touring Amazonia on $1,000 per day, which could easily be a high-impact form of traditional luxury tourism. A more precise application of the ecotourism concept might apply to ecologically low-impact touring of relatively intact natural ecosystems, but that would include a remarkably small set of the phenomena to which the term has commonly been applied. Ecotourism is then a socially contested term used to define, legitimate, promote, and constrain a wide variety of nature-based tourism development schemes.

Perhaps we could gain greater clarity through reference to sustainable development, defining ecotourism as a form of nature-based tourism that contributes to sustainable rural development. The analysis of transnational ecotourism as a form of sustainable development is therefore a way for us to tease out the implications of the wide variety of applications of both the ecotourism and sustainability concepts and one that requires us to explore the connections between transnational processes, national development trajectories, regional political economies, and local efforts to provide a reliable economic base for rural communities as well as local control over decision making.

The remainder of this lesson explores ecotourism in Belize to illustrate the complexities of sustainable development. We examine Belize's ecotourism industry because it has taken a conscious effort to enact ecotourism. Between the 1970s and the 1990s, tourism was second only to sugar production as Belize's primary source of foreign exchange and its fastest-growing industry. As a result of ecotourism's importance, the government of Belize placed increased emphasis on environmental protection, making commitments to use tourism to protect rather than destroy the environment. By 2011, tourism-related activity represented one third of Belize's total national economy. Belize is not a "beachy" country, so tourists come to visit rainforests, wetlands, mangrove coasts, and coral reefs to view both nature and archeological sites. Ecotourism accommodations range from small rustic lodges built with local materials traditionally used by the Maya to luxury jungle resorts with pools, bars, private cabanas, and landscaped gardens. What's the reality of ecotourism development in one small country? We briefly examine some of the paradoxes of ecotourism, which highlight that to achieve sustainable development—that is, maximizing economic growth, social equity, and environmental protection—there are inevitably trade-offs among the three systems.

ECOTOURISM AND NATIONAL DEVELOPMENT IN BELIZE

One of the key impacts of globalization on the nation of Belize has been its rapid entrance into the transnational ecotourism market. The Belizean government has made a policy commitment to environmental stewardship to prevent the degradation of coral reefs, wetlands, and rainforests, and in Patty Pattullo's terms, to utilize tourism "to protect the environment rather than destroy it and so contribute to sustainable development" (1996, p. 117). However, such a government commitment may prove to be unsustainable in the face of growing transnational pressures to open its rich natural resource base to **transnational corporations** (TNCs) and to repay a mounting international debt. Belize's resources are attractive to tourists but also to TNCs as exportable raw materials. If ecotourism can't provide the income the country needs to support its citizens and pay its debts, resource exports will.

The social sustainability of Belize's nature tourism development trajectory will depend upon its ability to provide a reliable economic base that rural communities can depend on. The ecological sustainability of Belize's nature tourism path will depend upon its ability to offer sufficient economic incentive for the government and landowners to forego more ecologically destructive economic alternatives, as well as the willingness of those social actors to keep the scale and nature of tourism facilities within ecological limits.

RAINFOREST TOURISM IN THE ORANGE WALK DISTRICT: CHAN CHICH LODGE

Belize's western rainforests are sparsely penetrated, inhabited, and developed. The Orange Walk District in northwest Belize is the center of the nation's sugar industry. In the far west of Orange Walk, cane fields give way to tropical forest, allowing for the development of nature tourism. Within a few kilometers of the Guatemalan border, the Chan Chich Lodge offers a unique luxury rainforest experience. Chan Chich is a private reserve originally owned by the nation's largest private landowner (who died in 2010). He was a seventh-generation "white" Belizean and the wealthiest person in the nation. His initial plan for his Orange Walk estate was to clear the rainforest and develop the land as an enormous citrus grove. Part of his land was already in orange production when his expansion plans inspired a "save the rainforest" campaign. Widespread national outrage at the sale of the major part of his 700,000 acres (over 12% of the nation) to two Houston-based investors and Coca-Cola Foods for under US$9 per acre created major political obstacles to this agroexport scheme. Seizing ecological resistance as an opportunity, he embarked on an "ecotourism" initiative, developing part of the private rainforest for nature consumers while selling off only a portion for agricultural development. His Chan Chich Lodge was featured on a Discovery Channel special soon after opening in 1989 and immediately became one of the premier jungle lodges in the nation.

Chan Chich Lodge is the one of the most expensive rainforest tourism destinations in the country, with visits during high season ranging from $500 to $1,000 per day. It is located in dense jungle amid numerous unexcavated archeological sites. It is also located within what amounts to the private "nation within a nation" of the owners. Access to Chan Chich is through a private airport, the second largest airport in Belize. The airport is located in the privately owned town of Gallon Jug, where tourists are met by luxury tour buses that take them to the lodge on a private paved road. After crossing the private suspension bridge, tourists enter the ancient Mayan plaza, which now hosts the lodge building, pool, bar, hot tub, and 12 luxurious private cabanas amid carefully landscaped gardens. Chan Chich attracts wealthy Northerners searching for a rainforest experience within a bubble of Western amenities. In addition to an extensive network of trails, the lodge offers horseback riding out of private stables, canoeing on the private Laguna Verde, air-conditioned bus tours of the owners' agroexport enterprise, and international cuisine provided by its American chef. The lodge is managed by an American expatriate couple, whose American expatriate relative serves as bartender. The rest of the staff is Belizean, drawn primarily from the sugarcane fields of the Orange Walk District. The lodge grounds are elaborately landscaped and require constant maintenance to keep the jungle from reclaiming the site. Belizean workers are endlessly on hand and knee, pulling weeds and trimming flowering plants.

The quality of the rainforest experience offered at Chan Chich is truly remarkable, with numerous species of rare fauna wandering through the plaza. A 10-minute walk into the jungle over Mayan ruins offers glimpses of the local wildlife for which most tourists come to the rainforest. The constant raking of the elaborately marked trail system by the Belizean staff provides relatively risk-free access to an ecosystem hosting numerous deadly snakes. Most of the amenities provided in the lodge and cabanas are purchased in Miami, and in-room water coolers offer the owners' own brand of bottled water. Electricity lines follow the private road from Gallon Jug, and most food supplies are brought in from outside of the estate. Roof thatching is from local materials, and the tropical hardwood for construction comes from the jungle clearing of the agroexport operation, cut at the owner's commercial sawmill.

In contrast to the multistory homes of the American expatriate senior staff, the Belizean tourism workers live with their families in two well-hidden compounds, one of which is immediately adjacent to the lodge's open-burn dump. The housing, electricity, and water are provided to the staff for free. As most regional employment outside of the estate is in the sugarcane fields that dominate the Orange Walk District economy, jobs at Chan Chich are quite attractive. Cane field work is long, hard, and dangerous. In contrast, a Chan Chich waitress will earn roughly double the wages of an agricultural worker for a 9-hour workday. While the bulk of employment is in kitchen staff and grounds maintenance, the three skilled guide jobs offer better wages and slightly more autonomy. But even for the guides the work is often unfulfilling. Ten-hour days, 6 days a week filled with raking miles of trails is boring work, with actual tour guiding offering brief moments of respite. There is substantial resentment of the American expatriate management and the impossibility of advancement beyond guide work. This is despite the fact that the local environmental knowledge of the guides is truly astounding. The Belizean workers are aggressively supervised by the vigilant Americans. The master–servant relationship between the "white" managers and mestizo and Mayan workers sets the tone for the deference that Northern elites expect from local workers.

The long-abandoned town of Gallon Jug to which tourists arrive was rebuilt by the estate owner to serve his plantation operations and includes one of his three homes, which sits atop a landscaped hill overlooking the town. The remoteness of this frontier agroexport operation has produced a classic company town, where agricultural workers live in company housing, shop in the company store, and have no local alternative employment options. The nearest non-estate-owned town is over 30 miles away, so agricultural and tourism wages are immediately recirculated into the owners' private economy.

In terms of ecological protection, the lodge has served to provide fairly high returns to the landowners from an intact rain forest. It has managed to keep the scale modest by keeping the cost to nature consumers high, thus limiting the clientele to the top of the global stratification system. However, the origins of the lodge and its primary role were not income generation but rather legitimation of the owner's status as a dominant economic actor in the nation. Providing a private nature preserve offers political cover for forest-clearing development schemes. However, private preserves exist at the whim of the landowners and therefore offer no guarantee of long-term protection. Unless national protest can pressure the Belizean state to intervene, the land base of this preserve may be put to whatever use the landowner desires. The fact that the lodge is an adjunct to forest-clearing agribusiness and represents the primary route of capital penetration into otherwise "pristine" rainforest indicates that, rather than providing sustainable development for rural populations, Chan Chich provides the primary source of local ecological disruption where little or no rural population previously existed in recent history. However, it does provide the only economic counterweight to more ecologically destructive agroexport and resource extraction schemes.

In terms of social sustainability, the relationship between American managers and Belizean staff is problematic. The enormous control leveraged on workers in this isolated jungle outpost, the impossibility of locally owned tourism development, and the limited opportunities for occupational advancement provide similar relations of production as seen in a traditional plantation economy. As the workers are brought in from the non-rainforest areas of the Orange Walk District to populate company towns, it is impossible to speak of sustaining indigenous rural communities. Local populations have no decision-making authority over local ecosystem uses. In addition, although Chan Chich does provide jobs for a number of families, the limited employment capacity of this single facility is inadequate to provide for a fully sustainable local economic base.

FOREST TOURISM IN "THE CAYO": MOUNTAIN PINE RIDGE AND GAÏA RIVERLODGE

The Cayo District is Belize's western mountain frontier, known for its dense jungle, rugged mountains, sparse population, and lack of economic development. Within "the Cayo," the Mountain Pine Ridge is an ecologically unique region. The state-designated Mountain Pine Ridge Preserve protects the largest expanse of pine savanna ecosystem in Belize (although not from the invasive pine beetle that has ravaged the forests in recent years). Entrance to the preserve is through a single dirt logging road with access controlled at a gated government checkpoint operated by the Forestry Department. Access into and within the Mountain Pine Ridge Preserve is by logging roads, and little additional transportation infrastructure has been constructed to facilitate tourism.

The forests of Mountain Pine Ridge have been selectively logged since the 1930s, and the state still sells logging concessions within the preserve (much like a national forest in the United States). The logging is an export-oriented operation, with unprocessed logs and lumber cut at small local sawmills shipped to the United Kingdom, Japan, and the United States. Most of the logging operations are Belizean-owned. Although select logging allows for fairly rapid regrowth of the forest, the necessity of firebreaks, logging roads, and wet weather skidding produces significant erosion problems. The preserve includes spectacular wild rivers with numerous undeveloped falls, caverns, and mountain peaks. The elevation provides a mild climate, while the surrounding geography allows for quick access to tropical rainforest at lower elevations with some of the densest jungle in all of Belize.

Nature tourism facilities in the Pine Ridge rely on access to small and large parcels of state-owned land within the Cayo, including Caracol (the largest Mayan archeological site in the world) and Chiquibul National Park (a premier expanse of ecologically rich jungle habitat). Daily tours to these and other state-owned natural wonders provide the primary attraction for tourists, and the fees for these guided day trips serve as a primary source of revenue for small local tourism operators and nature guides. The land within the preserve is a mix of private and public land as much of the private land was not nationalized at the time of "preserve" designation. Most of the private inholdings are foreign-owned, the majority of those landowners being Americans.

There are four major nature tourism lodges within the preserve. Three of these are foreign-owned and were built quickly with large initial capital investments. The Gaïa Riverlodge, the only Belizean-owned major lodge within the preserve, has been built slowly over the years with comparatively meager capital investments. It was originally named the Five Sisters Lodge after a local ecosystem feature, the magnificent Five Sisters waterfalls that it sits adjacent to. The name was recently changed to Gaïa Riverlodge, a term that has no local significance but that appeals to global ecotourists. The lodge began with a mestizo and creole family's purchase of 10 acres of land in 1991 that included the Five Sisters waterfalls and the land immediately above it on the banks of Privassion Creek. The owner and his family began constructing a small lodge building and four cabanas from local materials traditionally used by the Mayan inhabitants of the region, including palm frond thatching for which the government collected royalties for extraction from the preserve. The lodge opened in 1995 and has been slowly expanded with reinvestment of profits generated from the initial four cabanas. Gaïa Riverlodge's 14 cabanas and a lodge building together can host as many as 45 guests in peak season.

In the early years of operation the lodge had no electricity and relied on propane tanks and kerosene lamps. Eventually, a small hydroelectric dam was constructed above the falls to provide a local renewable and independent power source. Food for the lodge is purchased in nearby San Ignacio. Fresh water is provided through rainwater collection tanks. "Gray water" is treated on site, and sewage is fed into an in-ground septic tank, which is pumped out and transferred to the district landfill. This family-owned lodge is the least expensive option for ecotourists within the 300-square-mile preserve and its 10-acre land base remains the smallest of the four private lodge inholdings.

In addition to family labor, the Gaïa Riverlodge employs as many as 25 people in season and 19 people off season. As the lodge is rarely full off season, much of the May-through-October work is in maintenance and construction. The numerous lodges in the Cayo compete for trained personnel, keeping wages relatively high and demonstrating the economic advantage of competitive over monopolistic tourism development for rural populations. Compared to local logging and agricultural employment, tourism jobs at Gaïa Riverlodge still provide poor wages but good benefits and security for those fortunate enough to be a part of the year-round staff. An experienced guide still earns substantially less than a successful family farm might earn in the region. However, many local residents prefer tourism work as it is viewed as more skilled and more rewarding and it provides the possibility of upward social mobility within the industry. Much of the Gaïa staff has experienced upward mobility, with some moving from waiter positions through guide work to high-level managerial positions. Loggers earn more money, but the work is difficult, dangerous, and insecure. For year-round staff, off-season employment is rotated on a 1-week-on, 1-week-off basis, which keeps the staff employed year-round but only part time. This arrangement helps to mitigate the problem of seasonality in employment, which is a common obstacle to the social sustainability of ecotourism.

The lodge provides housing and food for its employees, as is the norm for remote tourist facilities. Most employees are from San Ignacio, the largest town nearest the preserve, and most of the wages are spent in San Ignacio, contributing to the local economy. A smaller share of the wages is spent in San Antonio, a small village just outside of the preserve entrance. Local lodge operators view logging as the primary threat to their nature tourism investments and pressed the government for greater restrictions on logging as the disruption of forest ecosystems, erosion, fires, siltation, and degradation of scenic views reduce the quality of the nature tourism experience. Their concern is that nature consumers may choose to avoid working landscapes in favor of wilderness areas as the global competition to attract rainforest tourists has largely become a war of authenticity among tropical nations. The irony here is that logging provided the transportation infrastructure that made nature tourism possible in the Mountain Pine Ridge, and now the local tourism industry that logging inadvertently facilitated has become the primary force opposing the continuation of the logging industry. If logging is displaced by tourism, tourism will have to expand in order to provide enough employment to sustain local populations. That expansion of nature tourism would in turn present ecological threats of its own.

The government of Belize, in league with nature tourism investors, would like to create an elaborate network of jungle lodges in the Cayo using the Mayan ruins as focal points for development (a model pioneered by Chan Chich Lodge) as part of a five-nation regional tourism initiative ("La Ruta Maya"). Such a system of lodges and trails would penetrate remote parts of Mayan country in the least developed region of Belize. Nature tourism development would then emerge as the primary threat to undeveloped jungle ecosystems as well as the subsistence economy of the Maya who inhabit them. The extension of roads, funded by World Bank loans, into remote jungle areas to make nature tourism possible simultaneously makes agricultural and logging development feasible by putting them closer to potential export markets, thus encouraging forest clearing. Such a development would therefore require the state to confer protected park and preserve status upon additional parcels of jungle to protect its investment in nature tourism.

Although the state wants to expand ecotourism revenues, it also wants to expand revenues from natural resource extraction. In June 2005, oil was discovered in Belize. Drilling began in 2006. While oil extraction offers the possibility of increasing revenues (US$380 million was generated between 2005 and 2012) to a deeply indebted state, and providing economic expansion in a country with a 60% poverty rate, it also threatens the protected lands and marine reserves that form the basis of Belize's ecotourism economy. While the onshore oil concessions have been rapidly developed, the offshore concessions resulted in significant environmental protest. On April 18, 2013, the Belizean court invalidated the offshore oil concessions citing a lack of environmental review, and effectively banned offshore oil development. The threat of oil development on the largest barrier reef in the Western hemisphere caused significant political mobilization. A petition drive drew enough support to trigger the nation's first "people's referendum", which attracted more than 10% of the eligible voting population of Belize. The referendum vote supported an offshore drilling ban. The long-term investment of the private sector in ecotourism, combined with the development of a significant domestic network of environmental organizations (see Lesson 18) combined to generate resistance to the shift toward extraction (especially in the barrier reef which formed the early basis for the emergence of an ecotourism economy). The Belize Coalition To Save Our National Heritage (formed in response to the April 2010 Deepwater Horizon spill in the Gulf of Mexico) drew together over 40 domestic and international nongovernmental organizations (NGOs) in support, representing every corner of the country. Clearly, the generalized threat to the reef from an offshore drilling accident has played out differently from the more localized, site-specific threat from onshore oil fields where drilling continues. Where onshore oil development poses mostly local trade-offs between extraction and ecotourism development, the threat of a major offshore oil spill that could undermine the entire reef-related ecotourism economy led Belizeans to choose environmentally protective ecotourism over potentially destructive extractive development.

THE PARADOXES AND TRADE-OFFS OF ECOTOURISM

The specifics regarding the case of Belize allow us to highlight some of the inherent questions of both ecotourism and sustainable development and to highlight some of the questions that serious attempts at sustainable development must address. For instance, who benefits? Whose economic growth is maximized? Which social groups make decisions about development? Do locals benefit? Does the state? How are benefits distributed? What's protected? At what cost? Recall that sustainable development, and ecotourism as an example of it, attempts to maximize economic, social, and ecological systems. Can ecotourism, as a form of sustainable development, really provide for sustained economic growth, sustained social equity, and sustained environmental protection?

We begin by highlighting the economic system and examining local employment. The cases demonstrate conflicts regarding who gets the best jobs as well as trade-offs between more employment and less environmental protection.

One of the best jobs in Belizean ecotourism is tour guide. In Belize, the state has developed a system of certification and regulation of nature tourism guides. With the assistance of a loan from the Inter-American Development Bank, the state contracted with Northern academic and private sector tourism consultants to design a system to guarantee the quality and ability of tour guides. Through the Belize Tourism Board, the state established a series of mandatory courses leading to legal certification of nature tourism guides. Tour guides are required to pay a license fee in order to be legally employed in the industry. The licenses are available only to those who have completed the required courses. A steep fine has been established for those found engaged in guide work without appropriate certification and licensing.

This program of tour guide standardization and control has a big impact on who remains in guide work and who is likely to enter guide work in the future. A key limiting factor is literacy and access to formal education. Belize is a nation where five different languages are spoken. Those with limited English reading and writing skills are less likely to pursue the required formal course work and to pass those courses if they try. The program therefore excludes many guides with extensive local environmental knowledge in favor of those with solid literacy but perhaps little local knowledge. In the rainforests of western Belize, literacy rates are lower but knowledge of rain forest ecology is obviously higher. The value of that indigenous knowledge has been decreased, while the value of formal academic skills has been increased. As the program has been implemented, fewer rainforest dwellers have been employed as guides at the same time that more formally trained guides from coastal Belize now explain rainforest ecology to nature consumers. If a goal of nature tourism as sustainable development is to provide a way for indigenous environmental knowledge to be parlayed into a source of livelihood for local populations, such changes in the structure of the nature guide industry move away from sustainable development.

The number of people employed and "economically sustained" through ecotourism is often in direct relationship to the amount of environmental degradation caused by the enterprise. In other words, in terms of the scale of specific ecotourism development schemes, smaller-scale operations often employ fewer people and have fewer negative environmental impacts. The experience of Chan Chich Lodge shows that relatively small-scale operations can increase their employment capacity by providing more tourist amenities (pools, gardens, stables, etc.), but each of these comes at greater ecological costs. The concept of scale therefore relates not only to the size of the facility in terms of the number of tourists accommodated but also to the number of built amenities and the level of luxury in which each individual nature consumer is accommodated. Larger-scale operations are likely to provide more jobs, even though the increases are likely to be greatest at the lowest level of employment (waiters, maids, grounds maintenance workers) rather than the higher levels (chefs, managers, accountants, guides, bartenders). However, those increases in the number of tourists or levels of luxury in order to boost the social sustainability of the enterprise clearly decrease the ecological sustainability of the enterprise in terms of level of natural resource demands and waste production.

This process can be seen at Gaïa Riverlodge in the Cayo, where expanding occupancy requires additional clearing of riverine slopes and the construction of additional amenities (a new bar at the base of Five Sisters falls) reduces the undisturbed quality of the local environment. As facilities expand and resource inputs and waste outputs increase, gains on the social side of sustainability become trade-offs with the ecological side. Without a careful and conscious balance, ecotourism development begins the slide into traditional tourism development, where ecologically low-impact tourism is abandoned in favor of ecologically higher-impact tourism of decreasingly intact ecosystems. While these kinds of changes in the ecological impact of nature tourism may not threaten local environments to the extent that all but the most discriminating nature consumers abandon the destination, the changes do mean that such a rural development scheme can decreasingly be defined as sustainable. As ecotourism becomes traditional tourism in a natural setting, social sustainability may increase (in terms of jobs) but ecological sustainability is lost, except in the relativistic sense that such development may still be more environmentally protective than resource extraction and export agriculture. The problems of maintaining appropriate scale, keeping ecological impacts minimal, and providing sufficient local employment while effectively competing with other potential uses of local ecosystems, notably resource extraction, lead us to the next paradox of ecotourism.

What is sustained by ecotourism? How does the environment fare? What are the costs to the ecosystem? There are numerous ways that the environmental system is affected by ecotourism.

Although the "eco" in ecotourism often implies that tourism may be ecologically benign, even low-impact tourism brings new sets of ecological withdrawals and additions to intact ecosystems. Low-impact is not no-impact, and even the most responsible ecotourism operators must recognize that nature would be less disturbed without their operations in remote and ecologically sensitive parts of the globe. Hence, ecotourism development in untouched and unthreatened ecosystems is, in and of itself, an ecologically disruptive force. Such unnecessary intrusions upon nature, however mild, may be justified on the grounds that the exposure of nature consumers to these natural treasures increases their awareness of and dedication to the urgent need for environmental protection. As a consciousness-raising tool, low-impact ecotourism may generate more general environmental protection than local environmental destruction. Nevertheless, at the local level, ecotourism does represent a primary, and perhaps the singular, ecological threat to "wild" nature in many parts of the world. That is, low-impact ecotourism connects ecosystems to the global economy. In areas with no human populations or hosting indigenous subsistence-oriented economies, this can only bring ecological and/or social threat.

As noted, infrastructure expansion is one of the most obvious ways that ecotourism disturbs the environmental system. Ecotourism needs roads, dwellings, toilets, and more. Local roads are necessary to take tourists to remote regions. Typically, ecotourism either follows existing roads, which were built for extractive industries, or requires that new roads be built. In the case of the Mountain Pine Ridge, ecotourism occurs alongside logging and access to ecotourism lodges is ironically facilitated by the extractive industry. Ecotourism generates value from sustaining resources in place (scenic ecosystems) rather than removing elements of the ecosystem and sending them to distant markets. Here, ecotourism competes with extraction for policy protection from the Belizean government. By following a logging path, the state can generate short-term revenue for itself, private capital investors, and local populations. The ecotourism path generates less revenue, though ideally over a longer period of time. States that need to increase immediate capital flows for debt repayment are unlikely to prioritize more sustainable tourism development over less sustainable extraction development. This means that international debt is likely to cause governments to prioritize less sustainable fast moneymaking schemes over more sustainable options. Private landowners may have similar fast-money priorities as well. Recall that Chan Chich was created only in response to public outrage that the land would be sold for export-oriented development.

When ecotourism emerges independently of extractive industries, new roads may need to be built. Here, ecotourism is aimed at bringing economic development to remote regions with intact ecosystems that have yet to be integrated into the global economy. Then, new transportation infrastructure becomes the first requirement of ecotourism development. Even if infrastructure is intended to facilitate ecologically low-impact tourism rather than traditional luxury tourism, the new roads (and airports) constructed by states, funded by international financial institutions, and promoted by private investors will represent the primary vectors of capital penetration into intact ecosystems. Ecotourism then becomes the vehicle of environmental disruption in otherwise undisturbed ecosystems, making it more difficult to view ecotourism as environmentally protective. This new infrastructure will make other potentially less sustainable economic activities (such as logging, mining, or agriculture) viable in previously inaccessible locations.

Finally, who decides? Who controls the process? What is the social system in which decisions and processes are developed? In Belize, two groups play key important roles: ecotourists and the government.

The ecotourist plays a large role in who decides. Like the definition of ecotourism, the definition of what constitutes an ecotourist varies widely. Nature tourists run the gamut from those using extensively modified nature (ski slopes, golf courses, etc.) to those using relatively undisturbed nature (all-terrain vehicle enthusiasts, jet skiers, etc.). Ecologically low-impact nature tourists tend to prefer lower-impact activities (hiking, canoeing, etc.) in relatively undisturbed nature. For this subgroup of nature consumers, the extent of the negative environmental impact of their nature-consuming activities is largely dependent on their proximity to the nature tourism destination and the total cost of their activity. The greater the distance they must travel to access ecotourism and the more money they spend to engage in ecotourism, the greater their negative impact on the global environment. Most ecotourism locations in the Global South are dependent on transnational ecotourists. These long-distance ecotourists may have the greatest negative environmental impacts despite their intention of engaging in ecologically low-impact forms of touring intact ecosystems and the value that they place on environmental protection. Despite their environmental awareness and concern, their global ecotourism endeavors require enormous levels of ecological withdrawal and addition.

What are the origins of the capital ecotourists' need to tour? The paradox is that this need is likely generated from ecologically destructive economic activities and investments in such activities. The surplus wealth that allows for the emergence of a group of relatively affluent Northern ecotourists who can be globally mobile is largely generated from the destruction of other ecosystems in other places, where other local populations pay the environmental, health, and cultural costs of production. Thus, even low-impact, environmentally conscious nature consumers seek to experience and protect some ecosystems by indirectly destroying other ecosystems, unless they fund their leisure travel from ecologically sustainable enterprises and investments.

The analysis brings us back to the paradox of transportation, but here at the global level. Transnational ecotourism requires vast expenditures of finite energy resources for inessential activities. Most transnational travel is fueled by high-altitude combustion of nonrenewable fossil fuels in jet aircraft. Any human activity that depends on the increased use of nonrenewable resources for a completely nonessential luxury activity accessible to only a small minority at the top of the world's wealth stratification pyramid can hardly be considered a form of sustainable development. Transnational ecotourism may promote relatively sustainable development in a specific ecologically threatened location but clearly cannot be considered ecologically sustainable as a global enterprise. If we accept the premise that air travel itself is a significant threat to sustainability in terms of ecological withdrawals (fossil fuel depletion) and ecological additions (greenhouse gases, ozone layer destruction), then the booming transnational tourism industry and even its ecologically conscious subindustry, ecotourism, represent more of a threat to, than a promise of, a more sustainable global development path. For the most part, low-impact ecotourism requires that nature consumers think globally but tour locally.

Where ecotourism utilizes public lands protected by the state in parks, preserves, and refuges, the sustainability of ecotourism is dependent upon national development policy and orientation. That orientation will determine the extent to which public lands are managed in ways that are compatible with ecotourism and long-term ecological protection. As long as the state is dependent on ecotourism, public lands will be managed in ways that allow for that, even where other economic enterprises are permitted. Where ecotourism primarily uses privately owned land, the survival of ecotourism is wholly dependent on the economic choices of private landowners. In general, national development trajectories are less subject to rapid reorientation than private investment decisions, which may respond more immediately to shorter-term market opportunities.

The primary threats to state development orientation in terms of environmental protection and long-term management of public lands that is consistent with ecotourism development are the transnationally generated pressures originating from the IFIs. **Structural adjustment** policies promote the opening of national resource pools for TNCs in the interest of rapid national revenue generation to facilitate debt repayment. Debt crises and consequent structural adjustment policies therefore make national governments more likely to respond like private landowners to opportunities for quick profit and less likely to prioritize long-term sustainable development goals. Free trade reduces the authority of nations to set their own development priorities and agendas and undermines environmental protection initiatives necessary to promote sustainable ecotourism development. Ecotourism based on private land is primarily threatened by more lucrative short-term profit opportunities (as in the case of Chan Chich). Ecotourism based on public lands in nations with a large economic stake in tourism revenues is primarily threatened by the pressures of the IFIs to convert sustainable public land uses to rapid liquidation as a condition of further loans, entrance into free-trade blocs, or loan interest payment plans. The IFIs thus encourage states to prioritize short-term gain over long-term social and ecological goals. The IFIs have encouraged Belize to increase investments in agroexport production and extraction as a means by which to "stabilize" the national economy. However, agricultural and natural resource exports are subject to wide annual fluctuations in world market prices and have not historically been a source of economic stability for Southern nations. And agroexport and extraction are the primary threats to ecotourism development. Within the context of the global political economy, ecotourism based on the use of public protected lands probably has a greater chance of long-term social and ecological sustainability.

Sustainable development must ultimately be rooted in the relationship between specific human populations and specific ecosystems located in specific places. However, the main socioeconomic and political forces determining the relationships between human populations and natural systems are transnational and distinctly placeless. The TNCs and IFIs that increasingly determine the trajectory of natural resource utilization often operate with little regard for the specificities of places or the communities that inhabit them. Theoretically, ecotourism development can be designed and implemented in ways that meet both the ecological and social requirements of sustainable development in specific places. However, such local development does not occur within a macrostructural vacuum. In Belize, the impacts of the global political economy can be seen from the broad state reorientation toward unsustainable agroexport expansion down to the restructuring and redistribution of ecotourism guide employment. Therefore, if we are serious about pursuing sustainable development, we need to fully consider what is necessary to create the sociopolitical space in which communities may chart a sustainable development course in any specific place.

CONCLUSION

As you've now seen in both the global-level conflicts between the Global North and the Global South at the United Nations Conference on Environment and Development and the national- and local-level paradoxes involved in establishing ecotourism-based development, determining the appropriate balance and acceptable trade-offs between meeting human social and economic needs and protecting the environment from which those needs must be met is complicated. It is also clear that natural science can offer us guidance toward sustainable development in terms of what impacts ecosystems can bear but can't offer us much direction in terms of determining how socioeconomic trade-offs could or should be negotiated. Environmental sociologists can provide analyses of what, how, and why various social needs, goals, and groups compete or coalesce around different ways of operationalizing the sustainable development concept.

The three broad theoretical approaches to sustainable development can each be applied to the specific case of Belizean ecotourism as sustainable development. From a free-market environmentalism perspective, ecotourism could be made more sustainable with the creation of zero-emissions, renewable energy–based global transportation systems. With full knowledge of the ecological impacts of extractive, agroexport, and ecotourism industries, consumers in the Global North can choose to boycott products that compete with ecotourism development and to frequent ecotourism enterprises that provide the greatest local social and ecological benefits. From a policy/reformist perspective, governments can choose to place limits on the scale of ecotourism enterprises and the enterprises that compete with them. They can also designate and enforce protected status on fragile ecosystems and make policy commitments to more ecologically benign development paths. Globally, they can establish debt relief policies that reduce the pressure on indebted countries to sell off their natural resources for short-term liquidity. From a critical structural perspective, free markets could be subjugated to social and ecological priorities, barring private landowners from acting in ways that produce environmentally and socially destructive outcomes and requiring governments to respond to the needs of their populations rather than international investors. Redistributive policies could be used to alleviate poverty without economic growth, so the need for Southern communities to organize their economies and ecosystems around the interests of wealthy Northern ecotourists would be diminished.

Ultimately, truly ecologically and socially sustainable development can be achieved only by making some tough collective decisions about what will be sustained and for whom and how social and ecological costs and benefits will be distributed. Such collective decisions are political; therefore, sustainable development is political. While sustainable development as a concept may have emerged as an effort to make an end run around conflicts between the economy, the environment, and distribution, sustainable development as a genuine enterprise will likely require that those conflicts be addressed directly. And it is the resolution of those conflicts that will prove to be the truly difficult work.

SOURCES

Buttel, Frederick. 1998. "Some Observations on States, World Orders, and the Politics of Sustainability." *Organization and Environment* 11(3):261–286.

Gould, Kenneth A. 1999. "Tactical Tourism: A Comparative Analysis of Rainforest Tourism in Ecuador and Belize." *Organization and Environment* 12(3):245–262.

Humphrey, Craig R., Tammy L. Lewis, and Frederick H. Buttel. 2002. *Environment, Energy, and Society: A New Synthesis.* Belmont, CA: Wadsworth.

McMichael, Philip. 2011. *Development and Social Change: A Global Perspective.* Thousand Oaks, CA: Sage Publications.

Meadows, Donella H., Dennis L. Meadows, Jorgen Randers, and William Behrens III. 1972. *The Limits to Growth.* New York: Universe Books.

Mol, Arthur P. J., and Gert Spaargaren. 2000. "Ecological Modernisation Theory in Debate: A Review." *Environmental Politics* 9(1):17–49.

Pattullo, Patty. 1996. "Green Crime, Green Redemption: The Environment and Ecotourism in the Caribbean." In Helen Collinson, ed. *Green Guerrillas: Environmental Conflicts and Initiatives in Latin America and the Caribbean*, pp. 178–186. Nottingham, UK: Latin America Bureau Russell Press.

Rudel, Thomas K. 2005. *Tropical Forests: Paths of Destruction and Regeneration in the Late Twentieth Century.* New York: Columbia University Press.

Sunderlin, William. 1995. "Managerialism and the Conceptual Limits of Sustainable Development." *Society and Natural Resources* 8:481–492.

Sutherland, Anne. 1998. *The Making of Belize: Globalization in the Margins.* Westport, CT: Bergin and Garvey.

World Commission on Environment and Development. 1987. *Our Common Future.* Oxford, UK: Oxford University Press.

Conclusion: Unanswered Questions and the Future of Environmental Sociology

Kenneth A. Gould and Tammy L. Lewis

Throughout the preceding 20 lessons in environmental sociology, some inter-linking themes emerged that coincide with the four parts of the book. These themes summarize what environmental sociology is and what we definitively know:

1. Historically, sociologists have separated social and ecological systems; however, environmental sociologists have sought to integrate these systems both theoretically and empirically.
2. Environmental problems are the result of human social organization, and as such, their solutions are not simply technical but require changing human social organization.
3. The negative effects of environmental problems are not equally distributed; less socially powerful groups suffer more than others.
4. There are varied responses to environmental changes; those that attempt to alter human social organization have a tall task and face resistance. There is no single or simple answer to solving environmental problems.

The preceding lessons in this book presented you with a broad overview of the kinds of questions environmental sociologists ask and the kinds of analyses they construct. Clearly, this book could not present *all* of the questions environmental sociologists have asked or *all* of the analyses they have constructed. But even if it could, it would still not include all of the questions environmental sociologists *could* or *should* ask or all of the analyses they *could* or *should* construct. And we do not pretend to be able to envision and list all of those here (see Appendix A for a partial list). What we can do with the few pages that remain is to suggest some of the questions that we believe most need to be addressed by environmental sociologists in the near future and to suggest the kinds of analyses that we see as most pressing for environmental sociologists to construct.

THE CITIZEN QUESTIONS—NO EASY ANSWERS

Throughout many semesters of teaching environmental sociology, students have confronted each other and us with the following question: What should we do to solve environmental problems? The lessons in this collection demonstrate how environmental problems are created by social arrangements and how the features of those social arrangements shape our collective responses to (or failures to respond to) environmental problems.

What can be done to address environmental problems? What can we do? How do we create social change? Where do we start? At what level should change be directed? Do we need to work simultaneously at changing individuals' opinions and actions and institutions' organization and practices? How do we begin to create a sustainable world?

The analysis inevitably leads to questions of our goals. What do we want? What's the desired end? What alternatives are available? How do we get outside the box? As sociologists, we understand that what seems "natural" and taken for granted is socially constructed and, thus, socially changeable. We encourage our students to reconstruct and envision new social arrangements. Some of their constructions and ours are utopian. However, given that students now also understand that power relationships are part of what keeps environmental problems problematic, we can also think about how we can make pragmatic (not just hopeful) steps toward these utopias. We can analyze various strategies. Should we form a green army that storms capitalist headquarters? Work to elect leaders who prioritize environmental and social issues? Join labor movements? Become teachers? Move to the woods?

In the 2005 book *The Logic of Sufficiency,* Thomas Princen posed the following set of questions:

> What if modern society put a priority on the material security of its citizens and the ecological integrity of its resource base? What if it took ecological constraint as a given, not a hindrance but a source of long-term economic security? How would it organize itself, structure its industry, shape its consumption?

How we proceed will depend on what we value. We ask our students to define "the good life," "development," what they want for their futures. Despite being bombarded with media messages, advertisements, and a dominant social paradigm of "more is better," our students (and hopefully you, too) now question these basic social assumptions. A higher gross national product per capita is typically not part of student responses to questions about their visions of their futures. We hope you are also thinking about quality of life, not just quantity of stuff.

It would be nice if we could close this book by offering you "50 simple things" you could do to bring the social system–ecosystem interaction into better balance. Of course, by now you are familiar enough with the sociological perspective on environmental problems to understand that we think the solutions are not simple, nor do they rest solely on the changed behavior of individuals. More important than changing individuals is changing the relationships among them.

While it is nice to think that changing social institutions and social processes in ways that are more protective of the environment will ultimately be good for everyone, the lessons that have preceded this one illustrate that with social change, the distribution of social and environmental costs and benefits can be, and often is, quite uneven. How the costs and benefits of pro-environmental changes are distributed is likely to have a substantial impact on who supports those changes and who opposes them.

A SOCIOLOGICAL ENVIRONMENTAL IMAGINATION

In looking to solutions to environmental problems, C. Wright Mills' classic 1959 piece on **"the sociological imagination"** in the book by the same name and the chapter titled "The Promise" presents a still-useful analysis. Mills differentiated between "personal troubles" and "public issues." Personal troubles are within the scope of the individual and may be addressed by private strategies. However, what many of us experience as our own problem may also be shared by many other people. When this is the case, what seems to be very personal is actually what Mills called a public issue; however, we often fail to see it in this way. For example, say that you live in the city and suffer from asthma. You may consider yourself sickly and do what you need to do to manage your condition. This is a logical private strategy to your problem. However, if you step back and look at other people who live on your block, you might notice that a lot of people on your block have asthma. If this is the case, your personal problem is actually a public issue. The cause of public issues is not an individual defect; it is related to how we have organized society. Thus, your asthma may have little to do with your personal genetic makeup, but instead, it may have a lot to do with the polluting industries in your neighborhood. Public issues such as this can only be fully addressed by changing how we organize such things. The nature of social organization creates public issues, which in turn affect many individuals. Public issues must be addressed by public strategies. Individuals can change their "selves" but alone cannot change those institutions that create public issues and, thus, affect their lives. Public issues must be addressed collectively.

Environmental problems are "public issues," and as such, their solutions cannot be found in individual behavioral changes alone. The solutions to environmental problems will be found in changing social institutions and processes. One thing that we hope the preceding lessons have made clear is that environmental problems are not simply the result of greedy corporate executives, ill-informed consumers, or careless workers, whose bad individual behavior can be adjusted with better environmental (and perhaps moral) education. While we agree that greed, consumption, and work all play a part in the imbalance between social systems and ecosystems, the problems stem from the way these behaviors are woven into our existing social structures, norms, and roles. From a sociological perspective, it makes little sense to try to "fix" individuals if the roles they play and the decisions they make in regard to the environment are largely generated externally, from the social order they participate in.

Changing that social order to address environmental problems will be one of the great collective public issue challenges of our era. How, then, shall we proceed?

BACK TO THE CLASSICS

We know that our productive system and the ecological system are linked: Increased production creates increased environmental additions and withdrawals that lead to environmental problems; these environmental problems restrict further production. In his classic 1980 book *The Environment: From Surplus to Scarcity*, Allan Schnaiberg termed the tension between productive expansion and ecological limits the "socio-environmental dialectic." He asked how the tension between the two can be reconciled.

Schnaiberg identified three ways the dialectic has been synthesized historically: (1) the **economic synthesis**, (2) the **managed scarcity synthesis**, and (3) the **ecological synthesis**. These come about by the choices of social-political actors engaged in the treadmill of production. For each of these syntheses, he considered what would happen with production, the environment, and social inequality. Let's look at what he projected.

The *economic synthesis* continues with production expansion and accelerates the treadmill of production. The result is increased ecological additions and withdrawals, as well as increased inequality, in part due to the use of high-energy technology and the displacement of workers. Politically, a great effort is required to deal with social welfare issues. Schnaiberg argued that under this scenario the social future will play out as "the rich rob the poor."

The *managed scarcity* synthesis involves reducing or altering production to some extent to protect aspects of the environment, largely through mild forms of state intervention. Socially, the protection costs are unevenly distributed, with the poor taking most of the burden. This constitutes "business as usual," at least in the United States.

The third synthesis, the *ecological synthesis*, reconciles the social and the ecological systems by decreasing both production and inequality. Here, we use Schnaiberg's words:

> If the ecological synthesis could be achieved, it would be the most durable of the three. Production organization, once set around the biospheric capacities and flows, would require only small adjustments over time to maintain a sustained material production. . . . No eternal social peace is guaranteed by such a synthesis, though. Changes over time in the social and political structure could lead to increased pressures for production expansion. Capital accumulation

could grow within certain groups, leading to constituencies favoring either managed scarcity or economic synthesis. . . . The ecological synthesis is the most difficult to anticipate because it represents a major departure from managed scarcity. . . . The transition from managed scarcity to ecological synthesis is likely to be a long and painful one, if it does take place. (p. 426)

Powerful growth coalitions and treadmill actors make this path socially and politically difficult. They will resist both ecological limits to production and more equitable social distribution of costs and benefits.

How do we create changes? How do we move toward an ecological synthesis? How can we change production to change the ecological and social systems? Schnaiberg argued that it would be tough to do this industry by industry or through the whole economy without causing social problems. A possible route is through state intervention. Again, in Schnaiberg's words:

The task is a monumental technical and political one. We must first estimate a biospherically and geopolitically feasible, sustainable production level for the society. And then we must decide how to allocate the production options and the fruits of such production. (p. 431)

Schnaiberg laid out "a socio-environmental program" with seven elements designed to shift us away from high-energy, low-labor styles of production to low-capital, high-labor forms. For example, it calls for taxation of new fixed capital (to shift to low capital) and employment tax credits (to encourage labor intensity). These goals are reformist in that they can take place within our current capitalist political-economic system. However, it is likely that those who benefit most from the current conditions will resist them.

Another alternative socialist restructuring—has potential in that social welfare is treated seriously in socialist systems; however, historically, Schnaiberg argued, there has been variability with regard to how socialist approaches have interacted with the environment. For example, the Soviet Union destroyed many ecosystems, while China, in the middle part of the 20th century, used a Maoist strategy which "involved careful husbanding of resources and intensive use of labor." Today, countries in Latin America that are moving toward socialism, such as Venezuela, Ecuador, and Bolivia, have prioritized social welfare over environmental protection. In other words, socialism, on its own, is not the answer to reaching an ecological synthesis.

In the end, Schnaiberg's analysis of the treadmill of production suggests that the most fruitful path forward is in the formation of coalitions among social groups. He concluded his book by arguing as follows:

The treadmill of political capitalism was not built overnight, nor will it disappear in the short term. Sustained efforts at consciousness-raising, commitment to political conflict and the development of coordination between environmentalist and social equity movements may serve to take it apart, strut by strut. (p. 440)

Interestingly, another important thinker in environmental sociology, Frederick H. Buttel, arrived at a similar conclusion in laying out alternative environmental futures. In one of his last publications (2003), Buttel assessed four basic mechanisms of environmental improvement: (1) environmental activism/movements, (2) state environmental regulation, (3) ecological modernization, and (4) international environmental governance. (He also assessed green consumerism but largely dismissed it as a major source of reform.) He was concerned with understanding which is the most promising way forward for a "more socially secure and environmentally friendly arrangement."

> When all is said and done, the pressures for an environmentally problematic business as usual [Schnaiberg's managed scarcity synthesis] . . . have become so strong that citizen environmental mobilization is now the ultimate guarantor that public responsibility is taken to ensure environmental protection. (p. 336)

He saw environmental movements and activism as the foundation of reform. Fundamental to this are the coalitions that have been formed between environmental organizations and other groups. Some of these include coalitions with the anti-corporate globalization movement, the labor movement, the sustainable agriculture movement, the consumer movement, the anti-biotechnology movement, the genetic resources conservation movement, the Occupy movement, and the human rights movement.

In sum, both of these founding thinkers in environmental sociology came to the conclusion that there need to be coalitions of social movement organizations that come together to work both for ecological rationality and social equity. In other words, things will not get better "naturally." If we want to see a more fair and ecologically sound world, we must work collectively to make it happen.

A FUTURE FOR ENVIRONMENTAL SOCIOLOGY?

Environmental sociology has sought to integrate the natural environment into sociological analysis. What environmental sociology needs to do now is to take that integration and extend it into all aspects of sociology as a whole. Environmental sociology has largely remained a subdiscipline unto itself. The result has been that little of our analysis of the interplay between social systems and ecosystems has been infused into the other subdisciplines of sociology. If environmental problems are going to be solved in ways that enhance the general well-being of people, the relationship between social systems and ecosystems has to be an important consideration in analyses of the nature of work and labor, social institutions, science and technology, social movements, cities and communities, etc. That is, the promise of environmental sociology to fully integrate the relationship between human society and the natural world into the ways in which we think about what society is and how our goals for society can be achieved has yet to be fully realized. The ultimate goal for environmental sociology ought to be that there will no longer be such a thing as "environmental" sociology. Instead, sociology, the study of society, will, by definition, be fully inclusive of the ways that societies are shaped by and reshape the natural world.

Within such an environmentalized sociology, the study of labor and work would, by definition, include consideration of the environmental health of workers, the ways in which labor participates (or fails to) in natural resource decisions, the impacts of the distribution of remuneration from labor on the natural world, and the ways in which workplaces and the organization of work enhance or degrade environmental quality. The same would largely be true of the sociological study of institutions, culture, race, gender, law, religion, etc. Environmental sociology will be successful when it becomes unthinkable to attempt to analyze aspects of social life without consideration of, or reference to, the natural world that, ultimately, provides the context in which social life happens. To be a sociologist would then require an environmental analytical lens as part of the larger sociological lens. Without the relationship between social systems and ecosystems in the equation, the sociological imagination is only partial and ultimately flawed. In the end, we agree with Catton and Dunlap's call for a New Ecological Paradigm in sociology (see the Introduction to this book).

LOOKING SOUTH

We find some hope for a more fully environmentalized vision of sociology in the scholars and scholarship of the Global South. As you read in Lesson 18, most Southern environmental movements and activists do not view environmental problems and development problems separately but rather as a cohesive matrix of production and distribution issues. Such a Southern view resonates with the approaches suggested by Allan Schnaiberg and Frederick Buttel. Therefore, one path for the social organization of environmental sociologists we see as promising is greater intellectual exchange with scholars in the Global South.

As we noted in the Introduction to this book, because of the way that sociologists have organized themselves professionally, there has been only limited organized intellectual exchange between U.S.-based environmental sociologists and our colleagues in other countries. There has been a concerted effort to foster greater interaction between U.S. and European environmental sociologists, and those exchanges have invigorated the subfield. Given that most of the environment, and most of society, is encompassed in the geographical and social space often referred to as the "Global South" and that the tendency in the South is to take a more holistic view of environment and development, we believe that a concerted and sustained effort at fostering similar intellectual exchange between Northern and Southern environmental sociologists is crucial to the future of the subfield. In other words, environmental sociologists need to consciously organize to change their patterns of social relationships too.

SOURCES

Buttel, Frederick. 2003. "Environmental Sociology and the Explanation of Environmental Reform." *Organization & Environment* 16:306–344.

Catton, William R., and Riley E. Dunlap. 1978. "Environmental Sociology: A New Paradigm." *American Sociologist* 13:41–49.

Mills, C. Wright. 1959. *The Sociological Imagination*. New York: Grove Press.

Princen, Thomas. 2005. *The Logic of Sufficiency*. Cambridge, MA: MIT Press.

Schnaiberg, Allan. 1980. *The Environment: From Surplus to Scarcity*. New York: Oxford University Press.

Appendix A: Twenty Questions in Environmental Sociology

The 20 lessons in environmental sociology have, we hope, opened your eyes to new ways of seeing human–environment relationships and have raised new questions about these relationships. Below, we offer you 20 *questions* in environmental sociology that we have compiled from the contributors to this volume. We hope that you will join us in looking for the answers.

1. Our understanding of the environment is socially constructed, yet the consequences for our actions on the environment are real. What are the key channels through which we receive information from the "real" environment?

2. How do we create incentives for investors to prioritize investment in workers over production technology? Is this possible?

3. Will access to more information from a wider variety of sources enable us to better understand the structural causes of environmental degradation?

4. Will a democratization of research and development decision making result in a more environmentally sound and socially just technological trajectory? What parallel or preceding social changes might have to occur to make pro-environmental and pro-equity outcomes of a democratic research and development process more likely?

5. What types of changes to the industrialized agricultural system can maintain adequate food supplies while decreasing environmental degradation and social inequality?

6. What types of environmental change are associated with human migration? What are the impacts of migration (forced or voluntary) on environments in the sending and receiving areas?

7. At what point can lowering the global birth rate counterbalance growing consumption?

8. How will we reduce our overall energy demand? Will we live with less or continue the search for alternatives? How will costs and benefits throughout an energy transition be distributed?

9. How do the structured interests of the medical establishment militate against addressing environmental health? How could those interests be restructured?

10. People have an interest in protecting both their economic well-being and their health and the health of their environment. But how do they prioritize those interests when trade-offs are necessary? What role do organizations, such as

businesses, unions, and environmental organizations, play in shaping individual perceptions and priorities?

11. Can capitalism be "greened" to be an environmentally friendly system? What changes are needed to create an "ecological synthesis"? What are our economic goals? Are there other forms of organizing the economy that create "the good life"?

12. In addition to environmental movements, there are a number of other social movements in the United States, such as labor, civil rights, and feminist movements. Which elements of the environmental movement are likely to engage in alliances with these other movements and why?

13. In what ways can the broad understanding of environmental movements in the Global South filter their way "up" to the narrower environmental discourses of the Global North? How might this affect the actions of U.S. environmental movements? What types of alliances and campaigns between movements in the Global South and Global North could create widespread improvements?

14. How do societies address the environmental needs of communities when those needs conflict with those of national economies or the global environment?

15. How can we combat climate denial in ways that lead toward effective social responses to climate change?

16. How might anti-imperialist and anti-racist political struggles be linked to environmental sustainability?

17. If social inequality is at the root of the global ecological crisis, what does that suggest about the ways in which we typically think about environmental sustainability?

18. Can the overall quality of life for individuals, families, and communities be improved while reducing the aggregate negative impacts of society on the natural environment? If so, how?

19. The scientific establishment has to some degree been corrupted by the influences of corporations and the military (among other powerful interests). To what extent is there potential for the sociological establishment to be corrupted by similar influences?

20. How can environmental sociologists communicate their structural understandings of the causes of environmental change to a broader public and to key decision makers so that they can make a difference?

Index/Glossary

Achuar, 319–20
Achuara Jivaro, 319
additions, 37–38
Advanced Technology Program, 83
advertising
    consumption and, 81
    food production and, 200 201
    global media and, 89–90
    naturework and, 18–19
advertorials, 89
affines (in-laws), 319
affluence, ecology of, 301
Afghanistan, 324–26
AFL-CIO. *See* American Federation of
    Labor-Congress of Industrial
    Organizations
African Americans
    CAFOs and, 221–22
    communities, 30
agenticity, 320
Agrawal, Arun, 327
agricultural revolution, 108–10
agriculture. *See also* alternative food and
    agriculture; conventional food and
    agriculture; food production
    community-supported, 202
    corporatization of, 193–94, 200
    environmental justice and, 199–200
    famine and, 128
    technology and, 108–9
Aguas del Tunari, 306
Agyeman, Julian, 206
aid agencies, 335
Akwesasne, 1
algae blooms, 225
Alianza PAIS, 311
Alkon, Alison, 206
Allen, Paula Gunn, 63
Alliance for a Responsible Swine Industry,
    217, 226
alternative discourses, 275

alternative food and agriculture: Refers to
efforts to reform food and agriculture
according to one or more of the following
objectives: healthy food, safe food, local
food, democratic food and agriculture,
socially just food and agriculture, and environmentally sustainable food and agriculture., 202–5

Amazon rainforest, 42
American Academy of Physicians, 151
American Community Survey, 119
American expansionism, 60–61
American Federation of Labor-Congress
    of Industrial Organizations
    (AFL-CIO), 294
American Forestry Association, 266
American Forests, 263, 266
American Lung Association, 151
American Petroleum Institute, 248
American Society for the Prevention of
    Cruelty to Animals (ASPCA), 273
American Sociological Association, 5
Amnesty International, 305
Anderson, Benedict, 57
anger, 251

animal rights: An environmental movement discursive frame that maintains that
all species have intrinsic rights to realize
their own evolved characteristics, and to
live an independent life free from human
direction or intervention., 273–74

antibiotics, 218
anti-globalization/greens frame, 274
Apollo Alliance, 280

applied science: The discipline of science
that utilizes existing basic scientific knowledge in the development of useful applications and technologies. Applied science is
primarily directed by corporations., 113

cosmetics industry, 18
cosmic factors, 5
Cox, Oliver, 30
"cradle to cradle" concept, 17–18
CSA. *See* community-supported
 agriculture
cultural anthropology, 315–16
cultural ecology, of nomadic pastoralism,
 322–26

cultural idealism: A theoretical perspective in cultural anthropology that emphasizes how cultural symbols, meanings, ideas, beliefs, and values affect the ways that people organize their social lives and both define and use their physical surroundings., 318, 320

cultural impacts, 168–69

cultural materialism: A theoretical perspective in cultural anthropology that emphasizes the effects of material factors-especially characteristics of the physical environment, technology, demography, and economic organization-on other aspects of sociocultural systems., 318–20

culture, 17, 317–18
Cuomo, Andrew, 243
CWRA. *See* Clean Water Responsibility Act

Dahl, Robert, 54
Darwin, Charles, 120–21
data, 102
Davis, Mike, 174–75
Dawes Severalty Act of 1887, 62
debt-for-nature swap, 309
debt relief, 350

deep ecology: An environmental movement discursive frame that centers on the belief that the richness and diversity of all life on earth has intrinsic value, and so human life is privileged only to the extent of satisfying vital needs. Maintenance the diversity of life on earth mandates a decrease in human impacts on the natural environment and substantial increases in the wilderness areas of the globe. It is based on the philosophical principle that human beings, like any other species on Earth, are part of the web of life. It proposes that human societies should be rebuilt in harmony with nature., 34, 269

Deep Ecology: Living as if Nature Mattered
 (Devall & Sessions), 34
Deepwater Horizon, 140

deforestation, in Ecuador, 130–33, 131*f*, 132*f*
Delta Works, 242
democracy
 diversity in, 78–80
 technological innovation and, 116–17

demographic transition: A description of population growth changes associated with low growth rates achieved through controlled fertility and low death rates achieved through modern healthcare and sanitation. Because of the cultural lag following technological change, birth rates remain high and population growth increases dramatically. Only when family planning norms adjust downward to account for longer life expectancies and higher survival rates among children will population growth slow and stabilize, indicating that a demographic transition to a "modern" society has occurred., 122–23

demography: The discipline in the social sciences that studies the characteristics of human populations, including composition and how populations change over time, 119

denial, 252
 climate change, 248
 cultural, 253–54
 implicatory, 251
 interpretive, 254 55
 overcoming, 257–58
 of self-involvement, 255
 socially organized, 252–53, 257–58
 strategies of, 253
Department of Agriculture, 196

depreciation allowances: Tax deductions that allow taxpayers (mostly corporations) to recover the cost of wear and tear, deterioration, or increasing obsolescence of property they own. This tax break allows firms to reduce their taxes and use the money they save to invest in new production technology (which often reduces labor demand and increases energy demand). In that way, depreciation allowances act as a public subsidy (in the form of a tax break) for firms to make investments that reduce employment and increase energy use., 75

deregulation: The process or act of removing or reducing government restrictions and regulations. Deregulation reduces the intervention of states in markets, giving more power to corporations., 86, 163

Descartes, René, 97
Descola, Philippe, 316–17, 319–20
The Desolate Year, 91
Devall, Bill, 34
development theories, 32
diachronic processes, 316
Dietz, Thomas, 152

disaster resiliency/sustainability: The ability of a community to withstand and recover from repeated disaster impacts over time, with minimal losses of life and property and little damage to the surrounding natural environment., 242–43

disasters, 231–32
    insurance, 237
discourse analysis, 263–75

discursive frame: A unique cultural viewpoint that informs the practices of a community of social movement organizations. Each discursive frame provides a cultural viewpoint from which the environmental organization acts. This discursive frame defines the goals and purposes of the organization and provides guidance for the actions of the organization., 264, 274–75

disembedding: Social relations "lifted out" of their local contexts and restructured across time and space., 21–22

distanciation: Global economies and electronic communication networks connect us to physically absent people in places that are geographically remote from us., 22

DNA damage, 148
doctrine of discovery, 61–62
domestic relocation, 74–75
dominance, 40

dominionism: The cultural, legal, economic, religious, and political construction of humans as the rightful dominant species on planet Earth., 58

double reality, 251
DuBois, William E. B., 30
Ducks Unlimited, 265
Dumping in Dixie: Race, Class, and Environmental Quality (Bullard), 165–66
Dunlap, Riley, 6, 32, 322, 328, 359
Durkheim, Émile, 5, 31–32, 110, 290

Earth Day, 6, 32
Earth First!, 101, 269, 306

Earth Policy Institute, 150
Easley, Mike, 227–28

ecofeminism: A theoretical approach that emphasizes hierarchy as the main factor behind the destruction of nature. Patriarchy allows males to mistreat not only women but nature, since the latter is also perceived as female. This theory also emphasizes women's special relationship with nature (e.g., being able to carry life). An environmental movement discursive frame that sees ecosystem abuse as rooted in androcentric concepts and institutions. Relations of complementarily rather than superiority between culture/nature, human/nonhuman, and male/female are needed to resolve the conflict between the human and natural worlds., 33, 271–72

ecoimperialism: The imposition of environmental ideas and practices derived from dominant societies upon subordinated populations, especially with respect to assumptions about the universality of Western definitions and objectives in the management of environmental resources., 310–12. *See also environmental imperialism*

ecological externalities: The environmental costs of producing a good or service that are absorbed by individuals, institutions, or societies as a whole but not included as costs of production by the producing firm. The costs of pollution from a production process may include increased health costs to exposed individuals, remediation costs borne by taxpayers through the work of local, state, or federal environmental agencies, or lost recreational enjoyment of ecosystems. In pursuit of increased profitability, firms tend to oppose environmental regulations and standards that aim to make them internalize pollution costs in their economic calculus through safer, waste disposal, waste treatment, or waste reduction., 72

ecological footprint: A metaphor for the amount of land necessary to sustain consumption and absorb wastes for an individual (or group or nation)., 19, 125, 125*f*, 321

ecological Marxism: A theoretical tradition based on Karl Marx's description and critique of capitalism. It emphasizes the contradictions of the system (e.g., class inequality) and the crises they create. It highlights the contradictions between the capitalist means of production and the environment., 36–37

ecological modernization theory: A theory based on the principle that capitalism possesses the institutional capacity to reverse existing environmental destruction and that it can become environmentally sustainable. The theory proposes modernization through the employment of green or environmentally sustainable technologies., 43–44, 279

ecological synthesis: A relationship between society and the environment in which demands for production expansion are routinely subordinated to environmental limits and the necessity of sustaining the ecological systems and processes. Under such a regime, demands for the alleviation of material deprivation are met primarily through redistribution., 356–57, 362

ecological violence: The disruption or destruction of ecosystems in whole or in part, whether intentional or otherwise. This can occur in an instant or over a long period of time, in what Rob Nixon calls "slow violence.," 53

"Ecologic Relations of Ethnic Groups in Swat, North Pakistan" (Barth), 322–23
Ecologist, 305
ecology, 4
  of affluence, 301
  movement, 5
economic cycles, 40

economic Darwinism: A theory that proposes that only the fittest individuals or organizations will prosper in a competitive economic environment. Representing socially constructed economic structures as natural processes, this theory views economic "winners" (firms or individuals) as inherently more "fit" than economic "losers," and so justifies outcomes as natural and thus morally acceptable., 68

economic determinism, 42

economic globalization: The ways in which economic activity is integrated on a planetary scale. While there has been some amount of transnational economic exchange for centuries, in recent decades levels of trade and investment across national borders have increased dramatically., 55–56, 86, 292, 298

consequences of, 307–10
environmental protection and, 287
in Global South, 307

economic growth: Increase in the amount of goods and services produced over time; often measured at the national level by gross domestic product (GDP)., 331
  over public safety, 232
  sustained, 82
economic inequality, 298
economic resource mobilization, 277–79

economic synthesis: A relationship between society and the environment in which environmental concerns are routinely subordinated to demands for production expansion and economic growth. Under such a regime, both ecological disorganization and inequality continually increase., 356

ecospiritualism: An environmental movement discursive frame that sees nature as God's creation and argues that humanity has a moral obligation to keep and tend the creation. Hence, natural and unpolluted ecosystems and biodiversity need to be preserved., 272–73

ecosystem: A complex set of relationships between living organisms and the non-living components of their environment. Ecosystem communities are linked together through energy flows and nutrient cycles., 3

ecotourism: A form of tourism in which "nature" is a major draw for the tourist and in which some effort is made to minimize the negative environmental impacts from tourism activities. Ecotourism is marketed toward those concerned about the environment and is often presented as a means to enjoy and preserve natural areas, although such claims are sometimes suspect., 285–86, 336–38
  in Belize, 338–44
  sustainable development and, 337–38
  trade-offs of, 344–450
  transnational, 348
Ecuador, 129–34, 131f, 132f, 311–12
education, treadmill of production and, 38
Ehrlich, Paul, 125
electricity, 107
  energy boomerang effect and, 149
  from nuclear power, 147
  in the United States, 140, 141f
Eliasoph, Nina, 252

elitist movement: A movement made up of individuals from powerful social groups; early U.S. environmentalism has been called an elitist movement, but more careful analysis shows that while the first U.S. environmental organizations were founded by rich, white, well-educated men, environmentalism has taken many forms by many types of people over time and across continents., 302–3

emotions, 251–53

empiricism: The theory of knowledge that asserts that knowledge comes from our senses-sight, hearing, taste, touch, and smell., 97, 102

Enbridge Inc., 63
Endangered Species Act, 53
energy, 137–38. *See also specific energy production methods*
    consumption patterns, 138–39, 139f
    demand, 361
    independence, 71–72
    renewable sources of, 148–52
    security, 71–72
    sources of, 140–48
    system-level changes in, 153

energy boomerang effect: The phenomenon whereby producing energy through alternative means increases the overall supply of energy, causing energy prices to decrease. These cheaper prices then encourage society to use *more* energy, deepening our dependence on unsustainable energy-intensive lifestyles and having little effect on the goal of decreasing our dependence on fossil fuels., 149

Energy: Overdevelopment and the Delusion of Endless Growth (Heinberg), 137
Energy Policy Act of 2005, 144
Enlightenment, 30–31
entropy, 37
environment
    classical sociology and, 30–32
    conventional food and agriculture system and, 197–202
    globalization of, 310
    jobs *versus*, 287–89
    natural, 23–24
    perception of, 100–101
    population and, 118–19
    productivity and, 69–70
environmental crises, 6
Environmental Defense Fund, 6, 269, 308

environmental degradation
    consumption and, 29
    global inequalities and, 41
    public health and, 268–69
    world-system theory and, 41

environmental health: Aspects of human illness that are caused by factors in the environment, including built environment, chemicals, and other exposures; focuses on the prevention of these exposures and reduction thereof. An environmental movement discursive frame that maintains that human health is the outcome of interactions with physical, chemical, biological, and social factors in the natural environment, especially toxic substances and pollution. Ensuring community health requires a livable and healthy community, with adequate social services and elimination of exposures to toxic or polluting substances., 264, 271
    case for, 182–84
    labor unions and, 294–95
    prioritization of, 361–62
    shift to, 180–82
environmental ideas, 317–18

environmental imperialism: The imposition of environmental ideas and practices derived from dominant societies upon subordinated populations, especially with respect to assumptions about the universality of Western definitions and objectives in the management of environmental resources., 326–29. *See also* ecoimperialism

environmental inequality, 56, 164
environmentalism
    civic, 279
    differences between Global North and Global South, 301–3
    free market, 333–34
    reform, 267–69
    in United States, 302–3
Environmentalism: A Global History (Guha), 301–2

environmentalism of the poor: Concern about the environment, especially when economic livelihoods are at stake; a term often used to describe environmentalism in the Global South., 301, 303–4

environmental justice: A theoretical framework and methodological approach to examining the uneven ways in which pollution and other environmental hazards are distributed among particular social groups,

produce the means of livelihood of a worker (the additional work that then produces a profit for the owner of the means of production). The term is also commonly used to refer to people for whom no work is available. The unemployed constitute surplus labor in an economy, as they are not being put to productive economic use., 109

labor unions: Organizations formed by workers to advance their collective interests. It is widely recognized that individual workers are disadvantaged when dealing with employers who control workers' access to the resources needed to survive. By acting collectively through a union, workers can bargain with employers in an effort to improve workplace conditions. Unions can also serve as a voice for workers in the political sphere., 38, 55, 268, 289–95

    capitalism and, 290
    domestic relocation and, 19
    in Sweden, 19
language, 16
latifundia (manor farms), 130
Latin America, imperialism in, 59–61
laws of thermodynamics, 37
lead poisoning, 184
legal gains and losses, 169
Leopold, Aldo, 101
less developed countries, outsourcing in, 74–75
lifestyle changes, 153
Lifton, Robert, 251, 255, 257
The Limits of Growth, 331
littering, 15
livestock wastes, 209–11. *See also* hog waste
Living in Denial: Climate Change, Emotions and Everyday Life (Norgaard), 255
lobbying, 83
locally unwanted land uses (LULUs), 168, 200
Lockie, Stewart, 203

logic of science: The philosophy of knowledge that underlies the scientific enterprise, informing its methods and theories., 96

The Logic of Sufficiency (Princen), 354
Lone Wolf v. Hitchcock, 62–63
Longhofer, Wesley, 309
Love Canal, 6, 183
Lovins, Amory, 44
Lovins, L. Hunter, 44
LULUs. *See* locally unwanted land uses

MacKinnon, Catherine, 58
Malthus, Thomas Robert, 31, 120–21, 127

managed scarcity synthesis: A relationship between society and the environment in which some of the negative impacts of social systems on nature are reduced through relatively mild forms of government intervention in the economy (such as regulation of pollutants and limits on access to natural resources)., 356

managers, 67
Manhattan Project, 95–96
Manifest Destiny, 60–61
manufacturing
    environmental protection and, 286
    FTAs and, 292
    outsourcing of, 74–75
Marcellus Shale, 146

market-based approaches: The use of the market by social movement organizations to achieve their objectives., 192, 204–6

Marshall, John, 61
Marshall Doctrine, 63
Marshall Institute, 248
Marx, Karl, 5, 29, 110, 127, 290
Marxist theory, 32, 35–36. *See also* ecological Marxism; neo-Marxist political-economy theories
Mason, Jim, 58
Massachusetts Institute of Technology (MIT), 143–44
material adaptations, 319
The Matrix (film), 97
McCarthy, Deborah, 171
McDonaldization, 23
McDonough, William, 17–18
McIntosh, Peggy, 175–76
McKibben, Bill, 63
McMichael, Philip, 192
Meadows, Donella, 17
megadams, 151
megaprojects, 237
Mendes, Chico, 308–9
Merchant, Carolyn, 58

metabolic rift: A Marxist term, popularized in environmental sociology by John Bellamy Foster, that describes the transfer of energy from the countryside to the cities when food produced in the former is sold in the latter. Soil nutrients decline in agricultural areas because they are transferred to cities, where they are disposed of as waste, creating pollution and health risk., 36, 127

methane, 141
 contamination, 146–47
Methanex, 78
methyl tertiary-butyl ether (MTBE), 78
miasma theories, 180
Micheletti, Michele, 203
migration, 361
Miljkosok, 256
Miller, Scott M., 145
Mills, C. Wright, 58, 355
Minamata disease, 182
Mishler, E. G., 180–81
MIT. *See* Massachusetts Institute of
 Technology

mitigation: The planning and implementation of strategies designed to lessen or
eliminate potential disaster impacts., 187–
88, 237–39, 242–43

modernity: The period in Western history
beginning approximately in the 16th or
17th century, characterized by the rise of
capitalism and the move away from medieval institutions., 99

modernization, 121–26
 ecological, 43–44, 279
 reflexive, 43

modernization theory: A theory popular
among U.S. policymakers during the Cold
War that explained global inequality as a
result of different levels of economic and
cultural progress rather than as a set of
innate, inherited, or moral characteristics.
Modernization was the theoretical foundation for foreign aid from the United
States during most of the Cold War period.,
39, 121

Mohai, Paul, 59
Mol, Arthur, 43, 334
Molotch, Harvey, 18
Monbiot, George, 202
monocropping, 121–22
monopolies, 42–43
Monroe, James, 59–60
Monroe Doctrine, 59–61
Monsanto Company, 91, 195*f*
moral control, 120–21
Morales, Evo, 307

moral hazard: The tendency of people to
engage in risk-taking behavior that they
would normally avoid because they have
insurance that will cover the costs of any
negative impacts., 240

Moran, Emilio, 317

MOSOP. *See* Movement for the Survival of
 the Ogoni People
Mountain Pine Ridge, 341–44

mountaintop removal (MTR) mining: A
type of surface coal mining prevalent in
Central Appalachia wherein mountains
are blasted apart to expose thin seams of
coal for coal extraction. This type of
mining leads to many environmental and
public health problems for nearby communities and ecosystems., 142–43

Movement for the Survival of the Ogoni
 People (MOSOP), 305–6
MTBE. *See* methyl tertiary-butyl ether
MTR mining. *See* mountaintop removal
 mining
Muir, John, 302
Mumford, Lewis, 107–8
Murphy, Wendell, 213, 226
Murphy Family Farms, Inc., 213
mysticism, 34

Naess, Arne, 34
NAFTA. *See* North American Free
 Trade Agreement

nanotechnology: The engineering of
matter on an atomic and molecular scale to
produce new materials and technologies
with at least one dimension sized from 1 to
100 nanometers. (A nanometer is equal to
one billionth of a meter.) Molecularly engineered materials are sometimes referred to
as nanates. Machines engineered at the
molecular scale are commonly referred to
as nanites or nanobots., 115–16

National Assessment of the Potential
 Consequences of Climate Variability
 and Change, 188
National Audubon Society, 263, 265
National Cancer Institute, 162
National Environmental Policy Act, 6
National Flood Insurance Program
 (NFIP), 239–41
National Institute of Environmental Health
 Sciences (NIEHS), 181
National Oceanic and Atmospheric
 Administration (NOAA), 198, 246
National Pork Producers Council, 228
National Security Agency, 87
National Wildlife Federation, 265
nation-states, authoritarianism of, 65–66
Native Americans, 34, 163–64, 317. *See also*
 First Nations
 reservation lands, 63
nativism, 129

political cycles, 40
Pollan, Michael, 70–71
polls, 247
pollution. *See also specific pollution types*
  cancer and, 162
  chemical, 69–70
  reform environmentalism and, 267–68
  uneven distribution of, 163–64
Pollution Prevention Policy (3P), 334
polybrominated biphenyls (PBBs), 182–83
polychlorinated biphenyl (PCB), 83–84
Pope Innocent IV, 62
The Population Bomb (Ehrlich), 125

population density: The average number of people who live in a specified area unit, usually a square mile or square kilometer., 119

population growth: A measure of changes in population over time by taking a population at one time and adding all the births and immigrants who arrive before a later time, while subtracting the deaths and emigrants., 31, 118–20, 123*t*

  in Ecuador, 130–34, 131*f*
  food production and, 31
  Global North/Global South and, 128–29

population: The number of people living in a specific geographical area at a specific point in time., 41, 118–19, 123*t*, 126*t*

  controls, 126
  environment and, 118–19
  pyramids, 123–24, 124*f*–125*f*
  as straw doll, 127–29
  tropical forests and, 129–34
Post Carbon Institute, 154
post-disaster mitigation planning, 238–39

post-industrial: A period in a society's development when the relative importance of manufacturing declines and the wealth generated by the service and information sector(s) increase. The contemporary United States is often referred to as having a post-industrial economy., 89

The Potential Effects of Global Climate Change (EPA), 187

precautionary principle (PP): Defensive public health approach to reducing or banning chemicals even in the absence of understanding whether or not they harm human health; a "look before you leap" approach that disallows the use of a new substance until it is proven safe., 189, 271

Preparing for an Uncertain Climate, 187–88

preservation: An environmental movement discursive frame that sees nature as an important component in supporting both the physical and spiritual life of humans. Hence the continued existence of wilderness and wildlife, undisturbed by human action, is necessary., 264, 266–67

PR firms. *See* public relations firms
Princen, Thomas, 354
Principles of Environmental Justice, 65
privatization, 84, 87
Proceedings of the National Academy of Sciences, 145

processual: Studying sociocultural systems as processes that are actively produced and transformed over time, rather than as static and unresponsive "things" or conditions., 316

productivity, 67–68
  communities and, 67
  environmental regulation and, 73
  environment and, 69–70
  technology and, 70–73
  workers and, 67

professionalized environmental organizations: Formal environmental organizations, registered with the state, with paid leaders and staffs, large budgets, lobbying arms, and extensive fundraising mechanisms, many of the U.S. environmental organizations follow this model., 301

profitability: Measure applied to assessing a business' income as compared to its expenses. Expenses include labor, material inputs, equipment, shipping, and marketing. Income is based on volume of goods and services produced and the price of those goods and services. A business is profitable when its income exceeds its expenses. Profitability is the goal of all business ventures in a capitalist economy. In classical and Marxist economics, profit is the return to an owner of capital goods or natural resources in any productive pursuit involving labor (or a return on bonds and money invested in capital markets). In Marxist economic theory, the maximization of profit corresponds to the accumulation of capital, which is the driving force behind economic activity in capitalist economies., 67, 113–14

  treadmill of production and, 38
profit margin, 67, 78
  global media and, 88

second modernity theory: A theory based on the principle that modern societies are making the transition to second modernity, a stage characterized by reflexivity or deep evaluation of our social institutions and ways of life. Scholars who subscribe to this theory disagree with the notion proposed by postmodernists that modern societies have already made the transition to "postmodernity.," 45–46

selective interpretation: The interpretation of events or ideas to produce desired or consistent emotional or cognitive states., 254

slurry: The liquid waste product created when coal is washed to remove the non- combustible materials like sulfur. Slurry is stored above ground in open impoundments with a capacity to hold millions (sometimes billions) of gallons of this coal waste, or it is injected underground into abandoned coal mines. In numerous communities, this slurry has leached out of the underground injection site and contaminated the water table with toxic metals and chemicals., 143, 215

social Darwinism: A Victorian theory associated with Herbert Spencer that posits that the relationship between humans and their environment has a "natural" evolutionary course that can be overcome through social action, particularly restraint on population growth among those groups considered less evolved., 120–21

social ecology: A theory built on the principle that the source of environmental problems lies in social inequality; that is, environmental problems are fundamentally social problems., 33–34

social equity: The least well-defined pillar of sustainable development; in reference to sustainable development, it refers to equality of opportunities for social groups to have a say in making decisions about the environment, and to have equality of access to a healthy environment., 82, 331, 334, 338

socially organized denial: The idea that what people ignore or pay attention to is a collective process that results as individuals follow appropriate norms of attention, emotion, and conversation., 252–53, 257–58

world-system theory: A theory built on the premise that the expansion of European colonialism beginning in the "long 16th century" (1450-1640) was capitalist in nature; that is, it was based on the search for wealth and profit. This expansion created a world-system containing a global stratification system in which the rich countries, the core, have exploited the poor countries, the periphery, for raw materials, new markets, and cheap labor. In between the core and the periphery lies the semiperiphery, a category that includes countries that either declined from the core or rose from the periphery., 39–42

World Trade Organization (WTO): An international body designed to advance trade liberalization. It facilitates the reduction of trade barriers between member states. The WTO is regularly the target of protests from environmental organizations and labor unions who believe that trade liberalization undermines worker and environmental protections., 77, 274, 296–97